"Neil Landau's sensational book *The Screenwriter's Roadmap* isn't about how to write a good screenplay. It's about how great screenplays are written. Neil takes you inside the mind and process of some of the most brilliant screenwriters working today. We learn why they did what they did, and see how great writing came to be. This book is essential reading for anyone interested in writing a screenplay, or, really, anyone keenly interested in how movies come to be made."
—Dan Jinks, Academy Award-winning film producer whose movies include *American Beauty*, *Big Fish*, and *Milk*

"Before I start any new script, I use Neil's 21 Questions as a roadmap to move forward. They're invaluable to me not only in helping point the way, but in revealing potential holes in the story."
—Randy Brown, screenwriter, *Trouble With The Curve* (Professor Landau's former student)

"Neil entreatingly tells you the rules that many of the great screenwriters follow, break, swear by, and swear at. These writers have made some of the most entertaining movies of the last 25 years and the book allows you inside their process. It is a huge treat if you want to learn to write or just love movies."
—Bernie Goldmann, producer, Goldmann Pictures (*Mirror, Mirror*; *300*; *Land of the Dead*); former senior executive at both Disney and Village Roadshow Pictures where he oversaw production of *Training Day*, *Oceans Eleven*, *Three Kings*, *The Matrix*, *Space Cowboys*, *Practical Magic*, *Analyze This*, *Miss Congeniality*, and many other blockbusters

"Asking the right questions is the only way to find the right answers. Neil Landau has done the ultimate service to writers by asking those 21 most relevant questions. Then he has gone beyond that: he has gotten twenty-one brilliant, generous, successful writers to answer those questions. The result is a stupendous compilation of the most useful information a writer can have at his or her disposal, presented in an original, accessible format. Buy two copies. One to keep at your work space, the other for your earthquake preparedness kit."
—Hal Ackerman, Co-Chair of Screenwriting Department, UCLA School of Film, Television, and Digital Media; author of the Harry Stein soft-boiled murder mysteries

"Neil Landau's *The Screenwriter's Roadmap* is the most circumspect and significant contribution to the ever-burgeoning field of books treating the subject that I have seen in years. Using clear, engaging language he gets to the root of those fundamental issues confronting not screenwriters alone, but all purveyors of creative expression. Reading his book, artists will achieve a fresh perspective on virtually every aspect of the craft and business of writing for the screen, from story through character to dialogue, scene, setting, conflict, theme, and more. Utilizing examples from worthy films, the author integrates application and theory. He demonstrates an uncanny eye for the elusive shape of seductive dramatic narratives. While this is more than any mere how-to, there are tons of useful hands-on advice that will expand and inform screenplays and screenwriting careers. I eagerly commend *The Screenwriter's Roadmap* not only to new but also experienced writers, and indeed, to all people who love good movies."
—Prof. Richard Walter, Chair of Screenwriting Department, UCLA School of Film, Television, and Digital Media; author of *Screenwriting: The Art, Craft and Business of Film and Television Writing*

"*The Screenwriter's Roadmap* is an incredible resource for aspiring and professional writers alike. Neil's clear and cogent approach to story will help you identify the strengths and weaknesses in your own work, and the accompanying interviews provide an invaluable insight into the creative life of a writer. If you want to see your words on screen, this book is a huge step in the right direction."
—Dan Mazeau, screenwriter, *Wrath of the Titans*, *The Flash* (Professor Landau's former student)

"*The Screenwriter's Roadmap* is like having a direct line to 22 of the world's smartest screenwriting minds. Through extensive interviews, Neil Landau and his fellow writers reveal advice, secrets, and tricks of the trade, from the macro level of concept and theme, all the way down to the smallest complexities of characterization. It's hard to think of an aspect of the craft not covered by this excellent book."
—Xander Bennett, author of *Screenwriting Tips, You Hack: 150 Practical Pointers For Becoming a Better Screenwriter*

THE SCREENWRITER'S ROADMAP

THE SCREENWRITER'S ROADMAP

21 Ways to Jumpstart Your Story

Neil Landau

Focal Press
Taylor & Francis Group

NEW YORK AND LONDON

First published 2013
by Focal Press
70 Blanchard Road, Suite 402, Burlington, MA 01803

Simultaneously published in the UK
by Focal Press
2 Park Square, Milton Park, Abingdon, Oxon OX14 4RN

Focal Press is an imprint of the Taylor & Francis Group, an informa business

Notices
Knowledge and best practice in this field are constantly changing.
As new research and experience broaden our understanding, changes
in research methods, professional practices, or medical treatment
may become necessary.

Practitioners and researchers must always rely on their own
experience and knowledge in evaluating and using any information,
methods, compounds, or experiments described herein. In using such
information or methods they should be mindful of their own safety
and the safety of others, including parties for whom they have
a professional responsibility.

Product or corporate names may be trademarks or registered
trademarks, and are used only for identification and
explanation without intent to infringe.

Library of Congress Cataloging in Publication Data
Landau, Neil.
  The screenwriter's roadmap: 21 ways to jumpstart your story/
  by Neil Landau.
  p. cm.
  1. Motion picture authorship—Handbooks, manuals, etc.
  2. Screenwriters—United States—Interviews. I. Title.
  PN1996.L25 2012
  808.06'6791—dc23
  2012021687

ISBN: 978-0-240-82060-6 (pbk)
ISBN: 978-0-240-82063-7 (ebk)

Typeset in Minion Pro and Stone Sans
by Florence Production Ltd, Stoodleigh, Devon, UK

For my sons, Noah and Zach,
who inspire me every day.

We stare at our own backyards, hack trails through the rainforest, paddle through overgrown rivers, wade into swamps even as something pulls thickly at our boots. When we reach what feels like a destination, we turn and map the way for others. But will we show them the trail, or force them to negotiate a muddy slope? Will we label the poison ivy, indicate where the river is shallow enough to cross? Or will we add serpents dangling from the trees? We cannot be trusted. We tell our readers, Trust me.

At our best, we don't make road maps so much as chart the territory, creating the stories of Frolicking Green Water Dragons and lost cities, finding order in the very stars—the uncountable but finite bodies that glimmer above us, always in view, always out of reach. In *A Mapmaker's Dream*, Fra Mauro decides the search for the ultimate map ends with the individual. "Wise men contemplate the world," he thinks, "knowing full well that they are contemplating themselves." It may be folly to imagine anything more universal, more objective, more true. Each of us stands at one unique spot in the universe, at one moment in the expanse of time, holding a blank sheet of paper.

This is where we begin.

Peter Turchi
Maps of the Imagination: The Writer as Cartographer
Trinity University Press: San Antonio, Texas
Copyright 2004, Page 236

CONTENTS

FOREWORD

Screenwriters always want to be finished, to get the script just right and reach their intended destination: The End. But what's the best way to get there? I originally created these "21 Questions To Keep You On Track" as a handout in my screenwriting classes at UCLA to help demystify the basics of screenplay structure and character development with a step-by-step approach. My rules. My way. But little did I suspect when I decided to ask these questions to 21 of the best screenwriters in the business (several of them my former students) that their collective points of view would substantially influence the way I teach and write. The author/professor became the journeyman/pupil. And now, in true Joseph Campbell "Hero's Journey" fashion, I am "returning with the elixir" for *you*.

This book does not deign to guarantee how to write a great screenplay in 21 easy steps. But it will show you many viable navigational routes and tools to manifest your screenplay's greatest potential.

When I began to compile my interview wish list, I had three main criteria: (1) a respected body of work; (2) a proven track record that has garnered significant critical and/or box office success; and (3) screenwriters whose movies have withstood the test of time and/or effectively captured the times in which they were written.

Each self-contained chapter offers an interview with a screenwriter whose work is emblematic of the specific topic. The book can be read chronologically or randomly. The movies cited are as current as possible and include films from multiple genres, with some timeless classics and a few of my personal favorites sprinkled in. My one caveat: the many *plot spoilers* within these covers. I apologize in advance, but such are the occupational hazards for citing and analyzing movies. Rosebud was the sled. Get over it.

From chapter to chapter, you'll find as much common ground as conflicting viewpoints. This was intentional on my part. From the outset, I welcomed dissension. For some of the interviewed screenwriters, the pre-planning/outlining phase is sacrosanct, while many others don't outline at all. Some believe that research is essential and integral to the discovery process, while others eschew getting too bogged down in facts and stats.

By far, the most polarizing topic was theme—with about half the interviewees in favor of defining and writing in service of theme, and the other half assiduously avoiding any kind of overarching universal truth to refrain from being pretentious and/or preachy. For the record, my position on theme is that it is dependent on a screenwriter's individual creative process, the specific challenges of that screenplay and, ultimately, what *works* vis-à-vis connecting with an audience.

Even though the thesis of this book is that *there is no absolute formula when it comes to writing a successful screenplay*, I still had to establish an accessible, baseline vocabulary. For this reason, I have utilized the terms "act one" to refer to the first quarter of the screenplay; "act two" to refer to the middle two quarters; and "act three" to refer to the final quarter of the screenplay. This continues to be the most popular structure utilized by the major Hollywood studios today, but it is, by no means, compulsory.

The use of this basic terminology, initially theorized and propagated by the very wise and astute Syd Field, is not intended to imply that I subscribe to this one structural paradigm. Still, I believe it's valuable to learn the fundamental rules before endeavoring to break them. Innovators usually learn from their predecessors. If you want to build a *better* mousetrap, it's probably a good idea to learn how to build a basic one first.

At the same time, this book will present numerous perspectives on the various types of screenplay structures. As you will discern from the accompanying 21 interviews, many of the most prosperous and highly-regarded screenwriters in the entertainment business rigidly adhere to the basic three-act structural paradigm, others do not, and a few actively rally against it.

After you've read the myriad approaches and examples of storytelling models, only you can decide which mode of construction best suits your screenplay. If you're waffling between possibilities, don't over-think it. Just choose the structure that most creatively excites and inspires you—and go for it.

I tell my students to write the script that only *you*, based on your unique perspective and life experience, could write. Let this book be your field guide to writing movies that are both entertaining and enlightening. Today's viewers are savvy and tend to take their entertainment seriously—even when it's pure escapism. We want movies to reflect us, provoke us, inform us, and inspire us. A great movie resonates and leaves an indelible impression.

As you embark on your screenwriting journey, pack a lunch and plan for the long haul. Expect delays and detours—during which time you may (temporarily) come to hate your work-in-progress, your premise and, by extension, yourself for having ever thought of it. But assuming you have talent and perseverance, whether you're just starting out or have ventured down this road before, rest assured that you can get there from here.

ACKNOWLEDGMENTS

Boundless appreciation to the illustrious 21 interviewees for graciously sharing their wisdom, insights, and anecdotes.

Highest praise and gratitude to my editor, Trisha Chambers, and to stellar editorial contributors Tom Austin, Trent Farr, and James Morris.

Special thanks to Dennis McGonagle and Carlin Reagan at Focal Press, and to these generous colleagues for their support, encouragement, and mentorship: Hal Ackerman, Alexander Akopov, Cary Brokaw, Julia Candler, Sorche Fairbank, Ralph Fowler, lifesaver Jordi Gasull, Walter Klenhard, Pamela Long, Cory Miller, David Stern, and Richard Walter.

And in loving memory of Arnold James Tappin III.

1

WHAT'S THE CATCH?

Clarify the Central Conflict of Your Premise

Many newer screenwriters have the tendency to begin their scripts without having a clue what their screenplay is about. I'm not suggesting this should be a source of shame. In fact, it's an essential part of the writer's discovery process. As you'll read in this book, even the most accomplished professional screenwriters stumble and flail as they mine for the gold in what might, on the surface, seem like a great, original idea. Screenwriting is a series of tough decisions. When facing the infinite possibilities that a good premise presents to you, how do you tame and contain it? How do you narrow it down and make it accessible? How do you get that overwhelming jumble of thoughts and ideas—Post-Its on the brain—to make sense on the page? For me, a helpful place to start is by clarifying the *central conflict* of the movie.

The "catch" of your premise is its inherent central conflict—the "but" embedded at its core.

During the research and development process (aka floundering and flailing), I think it's crucial that you clarify and define the central conflict of your premise. Choose an idea that you're not only terribly excited to write, but is also a concept that contains a strong *inherent conflict*. Embedded in the idea itself will be a *contradiction* which is usually articulated with the word "but."

The "but" will provide you with the foundation and "narrative drive" for the entire second act—or core—of your screenplay. For many screenwriters and storytellers, this is just instinctual. It's part and parcel of telling a good story with a beginning (setup), middle (complication), and end (resolution). The complication will be the "but" at the center of your premise.

Check out the following examples of strong, viable central conflicts. Notice how each one begins with a compelling character (or two or a whole family). Remember, a premise is only as good as the character(s) it challenges. There are no driverless movies, so be sure to figure out not only the narrative drive of your story, but also who's behind the wheel.

Notice the Central Conflict *in Each Idea:*

Erin Brockovich: a single mom takes on a giant utilities conglomerate, **but** she's uneducated and broke.

Little Miss Sunshine: a family of losers pins its hopes on a children's beauty pageant, **but** the road to victory is paved with misfortune and their finalist daughter is hopelessly gawky.

Knocked Up: a slacker adult must prepare for fatherhood, **but** he's still an immature child himself.

American Beauty: a depressed family man rediscovers his joy in life when he falls in lust, **but** with his teenaged daughter's best friend.

If your protagonist's active goal or Plan A (at the start of act two) is based upon desire versus necessity, it's probably not going to be strong enough to sustain 50+ pages in the middle.

Think of the second act as a big challenge that the protagonist *must* tackle and/or overcome—or else there will be consequences. If he/she can walk away or get out of trouble with the greatest of ease, then he/she's not worthy of our time or the price of admission. But, then again, as an audience member, you probably already knew that. An audience can collectively feel when a story runs out of gas. Plot propulsion is necessary for them to keep paying attention—not because they have nothing better to do, but because the characters and story are too irresistible to tune out.

Always ask yourself: what will happen if my protagonist doesn't accomplish his/her goal?

The *stakes* of your movie can be defined as the consequences for inaction. What does he/she stand to lose? If the answer is: nothing, then your second act is already too flimsy or lukewarm. Revise. Rework. Reconsider. Heighten the conflict. Strengthen the antagonist. Turn up the heat. Tighten the timeline to increase the urgency. Clarify the central conflict of your premise before you start writing. If you make a list of ten possible central conflicts, there's usually one that jumps out at you as the most fertile to really delve into and explore. *See Chapter 5 on Stakes.*

A good, viable central conflict will be brimming with possibilities.

In the early stages of developing an idea, if you hit a concrete wall right away, it's most likely telling you to make a U-turn or find another avenue. Or, sometimes it's through the demolition of this wall that you find a secret tunnel to a better conflict. Be open to every possibility. As Tony Gilroy discusses in the accompanying interview, his way in to a new premise is "almost always through a very small hole."

Mr. Gilroy also comments that he never consciously thinks about central conflict before he starts writing. And yet, when you examine his work, there it is:

Michael Clayton: a legal fixer, Michael (George Clooney), struggles to rein in a renegade senior law partner, Arthur Edens (Tom Wilkinson), after Arthur goes off his bipolar meds and psychologically spirals out of control—**but** Michael discovers that Arthur may be the sanest among them as he threatens to expose a dangerous corporate conspiracy.

Duplicity: two double-dealing corporate spies (Julia Roberts, Clive Owen) fall in love and team up—**but** can they ever truly trust one another?

The Bourne Identity: an assassin, Jason Bourne (Matt Damon) is being hunted by his enemies, **but** has no memory of his past.

As the central conflict deepens at the midpoint, the protagonist's outer conflicts (via an antagonistic force) provoke inner conflict.

The setup of your screenplay will usually be stronger if you start with a desperate protagonist. Introduce us to someone who's already at the end of his rope—and then it starts fraying. Even if the protagonist isn't overtly miserable, he will be more intriguing to us if we see a small crack or perhaps larger void in his initial "ordinary world." In some cases, this desperation can be very subtle, such as in *L.A. Story* in which the jovial weatherman (Steve Martin) from always-sunny Southern California tells us in a voiceover that he was so happy all the time that he didn't realize how unhappy he was. Or Ryan Bingham (George Clooney) in *Up in the Air* telling us how much he cherishes being a peripatetic frequent flyer who revels in superficial interactions; it's his *raison d'être* . . . but maybe there's something missing in his perpetual layover?

A desperate protagonist is primed to face a central conflict, inexorably leading to the midpoint of the screenplay (around page 55) where your protagonist is thrown for a loop by an external, unexpected plot complication. The midpoint is the middle of the central conflict, an event the protagonist doesn't see coming, and even better: something that more or less *blindsides* the audience. Being blindsided implies surprise and collision—force/counter-force—and this propels the plot from midpoint toward (explosive) climax.

Plot is revelation.

Ideally, as the plot unfolds, we're going to make vital discoveries about your characters, and some kind of hidden truth will come to light. If we know *everything* from the get-go, everything that follows is, by definition, anticlimactic. Make sure to deliberately dole out information and have your characters *earn* their discoveries. Audiences crave new information—so don't give it to them until you're good and ready. *See also Chapter 17 on Central Mysteries.*

Every scene needs to compel us forward because audiences are almost always more intrigued by what they don't know than by what they do know.

If you have a viable premise, acts one and two will pose a central question or mystery that demands an answer in act three. In other words, if the setup draws us in, and the unexpected complications keep us hooked, then the resolution will become tantalizing and inevitable.

In *Up in the Air*, Ryan (George Clooney) is as intrigued by the beautiful Alex (Vera Farmiga) as we are. But part of her allure is that she's almost too good to be true. As their relationship progresses and they develop a real connection at his sister's wedding, we want to get to know her better as well. But Alex remains elusive . . . until Ryan impulsively hops a flight and shows up on her doorstep—ready to declare his love. We feel his heartbreak and humiliation when he discovers she's (happily) married with kids because it mirrors our own shock and dismay at the revelation.

In *Rachel Getting Married*, we can see the effects of Kym's (Ann Hathaway) substance abuse and the tenuous challenges of rehab, but we don't fully grasp the depths of her inner turmoil until she deliberately crashes the family car into a tree. It turns out that Kym has a death wish; living with the pain of her past is more terrifying to her than dying. With her repressed Bohemian family walking on eggshells, trying not to set Kym off during her sister's wedding celebration, we wonder what happened in Kym's past that's so unspeakably shameful. This mystery is revealed in an emotionally raw, violent encounter with her mother (Debra Winger) when we discover that Kym is responsible for her little brother's accidental death; a horror that Kym can barely remember because she had been so high during babysitting duty. But this is the reality Kym must endure.

According to Aristotle, there are two kinds of plots: simple and complex. Both plots are viable modes for storytelling.

A **simple plot** is almost always "high concept" easily explained in a marketing tagline. An example of a simple plot is the blockbuster *Speed* (with Keanu Reeves and Sandra Bullock): there's a bomb on a bus and unless it gets dismantled, everyone dies but the bus can never travel less than 50 miles an hour. It's an adrenaline rush, a popcorn flick—fun for the whole family. I don't intend to suggest this pejoratively. There's a big difference between a "simple" plot and a "simplistic" one. In screenwriting, simple is a virtue.

Probably the story advice I offer most to my students is: "Keep It Simple." Simplistic, on the other hand, is not desirable and implies superficiality, predictability, and leads to a script that is uninspired, unfunny and unimaginative. Avoid at all costs. Simple plots work because they're like a ride. The audience straps itself in and understands the basic parameters. The twists and turns are usually about dangerous logistics and the conflict, at its most basic, is about good struggling to triumph over evil.

A **complex plot** is usually more layered, explores moral grey areas and encompasses greater character development. It's the difference between, say, *Iron Man* and *The Hurt Locker*. In the simple plot version of *The Hurt Locker*, Sergeant First Class William James (Jeremy Renner), would dismantle explosives and hunt down and kill one super terrorist. But the Academy Award-winning screenwriter, Mark Boal, and director, Kathryn Bigelow, present us with a complex war hero and the moral grey areas of battle. It's not simply good guys versus bad guys; it's about the inhumanity of war and the psychological toll it takes on myriad sides of the conflict. It offers no clean resolution. The characters face large challenges that could profoundly transform them—or root them deeper into their patterns and core identities. Whether they change a little, a lot, or not at all, they're evolving as the story unfolds.

The next time you're struggling with plot acrobatics, remember that audiences are most concerned with the relationships between characters.

Characters that engender no emotional investment as the central conflict unfolds, whether they're wholly likeable or not, are really just strangers moving through time and space on the page—and are a waste of time for everyone. In addition to your main character, who else populates your movie and has the greatest positive and negative influence on your protagonist? It could either be the antagonist or the "pivotal character"—such as a love interest, mentor, or confidant. In many great movies, the central relationship triangulates and involves two equally significant characters.

In *Juno*, she has two central "love" stories: one with Paulie (Michael Cera) the teenaged biological father of the baby in her womb, the other with Mark (Jason Bateman) the intended grownup adoptive father. Mark is the pivotal central relationship that fundamentally propels Juno's rite of passage from sardonic, apathetic teen girl into a more mature young woman.

In *Michael Clayton*, the central relationship is between Michael (George Clooney) and Arthur Edens (Tom Wilkinson), the senior partner whose life is spiraling out of control. But even as Michael struggles to neutralize the presumably insane Arthur, he begins to see the truth behind Arthur's manic rants—and this information is instrumental in helping Michael expose a high-level corporate conspiracy.

In *Rise of the Planet of the Apes*, the central relationship is between protagonist, Caesar (the ape) and his unofficial foster dad, Will (James Franco). Will raises Caesar from infancy through adolescence, and it's inevitable that Caesar will rebel against his authority. Will's influence on Caesar is essential to the story. The Alzheimer drug that Will had been illicitly testing on Caesar allows him to surpass the limits of his biology. But it is their personal relationship and years of nurturing that helps Caesar evolve into an animal leader capable of transcending the laws of man.

Your screenplay's central conflict is the core of an effective logline.

Your "premise" is the basic concept or idea for your movie. At some point, a studio reader or development executive will be required to boil the premise down into a one-sentence "logline." For a new screenplay to gain any traction in Hollywood, it needs to generate significant buzz and be handed up the food chain—from those who can merely recommend to those empowered to actually say "Yes." However, if the premise of your screenplay is too convoluted to summarize into a cogent logline—which will ideally contain a big "**but**"—then you will most likely have a problem getting past the initial gatekeepers. For this reason, clarifying the central conflict of your premise has become my all-important question #1.

Without a clearly articulated central conflict, you'll probably have an intriguing setup and possibly even a surprising end place, but the middle is mush. The center does not hold. Or there *is* no center, like an Oreo without the creamy insides—and where's the fun in that?

INTERVIEW: Screenwriter/Director Tony Gilroy

Tony Gilroy Filmography

Best known for:

The Bourne Legacy (also directed) (2012)
State of Play (2009)
Duplicity (also directed) (2009)
Michael Clayton (also directed) (2007)
    Academy Award Nominee (for both directing and original screenplay)
    WGA Award Nominee
The Bourne Ultimatum (2007)
The Bourne Supremacy (2004)

The Bourne Identity (2002)
Proof of Life (2000)
Armageddon (1998)
The Devil's Advocate (1997)
Dolores Claiborne (1995)
The Cutting Edge (1992)

NL: The idea behind Chapter 1 is the importance of clarifying the central conflict of your premise because if a really strong *central conflict* is embedded in the premise itself, it will often give you your whole second act. Something that is extremely clear in films like *Michael Clayton, Duplicity,* and *The Bourne Identity.* Is this something that you think about with an adaptation or an original? Do you start with character? Do you start with theme? Do you start with premise?

TG: I've never started with a premise. With a premise being a larger theme. That seems rather daunting. It's so hard to start anyway. It's just so hard to get started and get excited that the idea of starting with . . . I suppose you could start with the idea of revenge. But, the idea of starting with a theme: I've never approached anything that way. I think I always climb in through the smallest hole possible. The smallest way in is always the best thing for me. The more specific and small. Dowse your way through to find it. But, you've got to find it. I don't know if your idea or what the reader's idea of theme is the same as my idea. To me, the movie just has to be about something—about something that you can enunciate to yourself and that feels worthy of the scope of the movie. Something that feels like you can explain it to yourself. I've gotten very far down the road on things and have not been able to find it, so I've had to abandon them. I've never climbed in through something large. I always, always come *in through the smallest thing* I can find.

NL: For example, with *Michael Clayton*, did you start with the idea of an unorthodox, rogue attorney or with a "fixer" at a law firm?

TG: Yeah, I thought it was an interesting profession, an interesting character, an interesting job. And, you can smell fertility around certain things and you smell freshness. I don't know what you're going to do with a hit man anymore. How many people have dug that hole? I'm sure there's something fresh to say about it again. I'm sure there's some way of dealing with that. So, you're looking for a fresh piece of dirt and it seemed like there would be something promising there. And, I went exploring. I explored for a very long time.

NL: Do you do a lot of research before you start? Interviewing people who do this job or reading a lot of stuff?

TG: Yes, I do. I think it's one of the several great, incredible perks of this job is that you get to . . . if you have an appetite for it, if you're into it . . . you become an expert on a million different things in your life. A peripheral expert in a sense. Yeah, I did with *Clayton*. I spent a lot of time talking to lawyers, a lot of time reading about lawyers, and understanding big law and law firms and how they operate as these gigantic organizations. I live in New York and they all have their own identities and you gradually . . . *Clayton* was so fertile that there was just an incredible number of ways to go. That's the good side—it was hard to figure out which story to tell and it was fresh. It just smelled fresh. It probably had more personal resonance than I was aware of which was a motor on it. But, yeah, I went digging for quite a while.

NL: The Arthur Edens (Tom Wilkinson) character seems so instrumental to that story. In lesser hands, it would have just basically been Michael (George Clooney) versus Karen (Tilda Swinton). Arthur is just so complex and he's such a pivotal character in the journey. When did that come along?

TG: I don't remember exactly the chronology of how things reveal themselves, but I was very struck when I started to talk to people who worked in big law—huge, large law firms—about the amount of work that they were asked to do. The obsessive nature that the job entailed and the massive hours. Just the incredible demand of time. What would that be and what would that take? There was a lot of anecdotally well-known and apocryphal information about partners in law firms being very, very eccentric. There were a lot of people being rewarded for this type of behavior when they achieve power. A lot of really extreme personalities and really odd behaviors. And, then I had a couple of experiences with manic depression and it seemed to fit and all of a sudden there was a character. I think one of the first actual things that I wrote that probably made it into the movie was his speech at the very beginning. This is valuable. He started talking and that speech just came up. I wasn't sure what that meant or went. But, thought this was a great opportunity to have a character who has a mystical intelligence and an ability with language and it's a great place to orate and not be self-conscious about it and not have it be inappropriate. He just came alive. How he got here and what's going on with him. It's multiple tracks. I'm talking to lawyers who are telling me stories about bad documents. So, I started to dig into that whole side and the plot side came up at the same time. But, it was a very big explore. Some of them go very quickly, but that one was very big—lots of sailing around on that one.

NL: Arthur Edens is the cinematic cousin to Howard Beale [Peter Finch] in *Network*. The angry prophet filled with righteous indignation—and those arias—the music of language.

TG: You want to find some place where you can write like that where it's natural. It's the wardrobe that the person would wear. When we did *The Devil's Advocate*, I don't think I've ever had as much fun as I did writing those arias for Al Pacino [John Milton] because it was completely legit. You can't be too operatic. Most of the time you end up with people who the less articulate they are, the better off it is for the movie. So, when you find a character who has a legitimate right to be articulate in a certain way and then has a world view that you can climb into whether you believe it or not, you can really crusade behind it. So, Arthur [Tom Wilkinson in *Michael Clayton*] was that character. He was a cousin to Satan in that sense in just being able to swing completely free. I'm sure Paddy Chayefsky in the moment he realized what he could do with that character felt that he didn't have to hold anything back here. It's completely legitimate. You can't go too far. So, I'm sure there was that same exhilaration that you could get naked.

NL: Yeah, in a deposition no less.

TG: Yeah, exactly. I meant metaphorically, but yeah, you're right, he takes his clothes off.

NL: Given how intricate the plotting is, do you outline before you start writing?

TG: I do. I've spoken on that millions of times. I gather and gather and gather and gather and just build all kinds of ridiculous piles of paper and speeches and extraneous things that will never make the movie. And, just build and build and build until it just gets to some blister point where it can't go on any longer. All that indulgence. You have to hang on to some things as your career goes on. You have to hang on to indulgence and whatever passes for childlike wonder and innocence and confidence. But, the one thing you must get is that there has to be an extremely brutal part of yourself which is just unforgiving. So, at a certain point, you turn into the evil proctor of the story, and whatever doesn't want to be there, just disappears. To me, the real mark of an amateur is when you give someone a note on something to have them say, "Do you know how long I worked on that?" And, you want to just go, "Really?" Because I've thrown away years of work. In fact, it should actually get to the point where it feels incredibly cleansing and uplifting to throw things away. I'm never happier than when I'm cutting stuff out when I find stuff I don't need. Better than getting it, was throwing it away.

NL: You hear so much in screenwriting about stakes. Like, clarify the stakes, make the stakes high enough. I do find that it's very important. In *Michael Clayton*, the stakes are incredibly high because we're talking about global health and people being poisoned. But, then when you look at *Duplicity*, which is a completely different tone, equally intricate, and so satisfying, but the stakes so different. For Ray (Clive Owen) and Claire (Julia Roberts), they're pretty self-indulgent. They're out for their own satisfaction. How cognizant are you of stakes?

TG: It's a different target. I never concerned myself that much with the poisoning of the planet or what would pass as the shell of the movie. It's consistent with what I believe, but the stakes were extremely personal for him. The stakes were "Am I past redemption?" It was a movie for me about "too late." When it is almost too late to save yourself. The stakes for me were all personal for him. *Duplicity* was meant to be a game and fun. The stakes for them were love. Can two people who are just absolutely, completely corrupted, liars by trade, and rewarded for it . . . what do they do when they truly are in love? How does that work out? Even as a mature, experienced screenwriter, I've gotten pretty far down the road trying to build original material and realized that there wasn't enough of a desperate need for the hero. I don't think that's something that a traditional film can ever ignore. You have to come back to that, you have to be desperate. And, the more desperate it is, the easier it is to navigate.

> *P*eople have to want things desperately. It has to be important that
> something happens or that I get something or redeem something. The
> higher the desperation, the better the motor.

NL: As the audience, you're kind of playing with us, you're holding a card back, something that we'll have to wait until either the last third of the movie or the climax to reveal. Some of that is so great in your work because you play with chronology, showing us little pieces of this puzzle. It doesn't come together until pretty late. I think *Dolores Claiborne* was such a strong mystery.

TG: The book actually doesn't have any suspense in it. The book is structured in a bizarre way. Within the first ten pages, she basically goes in for questioning at a police station. She says, "I didn't kill the old woman, but I did kill my husband 20 years ago and if you get me a bottle, I'll tell you why." That did not work for the movie, so we turned it on its head.

NL: You have that great line: "I no more killed that woman than I'm wearing a diamond tiara." You have these great, iconic characters with super memorable lines. When you're structuring, probably at the outline stage, are you thinking, "Alright, I have to hold something back." Are you structuring everything like a mystery?

TG: I don't think you can tease people though. There's no rulebook. What's the most interesting way to tell the story and to hold your interest? There's been times when I've been irritated watching a film where you feel that they're just fucking with you. That's something I would be guarding against. You do not want to be a tease. It wants to be organic. *Duplicity* was all about the game of it. That was a very "gamey" kind of thing. Because you have a scene that you play three times, there's a lot of confection in that. It is by nature a puzzle. In general, I never felt that way in *Clayton*. To jump back when the movie jumps back isn't so much what happened as why does this guy seem to be acting the way he is acting? What got him here? It's just a way of framing the story that I think is most interesting. I would be very disappointed if anybody saw something and felt that I was being a tease. I'm not conscious of saying, "Oh, I'm going to keep this back." Information reveals itself dramatically. Sometimes it's better to tell everybody everything about the character right off the bat because it's what's outside them that's important. I've worked on films, I'm working on one now, where finding out about the characters is a very slow burn. There's just no opportunity to say who the person is beforehand, and as it reveals itself, it has a dramatic momentum to it. I'm trying to think where there's been movies that I've seen where you go, "Come on—you're just messing with me here." I wouldn't want to feel that I was doing that. It's not conscious. It's about what's the best way to tell the story.

NL: With *Michael Clayton*, the car bomb, and you're thinking, "Alright. What got him to this point?" Someone is actually trying to assassinate him, and we don't get to find out until pretty late in the story.

TG: If you tell the story chronologically, you never . . . and I'm sure at different points, we thought about it, but if you tell the story chronologically, you never get a chance to underline his real problem. You never get the chance to say, "God, I want to be here" and understand what he's going through. It was more about character than hiding a story energy.

NL: It's also a point of view thing because Michael, all he knows, is that he stopped to have a moment with those horses and then "boom" his car blows up. Then, we get to replay it and try to discover it as he discovers it. Is this a deliberate narrative strategy to reel us in at the so-called "inciting incident"?

TG: I speak against this any chance I get. I don't like the codification of screenwriting. I don't like the mechanical approach to learning how to do it or the three-act structure. These things are very destructive. They also lead a lot of people to think that they can do it when they can't. If there's a structure and a mechanics to it, then it leads a lot of people to believe that they'll be able to figure it out and that they'll be able to do it. I think that it also inhibits some people who should be doing it who are incredibly imaginative and disorganized in a way from building the skills they would need to tell their stories. The biggest thing is imagination. No one ever talks about it. It just can't get enough play. It's the business of making stuff up. I'm much more interested in someone who's got something wildly imaginative to talk about and show me that's a mess, that can't put it together, and doesn't have the ability to tell it right and is missing one of those pieces than I am about somebody who is a great technician who has no imagination and is essentially a journalist. That to me is the big missing piece in screenwriting education and screenwriting culture. There's many reasons why movies are bad. The biggest reason is that there's so many ways for things to go wrong. There's just so many events on the way to finally getting a movie done. When you direct a movie, there's basically 1,800 ways you can fuck up the movie every day and that's amplified all the way through the pre-production and the writing. So, it's hard to get something right. But, I'm talking about something else, I'm talking about how people approach what they're going to write about and how they're going to do it. You see so many people who have no respect for imagination or nothing to talk about, nothing to say. A 23-year-old kid who doesn't know anything who hasn't been anywhere who writes you a letter and says, "I want to be a screenwriter, and I've bought all the books." What can come out of that? Very little can come out of that.

NL: It's incredibly valuable to hear you say that. I didn't want to do a book that was going to codify or do one of those things that you're railing against.

TG: It's the lowest common denominator that everyone can talk about that equals the playing field. And, probably, most of those things do happen. You can probably do an algorithm that figures out the structures and God only knows, I probably fall into those. All I'm trying to do is be as imaginative as possible and write about something that's important to me in some way and have people who reflect everything that I've learned about human behavior and how complicated people are and how contrary they are and how mysterious they are. And, then tell it in a way that's not going to bore people and try to get it in under two hours. Those last two will lead you inevitably into what passes for technique. But it's imagination. There's not enough people making stuff up.

ASSIGNMENT

Write ten different one-sentence iterations (loglines) of your premise—each one containing a central conflict (expressed with either "but," "although," "unfortunately," "however," "even though," etc.). Does one of these jump out at you as the most viable? Which one has the strongest and most credible protagonist and central conflict to explore? Which one feels the least derivative of other movies: been there, seen that? Which one seems the freshest to you? Which one feels the scariest and most creatively challenging for you to write? Hint: this is the one for you to conquer. Write the story you're most afraid to tell and it will become your breakthrough script.

2

WHY ARE WE HERE?

Think of Setting and Time Period as Another Character in Your Screenplay

Write what you know, and if you haven't lived it: research. Wikipedia can be a good place to start, but you'll need to dig deeper. Search online for obscure articles and insights. Read memoirs, non-fiction, and novels set at the time. Watch movies and documentaries of and on the era. If finances and time allow: plan a trip to research and take a walking tour of your intended setting. Don't try to fake it. Readers can tell and it will undermine the story.

Here's what writer/director, Tate Taylor, had to say about filming *The Help* on location in Mississippi:

> I convinced [studio executives] that Mississippi is a character and you just cannot fake the South and you cannot fake Mississippi. So I really worked hard to get it brought there. Ninety-five percent of the locations were practical locations. I knew these homes. Skeeter's house—I threw up in that house in college. That's my college friend's parents' house—the Franklins. That stairwell: *Oh, yes.* I grew up in the house that Celia lived in, I grew up hunting and fishing on that land. I was told to never go on that land because the Lady Cat would shoot me—Cat Williams who owns the house. So, all this is personal. You had to go to Mississippi to get that feel.
> (Interview with Robert Harling, "Southern Gentleman,"
> *WGAW Written By*, February/March 2012, p. 33)

After decades of setting his best films in Manhattan, Woody Allen began venturing across the Atlantic into Europe: *Match Point* in London; followed by *Vicky Christina Barcelona*; and more recently *Midnight in Paris*. This delightfully whimsical film transports its protagonist, Gil (Owen Wilson) a frustrated novelist, from 2010 to the roaring 1920s, and later to the belle époque. This film is Mr. Allen's valentine to the City of Light, in the way his black and white masterpiece, *Manhattan*, illuminated the unique majesty of New York. Woody knows Parisian culture and history, and he juxtaposes past and present with his trademark neurotic character quirks, humor, and irony. As modern day Gil encounters the legendary literary and artistic icons of yesteryear—F. Scott Fitzgerald, Gertrude Stein, and Pablo Picasso—they impact his perspective of his current world and vice versa. Allen makes this fantastical interplay across time periods feel credible by presenting us with a Paris that's at once real, impossibly romantic, and ageless in its magic.

In-depth research often reveals characters and story.

True stories and anecdotes are almost always better than stuff you make up. Novice writers often mistakenly map out a screenplay first and *then* research the details. Fueling your imagination with the necessary background knowledge can help make you a stronger, more confident storyteller. If your protagonist is a chef, read autobiographies of famous chefs; study cookbooks; eat at suitable restaurants and ask for a tour of the kitchen. Better yet— interview the chef, the maître d', and the wait staff. I'm currently working on an animated movie that takes place in outer space, but all the details came from NASA and visits to Cape Canaveral, and my producer happens to collect space memorabilia.

In co-adapting *The Descendants* from novel to screenplay, Nebraska native director/screenwriter Alexander Payne spent the better part of a year living and observing the *real* Hawaii—off the beaten path—to get the nuance and texture of island life: the history, music, food, vernacular, and customs. Not everyone has that luxury, but the specificity of setting has always played a co-starring role in Payne's best work. Think of *Sideways* and you're immediately transported to the California wine country—and you are not drinking Merlot!

When it comes to telling the truth, we're all skewed.

Reality is subjective. No matter how well intentioned, everyone remembers the past from his/her own point of view. Or as author Jeanette Winterson observes: ". . . the curve of our memory is rarely a straight line." ("Behind the Masks: 'In One Person' by John Irving," *New York Times Book Review*, May 13, 2012). Your task as screenwriter is to interpret the facts in service of your characters, and to further your own agenda: writing a dramatically compelling movie.

Don't be afraid to take dramatic license.

Try to remain truthful, but don't get too weighed down by facts. Too much research can be a trap, if not a procrastination ploy. Once your imagination and notebook is filled with ideas and inspiration, put the notebook aside and start writing. You're not writing a documentary, so weed out the extraneous and don't try to impress the audience with all the great facts you dug up. Your characters and setting will be infused with the *spirit* of the facts. If you're writing a story that's "inspired by true events," it's usually necessary to compress time and consolidate several characters into one, or even to edit out some people altogether. Once the movie begins, the audience is more interested in the plot than a pedantic history lesson anyway. Instead, try to capture the *verisimilitude* of time and place; your film needn't be 100 percent historically accurate, but it does need to *feel* right.

A tale of two Bostons . . .

The Social Network, based upon the non-fiction book, *The Accidental Billionaires* by Ben Mezrich, offers its perspective on the rise of Facebook founder Mark Zuckerberg. His story is embedded in Harvard/Cambridge subculture at a very specific time: when cell phones were primarily used for actual talking, and only geeks were glued to their laptops 24/7. The opening scene in the campus bar sets the tone for everything to come. Mark (Jesse Eisenberg) is out on a date with pretty, down-to-earth, Erica (Rooney Mara). It's obvious that he likes her, but his relentless chatter, endless equivocating, and oblivious elitism are exhausting to her (and us). Erica tells Mark it's like dating a Stairmaster, drops a comment about finding jocks from the rowing team attractive, and excuses herself to go study. Mark apologizes, but insists that she doesn't need to go study. Erica asks why he's so sure she doesn't need to study. Mark tells her: "Because you go to B.U. [Boston University]," the intimation being that it's a big step down from the Ivy League—a stupid, thoughtless comment for such a deliberate, smart guy. It's a comment endemic to the movie's setting—insider-speak. And the last straw for Erica, who breaks up with him and walks out. Mark is left with a broken heart that no amount of success will readily fill. He's also got a chip on his shoulder against rowers. Enter two of the most handsome, strapping crew team members on the eastern seaboard: the Winklevoss twins (both portrayed by Armie Hammer) and their nascent idea for the college social network . . . leading to a smug rivalry that festers and blows up into a landmark lawsuit. The central mystery of the movie is the legal deposition, via flash-forwards and flashbacks. This is an origins story every bit as much as *Batman Begins*. Mark Zuckerberg may have been born in White Plains, NY, but Facebook was born at Harvard, an outgrowth of its founder's ravenous ambition and deep insecurities.

The Town begins in Harvard Square Plaza, during a bank heist at the Cambridge Merchant Bank, but the rest of the movie is set in Charlestown, a Boston neighborhood known for breeding bank robbers. This bleak place feels a million miles away from Mark Zuckerberg's Ivy League universe. The

Charlestown brotherhood would rather do time in prison than betray one of their own. Our antihero Doug MacRay (Ben Affleck) ends up taking bank manager, Claire (Rebecca Hall), hostage during their hasty escape. Doug releases her, but then keeps an eye on her back in Charlestown. He courts her and they begin to fall in love, all the while he keeps their relationship hidden from his cronies and the rest of the Charlestown criminal underworld. Doug yearns to move away and start a new life with Claire in Florida, but he's beholden to a ruthless money launderer (the local florist) who forces him to pull one last bank heist in order to protect Claire from being killed. The florist is representative of the traditions of this neighborhood: birthdays, weddings, and funerals—an immutable fact of life in any town, but also a nexus for malevolence in Charlestown. Doug is trapped in an impossible dilemma that's rooted in the only life—and place—he's ever known.

> So the next time you type: EXT. BOSTON, or NEW YORK, or PARIS into a script, be mindful that this city—and every other city and town across the globe—has many distinctive neighborhoods and personalities. A setting is often as multifaceted as the characters that inhabit it. The texture and nuance of time and place are integral to establishing the tone of your movie. Without context, a generic ESTABLISHING SHOT is meaningless.

INTERVIEW: Emmy Award-Winning Screenwriter/Director Jane Anderson

Jane Anderson Filmography

Best known for:

The Prize Winner of Defiance, Ohio (also directed) (2005)
Normal (2003) (teleplay and play *Looking for Normal*) (also directed) (2003)
    Emmy Award Nominee
WGA Award Nominee
If These Walls Could Talk 2 (teleplay) (also directed) (2000)
    Emmy Nominee
The Baby Dance (teleplay and play) (also directed) (1998)
    Emmy Nominee (for both writing and directing)
How to Make an American Quilt (1995)
It Could Happen to You (1994)

The Positively True Adventures of the Alleged Texas Cheerleader-Murdering Mom (teleplay) (1993)
    Emmy Award Winner
    WGA Award Winner

NL: Let's start with *The Prize Winner of Defiance, Ohio.* It seems to me there are so many parallels to life in our time, and yet, that particular story could only have been told in that time.

JA: The thing about doing some period pieces is, as a writer, you have to ask yourself, "Why are we watching this now, and how is it relevant to a modern audience?" Writers are natural researchers, we love reading history and non-fiction, and often we want to share our research with our audience, which can be a major mistake. We have to be very careful that our fascination with a time period or a place does not overtake the relevance or the entertainment value. Research is essential to giving your story richness, but you also have to have an overview of why you're telling the story in the first place.

The Prize Winner of Defiance, Ohio is a memoir written by Terry Ryan whose mother, Evelyn Ryan, had to accept the fact that, even if your husband is making you and your kids absolutely miserable, you have to support him no matter what. It was one of the hardest scripts I ever wrote because it was so difficult for me to understand how a woman could stay in a relationship like that for so many years. So what was I telling young women, or women my age who were watching this movie? Evelyn Ryan [Julianne Moore] is a hero, but am I also saying that it's heroic to stay in a bad marriage? So I had to figure out how to morally make peace with that as a writer. We do have a responsibility, no matter what genre we work in, that we are adding to the cultural language, and whatever message we put out there will be taken seriously. Even if it's an action-adventure, if you show people being gunned down, you can justify that as entertainment. But you also have to be keenly aware of what you're saying to your audience. And I've always been aware— I've always asked myself when I write a script, "What am I putting out there into the world? What message am I imparting?"

So here's Evelyn Ryan, an incredibly intelligent, creative woman, who is stuck in a small town, raising ten kids with an alcoholic husband [Woody Harrelson] who spends all her money. She is heroic because her objective in life is to get every one of those kids out into the world—intact. I felt it was important to end the screenplay with the daughter who wrote the memoir, to see her as an adult woman, whole, and creative, looking back on her mother's life. I asked Terry Ryan how she forgave her dad, how she was able to bear it all. And she laughed and said, "My mom taught us how to not take it to heart." When he had one of his horrible, drunken episodes, Evelyn taught herself and her kids not to take it personally. I wrote a scene in which he was in just this hideous rage, and she got him to start laughing at how absurd he was. With *Prize Winner*, I came up with a phrase for myself, which was, "Pain is inevitable, but suffering is an option."

Place is very important in this piece because it's the Midwest. There's something about the Midwest that I really admire. They're so incredibly hardy. In the nineteenth century, the people who moved out to the Midwest in covered wagons had to put up with locusts, and hail, and children dying of diphtheria, and freezing cold winters, and their crops dying on them, and they always got back on the plow. Always, always, always. I was writing the screenplay for *Normal* at the same time I was starting *Prize Winner*. Both are Midwest stories. And I actually went to Defiance to meet Terry and her brothers and sisters, and at the same time I was also looking at farm communities for *Normal*. What I noticed about the geography there—not only is it very flat, but everything is in rows. Very neat rows. The roads are very, very, very straight, and the fields at the edge of those roads—I would watch farmers plow, and it's like, one row, and then you turn around and go down another. As coastal people, we make fun of the Midwest personality because we feel it's not as creative, as rebellious, because of the straight rows. But you have to have straight rows to plant crops. And you have to have straight rows in order to get through all the tragedy that you face during a bad farm season. I've grown to love the straight-row culture. I find that culture a very rich canvas for a story because it gives my characters something to rebel against. *Normal* takes place in a Midwest farm community. It's about a man [Tom Wilkinson] who's been married for 25 years to his wife [Jessica Lange] when he realizes that he's a woman trapped in a man's body. That journey is all the more intense because of the setting. It wouldn't have been the same if I had set it in California, or Colorado, or the East coast. Although it might have been really interesting if it was set in the Deep South.

NL: More incendiary, though.

JA: It would be more incendiary. I wanted it in the Midwest because the play's called *Looking for Normal*, and the film is called *Normal*, and I was more interested in how somebody who's transgender and wants to hold onto their marriage gets back into a regular life. The South is very gothic, and that serves a different kind of story.

NL: Yes, it's almost like they couldn't have stayed in that life—they wanted to get back to normal, but "normal," at least in the South . . .

JA: There would have been wild drinking, and there would have been people with guns—which, of course, is a stereotype, but the southern states really do have a history of extremity. The Midwest has a history of people trying to tame the elements so they can have a regular life. And that dynamic fascinates me, for certain storylines.

NL: With Evelyn in *Prize Winner*, there's even an ongoing subplot where every time she gets in the car to go somewhere, she's derailed by either the kids uprooting the neighbor's flower garden or the car breaking down. She's trapped.

JA: Yes. It's a culture of deep responsibility—which is Evelyn's prison because she's *honorable.*

NL: Her children are her top priority. It's kind of ironic because at the end of the movie she wins the Dr. Pepper challenge, and one of the parts of the prize, besides some money, is a trip to Europe. And she ends up cashing the trip in to pay the mortgage. So it's literally the thing that could set her free to go explore the world, which would change her—but her roots are this house. And the children don't want to leave this house. It's in *Defiance,* I mean, that's no coincidence—

JA: I'm glad you nailed that because that was a very important theme I wanted to bring out. You see, I was handed the memoir, and had massive amounts of material to go through to decide what to dramatize. No one's life is a three-act structure. As the writer you need to pick and choose the themes of the person's life. Your job is not to make a documentary film, about a historic incident, or about the person's life—your job is to give it dramatic content, and make it artful. So, with *Prize Winner,* I picked some symbols. Evelyn Ryan had won a giant freezer in a contest. It was a perfect object of contention in the marriage because Kelly [Woody Harrelson] knew he'd never earn enough to fill it up with food. I had him bring home a little package of hamburger meat and it looked so pathetic when he put it in the bottom of that vast freezer. And then when Evelyn wins a supermarket shopping spree—well, she's able to fill that freezer all the way to the top. Once you know what you want to write about, the real-life incidents will sort themselves out—the symbols just flash at you.

NL: That freezer is such a central metaphor for the whole family because when it's first delivered, the emptiness reminds the husband of his own hollowness. He even proceeds to beat up the freezer in one scene by smashing it and trying to throw it out of the house. Of course alcohol fills up the emptiness in him—or so he thinks. It actually creates more emptiness. Then Evelyn fills the freezer with sustenance, and he's jealous of how she filled it. It's like this peace they make because it needs to be filled, but *he* can't be the one to fill it.

JA: Exactly. Exactly.

NL: And at a certain point, when she isn't winning any of the contests, it does empty out, and when the freezer is empty, the glue that holds the family together is love, which you can't fill a freezer with. It's very beautiful, very poetic. Okay, so let's talk now about *If These Walls Could Talk 2* for HBO. Was that also in the Midwest?

JA: It was vague. That whole piece was about *time.* I don't think our producers were ever really clear—I kept asking, "Where are we, where are we?" We all vaguely decided it was the Midwest, but really time was more essential. It was the early '60s. Like, 1961. And then it skipped to 1972, which was when feminism had come on the scene and suddenly lesbians were acknowledged, and then the present day, where you could be married and have a baby.

NL: You focused on the issue of gay rights—being able to visit your sick partner in a hospital and make decisions.

JA: Yes. You're a wife and you aren't.

NL: Right, the feelings of exclusion. So rooted in the time, and the specificity of how much they loved each other, and how it was almost like you saw this really powerful woman and how she shrunk back, so diminished.

JA: And I used objects in the house—such as the bird collection—to address the assumption that if you're a relation, even if you're a distant relation—that you were entitled to have everything in the house. In one scene, Elizabeth Perkins' character [Alice] wanted to have the bed.

Vanessa Redgrave [Edith] came up with a brilliant idea. She said, "Wouldn't Alice want to measure the bed to see what size mattress she would want?" I called props and told them to get us a tape measure from 1961. It intensified the scene. Alice even has her daughter hold one end of the tape for her, which intensified the ugliness of the whole scene.

NL: Invasion of territory.

JA: The invasion of territory. The bed was another symbol because, of course, the bed is your marriage bed, where we assumed they made love and slept together for decades. I deliberately had Edith lay out Abby's [Marian Seldes] jammies on her bed and put the pillows out. Then grieving on the bed, and then having the bed removed. So again, I think imbuing objects with emotional symbolism is essential.

NL: Let's segue to another HBO movie, *The Positively True Adventures of the Alleged Texas Cheerleader-Murdering Mom*, which was set in Channelview, Texas.

JA: Oh, place was essential. Essential. I went down there. With any assignment I've ever had that's tied to place, I've always said to the producers, "You need to send me down there." Going down to Channelview answered a lot of questions I had. HBO handed me an article about a woman who was going to murder another woman over a cheerleading position. It was so absurd—it was so ridiculous, I had to know what kind of environment could possibly create such a situation. When I went to Channelview, it was all answered for me. First of all, it stinks—it's a refinery town—Channelview is named after a water channel that's choc-a-bloc with plastic and oil refineries, so you can smell this place from 20 miles away. It's poisonous! Not only that, when you travel through the suburbs, there are signs on the front lawns saying there are pipes running underground, carrying oil and gas and flammable liquids, and to beware. Then, on top of the ground, there were firework stands, everywhere you looked—on top of flammable ground! And then guns, guns are also such a part of the culture. I found a documentary about danger in the workplace, and they did a piece on Channelview because one of the refineries blew up and killed a hundred workers. So I immediately included that in the screenplay. It's that sense that anything could happen. Anything could blow up in this town in Texas.

> *When you live in a place where anything can blow up, your behavior is going to be reckless, and a little desperate, and a little survivalist.*

It's a survivalist kind of community. Survivalists feel that anything is okay to protect your children, including hiring someone to kill the mother of a rival—so that's why place was essential.

NL: There was also the idea of the large, Texan lifestyle, and Wanda Holloway's (Holly Hunter) desire for status.

JA: Exactly. It's near Houston. So, the ex-husband Tony [Gregg Henry] lives in a suburb out in Houston where the homes are fancier, and when we went into their house, everything in the house was for show. I remember they had a huge bookshelf with those book series that are all leather-bound, 'cause they look good.

NL: They've never been cracked open.

JA: Yeah. And they had a dog, what are those—are they Shar Pei? They're hairless and ugly, but they're really expensive. I also noticed the way the family dressed. His new wife had to have the good jewelry—and when we visited Wanda, she dressed very well, but she still lived in Channelview, in a very ordinary tract house neighborhood with the flammable gas pipes running underneath, but she still had big Texan hair, and a need to wear big high heels, look hot, and spend money.

NL: There's a great line, where she finally gets arrested, and she asks the cop, "What do I wear to jail?"

JA: Then the cop says to her, very helpfully, "You might wanna take your jewelry off." It is the culture of that particular part of Texas, the culture of appearance.

NL: Setting plays a significant role in *The Baby Dance*. The infertile wealthy couple [Stockard Channing and Peter Riegert] in Brentwood, that environment—their home was very modern and sterile, and then they went to Louisiana where it was very green and there were stray dogs.

JA: I had gone to Louisiana before. Things always grow so well in the southern environment . . . cats always having kittens and dogs always having puppies. It's very hot, and it's very wet—any seed that falls in the ground sprouts. So, yes, I wanted to take the LA couple and put them in an environment that added to the distress of being infertile. But along with the fecundity comes poverty, and what do you do with all those cats and babies and dogs and plants? So yes, it was the perfect environment.

NL: And bingo! I remember the Bingo balls, at the beginning, the way it opened.

JA: Yes. I hadn't thought of that until I went down to Louisiana and I went to a bingo parlor. I didn't realize it was such a vital part of the culture.

NL: Much like the randomness of an egg being fertilized, and that's exactly what I thought of . . .

JA: I love that image.

NL: And the same with *Prize Winner*, and another movie of yours, *It Could Happen To You*. I started to think about the role of luck. It's a big lottery, one in millions, and how many sperm are swimming toward . . .

JA: Exactly, yes.

NL: And, *Prize Winner*, with the contest—and how one thing can change your life—how it can either break it apart or bring people closer.

JA: My family was well off, and I've always asked myself, why did I get to be born into a situation where I would never have to worry about money, and where every opportunity I ever wanted, I could have—education, etc. I had parents who encouraged my creativity—why am I so lucky? Why did my soul, or whatever, land in this family, and why are there so many people who were born in such miserably heartbreaking situations? It's so unfair, and that's why luck is—why I need to keep writing about it, I suppose. With *It Could Happen To You*, at the end of the day, it's not my piece because it's been rewritten, but the themes are all there. I wrote that after my dad died as a celebration of his generosity. Because the thing is, if you have a generous heart, you will be paid back ten-fold. That was the theme. So with the cop and the waitress—luck got them that money. But the ex-wife was furious and took it away from them, and they were poor again. But because they had been so generous with what they were given, New Yorkers paid them back ten-fold. And that is my fantasy about life—that if you are generous with what you have, even if you're not paid back in a monetary way, you will be paid back spiritually and emotionally. You will have friends. I've seen people when I travel—incredibly poor people who will share everything. And that was a theme that I wanted to get out into the cultural [consciousness].

NL: One last question. When I teach, I always ask screenwriting students, "Where's the heat of the piece?" And in *Prize Winner*, you go right to the heat, I mean, his drunken rage gets very hot. And the scene when the milk spills, and the glass cuts her—those are really hot scenes. Of course not every scene can be hot, so you keep building and building, but I think part of the heat is generated from the collision of the positive and the negative. So when you're going to this place to do your research, are you always looking for the positive and negative attributes of the place?

JA: The contradiction in the place, yes.

NL: You know, love is the ultimate positive, and fear is the ultimate negative—and so it's interesting how that coalesces around the idea of how it could happen to you—the lottery ticket itself is neutral, in a way.

JA: Yes. Your will, your dreams, your hard work, the choices you make, determines what kind of life you're going to have. Nothing you do will ever guarantee that you'll have fame or money or success because life isn't always fair. But you do have control over whether you're going to act decently and stay creative or whether you're going to let joy into your life. And that's what you have to remember in this crazy business of ours. Keep getting back on the damn plow. And at the end of the day, thank your lucky stars that you get to tell stories for a living.

ASSIGNMENT

How do time and place inform and enhance your premise? How do the regional and cultural traditions of setting influence the decisions and evolution of your characters? Make a list of the ten most prominent or marked characteristics of your principal setting. How are these elements integrated into your scenes? Can you more effectively layer your scenes with the dimensions of sight, sound, smell, taste, touch and any other environmental influences?

Why does your screenplay start "today" versus yesterday or a week/ month/year/decade ago? Make a chronological calendar of what happens and when in your screenplay. What is the total duration of your story? What time of year is it? What's the weather like? Does the story take place over a holiday or special occasion? What visual cues are you providing which are specifically linked to character and place versus generic/clichéd?

3

WHO ARE WE ROOTING FOR?

Create an Iconic Protagonist with a Core Contradiction

What makes iconic characters so enduring? Their unique perspective of self and the world around them. If you strip away their external (metaphorical) masks and armor, at the center of their being will be a **paradox**. She's both a tough FBI agent and a fragile girl (Clarice Starling) in *Silence of the Lambs*. He's a seemingly fearless adrenaline junkie who's totally unable to function with any emotional intimacy (Sergeant First Class William James in *The Hurt Locker*). He's a seemingly fearless archeologist/adventurer, but he's afraid of snakes and commitment (Indiana Jones). In *The Professional*, Leon (Jean Reno) is a cold-blooded assassin, but a nurturing father figure to orphaned young Mathilda (Natalie Portman). Embedded in this paradox is vulnerability, and this creates our **rooting interest** in our protagonist—whether he/she is inherently likeable or not.

Attracting a movie star requires a magnetic role on the page.

Obviously, casting plays an integral part of any iconic character. It's the perfect marriage between actor and role. Many screenwriters like to cast their ideal actors—living or dead—in their heads as they write. In works of fiction, the most fully realized characters tend to be drawn from our own lives. What came first, the chicken or the egg, the role or the actor's interpretation of the role? For the screenwriter, the goal is to draw inspiration from these fully realized iconic characters and hatch your own fresh creation.

Iconic protagonists will often need to relinquish what they perceive to be their greatest strength.

The protagonist introduced in act one will have his/her own set of priorities, values, routines, and basic *modus operandi*. But the crises in the film will usually challenge him/her to reevaluate, recalibrate, and come to the realization that their best instincts are what brought them to this breaking point. As a result, most well-developed protagonists will initially be forced (usually) by circumstances *beyond their control* to surrender their behavioral "crutches" and find a new way of being.

In *American Beauty*, Lester (Kevin Spacey) starts off complacent but is thrown into the unknown when he is fired and ultimately grows to become the man he lost sight of along the way. In *Six Degrees of Separation*, Ouisa (Stockard Channing) walks out on her pretentious husband and their elite lifestyle, seeking a more authentic fresh start. In *Juno*, our teenaged heroine (Ellen Page) grows through the journey of her pregnancy from a snarky child into a genuine and sincere adult and expectant mother. In *Little Miss Sunshine*, Richard (Greg Kinnear) has to capitulate his "surefire" path to success, but in accepting his current (uncertain) lot in life, he finally recognizes how lucky he is. In *The Dark Knight*, after losing the only woman he has ever loved, Batman becomes the purest form of hero by accepting the mantle of villain in order to save Gotham from itself.

Iconic protagonists are forces of nature to be reckoned with, so underestimate them at your own peril.

In the Coen Brothers' *Fargo*, Marge Gunderson (Frances McDormand) is a cheerfully innocuous pregnant wife—and a badass cop with the dogged investigative skills of a bloodhound. In the Coens' *The Big Lebowski*, The Dude (Jeff Bridges) is a cowardly stoner who manages to crack open a complicated kidnapping plot and to defeat the German nihilists. In *Forrest Gump* (Tom Hanks), our mentally challenged hero is instrumental to major historical events. In *The Godfather*, Michael Corleone (Al Pacino) is a righteous war hero who emerges as a ruthless mafia kingpin. In *Black Swan*, Nina Sayers (Natalie Portman) is a ferociously determined prima ballerina whose perfectionism and delusions turn her into a killer. In *Lars and the Real Girl*, Lars Lindstrom (Ryan Gosling) develops an increasingly intense bond with his blow-up doll/girlfriend, Bianca. In *The Graduate*, Benjamin Braddock's (Dustin Hoffman) unabashed resolve to get the girl of his dreams, Elaine Robinson (Katharine Ross), transforms him into a warrior. And, consider the fierce determination of Maggie Fitzgerald (Hilary Swank) in *Million Dollar Baby* and Mattie Ross (Hailee Steinfeld) in the remake of *True Grit*. Each iconic protagonist withstands an endurance test, for better or worse, and we remember them for their fortitude and tenacity.

Iconic protagonists have a unique sense of style.

Some actors work from the "inside-out" (psychology dictates external appearance), and some work from the "outside-in" (external descriptors help reveal inner psychology) when it comes to their characters' external attitude and fashion. As screenwriters, we need to consider a similar approach when it comes to dimensionalizing our characters. For example, when we envision James Bond, we immediately picture a dapper black tuxedo.

In *Drive*, the Driver (Ryan Gosling) is emotionally guarded and silent, an enigmatic rogue who lays low and stays anonymous. (We're never even told his name.) But his sense of style is contradictory. Throughout the film, he wears a flashy silver jacket emblazoned with a scorpion. Maybe it's his lucky jacket, his talisman? Maybe he just thinks it's cool? Or maybe he defies anyone to mess with him. It's his paradox. He's mysteriously laconic and undeniably captivating.

In *Hotel Rwanda*, the cool, always-in-control posh hotel manager, Paul Rusesabagina (Don Cheadle), never goes to work without his impeccable suit and tie. But as civil war erupts all around him and threatens to destroy his family and livelihood, Paul starts to emotionally unravel. In one of the film's most memorable scenes, Paul locks himself in the hotel men's room to regain his composure amidst chaos, but he's totally overwhelmed. He looks at himself in the mirror and struggles to knot his tie, in order to maintain appearances to his staff and guests. But his hands are shaking too badly; the simple act of knotting his necktie has become impossible. We watch as Paul yanks off the tie and slumps to the floor, sobbing. If clothes make the man, then this man's spirit has been irreparably broken.

See also: Annie Hall (Diane Keaton) wearing men's ties and baggy clothes; Indiana Jones' trademark brown fedora and whip; Alex Owens' (Jennifer Beals) off-the-shoulder, cut-off grey sweatshirt in *Flashdance*; Princess Leia's (Carrie Fisher) white robe and dual-braided hair buns in *Star Wars*; the multiple piercings and body ink in *The Girl with the Dragon Tattoo* (Rooney Mara); and the swaggering Captain Jack Sparrow (Johnny Depp) in *Pirates of the Caribbean*, channeling his inner Keith Richards, in kohl eyeliner, rocker dreadlocks, gold teeth, twin-braided goatee, sparrow tattoo, silk tweed frock, and ubiquitous red bandanna.

Iconic protagonists have idiosyncratic voices and attitudes.

If you cover up the character's name on the page, your reader should still be able to identify who's speaking *because no one else in the screenplay sounds the same.* Here's Juno MacGuff's (Ellen Page) summation of her birth mother:

          JUNO
Oh, and she inexplicably mails me a
cactus every Valentine's Day. And I'm
like, "Thanks a heap coyote ugly.
This cactus-gram stings even worse
than your abandonment."

And here's Mark Zuckerberg's reply to a prosecutor asking if he has Mark's full attention:

> MARK
>
> You have part of my attention. You have
> the minimum amount. The rest of my
> attention is back at the offices of
> Facebook, where my colleagues and I are
> doing things that no one in this room,
> including and especially your clients,
> are intellectually or creatively
> capable of doing. Did I adequately
> answer your condescending question?

See also: Richard Hoover (Greg Kinnear) and his Nine-Step "Refuse to Lose" program, not to mention his (self-imposed) mute son, Dwayne (Paul Dano) in *Little Miss Sunshine*; Jonah Hill as the trash-talking, schlubby horn-dog Seth in *Superbad*; and the "money" L.A. hipsters (Vince Vaughn and Jon Favreau) in *Swingers*.

Iconic protagonists are virtually always their own worst enemies and harshest critics.

They insist on clinging to their neuroses—which Freud defined as the "separation from Self." They also tend to be self-destructive underdogs living in the shadow of former glory: Randy "The Ram" Robinson (Mickey Rourke) in *The Wrestler*. Or jealous, rudderless bachelorette, Annie Walker (Kristin Wiig), who sacrifices her last morsel of dignity in a pitifully funny game of one-upmanship in *Bridesmaids*. Or, the ne'er-do-well, divorced weatherman, David Spritz (Nicolas Cage), in *The Weather Man*, who will do anything to rouse his apathetic teenaged daughter; to win back his disparaging ex-wife; and to earn the approval of his weary, hypercritical, Pulitzer Prize-winning father (Michael Caine).

Their identities and personalities run to extremes.

What do they yearn for? What do they fear most? These positive and negative polarities will generate the spark that fuels their dramatic journeys. Melvin Udall (Jack Nicholson) in *As Good as It Gets* is a sexist, homophobic, misanthrope who writes romance novels. Tony Stark (Robert Downey, Jr.) is a flashy playboy science nerd in *Iron Man*; Aron Ralston (James Franco) is an extreme thrill seeker who goes off the grid without telling anyone where or when he'll be back, and then must endure the longest *127 Hours* of his life. A useful question to ask as you endeavor to create your own iconic protagonist is: *Who does that?*

They transcend our expectations and they dance to their own rhythm.

Some of my favorite iconic protagonists literally love to dance: *Billy Elliot* (Jamie Bell); John Travolta as Tony Manero in *Saturday Night Fever* and Vincent Vega in *Pulp Fiction*; Lieutenant Colonel Frank Slade (Al Pacino) in *Scent of a Woman*; and the indefatigable Napoleon (Jon Heder) in *Napoleon Dynamite*. If they can't dance or have two left feet, then we're treated to another distinctive character trait. As you layer your characters, be mindful of music and sound. What's the soundtrack that defines them? What's playing on their iPods? What kind of music is playing on the car radio as they drive and bop their heads to the beat? Do they hum to themselves when washing the dishes? Do they find the sound of birds tweeting melodies relaxing, or do they want to pick them off with a BB gun? Do they play any musical instruments? Do they sing in the shower? Do they hate karaoke as much as I do?

Characters are defined first and foremost by their actions.

Novice screenwriters tend only to focus on how their characters speak. But movies are a *visual* medium, so when you're introducing your main characters don't presume that their dialogue will define them beyond the superficial. Dialogue will usually serve their *personas*. But their actions and the subtext of dialogue is often what truly reveals who they are.

In *Broadcast News*, handsome, fledgling, wannabe anchorman Tom Grunick (William Hurt) comes back to network news producer Jane Craig's (Holly Hunter) hotel room for some sage advice; Jane is a little spitfire and attracted to Tom—not for his brains but for his sex appeal. He's ambitious and isn't beyond using his charm to advance his career, but he's also not interested in going to bed with her just yet. She flirts. He parries. They're at cross-purposes; he's more interested in her mind than her body. In a later scene at the newsroom, Tom observes Jane at work and is blown away by her producer acumen. He asks her to teach him what she knows. But she's not interested in teaching remedial reportage to this neophyte. He could turn and walk out without saying another word, but he decides to confront her on her fickleness. Tom asks her pointblank if she's unwilling to help him on a professional level in retaliation for his rebuffing her sexual advances in her hotel room. Jane looks at him and says:

                    JANE
          Oh, please.
               (then, almost gently)
          You're gonna have to understand
          something. This isn't personal.
She exits.

The inference is that he's totally wrong and she would *never* be so juvenile and petty. But both he and the audience can see right through her and her words are the exact opposite of the truth; she feels rejected and humiliated, so now she needs to put him in his place.

The key to an iconic character is (usually) an enigmatic backstory.

In the *Bourne Identity* films, Jason Bourne (Matt Damon) must overcome his past as an assassin—even though he's suffering from amnesia. In the present, he's an "innocent" hero being hunted by his enemies. In his past, he was the hunter. How can he disavow and overcome a backstory that he can't even remember? And just how dark was his sinister past?

It took three movies before we knew anything about Indiana Jones. And three to get to the bottom of the Luke Skywalker and Darth Vader relationship. Indy doesn't want to talk about it, and Luke doesn't even know about it.

In *The Aviator*, we see Howard Hughes' (Leonardo DiCaprio) mother bathing him as a child, and we wonder if this might be linked to his legendary OCD (clean = safe, nurtured), or maybe some kind of Freudian mommy complex that may have led to his attraction to the buxom Jane Russell?

In *Catch Me If You Can*, we meet youngster Frank Abagnale, Jr., and witness firsthand how his mother's divorcing his unsuccessful father (Christopher Walken) creates a lasting void in Frank's life. It's not until the latter third of the movie that we come to understand that his mother's abandonment has motivated virtually all of Frank's con games. For all his masquerades, all Frank truly wanted was his family back together, basking in the glow of another Christmas tree.

In *The Silence of the Lambs*, Clarice Starling (Jodie Foster) has a painful childhood secret about her failure to save the crying lambs from the slaughterhouse at her uncle's ranch. Hannibal Lecter coerces Clarice to reveal this private shame—as "quid pro quo" for his further insights into the current Buffalo Bill serial killer case. Clarice's backstory is inextricably linked to the climax and resolution of the film. When she is finally able to locate Buffalo Bill, she *must* enter his lair alone and overcome her inner demons from her past. There is a terrified, screaming woman being held captive in a pit in the maniac's house, and this time Clarice isn't going to run away from saving this "lamb." At the climax, it's Clarice flailing helplessly in the pitch-black basement, with Buffalo Bill (in night vision goggles) moving in for the kill. But Clarice's bravery and intuition wins the day. As our iconic heroine slays the beast, the bullets from her gun blast through the wall behind him and the light, literally and figuratively, overcomes the darkness.

> The screenwriter's goal is to create an iconic protagonist and then see how he/she performs under pressure. Set up their unique strengths and weaknesses; force them out of their comfort zones; find their core, primal fears and ultimate desires; identify their blind spots and challenge their limitations—pushing them to the edge.

INTERVIEW: Screenwriter/Director Steven Conrad

Steven Conrad Filmography

Best known for:

Identity Theft (2013)
The Secret Life of Walter Mitty (2013)
The Promotion (also directed) (2008)
The Pursuit of Happyness (2006)
The Weather Man (2005)
Wrestling Ernest Hemingway (1993)

NL: Let's talk about how to create an iconic, memorable protagonist by really pushing your characters to the edge and by metaphorically making them walk over fiery coals or broken glass in order to get to their goal. Some of your characters even have milkshakes or fast food thrown at them. It's amazing how you have created people who are just so well intentioned and, yet for the most part, are very unlucky. They are really strong survivors who often start off as pacifists, but by the end, are fighters/warriors. My first question is what attracts you to these characters because it's a very recurrent theme in your work.

SC: I always hope for uncovering a story that will be familiar to me in one way or another. I can't sit down and make pages if it doesn't seem like it could appear in one way or another in my life. So much of the movie market is fantastical—even when they're sold as romances, they're fantastical. They're a series of events that could simply never happen to anybody. There's a place for those movies for sure, but that shouldn't be a demand on every writer. For my part, I can't do it unless the story reminds me of a struggle, one way or another, that I've had to fight through. It doesn't have to be the actual event though. In fact, none of the things that I've written about are things I've specifically lived through, but it's the wish or the hope or the expectation behind the events I seem to need to be able to call to mind from my own life.

I write, in one way or another, about all three of those things: wishes, hopes, and expectations; that's elemental to me, the relationship of a character to those things. But I regard them as pretty different phenomena. If a character's wishes remain outside his grasp, he can quickly make peace with that—it happens to everybody on a daily basis. But imagine a character who has to handle the fact that his hopes might elude him. That starts to get a little closer to what's critical. It's harder to come to grips with. And if you create a character who has to struggle with the fact that even his basic *expectations* might go unmet, now, you're starting to get something cooking, boiling, heating up. There's a promise of conflict because that will probably make a person react. It'll make someone stand up. For my part, I try to push stories to a place that's even more urgent than that, where the character struggles with the fact that he may not even get what he *deserves*. This type of movie brings out elements of characters which may allow them to be more remarkable because their fight is not the one that we see represented most often through film narrative. There are obviously really terrific examples of this sort, from *Breaking Away* to *Planes, Trains and Automobiles*. In fact, the movies that we had from film's inception are probably closer to that quotient than any other, but they're not produced en masse anymore.

I guess I mean a story where a guy feels he deserves to be treated fairly, decently, and earnestly. To have goals that are common and to have those frustrated. You don't have to write a movie that's super real to get that energy. *Raising Arizona* has that mass in it and it makes Junior unforgettable. What does he want? He wants a family. So, I guess that's it for me . . . getting it to that place where a character realizes he may not get what he deserves.

NL: It's a sense of some kind of personal justice. The movie, *Kramer vs. Kramer*, comes to mind because you know that great scene where he has to get a job on Christmas Eve or he's probably going to lose custody of his son. How people are on completely different planets in a way because he comes in, ready for his interview, and they're like, "Hey, we're having a Christmas party, just come back after the holidays."

SC: Yeah, and knowing he's so desperate. It's a secret between the main character and the audience. A story can benefit from this design—where the audience knows elemental facts many of the story's characters don't. An example from my stuff that works like this I guess is *The Pursuit of Happyness*. None of Chris's colleagues are aware of the desperate conditions of his personal life, and there is a lingering threat they may figure it out. It's a little like that horror movie quotient where the audience knows something that the main character doesn't—that something's lurking around the corner. They're not totally different—those blueprints.

NL: In *The Pursuit of Happyness*, when Chris [Will Smith] goes to the potential client's house with his son and he gets invited to be in the Skybox at the game. First, he doesn't want the guy to know that he doesn't even have a car.

SC: Yeah, it works along those lines for sure.

NL: And, then the heartbreak when the guy just casually says, "No, no . . . it's great you can hang out with us, but I have no interest in giving you my business."

SC: That movie, for me, I didn't know quite what to do with it until I watched *Umberto D* [directed by Vittorio De Sica (1952)] It's about this guy who's walking around desperate to pay the rent, and he can't, and no one knows. It takes place in a very fixed period of time, like *Pursuit* does, but it's even smaller. Somehow watching that movie allowed some possibilities that I wasn't imagining before. *Bicycle Thief* is also an obvious model for that one. But, I don't know, for some reason, *Umberto D* got into my bones.

NL: In talking about your body of work with *The Weather Man*, *The Pursuit of Happyness*, and *The Promotion*, which you also directed, there's a lot of father/son issues running through your stories. They show men trying to figure out what it means to be a successful father. How far they'll go. In *The Pursuit of Happyness*, when Chris is trying to make the train station a magical experience for his son, Christopher [Jaden Smith], so that it's not so devastating. It reminds me of *Life is Beautiful* in the concentration camp or in *The Weather Man* with how he just wants to help his daughter, to bond with her with the archery lessons and when he takes her to New York. In terms of the father/son stories and the stories of marriages in trouble and divorce, would you say you're a cynic or an idealist or somewhere in between in terms of getting and holding a family together and being a good parent?

SC: It really is the fight of your life—to do that job well, it ought to come to feel like that. It's monumental, this promise to have everybody that you say you love to be well-served by you one way or the other. There's probably nothing more important, so why shouldn't we write about it? Share what apprehensions, insecurities we have about doing it, doing it well? I guess the trick is to make it interesting. An important thing to keep in mind may be that screenwriting is so much more closely aligned with telling a story at a campfire than it is with reading a novel. You're saying to someone, "Hey, sit down, don't move, I'm going to talk for two hours." Your obligation then obviously is to be interesting, to make somebody sit still, to pin the audience down. That's a knack. It's up to someone else to say that it's a talent, but there's no getting around the fact that it's a knack. You remember kids from growing up who could do that—pin you down with a story. If you have that knack you have a fine head start. But even as you start to apply more graduated notions about the craft of writing—like say theme development or exploration or something, I think it's worth remembering all the while that you're mostly trying to pin someone down with a tale—that the gist of all of it is as uncomplicated, and as difficult, as the challenge of a campfire story.

NL: There is a similarity between the campfire story and a movie because you're sitting in the dark and you're watching flickering light and you actually *want* the story to be good, you *want* to stay engaged. Keeping the fire going is the real talent of a screenwriter. In terms of craft when I look at your work, the stakes always seem to come back to the children, being a good father and doing this for your child because ultimately, it's not so much about getting the job or getting the money, it's about what that represents. The other thing that you seem to weave into your work that heightens the stakes is the idea of really strong contrasts between characters. For example, in *The Weather Man,* you've got David [Nicolas Cage], who nobody respects. People throw things at him. His dad [Michael Caine] is a Pulitzer-prize winning author, and if that isn't bad enough, he's terminally ill. It makes David just feel so much worse about himself at every turn. When he takes his dad to the hospital, he can't even buy him a cup of coffee correctly. I was thinking about the comparison between the idea of David trying to be a good enough dad in contrast to the guidance counselor who's a pedophile. The exact opposite. I was wondering how consciously when you're mapping out a story, you think about showing these strong contrasts between your characters? How deliberate is it?

SC: I think that just happens along the way—it's not something I consider at all before I start writing. I tend to think about very little early on other than figuring out what a character is stirred up about. Someone pointed out to me a few months ago, that none of the main characters in any of my stories have friends. And, that was news to me. It turned out on reflection that it was true. It was this thing I had been doing without having any sense that it was a rule for me, but I guess it is. For whatever reason, I've chosen to write about characters who have no one to confide anything in. It's true in my new movie, *The Secret Life of Walter Mitty,* too. I don't know why. Maybe it works better for me if there's no one there to throw a life vest.

For me, it cooks better when the character is left entirely to himself to root out the solution to his problems.

The people that I put around the main character seem to be there to draw out whatever aspects and attributes, qualities of this character that I think need to be called upon to save him. Anybody else in the movie is there to make this character clear to himself. It helps me to bear in mind that an ending, in terms of character, doesn't always imply change. You become accustomed to thinking about characters in terms of arcs because it's part of the vocabulary of collaborative filmmaking. It's a regular note you get from studios—this arc thing which promises that you're going to watch a character change. I don't recognize that from real life all that much. I'm generally suspicious of people who have immediate changes. I think all of us are. People who find God. People who overpromise. On Tuesday, he's a terrible dad, but by Wednesday morning, there's a note on the refrigerator that says,

"Everything's going to be better now." I'm just suspicious of that. The thing that I recognize more from life is the people who just won't change. I don't think that that's a bad thing. I somehow have come to depend on characters having to stay the same while they have to change the elements around them. It's not my idea, it works really well in all sorts of movies. *Meet the Parents* is that kind of movie. Greg Focker undergoes zero transformation, none. All he has to do is endure, until the people around him change. That's true of *The Pursuit of Happyness* too, in that whatever was in this guy on page 1 was still there at the end of the movie, but he had to fight for the opportunity to demonstrate it.

NL: They seem to change a little bit to me. In the Fockers' example and in *The Pursuit of Happyness*, they start off having a little bit of shame for their circumstance because they are proud and hard-working and feel they deserve better. I feel that the reason that people can prey on their weaknesses is because they do have this insecurity and this doubt. I could be wrong, but it seems to me at the end that they're not willing to be their own worst enemy anymore. I think that the people around them prey on that, and then they stand up and just say, "Look, I don't give a shit what you think anymore. This is the truth, this is who I am, and if you don't like it, screw you." And, in the beginning, they seem to want more approval than that.

SC: Yes, but isn't that the same as saying the events of the movie are there to draw out the character's best self?

NL: Absolutely. Yes.

SC: I use that a lot. I expect that what the character is going to undergo will make that happen. I won't start a story unless I feel that that's already there with my character. Mostly the way I think of it is that they're making a sound that nobody can hear. And, then the conditions around them have to change, have to come to them slightly. That the person had this potential the whole time and went and made events happen in order to draw out the promise of themselves. The point I'm hoping to make is that you might help your story if you resist some of the assumptions that seem to come with film writing—like arcs are necessary, or that genre lines have to be respected all the time. The genre thing—is it a comedy? Is it a drama? It's a drag because if you think about our early films, like Charlie Chaplin's films, they were at once very beautiful and sad—and very funny. There weren't genres then. So, when a filmmaker was making films without giving genre a thought, he made movies like that. It was an instinct to be all those things. When Chaplin was free to do anything, he aimed at doing a lot. It's a sound instinct, I think, even though you'll be pushed into narrower ways of thinking about movies now.

NL: So much of it is dictated by the marketing machine.

SC: Well, one way to resist the machine aspect of filmmaking is to make work you hope an artist can latch on to. My things only ever get made because an actor now and then wants to make them. I haven't made one yet, and I don't see it happening anytime in the near future, where the studio says we just have to make this movie. They only ever get made because I catch a break when an actor reads the script and says, "This might be good to perform." It's helped me to keep in mind that I'm not writing a book; it's not a finished thing. It's just a blueprint for other craftspeople to come in and use to do their thing—a director, an actor—and *that* becomes the draw for the audience— what the director, actor, production designer choose to *do* with the thing, not what I did with it. Scripts that spell everything out emotionally don't leave actors places to go and may be lessening the prospect they get made.

NL: Going back to the idea that your characters don't have any friends. Seems to me that maybe whether it's conscious or not, it helps raise the stakes of the story, which is another issue you hear a lot about from the studios. But, for example, if they don't really have any friends, you get the sense that the spouse was the best friend. And, then something goes wrong, usually due to finances, so that not only are they losing their marriage, but they're also losing their best friend which raises the stakes. Then, all they have left is their children, which is already the most important relationship in a parent's life, but it makes it even more dire at that point. When you're figuring out a story, do you consciously think about, "Well, the stakes aren't strong enough"? Or, is it a very organic process where it just happens from instinct?

SC: I don't think about it, but probably when I'm working on a story where the sense of what's at stake is weak, I'll just abandon it without realizing why— I'm sure that's a regular feature of the stories I quit on—that not enough is in the balance. I think decent writers have a pretty natural sense of this though and lean toward stories where something significant is in the balance. The good ones find stakes where you haven't looked before exactly, engage you with characters who aren't commonplace, and create conflict from sources you weren't quite expecting to get it from.

NL: Back to the loner character, who only has to ultimately rely on himself because he's not going to have somebody throw him a life vest, is that why you use voiceover in your screenplays? Is that a function of the character not having anyone else to talk to?

SC: Yeah, I guess it just seems better to me to create a character who's found himself in a fight and looks back at the corner and there's no cut man around. Voiceover can draw this out. But, initially I decided that it ought to be leaned into because you hear most of the time that you're not to do it, that it's regarded as a cheap trick and is elementally fake. And, sure that's true, but it's also true that every single aspect of a film is fake. Movies are pretend, so the idea of putting some restriction on how fake they ought to get seems silly to me. So I thought, if no one is doing voiceover because you hear in school that you shouldn't do it, that it might be a good thing to do. I thought it could work if what you're hearing is a surprise to the person who's thinking it and not just the character telling you the story, voiceover that is just then dawning on the person who's thinking it. I don't do it anymore. It kind of came and went for me. But I like it. But it's just one way, it's not *the* way. I just like to watch realizations about the world dawn on characters. How unkind it is. How little it cares for you. How splendid it is. Again, Chaplin did this exquisitely—no voiceover—but it can be a way there sometimes.

NL: In *The Pursuit of Happyness*, the voiceover spells out a strong theme, which is that there's supposed to be an "i" in happiness. The idea of telling the story with that particular voiceover and bringing in the stuff about Thomas Jefferson. Where did that come from in your storytelling and do you consciously think about theme when you start writing or is it just something that emerges?

SC: No, I never add that layer of complication to it. I really try to stick to a basic plight and trying to create a question for the audience over what might happen next. I guess I bury any sense of theme. I guess the Jefferson stuff popped into my head because the challenge Chris faced felt American to me.

NL: Did you see happiness misspelled on a wall somewhere?

SC: No, I just wanted to draw out this idea that Chris knows that his child is not going to be excellently looked after for most of the day—that Chris is completely aware of that but has to undergo it anyway. It seemed like a clear way to communicate a feeling that most of us have to want to exceed our conditions. Very little of what I write I actually draw from things that happen. I love beyond all else the feature of movies that they're pretend, as I was mentioning. I think most of the people who make them, myself included, wouldn't fare well out in the real world. Maybe we come to movies exactly because they're made up, and they let us live in a world where things don't work the way they do normally. There's probably a reason why none of us are in the army. I hope to help make films soon, in fact, that have less of a real sensibility in terms of storylines and settings, that aim for Alice in Wonderland grandeur. I'd like to see how far that can go and still be about humans.

NL: How much pre-planning do you do before you start writing? Do you outline?

SC: No, I never do. That's created problems for me because you have to do it if you're going to work in the system. People expect it, but it's a challenge for me as I'm bad at it. But maybe it ought to be a challenge for a good writer to be able to come up with something interesting before he writes it. It ought to be impossible to do that, maybe, to fully imagine something before you sit down and devote all the hard work and hundreds of hours it takes to do something well. I wish I could. I see the assets of it. It just doesn't directly work for me. I generally just sit down and wait for something to occur to me that's interesting.

NL: In *The Pursuit of Happyness*, you have a pretty defined structure because it's inspired by a true story and you know you're starting with a guy who is just struggling so hard to get through it.

SC: The proposition from the studio was to tell Chris Gardner's life story and that could have meant birth to where Chris Gardner is now. Nobody early on identified that two-month period as our narrative. But luckily, nobody asked me to pitch a take on it. I had made movies with the producer Todd Black before—we're friends. And I think that Will Smith was okay with letting me go away for a little bit and just seeing what I came up with. So I was allowed to spend the time writing pages which ended up in the garbage can until I saw the one that could possibly have a story in there. I don't know if I would have been able to find that if I had to pitch it a whole lot. So much of what's good about good movies would be impossible to pitch. If you list your ten favorite movies, I wonder if you can imagine anybody pitching them in a room in 20 minutes. *The Big Lebowski*? Something good is going to get left out. So I got really lucky with the development of *The Pursuit of Happyness*. I guess that only really works if you have a personal relationship with the bosses and have earned a little faith that if you turn in something that doesn't work, the producer knows "Well, give him another week, he'll fix it." Where they know you'll do the hard work it takes to find some common sense of accomplishment with it.

NL: Do you start off with any loose benchmarks? Do you write in a linear way? Or, do you just start with a particular character and think, "I'll see where it takes me"? Maybe it's different on each project.

SC: No, I guess I jump all over the place and try to find enough scenes to put them together. Then they line up in a way where I start to see a little bit of a path somewhere. Then I go back and rework the scene to more clearly mark that path.

NL: What would you say you've learned the most from seeing your work go from page to screen? Whether with Gore Verbinski or Gabriele Muccino or directing yourself with *The Promotion*—how has that influenced your writing process?

SC: I guess when the stories are on screen you get the chance to watch the audience's body language while they're in the middle of them—you can see, clearly, what bores or excites them, when they're tuned out or engaged. When they're tuned out, you think to yourself, "Okay there's a good part coming up in like four minutes" and you start wishing that good part would hurry up and come. So I guess you learn to try to put more good parts in. Because during the good parts you hit a height where the score and the performance and the idea all coalesce, and there's this feeling of: "I'm glad to be sitting here in this theater right now."

NL: It's magic.

ASSIGNMENT

How do you decide who your dominant protagonist is? In general, he/she will be the character who: (a) has the most proactive goals; (b) has the most to lose; (c) changes the most in the course of the story. Now it's time to peel away the outer, superficial layers (masks, defenses, personas) and *dig deeper* into what really makes them tick.

Answer the following questionnaire from the first-person POV of your protagonist:

The Character Game

What is your name?
How old are you?
Where are you from?
Where do you currently reside?
What is your favorite item of clothing or personal accoutrement?
What is your most favored room in your house? Why?
You walk into a bar, what do you order to drink?
What do you consider to be your best and worst physical features?
What is your worst vice?
At the start of the movie, what is your highest priority?
Who are you closest to in your family—(meaning spouses or blood relatives)?
Who do you call in an emergency?
Who in your circle of family/friends/coworkers could most likely betray you? Why?
Have you ever committed a crime? What did you do? Did you get caught?
You find a wallet containing $500 cash and a driver's license—what do you do?
Do you have any pet peeves?
What do you consider to be your biggest weakness (Achilles' heel)?
What do you consider to be your greatest strength?
What is your credo/philosophy in life?
What has been your biggest accomplishment thus far?
Key regrets?
What is the biggest misconception about you?
What is your most vivid childhood memory?
Have you ever been in love? When? With whom?
Do you believe in God, and if not, what do you put your faith in?
What is your ultimate wish for your life—if you could have or do anything?
What do you hate most about yourself?
What is your innermost, core fear? Why does that frighten you?
Do you have a secret? Something you've never told anyone or perhaps only a select few?

4

WHAT'S THE POINT
(OF VIEW)?

Add Dimension to Characters via POV, Subtext, and Dialogue

Once you've chosen the genre, tone, premise, and perhaps central relationship and conflict for your movie, you then need to decide on the point of view (POV). Is this a single, main protagonist story told in linear time? Is this a dual protagonist story? Is it a multi-protagonist story? Kaleidoscopic? Ensemble? The possible answers to many of these questions can be found in Chapter 8 on Structure. But POV is often more than a structural concern. It's also an issue of your characters' unique voices and perspectives. Are you telling the story from the POV of the good guy or the bad guy—or both? Is the protagonist looking back and reflecting on his life or are we taking the journey with the character and witnessing his discovery firsthand?

There are two basic points of view: objective and subjective.

Objective POV is a general, expansive, more or less "neutral" POV. It shows us all events, and is not limited to the protagonist's presence in scenes or his/her POV. Examples: *Rise of the Planet of the Apes, Contagion, Michael Clayton, The Bourne Identity, The Dark Knight, Magnolia,* and *As Good as It Gets.* If voiceover is used, the voice will be an external, omniscient narrator versus the voice of a character in the movie (which would render it subjective).

Subjective POV is a limited POV wherein we see everything—or almost everything—from one or more characters' perspectives. Singular or multiple subjective POV movies will often incorporate a specific character's voiceover and/or flashbacks, so we can see the effect of backstory and memory that has informed this subjective reality.

In *The Iron Lady,* we meet Margaret Thatcher (Meryl Streep) as an old lady having breakfast with her husband, Denis (Jim Broadbent). They chat about the price of milk and we experience their close bond ... until Mrs. Thatcher's secretary enters, and we realize that Denis is a figment of Margaret's imagination; her husband recently passed away, but she can't let go. She's also in the early stages of Alzheimer's. The film subsequently cuts back and forth in time according to Margaret's memories, and Denis remains omnipresent as her confidant until the end.

Other examples of subjective POV: *Juno, Martha Marcy May Marlene, Fight Club, Memento, The Sixth Sense, Amélie, Shutter Island, Extremely Loud & Incredibly Close, The Opposite of Sex, Brick, The Big Lebowski,* and *Up in the Air.*

Subjective POV can also be used as a heightened storytelling device—in which the camera itself plays an active role in the plot. *Paranormal Activity, Cloverfield, Open Water,* and *The Blair Witch Project* effectively spook us by utilizing "found footage" (revealed either up front or at the end). *Buried* gives us the claustrophobic POV of U.S. truck driver Paul Conroy (Ryan Reynolds) who's buried alive in a coffin in Iraq—with only a lighter and a cell phone at his disposal.

In the true story drama, *The Diving Bell and the Butterfly,* the POV is the ultra-limited perspective of *Elle* magazine editor Jean-Dominique Bauby (Mathieu Amalric), who suffers a debilitating stroke and is totally paralyzed—except that he retains movement in his left eye. The story is primarily told from the POV of Jean-Do's one functional eye, so when he blinks, the screen goes momentarily black. We can vicariously experience his severe limitation, along with his boundless determination and courage. And, how's this for inspiration? Jean-Do can only communicate by blinking his left eye to correspond to a prescribed sequence of letters and numbers—and he still manages to get his writing done!

Some movies offer both objective and subjective points of view.

The Hunger Games is primarily from Katniss' (Jennifer Lawrence) POV, but co-screenwriter/director Gary Ross also added the POV of the high-tech surveillance control room (not in the novel) to illustrate the power and domination of puppet master, Seneca Crane (Wes Bentley). This control room provides an omniscient perspective to monitor and manipulate the games.

In Ken Kesey's landmark novel, *One Flew Over the Cuckoo's Nest,* the story is told in the first person narration of Native American Chief Bromden (also known as Chief Broom) who tells the story after he has escaped from the hospital. Chief Broom tells the story from his subjective POV, even though he suffers from paranoid hallucinations. The Chief is also mute and deaf, which provides him with a sort of all-access pass to privileged information. In the movie version, the story unfolds objectively with no voiceover or first person POV. We empathize with antihero Randle McMurphy (Jack Nicholson), but the story is told about him rather than by him. And at the end of the movie, his perspective is eviscerated via lobotomy.

When writing a subjective POV, determine whether the audience knows more than the protagonist—or less.

In *The Silence of the Lambs*, Clarice arrives at a house to follow up on a lead in the case. We know that the man who answers the door is actually Buffalo Bill, the notorious serial killer she's been hunting all along. Unfortunately, she doesn't realize it until she's inside his lair in a dangerously compromised position.

In *The Girl with the Dragon Tattoo*, Blomkvist (Daniel Craig) re-enters the house of Martin (Stellan Skarsgård), not realizing that Martin is already on to him. But we already know and this fuels the taut suspense in the scene, as Martin notices the missing butcher knife and lures Blomkvist into his torture chamber.

In *Spider-Man*, we know Norman Osborn (Willem Dafoe) is actually the Green Goblin well before Peter/Spider-Man (Tobey Maguire) realizes it. In *Michael Clayton*, we witness the plot to murder Arthur Edens (Tom Wilkinson) well before Michael (George Clooney) could hope to anticipate it and protect him.

Conversely, check out these examples of movies in which the audience knows less than the protagonist:

The opening chapter of Quentin Tarantino's *Inglorious Basterds*, set at a French dairy farm in 1941, is a master class in POV and suspense. The scene unfolds from multiple perspectives and in three different languages: French, German, and English. When the S.S. Colonel Hans Landa (Christoph Waltz) arrives with his Nazi soldiers hunting for Jews at the home of French farmer, Perrier LaPadite (Denis Menochet), it doesn't appear that Monsieur LaPadite has anything to hide. But as the scene slowly progresses, we discover the Dreyfus family hiding under the floorboards. As Col. Landa enjoys his fresh glass of milk, he charmingly coerces LaPadite to come clean. Landa does so, at first, in English—which he knows the Dreyfus family does not understand, and then he switches back to French (all subtitled in English). After he casually bids adieu to LaPadite, Landa signals to his soldiers. They enter the farmhouse and riddle the floorboards with bullets, decimating all but one daughter of the Dreyfus family—who manages to escape. In this example, LaPadite knew the Dreyfus family was hiding all along, but the audience doesn't discover his secret until almost the end of the scene.

See also: Rachel Getting Married, Garden State, and *Ordinary People,* in which we experience the aftermath of a tragic event—its ripple effects—but we don't usually discover the full truth until the last third of the story.

Tell the story in the cut.

A great deal of screen storytelling is done in the transitions between scenes. Actually, many filmmakers believe that what you *cut from* and what you *cut to* are even more vital to story progression than the content of the scenes themselves. Today's audiences are quite proficient at filling in those "blanks" with their imaginations. In *Tootsie*, when Michael Dorsey (Dustin Hoffman) is told by his agent that no one will hire him on either coast, and Michael challenges him with, "Oh no?"—we immediately CUT TO: Michael making his way down the street dressed as Dorothy Michaels. He first appears in a sea of urbanites, but then we recognize him and make the logical leap. We already know from the prologue that Michael is proficient with stage make-up and adept at altering his appearance to suit various male roles. We don't need to see him making the female transformation. The dynamic cut is from the static shot of Michael, at a career impasse in his agent's office, directly to his alter ego, Dorothy, navigating Madison Avenue in high heels, blending in, but off-kilter. And one of the greatest comedies of all time is off and running.

With an unreliable or withholding narrator, the audience knows less than the protagonist.

In *The Usual Suspects*, *Fight Club*, and *Atonement*, each narrator has an agenda to keep the full truth from us until the climax.

In *American Beauty* and *Sunset Boulevard*, the narrators withhold crucial information from us about their untimely demises. We know from the beginning that things aren't going to end well for them, but we don't know when, how, or why.

Sometimes an unreliable narrator is just forgetful. *The Big Lebowski* is narrated by The Stranger (Sam Elliott) who starts telling the story about The Dude, but then loses his train of thought. To tell you the truth, for many years I believed this movie was narrated by the tumbleweed, but he's actually a cowboy that the Dude happens to meet at the bowling alley—and the man to whom he tells his story.

In paranoia or psychological thrillers, we're usually in the same (subjective) POV as the protagonist.

In this way, we get to experience his/her limited perspective—intensifying the suspense. If you go this way, try to keep this fixed perspective consistent.

In *Take Shelter*, we see family man, Curtis (Michael Shannon), becoming increasingly paranoid that the world is a lethally dangerous place and on the verge of the apocalypse. As he fortifies a bunker to protect his family from impending doom, his wife, Samantha (Jessica Chastain), and the audience can see that he's becoming more and more delusional. The film allows us to see both perspectives: his and hers. It's excruciating to watch, but a potent character study with an inevitable conclusion that is provocative and surprising.

See also: Black Swan, Shutter Island, Rosemary's Baby, and The Tenant.

Dual protagonist POV provides us with a parallel narrative and the expectation that both worlds will intersect—which may or may not occur.

In The Girl with the Dragon Tattoo, we first meet journalist Mikael Blomkvist (Daniel Craig) in damage control mode from a bruising scandal at his magazine, and then separately get introduced to Lisbeth Salander (Rooney Mara) at a rare in-person meeting with her boss and their client. Here, we're shown two separate lives that collide via necessity—as they come together for a common goal.

In the instances of The Departed, Donnie Brasco, and Breach, we are introduced to hero and antihero at cross-purposes, and both are operating under the shadow of deception and duplicity.

In the parallel narrative, Julie & Julia, we are crosscutting between two totally separate protagonists, writer/blogger/aspiring chef, Julie Powell (Amy Adams), and legendary master chef, Julia Child (Meryl Streep); their distinctive worlds; and time periods. The glue between the two narratives is lots of butter and each woman's passion for French cooking. The two women never meet, but they do sort of come together in the last scene; after Julie views Julia's reconstructed kitchen at the Smithsonian Museum and exits, the display kitchen magically transports us back to the day when Julia received the first published copy of her famous cookbook, The Art of French Cooking.

A Rashomon POV (inspired by the Akira Kurosawa masterpiece) provides us with several different perspectives on one event—and lets us form our own conclusions.

Variations on this POV include the heist thriller, Before the Devil Knows You're Dead, in which we witness the violent armed robbery of a jewelry store from multiple points of view. See also: The Usual Suspects, Courage Under Fire, and the animated Hoodwink'd.

In Amores Perros, we see a terrible car wreck from the POV of three different characters, each connected by their love for dogs. 21 Grams shows us the impact of a fatal car accident on three different protagonists. In Babel, an antique rifle ultimately links four different families on three continents. These last three examples each utilize a fractured narrative timeline to increase urgency, mystery, and suspense. See Chapter 20 for my interview with screenwriter Guillermo Arriaga.

What We Talk About When We Talk About Dialogue . . .

Unless you happen to be the reincarnation of the late great Paddy Chayefsky, when it comes to writing effective dialogue: less is more. There are also other great current dialogue maestros still alive and thriving—many of them interviewed in this book—plus Woody Allen, Judd Apatow, Diablo Cody, Aaron Sorkin, Quentin Tarantino, and other exceptional wordsmiths.

In addition to editing out the extraneous words that don't inform on character and/or advance the plot, here are some tips for honing your dialogue skills:

Dialogue is not real speech.

Movie dialogue needs to be somewhat heightened and "pop" off the page more than our everyday conversations. It also needs to be much more economical, distinctive, and focused on driving the plot forward. There are many exceptions to the rule of brevity, especially when it comes to comedy; if dialogue is laugh-out-loud funny, whether it's on point or not: don't cut it!

Each character needs to have a distinctive voice and attitude.

No two characters will look at the same situation in the same way. It's not just a manner of speaking; it's driven by character. Even if your characters were raised under the same roof and attended the same schools, each person needs to have a unique manner of speaking. Find words that only one character tends to use in order to distinguish his voice from others. Some characters are laconic, others are motor mouths; some characters use their smarts as a weapon—such as Mark Zuckerberg (Jesse Eisenberg) in *The Social Network*. Some characters use their words sparingly to remain elusive and therefore powerful—such as the Driver (Ryan Gosling) in *Drive*.

Before writing a scene, it's essential for you to know where the characters have just come from and where they're going next. Where they just came from might be the previous scene or maybe we haven't seen them in the screenplay for many pages; the important thing is that the writer knows where they've been. Did your character just have a big fight with her husband and now she's trying to be buoyant at a business meeting? Did another character just get fired from his job and now he's picking up his son at a play date?

There's a difference between a persona and who a person truly is.

In *The Devil Wears Prada*, Miranda Priestly (Meryl Streep) has a hyper-judgmental, sardonic voice in the workplace, but in Paris when Andy (Anne Hathaway) visits her in her hotel suite, we see a very different Miranda—sans make-up and too exhausted from her impending divorce to put on her usual airs of superiority; she's genuine, vulnerable, and it's the first time we get to hear her true voice:

                    MIRANDA
Another divorce splashed across
Page Six. Just imagine what they're
going to write about me: "The dragon
lady. Career obsessed. Snow Queen
drives away another Mr. Priestly."
... I don't care what anybody
writes about me. But my girls [twin
daughters] ... it's just so unfair
to the girls. It's just another
disappointment, another letdown.
Another father figure.

But after displaying too much emotion for comfort, Miranda puts up her "mask" again and keeps Andy at a professionally appropriate distance. Andy asks Miranda, with heartfelt compassion, "Is there anything I can do?" And Miranda coldly responds: "Your job."

Great dialogue is all about subtext.

Studies have proven that communication is somewhere around 93 percent body language and only 7 percent verbal.

This statistic translates to the huge importance of subtext. Aristotle wisely espoused that characters are defined by their actions. Needless to say (irony intended), characters are usually defined by what they do more than by what they say. How many times in your life have you asked someone if he/she is mad at you and the verbal response is "No," but the body language tells a different story: arms crossed, back rigid, or no eye contact? We all know that what people say is often the exact opposite of what they mean. The trick is *writing* it.

In *Annie Hall*, when Alvy (Woody Allen) first comes over to Annie's (Diane Keaton) apartment and they have a glass of wine and get to know each other on the terrace, check out how the subtext is articulated:

Throughout the following exchange we see subtitles on the screen in the manner of a foreign film. The subtitles show what the characters are thinking as opposed to what they say.

                    ALVY
        (gesturing to a series of
    photographs on the wall)
    Did you take these? They're great.

                    ANNIE
        Yeah, I—I—I dabble.

Title: I dabble? Listen to me—what a jerk.

                    ALVY
          They're very interesting. They have—
          a—a—quality . . .

Title: You are a great-looking girl.

                    ANNIE
          I'd like to take a photography
          course.

Title: He probably thinks I'm a yo-yo.

                    ALVY
          Photography is an interesting art
          form because a real set of aesthetic
          criteria haven't emerged yet.

Title: Her legs are great and what a great ass.

                    ANNIE
          Aesthetic criteria—you mean—whether
          it's a good photo or not?

Title: I'm not smart enough for him. Hang in there.

                    ALVY
          The medium or material of photography
          becomes a condition and enters into
          the total effect.

Title: Thank God I read that article by Susan Sontag.

                    ANNIE
          To me it's all instinctive. I just
          feel it. I try and sense it, not
          think it so much . . .

Title: God, I hope he doesn't turn out to be a shmuck
like the others.

                    ALVY
          Of course, but an over-riding
          theoretical sense places it within
          the perimeters of social perspective—

Title: Christ, I sound like FM radio. Relax.

In *The Town*, Doug (Ben Affleck) follows bank manager Claire (Rebecca Hall) to a laundromat to determine if she's been talking to the FBI about the identity of the gunmen who robbed her bank. She doesn't realize that he was the masked robber who'd taken her hostage. When she spots a blood splatter on the white blouse she was wearing during the bank robbery, she breaks down, crying. She believes Doug is just an innocent bystander, a stranger. She's embarrassed and apologizes for her display of tears: "I'm just having a bad week." Doug responds: "I understand." She has no idea how much he understands. Doug asks her out on a date and she accepts. When he picks her up outside her apartment building, she wants to be fun and carefree, but the robbery is still weighing too heavily on her. She confides to Doug about the ordeal. The audience knows the truth, but Claire is completely in the dark. She tells him she was blindfolded, and the gunman (Doug) told her to keep walking until she felt the water on her feet. Check out the double meaning in their dialogue—another form of subtext:

> CLAIRE
>
> Longest walk of my life. I kept feeling like I was going to walk off a cliff.

> DOUG
>
> I'm sorry.

> CLAIRE
>
> It's not your fault.

He determines that she never saw the robbers' faces, but she's certain that she would recognize their voices if she ever heard them again. Doug's reply: "It'd be harder than you think." The real meaning in the scene is what *isn't* being said. That's subtext.

Effective dialogue is about power dynamics.

In the opening scene of *The Social Network*, the more Mark (Jesse Eisenberg) prattles on about his perfect SAT score and ambition to get into the elite Porcellian Club—ostensibly to impress Erica (Rooney Mara)—the more he succeeds at alienating her. He's trying too hard, but he can't seem to censor himself; his intellect outshines his charm. For the future founder of the social network, the guy's got zero social skills. He keeps trying to dig himself out from under the rubble of his words, but he can't. Mark wants to feel important and powerful in this scene because he's easily the smartest person in the crowded room. But Erica is in the power position because she's pretty, and Mark believes that she's more interested in muscular jocks on the crew team than she is in playing verbal ping-pong with him.

I highly recommend that you check out a book called *Impro* by Keith Johnstone. It has a wonderful chapter on status. There is also *Games People Play* by Eric Berne for the transactional therapy take.

Good, snappy dialogue will often overlap.

Lively characters often talk at each other rather than to each other. Urgency is the lifeblood of dramatic heat, so characters don't necessarily have the time or patience to speak in complete sentences. Unless you're writing proper, upper crust, exceedingly polite characters, don't be afraid to let them interrupt each other. Cutting people off mid-sentence can also be a form of a power struggle: *Listen to me. No, you listen to me.* Who gets to talk, when, and for how long are decisions the screenwriter needs to make. And don't shy away from conflict.

Check out this excerpt from *Broadcast News* set in a high-pressure network news editing room:

                    JANE
             (consulting notes)
        Go back to 316, Bobbie. The sound
        bite in the cab—it starts, "I don't
        know how I'll feel . . ."

                    BOBBIE
        We could . . .

                    JANE
             (interrupting)
        Please, Bobbie, we're pushing.

As Bobbie expertly reverses the tape, Tom's [William Hurt] face appears in glass doorway and then he enters the already crowded room—Jane's [Holly Hunter] eyes click to him briefly. She makes not a move to welcome him. He pauses, but is committed and tries to find a place for himself against the wall.

                    TOM
        They said I should observe the . . .
Jane is distracted by the noise. Tom leaning over towards her.

                    TOM
        They said it would be okay if . . .

>   JANE
>   (incredulous)
>   We're working here!! You can stand
>   over in the uh, uh, uh . . .

She momentarily can't think of the word 'corner.' Then
back to Bobbie:

>   JANE
>   Play back the last line . . .

>   BOBBIE
>   He said something about . . .

>   JANE
>   (sharply)
>   Let me hear it!

Bobbie, taking the sharp commands with ever increasing,
yet still repressed resentment.
   The Assistant Director, BLAIR LITTON [Joan Cusack],
enters the editing room. She is about 26 and every night
since she got her job as Assistant Director she has been
the first to crack under pressure.

>   BLAIR
>   We'll need it in ten minutes. We're
>   putting it directly into . . .

Jane holds up a finger of warning to Blair as she picks
up a ringing phone and talks to Bobbie at the same time.

>   JANE
>   (into phone)
>   Craig, just a second—
>   (to Bobbie)
>   Let me hear it!

Memorable dialogue is informed by characters' obsessions.

What do your characters want to talk about versus what does the plot need
them to talk about? What's most important to them? What are their highest
priorities? Characters' highly specific neuroses provide them with their
voices.

In *Wonder Boys*, not only can James Leer (Tobey Maguire) effortlessly rattle off the names, exact dates, and specific methods of movie stars' suicides, but he can also do it alphabetically.

In *Sideways*, Miles (Paul Giamatti) has a prized bottle of wine—a 1961 Château Cheval Blanc—that he's been saving for a special occasion that might never come. And he will not, under any circumstances, drink Merlot.

Ideally, exposition and backstory will be conveyed on a subliminal level.

"Show, don't tell," is the #1 rule of screenwriting. But what does it mean? Characters don't need to explain everything they're doing because, hopefully, we can see them actively doing something. But when it comes to the past, unless you default to flashbacks, how can you get across the history between the characters? Find visual cues that are emblematic of the past. The most common picture that's worth at least a thousand words is a photograph. But photos tend to be overused for this purpose, so try to find other more expansive possibilities. Utilize a character's living space to articulate character. Is it organized or sloppy? Do they collect anything? What books do they have on their shelves? What food do they have in their refrigerator?

In *Se7en*, Detective Somerset sets a metronome every night before he goes to bed; it's the one sound he can control in the cacophonous urban jungle.

In *As Good as It Gets*, no one needs to tell us that Melvin has OCD; we can see how he locks his deadbolt locks over and over, always in the same sequence, and we also witness how he only washes his hands with a fresh bar of Neutrogena soap before he throws the new bar in the garbage. We also understand when he shows up at the café that it's his usual restaurant and his usual table—and he offends the waitresses and other diners, as usual. But no one has to explain the backstory to us. It unfolds through conflict. The best dialogue is often left unsaid.

Screenwriters tend to feel most productive when they're writing lots of dialogue. But never underestimate the power of silence on the page. Great actors can express volumes with their facial expressions, pauses, and body language. Of course, they need the screenwriter to have the confidence to weave nonverbal scenes into the script. Sometimes the best scenes can render the hero profoundly speechless.

INTERVIEW: Screenwriter Scott Z. Burns

Scott Z. Burns Filmography

Best known for:

The Man from U.N.C.L.E. (TBA)
The Bitter Pill (2013)
Contagion (2011)
The Informant! (2009)
The Bourne Ultimatum (2007)
Pu-239 (2006)

NL: Let's talk about the genesis of *Contagion* from the standpoint of character and your way into a story. You also play around a lot with perspective in both *Contagion* and *Pu-239*, where you start, go back three days, and then catch up. These are really intricate screenplays. *Pu-239* was based on a short story, but *Contagion* comes from you, right?

SZB: Contagion actually came from a scene in *The Informant!* There's a moment where Matt Damon's character, Mark Whitacre, is watching his FBI handler who's played by Scott Bakula on the phone. Scott coughs into the phone and Whitacre goes off on this riff, "Oh great, I'm going to get sick, then my kid's going to get sick and miss school, and then I'm going to miss work, and who's going to pay for all that?" I think on some level subconsciously I was fascinated by the Malthusian projection through the world that a virus would have. So, when we finished *The Informant*, [Steven] Soderbergh and I thought we would do a movie about Leni Riefenstahl, so I started doing research on that and then Steven called me and said, "I don't think I want to do the Riefenstahl movie right now, do you have anything else?" I said, "I've always wanted to do a pandemic movie like *Traffic* to explore the different aspects and how it affects people." And, he said, "Great, I'm in." So, then I began researching, and for me, research is a wonderful privilege of this profession in that if I decide to write a movie about a pandemic, I can go and have access to amazing scientists who want to speak to me and tell me about their lives. So, not only do you get the information, but you also begin to get ideas for characters because the people in the movie will have the same professions. The same thing happened in *Pu-239* where I spent time with some nuclear scientists at Los Alamos and some other places. Research is my favorite part of the process. So, I started learning about pandemic illness. The first thing that I saw was a TED Talk given by Larry Brilliant who is an epidemiologist, and I was able to go meet with Larry who said he would be supportive. He functioned as my rabbi through the whole entire process. Hooking me up with other epidemiologists and people at the Center for

Disease Control (CDC) and virologists and other folks who spent their life in public health and dealing with pandemics.

NL: Once you had the scientific basis of "this is plausible"—and what's so terrifying about the movie is how you see that something so small can be so devastating, just like with Patient Zero and the AIDS epidemic—then did you decide, "I want to tell this all over the world"? Sometimes it's hard because a lot of creativity is very mysterious and it just occurs to you. Starting in Hong Kong and then the affair and then leading to her husband and having her come back—was there a reason why you decided to have that particular way in to your story?

SZB: As I met with scientists and heard them talk about what their process was when something like this occurs, it became evident to me that there was a group of people whose job it is to work backwards in time to try and figure out where a virus comes from. That they're investigators and there's a procedural element to that. So, I liked the idea of someone having something to work back in time with as this thing rushes forward. But, then there's also the public health aspect, so Laurence Fishburne's character became a CDC official who would march forward in time with the disease. While simultaneously Marion Cotillard's and Kate Winslet's characters work backwards against the clock trying to find where this thing came from and what it was. I liked the tension between those characters and what that meant in terms of time because I knew those would be easy things to separate. The contrast in them drew me because as a storyteller you know that that's going to be two very different points of view right away. They form the spine of the movie, but at the same time, I felt that I needed characters who were not in the science community, who were essentially the audience's proxy, and that was Matt [Damon] and Gwyneth's [Paltrow] characters' family. They became very important to me because you saw how a decision or a misstep that the scientist made would reverberate through them. Then, I wanted a character who was a bridge, so I created Alan Krumwiede, the Jude Law character, who because he was a journalist and a blogger could play both sides of the fence and have the interests of both groups involved. That character really came to pass because there was so much that I learned in doing the research that I couldn't have one scientist talk that way to another scientist because they already have a common body of knowledge. I needed to come up with a character who could express these things in a way that was inflammatory, so that at times we want to agree with Alan Krumwiede and at other times we think he's a snake oil salesman.

NL: He is either the conspiracy theorist who is trying to get at the truth or maybe he's just trying to profit from it.

SZB: These four points of view became this box that I could build around the virus. You never see it. You only see what it causes.

NL: In classical dramatic terms, the virus is the antagonist of the story. But, there's also antagonistic relationships between people both with the hysteria and with people having their own agendas in their part of the world, "This is my responsibility, I do this . . . you do that."

SZB: What you learn very quickly when you start speaking to people in public health is that the virus is one problem, but human fear and panic and behavior and xenophobia and paranoia and ignorance and a whole set of other human foibles are activated during those times of stress. That was a big revelation to me about how much of a factor that is in all of these outbreaks throughout time. Whether it's the vilification of gay people during AIDS or the fact that the Spanish flu is called the Spanish flu because Spain was neutral in the First World War and they needed to come up with some name which wouldn't piss off any of the other countries—even though there's a lot of evidence that the Spanish flu came from the American army going all over the world.

NL: It seems the way to activate hysteria in any situation is to just have some prominent official say, "Stay calm, you have nothing to worry about." Because we technologically have viruses in our computers, I thought it was really brilliant to also show the spread of information electronically and how we can get infected with those viruses as well.

SZB: I learned doing research that there's a website where you can put in the serial numbers of your dollar bill, and it'll show you all of the places that your dollar bill has been and is likely to go. It's a lot of the exact same modeling that epidemiologists use for the spread of viruses.

NL: Do you have a planning process when you sit down to work? Do you outline? Do you do scene cards?

SZB: I don't really have an outline. What I do is make a list of every scene I can possibly think of that would be interesting. And, those accumulate during the research or just through thinking about the project and then they begin to organically take on an order. For me, I spend a lot of time thinking about transitions in film. In part, that is because that's what I know Steven thinks the most about. I try to tell the story in a cut which came from reading Walter Murch's amazing book, *In the Blink of an Eye*. He has this analogy that he makes: if you take a beehive and you move it a great distance while the bees are gone, they're actually able to find it again. But, if you move it actually a small distance, they get confused. I think the same is true of transitions and editorial. It's even true within small shifts . . . if you're cutting from a profile to a shot head-on, that will work, but if the camera isn't really moving all that much, then it ends up being an awkward jump cut. I think that happens in writing as well. If you make little incremental shifts, it sometimes is confusing, but if you move around, it forces the audience to start filling in. You activate their brain in the storytelling process. Like in *Pu-239*, when I was writing it, there was a Shiv scene and a Timofey scene—and a tension grew by bouncing back and forth between those stories that informed the language of the film. The same thing happened in *Contagion*. *The Informant* was different because Whitacre was in every scene. But, when you have these different points of view to shift, you can really advance the story and bring the audience in as your collaborator because they need to fill in some of those spaces. I'm a big fan of *Babel*, and multi-braided kinds of stories. However, I didn't want *Contagion* to be that. I wanted it to be where each scene hands off the story to the next scene, so it's really one story. But, the story is advanced through shifting perspective.

NL: There is also a trust that is developed with the audience. In *Pu-239*, initially we know that the two meet, and he's selling something and you create the mystery, "What is this Pu?" Then, we go back in time. Even if you didn't have that first scene, we intuitively know that if we spend a lot of time with one guy and then you just put him aside, that he's going to connect back with the story at a certain point eventually.

SZB: It was initially written that way where you spend a lot of time with Timofey and then you met Shiv. But, I think it was harder for the audience, which is why when I edited the film I thought we needed to tease . . .

NL: You needed to do the initial "these people are going to connect" in a mysterious way at the beginning, so that you wonder later about how and why.

SZB: I never took a screenwriting class. I've never read any of the books that people read and I suspect those books are really useful. I'm more interested in letting the story tell me how to tell it. I like the idea of starting a movie at the beginning of the third act, for like a second, as a tease, and then going back to the beginning. Because again, having the audience know that's in their mind, you can fuck with them in really good ways because they may think they know how you're going to get to that moment.

NL: Soderbergh likes that structure. Even in *Out of Sight*, it's great. Coming out of the bank, tearing off the tie and then looping back around.

SZB: And then, your responsibility is to get back there in a way that is logical, but not expected.

NL: When you have multiple characters all over the globe, do you work out the line of each of those characters separately?

SZB: You have to make four movies. You begin to understand why [Tom] Stoppard wrote, *Rosencrantz and Guildenstern are Dead*, because you realize there's a lot of time when your characters are off screen, and what's happening to them then? Even though, you might not end up shooting it, you do need to account for it in some logical way. Steven and I talked about that a little bit. I feel that my job as a screenwriter, once I've mapped out all four of those things which I will eventually put on note cards, is to say, "This is an interesting point in this story," especially if it comes on the heels of the moment in another story, and the juxtaposition of those two things is really going to propel things forward. But, the only way I know how to do that is to do the work of laying all four of them out and figuring out where you'd want to be in each individual story so that it contributes to the overall film.

NL: In all of the stories you've worked on, the timeline is really tight which helps with suspense because there's urgency right from the beginning: Timofey is about to die, decaying from the inside out because of the radiation poisoning and the pandemic is spreading. Do you have to know, this is Day 1, this is Day 2, this is what hour we're at? One of the things I loved about *Contagion* structurally is that you started it on Day 2. I hadn't seen that before. You almost forget about it and it gives you your great ending. Was that something you knew from the beginning and where did that idea come from?

SZB: In the very first version of the movie, I always wanted to end it by revealing how the bat and the pig met up—that to me was a mystery that I felt the audience would want to know. Then, through the editorial process, starting with Day 2 came later as a way of teasing that even more and underscoring that part of the movie had to be a detective story—and that's what science is at its best. I'm happy when people watch that movie and feel like it's pro-science.

NL: In *The New Yorker* review by David Denby, he points out how faith, religion, and God are not a part of the story at all. And, how when the chips are down and there's just complete hysteria, the characters all cling to science. I wondered if this was a very conscious decision on your part to leave out people going to church and praying?

SZB: There was an early scene at a mosque where you saw people in close proximity to one another, coughing, and there was also a scene in a Catholic Church where people are sick in line taking Communion, but the reason those scenes came to pass was because scientists had told me that there's a real issue every year when people go to Mecca during Islamic holidays because if someone is sick and you have a quarter of a million men in a tight space, they're going to cough on each other and then they're going to go back out into the world. There's always been a concern, and scientists have done some studies that outbreaks of diseases follow any of these sorts of pilgrimages, whether they're religious or otherwise. Steven and I wanted to get into that a little bit, not to condemn religion, but just to show how human beings congregating was an issue. There was also a scene that we wanted to do at an NFL football game which is another form of congregation and is just as much a type of worship in this country as anything else, but the NFL wouldn't let us. Even though, in the scene the way I wrote it, there was a sign on the scoreboard or a thing that came up on the scoreboard saying, "Please observe social distancing, wash your hands." But, the NFL was like, "No, we don't even want to go there." To me, science is our best bet in solving some of these problems and a greater understanding of the world of nature which, for me, is a very spiritual thing. For me, there is an environmental message in *Contagion* that is a part of how I think about the world which is why I was involved in *An Inconvenient Truth*. There is a moment when Al Gore does his slide show that he talks about how disease vectors will increase with climate change. There's a malaria band around the equator of this planet and as it gets warmer, that band widens and as it widens, it will start to engulf population centers that probably developed because they were outside of the malaria band. We're going to have a lot more sick people as the weather changes because population centers developed away from certain diseases. Human expansion is a part of what makes us vulnerable to certain diseases. We're getting in contact with animals in places we've never been before.

NL: I'd like to ask you a few questions on theme which has been the most polarizing question in this book. Half of the screenwriters I've interviewed say, "Don't ever think about theme just tell the story, let the audience figure out what it's about." "You want to avoid being preachy, pretentious, and thematic." And, then the other half say, "Theme is everything." "You absolutely must start with theme, you can build everything around that."

SZB: Flannery O'Connor said, "If there's no surprise in the writer, then there's no surprise in the reader." So, I think you may enter as a writer having a moral position or thematic expectation, but for me, the process of writing, hopefully, forces me to scrutinize that. I'm drawn to material where there's a lot of grey area. Sam Shepard said, "In the middle of a contradiction is where you find the most life." I think that's an important thing for people to understand in creating stuff and in their own relationships. So, that's where I come down on it. I like characters who are morally complicated. Mark Whitacre [from *The Informant!*] did steal quite a bit of money, but he was sick and he was manipulated by the government. I like when people walk out of that movie, and they're not sure how to feel about Mark Whitacre. I know that in Hollywood there's a tendency on the part of some to say, "Well, that's not satisfying," but my experience of film growing up is that it's immensely satisfying. When I saw *Dog Day Afternoon*, I fell in love with Al Pacino's character who is the basis for Shiv's character in *Pu-239*. He's a guy who does a lot of bad things for some really lovely reasons. I think a lot of human beings do that. So, to me, that is the theme—to investigate the kind of contradictions that life forces us into. Those have always been the characters that I want to write about.

> *When you start a project you have a position on something, it's impossible not to, but the challenge, if you're going to create good characters is to work against that and try and find the honesty in what makes people make their choices.*

NL: Any advice on writing great dialogue? In *Contagion* for example, you have so many people, how do you make each one distinctive? Were you able to base some of your characters on the people you met during your research?

SZB: A few things. One, I tend to mutter my script out loud as I go and really try and hear the language. I'm always amazed when people don't do that because you're not writing prose, you're writing something that's going to be spoken. Spoken language is different than written language. So, that's one thing. I think the second bit of advice I have is, or at least it's one of the things that I employ, do try and find people in the real world for these characters, and sometimes if you're lucky, it's a scientist that you've met or sometimes you can imagine your father if he was that scientist. I think Laurence Fishburne's character is a little bit like my dad on some level in terms of tone because I wanted his character to be the kind of guy you pick to get in front of the cameras because he is authoritative, which is why I was so thrilled that we ended up with Laurence in that role. Sometimes it's voices of people in the real world or characters from literature that you've read. I do think you have to pick a real person in the world and try and channel that voice while you're writing. Otherwise, everyone starts to merge and sound the same. Or, even going so far as to pick an affectation. Have someone say something like, "You know," a lot which I seem to do. Those are probably the three things that I try and do.

ASSIGNMENT

Eavesdrop on a real life conversation and write out the dialogue. Now "rake" the dialogue and prioritize the scene. Does the scene need to start at the beginning? Can you start in the middle and trust that we can understand the context based upon visual and verbal cues? Can we discern their backstory? If the people in the real life conversation sound too much alike, fictionalize and make each one distinctive. Analyze the power dynamics in the scene and who gets the last word.

5

WHAT'S AT STAKE?

Give Your Protagonist Something to Win and Something to Lose

The stakes in a movie can be defined as the consequences for your protagonist's inaction. In other words, what will happen if he *doesn't* become proactive in the face of the impending crisis in his life? Will he lose something of great value? I read a great many screenplays each year for both students and professional rewriting assignments. The most common weakness in lesser scripts is lack of dramatic tension—which is usually a symptom of: (a) no stakes; (b) low stakes; or (c) lack of clarity of what's at stake. Don't let this happen to you! Ideally, your protagonist will face a big challenge at the end of act one which will spark an *active* goal for him. This goal (or Plan A) is based upon necessity because if he doesn't accomplish it, there will be stakes.

The highest possible stakes in a movie are life and death.

In the thriller, horror, action-adventure, and science fiction genres, it's easier to establish stakes because the hero is usually battling against a nefarious villain, and the stakes are for him/her to stay alive and/or to save the lives of others—and there's almost always an urgent deadline. *See Chapter 13 on Ticking Clocks.*

In the classic action-thriller, *Die Hard*, police officer John McClane (Bruce Willis) gives thieves (posing as terrorists) a dose of their own medicine as they hold hostages in an L.A. high rise. The stakes are raised because his estranged wife is also trapped in the building. And the stakes are even higher because McClane is the *only person* inside the building who can solve the crisis. He's also a New York cop in Los Angeles—a fish-out-of-water—and he's up against the cunning, extraordinarily intelligent mastermind of this operation, Hans Gruber (Alan Rickman).

In *Contagion*, the worldwide medical community races to find the cure to a deadly epidemic before it turns into a pandemic and wipes out giant swaths of the global population.

The life and death stakes are much more contained and personal in *50/50* with Adam (Joseph Gordon-Levitt) fighting to beat the odds for survival of his cancer diagnosis.

In *Winter's Bone*, 17-year-old Ree Dolly (Jennifer Lawrence) struggles to keep her family together in an extremely poor, desolate town. Then, the Sheriff informs her that unless her degenerate, deadbeat dad shows up for his trial, Ree and her siblings will be homeless and penniless since he used their house as collateral for bail. She is stonewalled by all of her father's dangerous contacts in the local crystal meth business. Undeterred and fighting for survival, Ree risks her own life for the sake of her family.

In *Unstoppable*, a veteran train engineer (Denzel Washington) and his inexperienced, but brash young conductor (Chris Pine) must work together to stop a runaway train before it derails into a fuel oil tank farm, causing a major environmental disaster.

In the sci-fi thriller *Super 8*, a restless group of student filmmakers in a small town witness a calamitous train crash—and then must battle against an alien invasion.

When there aren't actual life and death stakes, the potential consequences need to feel like they're life and death to your protagonist.

In *Swingers*, hapless Mike (Jon Favreau) is still so emotionally raw from being dumped by his girlfriend that he spends the whole movie trying to fill that void. In one particularly uncomfortable yet hilarious scene, Mike leaves increasingly desperate messages on the answering machine of a pretty new girl (Nikki) he just met at a party. And we want to die *for* him. Mike had hoped that Nikki would be his ticket out of forlornness, but when she finally picks up the phone, she tells him never to call her again.

In *Little Miss Sunshine*, each time Richard (Greg Kinnear) phones his slippery agent, Stan Grossman, that call *feels* like Richard's lifeline to provide for his struggling family.

There's a terrific, high stakes sequence in *The Pursuit of Happyness*, in which single parent Chris Gardner (Will Smith) needs to sell the last of his bone density scanners in order to feed and shelter his young son. A homeless man takes off with one of Chris' scanners, and Chris chases him through the streets and subways of San Francisco *as if his life depended on it*. And later, Chris and his little boy find themselves in even greater dire straits, forced to sleep on the floor of the filthy men's room in the train station. Chris does what he can to spark his son's vivid imagination and turns the ordeal into a magical experience. This is a real low point for Chris, which raises the stakes for him to land that internship with Dean Witter.

This sequence is reminiscent of Roberto Benigni's masterpiece, *Life Is Beautiful,* in which a clownish father, Guido (Benigni), convinces his son that they're on a fun holiday and playing an elaborate game—in order to protect his little boy from the horrors of a Nazi concentration camp. Both films demonstrate how a shift in perspective can transform even the bleakest situations and temper the stakes.

Think of act two as a trap.

The second act of your screenplay is a battleground, and your protagonist has been drafted. He can't desert or opt out as a conscientious objector. He's both obligated and compelled to fight for a vital cause and against an antagonistic force whether he wants to or not. Why? Because if he tries to turn back or walk away from the challenge, the price—or *stakes*—will be too high. He stands to lose more than he can fathom. Put another way: what he stands to win is deemed less valuable than what he stands to lose.

Burn your hero's bridges so the road back to the relative safety of the "ordinary world" isn't even an option.

Without stakes, it's very difficult to launch a second act with enough dramatic tension or suspense, which will cause the middle of your screenplay to sag.

In *Mission Impossible 4: Ghost Protocol,* Ethan Hunt (Tom Cruise) and his Impossible Missions Force (IMF) are tasked with infiltrating the secret Kremlin archives to locate files identifying a mysterious terrorist, code name: Cobalt. But when the mission goes disastrously awry and a bomb destroys the Kremlin, the Russian government considers the attack an undeclared act of war. The U.S. President extracts Hunt from Moscow and activates "Ghost Protocol," a black ops contingency plan that completely disavows the IMF. Hunt and his team are to take the blame for the attack, but will be allowed to escape from U.S. government custody. Once free, they can finish their search and destroy mission against Cobalt—now identified as Kurt Hendricks (Michael Nyqvist): a Swedish-born, Russian nuclear strategist/crackpot hell-bent on starting a nuclear war. The only trouble is: Hunt and his team will have no U.S. government backup. It's Hunt and his handful of compatriots *out on their own*—and with no other alternative—to save the world.

Know what's most valuable to your protagonist at the start of the movie—and then place it at risk.

This will establish the positive goal (+) and negative stakes (–) in your screenplay. Notice the + and – push-pull in each of the following examples:

In *The Departed,* William "Billy" Costigan, Jr. (Leonardo DiCaprio) endeavors to prove his mettle and loyalty to the State Troopers' office, but if he gets caught as the mole by mob boss Francis "Frank" Costello (Jack Nicholson), Billy knows he's a dead man. At the same time, officer Colin

Sullivan (Matt Damon) wins a promotion to supervisor, but if he gets unmasked as a crooked cop under the thumb of the same mob boss, Colin's going to prison for life. Two Irishmen on opposite sides of the law. Ironically, the ostensibly "good" cop (Colin) is the scumbag, and the renegade informant (Billy) is the righteous one. What Billy values most is to achieve his lifelong dream of becoming a full-fledged police officer. What Colin values most is his relationship with his mentor and father figure, Frank Costello, and the power that Colin has amassed by playing both sides of the game.

In *The Town*, Doug (Ben Affleck) stands to lose both his band of thieves (his *de facto* family), and his new love, former bank manager, Claire (Rebecca Hall), if she finds out the truth about his role in the bank robbery.

In *Rise of the Planet of the Apes*, the ape (Caesar) stands to lose both his freedom and the one father figure he's ever had, Will (James Franco).

In terms of stakes, romantic relationships are emotional high wire acts—and there's no net.

Regardless of age, most protagonists are immature in one area of their lives and the experience of the movie will compel them to grow up. On a certain level, *all movies are coming-of-age stories*. The common fears of intimacy, commitment, and abandonment continue to haunt many characters well into their prime. Bridget Jones (Renée Zellweger) yearns to win the heart of Mr. Right—or else she will continue to face her sense of loneliness. Andy (Steve Carell), aka *The 40-Year-Old Virgin*, just wants to lose *it*—or else he'll always be sexually frustrated and despondent.

In *Up in the Air*, unrepentant bachelor Ryan Bingham (George Clooney) impulsively hops on a plane to (uncharacteristically) declare his love for Alex (Vera Farmiga). What's at stake for Ryan at this point in the movie is his newfound appreciation for family. Unfortunately, when Alex comes to the door, Ryan discovers that she's married with kids—and he is heartbroken.

Teenagers offer us another more innocent perspective—where almost *anything* can feel like life and death stakes. In *Twilight*, Bella (Kristen Stewart) has an undying devotion for handsome vampire Edward (Robert Pattinson). Her teenaged angst suggests that she'd rather die than live without him. Young love will go to any lengths to be together. Whatever. Blood is thicker than raging hormones. *See interview with* Twilight *screenwriter, Melissa Rosenberg, in Chapter 19 on Dramatic Fire.*

In the Swedish horror film, *Let the Right One In* (remade in the U.S. as *Let Me In*), a victimized 12-year-old boy, Oskar (Kåre Hedebrant), dreams of revenge against his bullies. Then he meets Eli (Lina Leandersson), a mysterious, outcast girl who seems to be allergic to the sun and food, and can only enter a room if invited. Eli gives Oskar the fortitude to fight back against his bullies. But when he realizes that Eli is a vampire who needs fresh blood in order to survive, Oskar is faced with a moral dilemma: even if she would never harm him and she has the power to make him invincible, how can he love a serial killer?

For teenaged angst supreme, check out the iconic scene in *Say Anything* in which the underachieving Lloyd Dobler (John Cusack) stands outside the beautiful class valedictorian Diane's bedroom window, holding his boom box over his head, blasting Peter Gabriel's "In Your Eyes." What's at stake is losing the girl he loves more than anyone or anything in the entire world.

In *Sideways*, Jack (Thomas Haden Church) is chased away from a one-night-stand by his date's bruiser boyfriend who threatens to kill him. He takes off—butt naked—and arrives back at the motel . . . only to discover that he left his wallet and his *wedding ring* (!) back at the scene of the tryst. Now Jack and his best man, Miles (Paul Giamatti), must go back into enemy territory or else Jack's fiancée will kill him. Jack finally realizes he's a careless cad and vows to clean up his ways. This is his moment of truth; at stake is that he still very much loves his fiancée and will do anything not to derail their wedding plans.

In *Tootsie*, it's clearly established that protagonist Michael Dorsey's (Dustin Hoffman) reason for being is his acting career, but as the plot thickens and his ruse of masquerading as Dorothy Michaels succeeds beyond his wildest expectations, he falls in love with his gorgeous co-star, Julie (Jessica Lange). And now the stakes are higher than ever: love. Unfortunately, he can't have fame *and* love without truth. In the end, he becomes a better man from being a woman. But he can't earn the reward until he grows up, comes clean, and suffers the consequences.

When it comes to stakes, the present will always supersede the past.

No matter how substantial the events of the past were, the past is over, and the present is here and now.

The parallel narrative film, *The Debt*, takes place in both the past (1965–66) and the present. In the present, we meet retired Mossad agent, Rachel Singer (Helen Mirren), and come to learn that she's lived the last 50 years with a painful, haunting secret. Back in 1965, Rachel (portrayed in the past by Jessica Chastain) and her associates had been tasked with capturing a notorious Nazi war criminal, Dieter Vogel (Jesper Christensen) known as the "Surgeon of Birkeanu," and transporting him to Israel to be put on trial. However, when their mission was compromised, young Rachel had been forced to shoot Vogel. Vogel is presumed dead, and Rachel and her cohorts agree to justify his murder with a lie that Vogel had been trying to escape. This dark secret comes to light in the present when Rachel discovers that Vogel is actually still alive and a patient at a hospital in Ukraine. The stakes of the past now have a potentially devastating impact on the present; in addition to an aged, ostensibly senile war criminal having escaped punishment for his past atrocities, Rachel's legacy is now at stake.

This is exacerbated by the book Rachel's daughter, Sarah (Romi Aboulafia), has written about her mother's heroic mission—for which Sarah is being lauded at a literary celebration. Rachel fears the truth could irreparably damage her daughter's reputation and thus their relationship. In the end, Rachel locates Vogel and kills him in self-defense. Having finally settled this old score, Rachel could choose to walk away and keep her secret hidden. Instead, she leaves a note explaining the truth for a reporter to find. Now that she's finally fulfilled her mission, she's ready to accept the consequences. As horrendous as it was, the past is now over, but Rachel still has the opportunity to overcome its stigma in the present.

> Where is the heat in your script? Seek out your characters' positive/negative goals and corresponding consequences. Every battery has a +/– charge. This is how energy—and the best drama—works.

INTERVIEW: Academy Award-Nominated Screenwriter Sheldon Turner

Sheldon Turner Filmography

Best known for:

By Virtue Fall (also directing) (2013)
X-Men: First Class (story) (2011)
Up in the Air (2009)
    Academy Award Nominee
    WGA Award Nominee
The Texas Chainsaw Massacre: The Beginning (2006)
The Longest Yard (2005)

NL: The Longest Yard is all about pushing characters to the edge, confronting fears, and raising stakes. Paul Crewe (Adam Sandler) is a character that starts out very self-absorbed and hedonistic, but gets humbled, very quickly when he's thrown into prison. Can you talk about the process of adapting it from the original film—what new things you brought to that character, and how you got inside him?

ST: It's a fascinating thing because if you speak to many filmmakers they'll cite the movies of the 1970s and 1980s as being really influential, myself included. So you look at a film like *The Longest Yard*, which was really a product of that time, I mean Burt Reynolds was an asshole in that, unapologetically so. What it gives you is an apparent arc, there's somewhere to go. I thought it was important to retain the 70s spirit of it, and when I came on to that project, Adam [Sandler] was producing along with his partner Jack Giarraputo, but it was never going to be Adam. So initially, it was designed as sort of a Brad Pitt, or a Vince Vaughn, or an Owen Wilson, and we developed it like that with a certain swagger to him.

You didn't like him, but you couldn't take your eyes off him. And then putting him in an extreme situation, and there's not much more extreme than prison, and if I'm being cynical, I'll say that change doesn't happen after the age of 14 without a gun to your head. And I think the equivalent of that is prison. So I kept pushing, let's push him to a place that he does wrong. He doesn't do it because he's going to save his mom's house, he doesn't do it because he's going to help an old lady cross the road; he's doing it because he's a douche—and in a sports world where it was an easy transmogrification into the twenty-first century, you have this sense of sports entitlement, even more so than it originally was, because now we have these athletes from the age of ten who are anointed and essentially allowed to go through as spoiled brats. And that was always who Paul Crewe, the twenty-first century version, was going to be. Someone who absolutely had never been told, "No." And then to put him in a place where everyone's going to tell him what to do, that's what hooked me, and the potential of a remake.

I love the movie, so I had to make sure that in loving the original I wasn't beholden to it. I didn't feel a huge onus to carry on. There's a criticism that it's too similar, but I think it's in where you choose to deviate, and for us that place is always character, it was always a sense for me of not just updating and saying, "Oh, now he's got an iPad," but a sense of how a guy, who was born of a culture that's so much more entitled than Burt Reynolds, would have been. Now for me, we were very lucky that we got Adam to do it because he is inherently likeable. Likewise, if it wasn't George Clooney in *Up in the Air*, I think the trip would have changed. I think what's made Adam so successful is he has an acute sense of what he can get away with on film and an acute sense of his persona, and he accepts it. But he also knows that it enables him to push those characters a little more. Where I've proposed something to other actors that is going to give us that arc and show that flaw early on, they're opposed to it because they're frightened that they're going to lose an audience with it. So I think it's a combination of static character before you even integrate it with an actor, and then once an actor comes on, trying to make that work in a way where we have to be aware of how likeable that person is, and work within the framework of that.

NL: The prison system really helped you with that because I think, whenever I have students who say, "How do I make a character more likeable or more approachable?" I say, "You have to look for their vulnerability." By throwing him in prison early on, you created a conflict with those guards right away.

ST: It's a huge part of it. I think you can have organic growth because getting back to the sense of people—the smell test for audiences—I think they know when something's not real. So for Paul Crewe, I think a lot of that had to be organic. It couldn't just be, "Now I'm behind prison bars, and I'm going to turn into the great humanitarian." He had to lose something, he had to lose a friend, he had to see that there were true stakes there, that there was the possibility of being that 75-year-old man who had been in prison for 40 years, and the terror of that, and then ultimately the character choice of, "I'm not going to throw this game. And I don't care what the expense of that is."

For me, it's always been that personal thing. Because, while it might not be saving planet Earth, it's still about the relationship that we identify with. We all know what it's like to not have the love of a father, to feel like you have to earn more of that love. I think moviegoing is a very selfish endeavor in a good way. It's selfish in that, for instance, biographies always sell well, not necessarily because we give a shit about Winston Churchill, but because we care about how Winston Churchill can help us. I think it's not dissimilar for a movie if you can help make people feel like: what would I do if I was in a prison like Paul Crewe? If we can play to the selfishness, the good selfishness, of an audience, I think it's a great thing. There's a reason Steven Spielberg has a movie about the invasion of planet Earth, but it opens up like *Kramer vs. Kramer*. Because it's all about making people feel like this is a world they identify with. And that was always a struggle, truthfully, with *The Longest Yard*, because there was always the higher pitch comedy of Adam. There was the "Where do you get laughs?" but you don't do it where you're showing wedgies at minute one and then what should be a hard hitting scene when he goes to prison—because it's not all fun and games. It was a similar challenge for *Up in the Air*, where in early drafts of the film, before there was 12 percent unemployment, I was able to deal a little more fruitlessly with fired people. There were a little more jokes, it was a little funnier; we knew we had that latitude. But then when the economy started to turn, it changed everything. You had to have more of a nobility, for lack of a better term, more of an obligation and responsibility to how you were going to portray that stuff.

NL: Like putting in the interviews with the real people.

ST: Right.

NL: In *The Longest Yard*, another big challenge is the fact that these characters are antiheroes. Yet we're cheering for the criminals in the big game, and we're completely wanting the warden, James Cromwell, to eat crow. It's a huge challenge though, and I wondered at any point, if you considered making him less of an antihero—like if you think of *The Fugitive*, he's innocent.

ST: That's a huge cloud in a good way. I'll tell you what the blessing was of *The Longest Yard*, which was my first film. The blessing was that we had

Jack Giarraputo as producer. It was a great process because it was extremely collaborative. I've never had a producer since then who's been that invested in the evolution of it. I remember an exec getting on the phone and saying, "Well, there's concerns of this and that," and because Jack's an 800-pound gorilla, he'd say, "No, you're totally wrong, you're an idiot. I'm sending it to Sherry [Lansing]." Most producers wouldn't do that, even if they had the power they wouldn't do that. So the beauty of working with a heavyweight producer like that, is they know when they can pull it, and when they have confidence in a script, it's a beautiful thing. For me as a writer, all I want is to feel protected. I just want to feel that if I do my job that someone's going to fall on their sword, if they believe in the project. And I think that's what producers don't realize. We, as screenwriters, are kind of the lion with the thorn and just waiting for somebody to pull that thorn out of our paw, and anyone who does, I think we'll be eternally grateful to. And not to deviate too far, but I talk to screenwriters all the time and invariably the question is, "What's your favorite studio? Who's your favorite exec?" And we all sort of go, "I don't really have one." Because, by and large, they don't have a sense of that fidelity; they're not trying to earn the loyalty, and I think that's to the detriment of Hollywood. I really think it's a problem.

NL: It's like a homogenization because there's pressure to hit the "four quadrants"—everybody every age that could play all across the country—but now it's global.

ST: At one point, we were toying with the idea of saying, "Well, where's the girl? Do we want to make a penologist come in and observe the prison?" And to their credit, you know Jack and Adam they said, "No way. This is a movie about guys and prison." And it didn't hurt the box office, we made two hundred million dollars.

NL: Because you have your bromance with Chris Rock, the kicker. It's a really sweet relationship. You know Paul is straight because he was with Courtney Cox in the beginning, but the two cell mates are the "love" story.

ST: Exactly, because all the time I'll talk about ideas that I love, and people say, "Why would women want to go?" And I think women go because they want to see a good story. It's not so selfish that they have to see a woman on the screen, just give me a compelling story. The same goes for me. I saw *Bridesmaids* and loved it. But I've got to tell you, on top of being funny, it's a good movie. It's got heart; it's really well done. And again, having those guys protect me, by saying, "No, we're not going to put a female in, we're not going to make Paul more likeable because we know what Paul's going through," was incredible because I've had the opposite happen where you write a character that you love and you push him, and then we go to the studio and they go, "He's not likeable." It's so frustrating, I can't tell you how often that's happened.

That was always the thing, and I give [director] Pete Segal credit because I was worried that it was going to be the big sort of Adam, which he does really well, but the problem is there aren't those types in prison. And there were times when, you had the wedgies and those sorts of things, but they never take you out of the film. That's what I think I'm proudest of with that movie—is that it doesn't overwhelm the sense of tone, because tone is everything. I think the problem, and again we talk about the 70s movies as being so influential, but we really don't learn the lessons of them. Because the thing the 70s talked about was pushing characters to the edge.

NL: Well, *Dog Day Afternoon* and *Network*—talk about pushing characters to the edge. Two of my all-time favorites.

ST: Absolutely, I'm a huge Sidney Lumet fan. And he did *Prince of the City*, a film that's probably going to be the most influential in the film that I'm going to direct, and what he did with Treat Williams' character by pushing him. I was watching *The Friends of Eddie Coyle* the other day, and it's the same kind of mystery. You don't know what's going on in the first 20 or 50 minutes of that movie, and I always think that was a great paradigm to work from. I think audiences will stay on if they're intrigued. *Die Hard* opened with a guy on a plane trying to stretch his feet, and once you understood that character and the plight that he was going through, then the explosions were even bigger than they could ever be because you cared about the guy that's in the middle of them.

NL: Would you say that movies are getting shorter now? It used to be 120 pages, now 110, and some people even like 100.

ST: I think it's why we respond to movies that are well done. And even the *The American*, a slow movie, owes a debt to the 70s. I watched *The Verdict*, another Lumet movie. What a movie.

NL: The pinball machine.

ST: It's awesome. There's even little moments like where he goes to meet the extra witness, and he's got a white carnation in his suit, and then he just throws it out. They never say it. You feel like now if we did that scene, we'd have to say, "Oh you're wearing the white carnation"—we'd have to point it out. I think that goes back to the central idea that we don't trust the audience anymore. There's this sense that they're stupid, and we're going to condescend to them. The best lesson I learned on this was from my attorney on the first script I ever went out with. There were moments I thought were particularly clever, and like a young idiot writer, I felt compelled to underline them in the script because I was so terrified that people would miss it. My attorney called me up and said, "Here's the problem, the dumb people aren't going to get it, and the smart people are going to be offended that you didn't think they were smart enough to get it." He was absolutely right.

NL: That's good advice.

ST: And the thing is you've got to trust in it. The problem is that from the standpoint of macro-Hollywood because there's so much material, there's also an inherent lack of respect. The assumption is, "Look at all these scripts, how hard could it be?" You and I both know, it's easy to write a shitty script, it's really difficult to write a good script.

NL: My script has taken 20 drafts, and I'm still doing little tweaks.

ST: That's the temperament of being a writer—the sense of knowing that the editing process is grueling, and just when you think you got it, you didn't get it, and you have to go back in and rework something. It takes a certain kind of mentality to do that, and that's why I say temperament's more important than talent, or as important, in this business.

NL: On the subject of preparation, as a writer, for *The Longest Yard*, how much research did you do? Did you go to the prisons?

ST: I did, but I think the reason I got hired was because I played college football. I think for Jack that was very important. So there was an inherent knowledge of how the game was played in writing those scenes. For me, I had to get a sense of, thankfully never having been in prison, getting a sense of how it operates now, as opposed to in the 1970s. You can't have a chain gang the way it operates in that movie, but you can have the equivalent now. So, a lot of this came from visiting prisons and getting tours, but also from just talking to professional athletes and trying to integrate the mentality of: "All my life no one's ever told me that's wrong. So I can steal a car, and get in a chase scene, and wait a second, you're going to arrest me now?" Just that sense of indignation of, "Do you know who you're dealing with?"

NL: In addition to research, how do you outline? What's your preference as to how much time you spend before you start writing an adaptation or an original?

ST: I have to start out with legal pads. I still love the organic sense of pen on paper. And my rule is, before I even start to write an outline, I have to fill a legal pad up with random thoughts, themes, ideas for scenes, musings about character, and dialogue. Once I get through that, then I start to actually get into the outline form. I hate outlining by the way. It's horrible, but it's so necessary. I always have a disclaimer, a little caveat when I hand in outlines, to a studio, I say, "Don't get too married to what's in it because there's a different process when you get on the page." I think that you realize more and more as you write: what is going to work in an outline and what is going to be difficult to translate into a script. I think there are people who write amazing outlines, but write shitty scripts. I think it's finding that balance in-between. What's great about what you do is forcing people to talk about it. It always changes everything when you say, "Tell me about your movie."

NL: What about theme?

ST: I'm big on theme. And even for a movie like *The Texas Chainsaw Massacre*, I had a theme. It's my guiding force, my narrative guide, through every scene in that movie. And the same goes for *Up in the Air*, and for any movie I write, there's got to be that underlying theme, even if it's something parenthetical or tertiary that comes in periodically.

NL: In *Up in the Air*, we don't really know that much about why Ryan Bingham is the way he is. Was that in the novel or earlier drafts?

ST: In the novel, they talk about the sister character as there is in the movie, and it was hoped that she would shed light on the distance that he keeps with everyone, including his family. I think ultimately suspicion comes from self-suspicion. This lack of trust, I think it's a necessity of doing that job. To me, at some point in doing a job like that, it becomes a part of you, you don't become a part of it. In order to do that, you make decisions, mostly subconsciously, of how I'm going to better be able to do this, not unlike a solider would in war.

NL: How much of the character do you need to know before you start writing?

ST: All of it for me.

NL: How do you decide what is going to bleed into the story, and what you're going to keep back, but allow behaviors to be influenced by it? Like Clooney likes being a platinum card member, he likes being a VIP.

ST: Which is certainly a character trait. I think for me, I write extensive dossiers about people, about characters. Where they went to high school, who their first girlfriend was, things that are never going to make it into the movie, but for me that makes them real. And then every once in a while things trickle through, and you don't necessarily know where it comes from. I think it helps with dialogue, it helps to really identify how these people speak specifically. I'm sure you read scripts where everybody sort of talks the same, and I think that's a function of not understanding the character. So for me, I want to know everything. And in fact the more stuff that's not going to make it on the page, the more stuff I want to know. Because then it really informs what he does and not really in a way that is methodical and didactic in terms of, "I know in my dossier in third grade he . . . so what do we do here." But just in an intuitive way, and that's where the challenge is to not feel constrained by your outline. I think there's two kinds of writers: There's the mechanical writer who goes through it methodically because scene 22 is going to pay off in scene 48, and then there's intuitive writers, which I consider myself the latter.

You do spend a lot of time on stuff that doesn't pay off, be it on projects that don't come together or be it on specific scenes that are never going to make it into your script. But you have to do that stuff, and I have to convince myself that those things actually serve a purpose. So that the scene that you and I are going to excise, which is never going to appear in any shape or form anywhere in the script, the soul of that scene will still be in the script.

NL: And for Ryan Bingham, it's being in control. As long as he's in control, of course, he doesn't feel vulnerable. And then, of course, love throws him off his game, and he has to let go of some control, and so it becomes his Achilles' heel. For your process, creatively, are there certain things that you need to know? Like, "I need to know what his weakness is . . ."

ST: All those things, and I also need to know the more idiosyncratic things. Everyone I think has a seminal moment in their lives. It doesn't have to be, "I got in a car crash," it can be something benign, but something that influenced their world view. I want to know what that is. More times than not, it doesn't make its way into a monologue in the movie, but sometimes it does. I have to know what their relationship with their father is, what their favorite kind of music is, what they listen to. What do they do when they get home? Do they turn on the TV? Do they go to the refrigerator and pop a beer? What is going on with this character when they're alone? What are the things that motivate them?

NL: So, we've seen how to raise the stakes for characters by using their yearnings and fears, how do you also incorporate the role of mystery? In *The Longest Yard*, there's a mystery embedded in the story because he doesn't want to talk about what happened in the past. So, the theme for me, which is a great theme because it's ironic, is that the truth will set you free. When he finally comes clean about his past, it sets him free even though, ironically, he could end up being incarcerated. Do you consciously think about giving your character a secret or something to obscure?

ST: Definitely. For me, it's never really a secret, it's more about having a whole profile of who this is, and finding the thing I want to bury. If it's after the creation of the character, I'll usually look through it and say, "That's something I could dole out," and you sort of circle it and go, "That's the main thing, that's why this guy is the way he is." It's the thing that he's going to guard most closely. And that's where you have a responsibility. I think we've all seen movies where we don't buy someone. I also think a movie's bad when the only way they can get information out is through alcohol. How many movies have we seen where the plan is, "Okay, let's have them get drunk together, and they'll share this moment"? I think that's a cheat. I don't think it works that way, and it feels inauthentic to me. So how do you put somebody in this situation? Again in *The Longest Yard*, we had the luxury of putting him in prison, but there are real challenges when you have a character like the OCD character [Melvin Udall as played by Jack Nicholson] in *As Good as It Gets*, who has been holding onto something for like 50 years.

How do you get a character in a situation where they're going to have an organic reason to reveal that thing that they've had so tightly wound up inside for so long?

NL: How has production and directing affected your writing?

ST: I'm always going to consider myself a writer because I love it, but it would be nice to have the option to direct when I feel that it's personal or where I feel that I can do it. It saves me every day. Part of the reason that I do it is because I think it's going to make me a better writer. Part of the reason, I think, we want to direct as screenwriters is because we have to think visually, even as we write it. You have to see that movie in your head before you ever write it, which is why I think so many writers make pretty good directors. I sat on a plane with Tony Gilroy for five hours and I talked to him about that very thing, with *Michael Clayton*, which is a movie I absolutely loved. Tony pulled it off. Tony did a 1970s movie that really did feel like it had a '70s flavor to it. He's one of the few, in the last decade I'd say, who has actually pulled it off. The way to become a writer is by seeing movies and understanding movies. There are things that impact you, and you don't know why. It's that thin line between being manipulated and being comfortable with it, and not feeling like you've been cheated.

ASSIGNMENT

Write a one-page protagonist monologue (in first person) explaining what you value most in your life on page 1, and how you are in some way desperate to protect it.

6

WHAT'S THE KRYPTONITE?

Determine Your Protagonist's Most Significant Weakness (Achilles' Heel)

Kryptonite is a fictional, radioactive ore from Superman's home planet of Krypton. It's the ultimate vulnerability of the otherwise invincible Man of Steel. It's also his fatal flaw that will be exploited by his enemies at every opportunity.

Character flaws are coping mechanisms, sometimes ones that are outmoded or just broken, and the plot happens to strip away the character's armor. In *As Good as It Gets*, Melvin Udall's (Jack Nicholson) physical weakness is Obsessive-Compulsive Disorder (OCD). He must lock the deadbolts on his front door with the same repetitive pattern, each and every time he enters or exits. So, in addition to washing his hands repeatedly, he can't step on sidewalk cracks and needs to bring his own sanitized plastic cutlery when he eats out. Melvin's disorder makes him feel extremely vulnerable, and as a result, he's a nasty, badgering, homophobic, anti-Semitic racist. His congenial gay neighbor, Simon (Greg Kinnear) refers to him as an "absolute horror of a human being." Melvin is also a misogynist—who happens to be a bestselling author of *romance novels* for his legions of female fans.

In one particularly memorable scene, a woman asks him how he manages to capture his female characters so well, and his response is:

```
                         MELVIN
          I think of a man, and remove reason
          and accountability.
```

But characters are defined by their *actions* more than by their words. And we come to discover that Melvin is all bark and no bite. A frightened monster cornered in the world. The story forces Melvin to strip away his armor and to reveal his true self—or else lose Carol (Helen Hunt), the waitress/single mom he's come to love. But it won't be easy. Defenses are in place for a reason, and intimacy can be terrifying.

A protagonist's Achilles' heel—physical and/or emotional—can take many different forms: maladies, madness, corruption, addictions, phobias, debt, defiance, vengeance, sins, low self-esteem, vices, blind allegiance, codependence, Narcissism, malice, hubris, and others.

Richard M. Nixon (Anthony Hopkins) in *Nixon*, J. Edgar Hoover (Leonardo DiCaprio) in *J. Edgar*, and the fictional Daniel Plainview (Daniel Day-Lewis) in *There Will Be Blood* are all plagued by debilitating paranoia.

Jason Bourne (Matt Damon) suffers from amnesia; Indiana Jones (Harrison Ford) from ophidiophobia (fear of snakes); Sheriff Martin Brody (Roy Scheider) in *Jaws* is afraid of the water; and the seemingly invincible Sundance Kid (Robert Redford) can't swim.

Mark Renton (Ewan McGregor) in *Trainspotting*, Brandon Sullivan (Michael Fassbender) in *Shame*, and the bride's sister, Kym (Anne Hathaway), in *Rachel Getting Married*, are all addicts. Sergeant First Class William James (Jeremy Renner) in *The Hurt Locker* is an adrenaline junkie. Leo DiCaprio as conman Frank Abagnale, Jr. in *Catch Me If You Can* is hooked on the thrill of deception.

Martha (Elizabeth Olsen) in *Martha Marcy May Marlene* suffers from Stockholm Syndrome. William Shakespeare (Joseph Fiennes) suffers from writer's block in *Shakespeare in Love* and will do anything to please his new Muse, Viola (Gwyneth Paltrow).

In *The Others*, Grace Stewart's (Nicole Kidman) children are allergic to daylight. In *Safe*, Carol White (Julianne Moore) is allergic to the twentieth century. *Bubble Boy* (Jake Gyllenhaal) is allergic to *everything*.

A hero's weakness can manifest as a "soft spot" for another person (or animal), causing a protagonist to break the rules.

How far will a character go to protect or help out a loved one?

In *Dog Day Afternoon*, Sonny Wortzik (Al Pacino) robs a bank to help pay for his lover's transsexual operation.

In *Rise of the Planet of the Apes*, Will (James Franco) risks his career to protect the ape (Caesar) that he's raised since birth.

In *Before and After*, a mother and father (Meryl Streep and Liam Neeson) go to extreme lengths to help their son cover up the death of his girlfriend—whom he's suspected of killing.

In *Million Dollar Baby*, seasoned boxing trainer, Frankie Dunn (Clint Eastwood) *breaks his own rule* (that women don't belong in the ring) when tenacious female boxer, Maggie Fitzgerald (Hilary Swank) convinces him to coach her. She helps fill the void left by his estranged daughter (Kate). We learn this via a few shots of "return-to-sender" letters Frankie receives from Kate. Apparently this has gone on for years. Significantly, Maggie's father (whom she adored) died when she was quite young. Frankie develops a soft spot for Maggie and trains her with all his might. Maggie becomes a champion fighter and earns money and prestige. Having originally underestimated her, Frankie now believes she's ready for the next level—with tragic results.

See also Chapter 7 on how antagonists exploit a protagonist's vulnerability.

While most character flaws are detrimental, certain character flaws are beneficial and make a protagonist stronger.

Defying conventional wisdom and/or refusing to bow to peer pressure or the majority rule can be a lonely road. In *The Help*, during the Civil Rights movement in Mississippi, it would have been easier for Skeeter Phelan (Emma Stone) to abandon the oppressed and mistreated black maids in her community, but she felt compelled to give the mostly illiterate maids a voice. While the film truncates the novel and oversimplifies its subject matter, there is no denying the powerful bond between Skeeter and her best friend's housekeeper, Aibileen Clark (Viola Davis). Aibileen risks her job and her life to speak up; this brave woman's Achilles' heel is that she can longer tolerate repressing her truth. Skeeter presents her with the vessel, but it's Aibileen and Minny Jackson (Octavia Spencer), who transcend their fears and limitations, and rise to the occasion.

Milk begins with our nation's first openly gay elected official, Harvey Milk (Sean Penn), narrating his "Only Read If I Am Assassinated Letter." Harvey tells us that gays were targeted because they were so visible, and as the face of the highly controversial liberation movement, Milk's main vulnerability was his conviction that *Separate is not equal*. Harvey Milk defies being categorized as a "tragic hero" because even though his untimely death (at age 48) was, indeed, a tragedy, he died for a cause that he passionately and vociferously believed in. His spirit lives on through his legacy.

Most character flaws are rooted in shame.

A sense of shame can be conscious or subconscious, omnipresent or sporadic. Shame is based in the belief that if people knew the real us, they'd ridicule, judge, reject and/or abandon us. It's the fear of *disconnection*. People tend to want to hide their weaknesses from others and from themselves. Character development is about excavating these dark or hidden places and bringing them out in the open so they can be examined with compassion. Some characters will fully conquer their fears and shame; others will find a healthier, less self-destructive way to live with them.

In *The Reader*, Hanna Schmitz (Kate Winslet) has successfully hidden her private shame (illiteracy) from the world, fearing she's unworthy in life and love. But when she meets an inexperienced teenaged boy, Michael Berg (David Kross), she's found someone more vulnerable than she, and, at first, wields her sexuality as power over him. It's their tacit agreement: she'll teach him how to be a man; he'll read literature to her. She's essentially a sexual predator—he's a minor, young enough to be her son—but they share a deep connection. But after their intense summer affair, she abandons him. It's not until much later in the story that Michael and the audience discover Hanna's shame, and the desperate choices she made throughout her life to hide it, including deciding to join the Nazi S.S. to avoid a job promotion that would have exposed her secret.

In *Brokeback Mountain*, Jack Twist (Jake Gyllenhaal) suffers from a bad case of unrequited love due to Ennis Del Mar's (Heath Ledger) internalized homophobia, expressed with Jack's oft-quoted line of dialogue: "I wish I knew how to quit you."

In *The King's Speech*, George's (Colin Firth) physical weakness is his unbearable stutter. His psychological weaknesses are his insecurity and shame. But through hard work with his speech therapist (Geoffrey Rush), encouragement from his wife (Helena Bonham Carter), and his own steadfast dedication, he manages to overcome it and deliver a rousing, unifying national speech by the end.

The crisis of the plot will inevitably bring unexpressed feelings to the surface.

Repression is a common character flaw. As you develop your characters, be mindful that they will have both conscious and subconscious goals. They might believe that they can control their environments and choose their friends and companions, but the one thing human beings cannot control is their emotions. Luckily, the ability to express the unexpressed can be extremely daunting for your protagonist, which is a very good thing for the screenwriter—whose primary purpose is to *externalize character psychology through dramatic conflict*.

In *Up in the Air*, Ryan Bingham (George Clooney) *consciously* wants to be alone in the friendly skies, racking up frequent flyer mileage and forging wholly superficial relationships. But his *subconscious* goal is to settle down and have a family. He seems to revel in bachelorhood, and lectures at symposiums about the unencumbered joy of an "empty backpack." But when a change in company policy threatens to crack the comfortable veneer of his career and saddles him with a challenging trainee Natalie (Anna Kendrick), he is compelled to reevaluate the void in his personal life. When he is ultimately returned to the friendly skies, they have lost their allure. He is a changed man, having realized that he needs to forge intimate, lasting relationships. He needs family. He needs love.

Repressed characters can be ticking time bombs, bound to explode at any time.

In life, everyone has a breaking point. Repressed jealousy might manifest as aggression. Unexpressed aspirations might spiral one into depression. Repressed hurt might turn into rage. An externally loyal, but privately disgruntled employee might become rude to customers and an embezzler. Feeling shunned might turn someone into a stalker. An overachieving child might rebel against parental expectations and become a cutter.

In the indie thriller, *Martha Marcy May Marlene*, Martha (Elizabeth Olsen) had been subsumed into a cult under the auspices of its charismatic, sociopathic leader, Patrick (John Hawkes). After she manages to escape, Martha goes to stay with her newlywed, type-A sister, Lucy (Sarah Paulson) and her architect husband, Ted (Hugh Dancy) at their Connecticut lake house. It's obvious to Lucy that something is "off" about Martha—who had disappeared two years ago. Martha is manic and wildly inappropriate one minute, withdrawn and hostile the next.

The audience experiences the escalating horrors of Martha's servitude in the cult via intercut flashbacks, but Lucy and Ted don't realize how emotionally scarred Martha is until much later in the film. Having no place else to go, Martha does her best to assimilate into Lucy and Ted's privileged life—and attempts to keep the sordid details of rape and murder a secret. Inevitably, during a cocktail party, Martha's terror of the past is triggered when she sees a bartender who either is, or reminds her of, one of the domineering cult leaders. And that's it: Martha has a psychological and emotional breakdown, screaming and thrashing, drowning in shame and sorrow. Martha has no idea who she is now, and faces a scary, uncertain future.

Antiheroes manage to succeed at their negative goals—which are usually illegal and/or misanthropic.

In Woody Allen's *Match Point*, a struggling but enterprising former tennis pro, Irish bloke Chris Wilton (Jonathan Rhys Meyers) gets a job as an instructor at a posh London tennis club. Chris becomes close to his student Tom Hewett (Matthew Goode), who introduces him to his British upper-class family, and Tom's sister Chloe (Emily Mortimer) quickly falls in love with him. Even though Chris knows that Chloe is his ticket into aristocracy, he can't resist his lustful feelings for Tom's fiancée, a sexy, aspiring actress Nola Rice (Scarlett Johansson). Chris and Nola have a brief affair, but then he breaks it off and marries Chloe—which affords Chris with prestige and a high-ranking career in the Hewett family business. Chris is on top of the world ... until he runs into Nola by chance and becomes obsessed with her. Nola, his *kryptonite*, becomes his mistress. When Nola gets pregnant with his child and pressures him to divorce Chloe and take responsibility, Chris can't fathom giving up his privileged life. His flaw is his uncontrolled desire—for her and for his life with Chloe—and he can't have both. Chris becomes an increasingly desperate, ruthless man. Woody Allen's earlier film, *Crimes and Misdemeanors* tells a very similar story—and the end result is identical. Both antiheroes get away with murder.

Tragic heroes are cursed by their vulnerabilities, and end up alone and alienated.

Check out the climactic shootout in the 1983 remake of *Scarface*, with the lone, paranoid, gun-crazy, power-obsessed drug lord, Tony Montana (Al Pacino) utterly overmatched by his enemies. Montana is crushed by his own hubris.

In *Black Swan*, Nina (Natalie Portman) is overwhelmed by her delusions, brought on by her infinite perfectionism . . . until it destroys her.

Requiem for a Dream revolves around a mother, Sara Goldfarb (Ellen Burstyn), and her drug-dealing, junkie son, Harry (Jared Leto). By day, Sara sits on a folding chair in front of her Brooklyn apartment building *kibitzing* with her busybody neighbors; the rest of her waking hours are spent glued to the TV. She's obsessed with a particular infomercial hosted by a self-help guru, Tappy Tibbons (Christopher McDonald). When Sara gets a mysterious (probably delusional) phone call inviting her to be a guest on the TV infotainment show, she jumps at the opportunity. It's her new lease on life, a chance to impress her neighbors and to show off her handsome son.

Sara goes on a diet so she can fit into the same red dress she wore to Harry's high school graduation. Unfortunately, she grows impatient with her slow weight loss, and gets a prescription for diet pills. Over the next few months, Sara becomes dangerously addicted to amphetamines. At the same time, Harry devolves into a hopeless cycle of heroin addiction and escalating violence. In the end, neither mother nor son can save one another from tragic physical and mental devastation.

In *The Departed*, State Police Special Investigator Colin Sullivan (Matt Damon) is a tragic antihero done in by his arrogance, duplicity, and allegiance to mob kingpin Frank Costello (Jack Nicholson). Meanwhile, our hero Billy Costigan (Leonardo DiCaprio), a righteous undercover cop, is unable to escape his own tragic fate when he's falsely accused of betraying Colin. Even though Billy knows that his own allegiance to Frank Costello was a ruse (he was a police mole), he is double-crossed and discovers that his top secret police record (the only proof of his undercover assignment) has been erased and that he'll never be able to prove his innocence to Internal Affairs. This is the *de facto* death of Billy's future as a legit police detective. It's particularly tragic because all Billy ever wanted when he accepted his undercover assignment was to overcome the stigma of his family's ties with the Boston underworld. He is later killed by a (crooked) State Trooper and, ironically, given a proper police funeral.

Meanwhile, Colin is ostracized, but arrogantly presumes he's escaped punishment for his treason ... until staff sergeant Sean Dignam (Mark Wahlberg) shows up at his apartment and assassinates him—leaving no trace of the crime. Billy and Colin were exposed and brought down by their blind allegiance to a corrupt system.

True heroes develop the courage to face their fears and overcome their limitations.

In *The Fighter*, prizefighter Micky Ward (Mark Wahlberg) must stand up against his self-destructive half-brother Dicky Eklund (Christian Bale) and rebel against his smothering manager/mother, Alice Ward (Melissa Leo), and his sisters. Micky's new girlfriend (Amy Adams) helps give Micky confidence in and out of the boxing ring. But in the climactic prizefight when Micky is getting trounced, Dicky stays in his half-brother's corner and gives him a motivational speech to push him to do better than he ever did. Micky then finds the inner-strength to battle back. The crowd is stunned as Micky wins by TKO.

In the true story *127 Hours*, mountain climber/adventurer, Aron Ralston (James Franco), must figure out how to extricate himself after his arm is caught under a crushing boulder, trapping him in a hidden crevice within an isolated canyon. Having forgotten to pack his Swiss Army Knife and rationing his food and water, Aron documents his death-defying 127 hours on his camcorder. As starvation, dehydration, and delusion overtake him, Aron recalls the most significant people and formative events in his life, and finally summons the inner-strength to cut off his own arm with a small multi-tool.

After severing his arm, he must then scale a 65-foot wall and walk eight miles before he can be rescued. In his hallucinogenic state, Aron has a vision of a mysterious little boy. In the bittersweet dénouement, a title card tells us that Aron's premonition came true. He met his wife, Jessica, three years later, and they had a son. Aron's near-fatal flaw was his perceived invincibility.

Character flaws can be overcome either by embracing or transcending them. In what way might your protagonist overcome this flaw by the end of the movie?

INTERVIEW: Academy Award-Nominated Screenwriter Susannah Grant

Susannah Grant Filmography

Best known for:

The Soloist (2009)
Catch and Release (also directed) (2006)
In Her Shoes (2005)
Erin Brockovich (2000)
    Academy Award Nominee
    WGA Award Nominee
28 Days (2000)
Ever After: A Cinderella Story (1998)
Pocahontas (1995)

NL: In both *Erin Brockovich* and *The Soloist*, your protagonists are real people, so I wondered how much research you did, how faithful you felt required to be with Erin Brockovich the real person and how much dramatic license you felt you might be able to take in constructing that character.

SG: I felt like there was an obligation to be really faithful. Because it had been a legal case, there were things I had to be factually correct about. In terms of character, I had been to a lecture that Nora Ephron gave the first year I was out here. She was talking about *Silkwood* and she said, "The truth is always interesting." I've always remembered that, and certainly Erin's truth—well, really anybody's truth—is interesting. So, I went into it with the idea that the answer was in the truth. That the answer to all of my problems would be found in the truth. The trick in a real story is that there ends up being a difference between the facts and the truth. The facts are often quite dull. For example, you have a couple that makes up and breaks up and makes up and breaks up as George and Erin did, but no one wants to watch them do this over and over because it becomes tedious. Instead, you can get to the truth of what their human conflict is by representing that quite faithfully without showing every fact of it. This was the first time I had done a real life story, so there was a big learning curve with a lot of trial and error. I'm sure I did a draft that was very factually correct, but functionally stultifying. Eventually, I found my way around to the essence of the truth. It all sounds like I knew it, and I did kind of know it intellectually, but I find the process of translating what I know intellectually into what I do creatively is always ugly and muddy.

NL: I know the feeling.

SG: After doing something for 15–17 years, I feel like I should not still be learning this on every script, but maybe that's the process. For almost every character I've written, there would always be the issue of likeability prior to my completing a script. It happens less so now because I have a bit of a track record.

NL: The protagonist's likeability factor was going to be my next question.

SG: Likeability is such a funny word. The nice thing is that it's never come up after I've written something.

> *I guess for me, if you can understand the motivation behind a character's behavior, you're not going to judge it as "likeable" or "unlikeable." So as a writer, you have to treat the character with compassion.*

You have to understand why she mouths off at everyone she meets. If you understand that before you start writing—where it comes from—what sort of need in her is being met by that behavior—what fear is being quieted or soothed by it—then it's not going to come off as unlikeable. It's going to come off as human.

Long ago, I had a bit of an acting background and I think that made a difference because that's always where you're coming from as an actor: understanding what the character wants, what the character needs, what their obstacles are, and how they overcome them. I think of things from that perspective, and it helps in terms of my own work.

NL: One of the things I tell my students when the likeability question comes up, which I almost never bring up, is to establish that they are vulnerable. I use Melvin Udall, Jack Nicholson's character, from *As Good as It Gets*, as an example. He was such a despicable person, but because he had OCD, we knew that he had a vulnerability. With Erin Brockovich, there's a self-destructive component to her mouthing off because it usually works against her. And, you're like, "No, don't do that." Although it certainly helps that she's funny because when she mouths off her insults are sharp and great. She's an underdog, a single mom with three kids barely scraping by, so we want her to succeed. As opposed to thinking, "Oh, you're a horrible person," our reaction to her outbursts is much more, "Don't, don't—can't you see this is a job? That you could make this work if you would just . . ." Ed says that to her later when he says, "Forget about law school, what about charm school?" Was Julia Roberts cast before you started the script?

SG: No, she wasn't, but at that time, if you were writing a female lead, you knew she would get the first look at it. I've never written with an actor in mind because I feel like I only get three to four months when the film is just mine and I can pretend I'm everyone. I'm writing, acting, directing, and shooting it. It's a nice little fantasy world. Now, I love everything that follows too. I love the collaboration, but I think if I didn't have my completely self-indulgent first draft without anyone else in mind I might be less generous.

NL: Regarding the evolution of the characters, what is your process on structure? Like in *Erin Brockovich*, she starts out as someone who is extremely desperate and has very few choices, but by the end, she's become strong and has lots of choices. It's pretty much a 180 turn. Do you work on an outline? Do you work with scene cards?

SG: I do work on an outline. I have a "quasi-system" that I picked up at some point in film school. I've completely modified it, and it's not even really a system. For some reason, it's a reliable dress dummy for me to build on, but it's not even something I could tell someone. I'm certainly not averse to systems; I just think it's really important for everyone to find the one that makes sense for him or herself. What I am adamant about is that I do think that the deification of the three-act structure is ridiculous. Three-act structure certainly works, but so do many others. You do hear people fretting over that page number when things are supposed to do whatever. That I think is something people should be loosely attached to. If something is working and you have a structure that's compelling and driving the story forward and you keep wanting to know what's happening next, you probably have a good structure whether or not it matches whatever those plot points are supposed to be. I think the shackling of yourself to the three-act structure is unfortunate for those who are starting out.

NL: It becomes very formulaic, instead of organically growing out of the characters.

SG: I heard a couple of writers talking and one of them said with a sort of panic in his voice, "I heard that Tom Stoppard said that the three-act structure is nonsense and you don't need it." And, the other person said, "Well, of course, he doesn't need it, he's a genius."

NL: That's true.

SG: Not that I'm putting myself in that category, but there are a lot of ways to write a really strong movie, and it's so exciting when you see one that's compelling all the way through and doesn't have any of those benchmarks.

NL: You're right. Basically, the only absolute I tell my students is that the goal of a well-structured screenplay is that the structure is invisible.

SG: Right. You're not done with all of your work until it looks like it didn't cost you anything.

NL: I've heard some actresses say, "A one-hour makeup job, you can tell I'm wearing a lot of makeup, but a two-hour makeup job, looks like I'm not."

SG: Exactly.

NL: What about theme? Is that important to you when you start to write?

SG: You know, it always is when I start to write, but then, that usually changes more than anything. I try not to overthink why I'm drawn to a particular piece of material. Why I want to write it. I try not to get too front-brain about that because I trust the unconscious more than the conscious. If I'm drawn to something I'm just drawn to something, and I do it. I find I have to go into it telling myself that I really am saying something. Otherwise, what's the point and how do you make your decisions? But, as I go along, that more than anything evolves. I find that there's actually something much more interesting going on between the characters. Theme is usually one of the last things to gel for me in a way that I'm comfortable with.

NL: I felt like the themes in *The Soloist* were more overt—I don't mean in an obvious way, but they were clearer to me. The idea between trying to save someone versus just being there for him was a theme that emerged.

SG: Right.

NL: I also feel that theme is what an audience would extract from a work, and people are going to extract different things. There was a theme of having a home—a sense of home—versus homelessness. Now, there were two scenes, in particular, that involved urine and this theme.

SG: Yes. We have found that pee is very funny.

NL: It is funny, but it's also how people mark their territory. Certainly that's true with the coyote pee and the raccoons, and there's also the scene where he's peeing in a cup.

SG: The thing that I liked about those scenes was how you deal with your own waste is a big separator between people who have a home and people who don't. It can give you the illusion of dignity. It's a funny movie to talk about because once Joe Wright [director] was on board, we had very little time to work together before the [WGA] strike. A lot of conversations that I wish could have happened over the course of three months were reduced down to six weeks. There's tons I love in that movie and I really like it, but I do wonder what it would have been if we had more time to dig in there. One thing we did end up talking a lot about was the notion of isolation which became the connective tissue between the two main characters.

NL: Just starting with the title, for example. Was Steve Lopez's book called, *The Soloist*?

SG: No, it wasn't. Steve's working title for his book was *Chasing Beethoven*. I was writing the script as he was writing the book, which is not that uncommon. Eventually, *The Soloist* became the title of the book as well. But, yes, the idea was that the title worked for both characters.

NL: They were both isolated in their own ways in the world. Steve Lopez had his ex-wife who he worked with and they had a son together, but they were apart. You also got the sense that she was still in love with him because there was this tension of a love triangle in a way between the bromance and her. Were some of those scenes invented?

SG: You know, all of those were. Actually, that was the one thing that Joe and I very amicably and respectfully disagreed on. Steve is married in the original script, but Joe kept saying, "Why is his wife in this movie?" And, I would say, "Because he has a wife." And, he would say, "She doesn't belong in the movie." And, I'd say, "We have to make her belong in the movie. Let's just keep working on it." But, he kept saying the answer was to remove her from the movie. We were really running out of time. It wasn't a situation where you thought, "Well, if I don't do it, they'll hire someone else," because what was on the page was what they were really going to shoot. I said to him, finally, "You're not going to be happy until you see this without the wife, are you?" He said, "No," so I said, "Fine, I'll do a draft without the wife in it." I worked for a day and a half and took out the wife. It actually did read better as a script, but I'm still not comfortable with it.

I did talk to his wife about it, and I said, "Look, the only way to put you in the movie is to make something of the marriage because if it's just a supportive wife without any tension in it, there's no point. You're fighting too much for screen time here to have a scene that doesn't do anything. The alternative is to get deep and real about your marriage, or push one aspect of your marriage and immortalize it in film forever." I think given those two options, she was happy to be cut from the movie. Steve had obviously made the choice to expose himself in this way when he sold the film rights to his book, but his wife hadn't made that choice. I wasn't comfortable on an ethical and personal level saying, "Let's not dramatize all these aspects of her character, but instead only this one because it will help us." It felt like we would have ended up skewing her. However, it still makes me uncomfortable because I still believe what Nora [Ephron] said about the truth.

NL: Let's talk about using voiceover and flashbacks to shed light on the past of the characters to contextualize their flaws. In *The Soloist*, there are flashbacks that try to answer the central mystery of whether Nathaniel was always like this. You wonder, how does a person go from that to here? And then, there was the voiceover of that inner schizophrenic voice. What were the ideas behind those choices creatively?

SG: Anybody who lives in the city walks by people on the streets who are struggling with some mental illness, so I thought, if we're going to do this movie, let's really show what everyone knows—that this is somebody's boy and that he wasn't born like this. He's a human being who has struggled with something that overtook him. Everyone understands that intellectually, but I hoped that watching it would be more illuminating or moving.

NL: It was.

SG: I didn't really think of the voices as voiceover. I thought of them as invisible characters, which is how Nathaniel experiences them. I have used voiceover before though. Originally, *In Her Shoes* had a lot of voiceover in it. Our director, Curtis Hansen, told me early on, "You know, when we shoot these scenes, we're not going to have the voiceover. Let's make the scenes work without it and then we can add it back in if we need it." Which he later told me was just his way of being polite; he didn't know me well enough to just say lose the voiceover. Everything did work better without it. It opens with a little bit at the beginning and then at the end when we hear her reading a poem. There are some times when it's great, like in *About a Boy* or *Casino*.

NL: American Beauty has a very effective voiceover and, of course, *Shawshank Redemption*.

SG: Whenever I'm inclined to do a voiceover, I try to challenge myself to come up with another way to convey the same information. You'll usually come up with something better.

NL: I tend to agree. I heard Billy Wilder speak once, and he said, "If the voiceover is not telling you something different from what you're seeing, cut it."

SG: Flashbacks are similarly tricky. When I was directing [*Catch and Release*], I asked the Director of Photography, John Lindley, if he could tell, when he's shooting a movie, which scenes will not make it into the final cut. He said, "I'm always suspicious when we're shooting a flashback." Ever since that conversation, I put a very high burden on any flashback I put in a script and make sure the scene is earning its keep.

NL: What's great in *Erin Brockovich*, is how you get a really strong sense of the past without having to flash back. One of my favorite scenes is how she puts on the tiara, and she's talking about winning Miss Wichita, and then George puts on the tiara. It gave you this touching scene that if you had flashed back, he wouldn't have been able to participate in the memory, which made it all the more vivid.

SG: I never thought of *The Soloist* scenes as flashbacks because we really told two conjoined stories. I'm trying to think if I've ever used a flashback effectively. Actually, I'm not even sure that I've used flashback period.

NL: Sometimes it's a storytelling crutch, and sometimes it's great to write them because it forces you to really know the backstory to figure it out. An exercise I do with my students is to ask them to write their protagonist's most vivid childhood memory. It can be good or bad, and sometimes those end up in the script, but almost never, and sometimes it just informs them later. Do you have an approach for when you're drawing your antagonist? Because what I love about your writing is all of the grey areas. In *Erin Brockovich*, there are several people serving the role of antagonist at the same time.

SG: I feel like I'm antagonist-averse because my antagonists are always very nebulous and internal. I mean, aside from *Pocahontas* and *Ever After*, those may be the only two that had clear antagonists. Everything else, you never saw who made the decisions. [In *Erin Brockovich*] PG&E was meant to be the antagonist, but it was just a building with different people representing it. Even though they were in its employ, they were in a way still victims of that corporation. With *In Her Shoes*, the antagonists are each other. There's no individual antagonist in *The Soloist*—it's schizophrenia. Sometimes I feel like I should make my life a whole lot easier and just have a villain. One of these days, I'm going to write something with a clear-cut, mustache-twirling villain.

NL: No, don't do that. It's worked out well for you this way. Howard Suber, who's been teaching forever at UCLA, says, "All villains are antagonists, but not all antagonists are villains." In your work, you have many antagonists along the way. In *Erin Brockovich*, before she even comes up against the corporation (PG&E), she comes up against various other people, and then it sort of crystallizes later in the movie when it becomes PG&E. But, at a certain point, George is also her antagonist. In *The Soloist*, I feel like it builds to that one scene in particular when Nathaniel threatens to gut him like a fish and kill him. As long as the tension is there, it works with one strong villain. I'm glad you are saying these things because this is another formula issue, where people say you have to have one main antagonist who you set up in act one and then have to track through. I think that's not always true.

SG: It's definitely harder to break those rules, so I'm always reluctant to tell people, "Oh, you don't have to worry, you don't need an antagonist," because it raises the degree of difficulty considerably both on your own work and then on the viability in the marketplace. But, if you're up for the challenge on both those fronts, I think it can be a lot more fun. The thing I also like to think about—and maybe this is why I never think about myself as having an antagonist—is the maxim that every villain is the hero of his own story. Nobody goes around thinking, "I am evil." Everybody can justify his or her actions in the context of his or her belief system as being noble. Occasionally, you have someone who is doing something naughty and they know it, but generally, people justify all kinds of behavior.

Todd Solondz's film, *Happiness*, is a great example of the compassionate portrayal of human behavior without judging or condoning the behavior. One of the characters is a child molester, and in his dramatization of this guy, Todd Solondz never says that what he's doing is good, or all right. He just shows you how this would happen—who this person is. Obviously, the character's behavior is completely reprehensible and repugnant, but if one were to write from that place—from a place of judgment—the end result wouldn't be nearly as compelling and human and real and terrifying as Dylan Baker's performance is in that movie. There's a real difference between endorsing behavior and understanding it.

ASSIGNMENT

Make a list of at least ten positive and negative characteristics (relative strengths and weaknesses) of your protagonist—both conscious and (perhaps) subconscious. Based upon this list, define your main character's chief vulnerability, and how he/she might (over)compensate for it via specific behaviors. How might this character flaw help and/or hinder your protagonist over the course of the story?

7

WHO'S THE BAD GUY?

Inject a Potent Antagonistic Force

My 11- and 13-year-old sons are my unofficial focus group on big studio movies. When I take them to the theater, I not only watch the movie, I watch *them* experiencing it too. When they get restless, I whisper to them: "Why are you bored?" And their answer is always the same: "There's no bad guy," followed by: "Can we leave?"

Antagonists can take many forms—and are not always personified:

- In *The Curious Case of Benjamin Button*, the antagonist is time.
- In *Contagion*, the antagonist is the epidemic.
- In *Jaws*, the antagonist is, of course, the shark.
- In *The Perfect Storm*, it's the hurricane.
- In *Juno*, the main antagonist is the unborn baby.
- In *2001: A Space Odyssey*, the antagonist is the computer, HAL.
- In *Requiem for a Dream*, the main antagonist is drug addiction.

All villains are antagonists, but not all antagonists are villains.

In *Erin Brockovich*, Erin (Julia Roberts) is challenged throughout the story by several lesser antagonists, including her bombastic boss, Ed Masry (Albert Finney); her next-door neighbor and lover, George (Aaron Eckhart); her rebellious son; and the uptight staff at the law firm. But the *main* antagonist— the monolithic utilities corporation, PG&E—is represented only by proxy through its phalanx of slick attorneys.

In *The Pursuit of Happyness*, there are several lesser antagonists to Chris Gardner (Will Smith): his fed-up wife, Linda (Thandie Newton); the homeless man who steals his bone density scanner; the manager at the motel who evicts Chris and his son (Jaden Smith); the gatekeeper at the homeless shelter. But the overarching antagonist is *poverty*.

In *The Help*, the main antagonist is racism in its many forms, both external and internal. It is then personified by the most overt queen bee in the neighborhood, Hilly Holbrook (Bryce Dallas Howard) and the coterie of ladies over whom she holds sway.

In many romantic-comedies, the love interests are each other's antagonists.

In the classic *When Harry Met Sally*, Sally is Harry's (Billy Crystal) antagonist because his greatest fears are intimacy and commitment, and Sally (Meg Ryan) falls in love with him.

In *500 Days of Summer*, the antagonist is elusive, noncommittal Summer (Zooey Deschanel) who is Tom's (Joseph Gordon-Levitt) source of joy and heartbreak. In *Tootsie*, Michael's (Dustin Hoffman) object of desire, Julie (Jessica Lange), is also his nemesis because if she discovers who he really is (a man in drag) then his masquerade will be ruined and he'll once again face the prospect of being an unemployed actor.

Forrest Gump doesn't have an antagonist in the traditional sense. When I interviewed the movie's Academy Award-winning screenwriter, Eric Roth, here is what he said:

> I think the complications of life would be the antagonist to Forrest Gump. I don't think it's any one thing. He might butt up against various things, but he's always very adaptable to make himself be himself during those things. . . . I think that's true mostly if you're going to do somebody's life journey—there's probably not just one person who's pursuing you—it's not a good or evil thing like that.

Following are some basic rules on the role of the antagonist. Be mindful that not every screenplay will adhere to all of these: the antagonist will be the primary (usually negative) person or force that most actively challenges or threatens your protagonist—thereby directly impeding your protagonist from attaining his/her main goals.

In *Catch Me If You Can*, Frank Abagnale, Jr. (Leonardo DiCaprio) is a successful con man with FBI agent Carl Hanratty (Tom Hanks), doing as the title says, trying to catch him. Hanratty is the antagonistic force.

In *Harry Potter and the Deathly Hallows*, antagonist Lord Voldemort (Ralph Fiennes) searches for the Elder Wand, the most powerful wand ever created. He needs it to overcome Harry's (Daniel Radcliffe) wand and make him truly invincible.

Antagonists often want something the protagonist (consciously or obliviously) possesses.

In *Enemy of the State*, Robert Clayton Dean (Will Smith) is a lawyer who becomes a target of a corrupt politician, Thomas Brian Reynolds (Jon Voight) and the National Security Agency when Robert receives evidence of a government official's murder, but doesn't know he has it.

In *Panic Room*, Meg Altman (Jodie Foster) and her daughter, Sarah (Kristen Stewart) become prisoners in their own house when it's invaded by armed robbers. Unfortunately, Meg doesn't realize that her place of refuge, the panic room, contains millions of dollars in a hidden safe.

In *Marathon Man*, exiled Nazi Szell (Laurence Oliver) keeps tormenting graduate history student, Babe (Dustin Hoffman), as Szell keeps asking "Is it safe?" Babe has no idea what Szell is talking about.

Antagonists tend to be parasites who outwardly seek to get power from others—through any means necessary: deception, theft, murder, manipulation—as opposed to protagonists, who tend to discover that their power lies within.

In *The Shawshank Redemption*, sadistic Warden Norton (Bob Gunton) exploits Andy Dufresne's (Tim Robbins) tax expertise. When a new inmate Tommy Williams (Gil Bellows) hears the details of Andy's case, Tommy reveals that while he was incarcerated at another prison, he'd met another inmate who claimed to have committed a nearly identical murder—suggesting Andy's innocence. Andy approaches Warden Norton with this information, but Norton fears Andy may reveal his corruption if Andy is released. The Warden protects his own interests and has Tommy killed, purportedly during an attempted escape.

In *Wall Street*, Gordon Gekko (Michael Douglas) is a corporate raider, charming, rich, and espouses "Greed is Good," but he's also merciless and will use the inside information of his employee, Bud Fox (Charlie Sheen) against him for his own profit.

Antagonists try to subvert the truth.

In *The Departed*, Colin Sullivan (Matt Damon) is a young criminal who has infiltrated the state police as an informant for crime boss Frank Costello (Jack Nicholson). Colin must serve Frank while hiding his true identity.

In *The Fugitive*, Dr. Richard Kimble (Harrison Ford) is accused of killing his wife. While the one-armed man committed the actual murder, Kimble discovers it was a conspiracy orchestrated by his presumed best friend, Dr. Charles Nichols (Jeroen Krabbé).

In *A Few Good Men*, Col. Nathan R. Jessup (Jack Nicholson) is a tough Marine who is supposed to protect the Marines under his command; instead, Jessup ordered a "Code Red" on a fellow Marine that resulted in murder. Jessup tries to cover up the cause of the murder from military lawyer Lt. Daniel Kaffee (Tom Cruise), who demands to know the truth. Jessup retorts with the now-famous line, "You can't handle the truth!"

Most villains do not change.

While their specific goals may change, antagonists end the story often as they began. They don't evolve or learn from their failures. Think of Voldemort from the Harry Potter saga; his actions haven't made him wiser. At the end, he's still an evil soul. The Joker, too, is an emotionally static character, as is Hannibal Lecter. If the villain were to change, to grow, then he would no longer be a villain.

The antagonist will often have the same goal as the protagonist—but with a negative or evil agenda.

The Joker (Heath Ledger) in *The Dark Knight* wants to rid Gotham of greed and corruption—and so does Batman. The significant difference is that Batman wants to clean up Gotham in order to save it; the Joker, on the other hand, believes that Gotham should be destroyed.

In *Se7en*, Detectives Somerset and Mills (Morgan Freeman and Brad Pitt) work tirelessly to arrest criminals. The serial killer villain, John Doe (Kevin Spacey) targets people who he finds physically and morally objectionable. The good guys and the bad guy want to clean up the streets—but their motivations and methods are completely different.

If your plot is lacking dramatic tension/conflict, you'll need to make your antagonist stronger.

Ideally, in acts one and two your antagonist will appear to be more powerful than your protagonist, and your protagonist will need to get stronger and bolder by act three in order to overcome this threatening force.

In *Precious*, the title character Precious (Gabourey Sidibe) is overweight, illiterate, poor and pregnant. She lives with her abusive mother Mary (Mo'Nique). Mary is such a monstrous mother, she was jealous of the attention given to Precious as a child, and allowed her then-boyfriend to sexually abuse her. Only at the end does Precious evolve from being weak and submissive to finally renouncing her mother.

In *Spider-Man*, Peter Parker (Tobey Maguire) goes up against Norman Osborn's alter ego "Green Goblin" (Willem Dafoe). While Peter/Spider-Man is a novice, still trying to figure out his skills, Green Goblin arrives in full force of his capabilities. At the end, Peter defeats the Green Goblin and forces Norman to reveal his true identity.

In many cases, the true antagonist is obscured and not revealed as the enemy until the climax.

In *The Silence of the Lambs*, Hannibal Lecter (Anthony Hopkins) serves the role of the antagonist in the first two-thirds of the story. He's terrifying enough: a cannibal and a serial killer. But look at the climax. Hannibal becomes a mentor/ally to Clarice—with no plans to harm her in the end. The real antagonist is Buffalo Bill (Ted Levine), the killer who wants to make a suit from the skin of his victims.

In *American Beauty*, even though we know Lester Burnham (Kevin Spacey) is dead at the beginning and is speaking in voiceover, we don't know how he died. Only at the end is the killer revealed as his next-door-neighbor, Col. Frank Fitts (Chris Cooper), a closeted homosexual whose murderous rage ignites when Burnham rejects his sexual advances.

In *The Usual Suspects*, after realizing that the entire narrative was actually an inspired off-the-cuff story told to Agent Dave Kujan by the weak, frightened Roger "Verbal" Kint (Kevin Spacey) we recognize that he has been the villain, Keyser Söze, all along.

The most iconic antagonists possess both positive and negative characteristics—and are uniquely flawed in both sympathetic and deplorable ways.

In *Silence of the Lambs*, Hannibal Lecter (Anthony Hopkins) is a gourmand and wine connoisseur, a brilliant psychiatrist, but also a cannibalistic serial killer.

In *Bridesmaids*, Helen (Rose Byrne) is pretty, ultra-generous, and the perfect bridesmaid to bride-to-be Lillian (Maya Rudolph), but because she is also highly competitive, passive-aggressive, and manipulative, she undermines maid-of-honor, Annie (Kristen Wiig), at every turn.

In *The Devil Wears Prada*, Miranda Priestly (Meryl Streep) is Editor-in-Chief at *Runway* magazine. She has style, wit, and intelligence, but she's also a hypercritical, manipulative bully who uses neophyte Andy Sachs' (Anne Hathaway) vulnerability against her by dangling the carrot of introducing Andy to high-level literary contacts if Andy can prove herself at *Runway*. Desperate for a career break (outside the fashion world), Andy's zealousness to please her persnickety boss threatens to destroy her personal life and self-esteem. Ironically, it's Andy's gumption that finally impresses the seemingly implacable Miranda. But, Miranda has another more vulnerable side which Andy witnesses when she sees her alone in her hotel suite—authentic and fragile—just after Miranda has discovered that her husband wants a divorce.

Some great antagonists are just pure evil.

Anton Chigurh (Javier Bardem) in *No Country for Old Men*, is a great recent example. He is tireless, ruthless, with the lifeless eyes of a shark and no moral compass—he's happy to kill on the outcome of a coin toss. Even the manner in which he executes is unique and gruesome: a captive bolt device made for putting down cattle.

Amon Goeth (Ralph Fiennes) in *Schindler's List*. He commits genocide and has no remorse, representing the evil of the Nazi Party. After finding that a maid hasn't cleaned his bathroom to his liking, he has a whisper of humanity as he considers letting her go. He gives her hope, but then decides to kill her anyway.

Hans Gruber (Alan Rickman) in *Die Hard*. What looks like a politically motivated hostage ploy is, in reality, a masterful plan to infiltrate the main vault in search of bearer bonds. The fate of the hostages is mere collateral damage to his ultimate, greedy goal.

In *The Dark Knight*, The Joker (Heath Ledger) tells the story about the origin of his scar, but he's an unreliable narrator: the story always changes. We think for a minute that the Joker has a sense of vulnerability, but ultimately he's just playing mind games with Batman.

Every villain is the hero of his/her own story.

Most antagonists don't believe that they are "bad." In fact, they usually feel justified, entitled, and downright righteous.

In *Misery*, Annie Wilkes (Kathy Bates) rescues her favorite author, Paul Sheldon (James Caan), after he crashes his car in a snowstorm near her remote cabin. As his "number one fan," Annie keeps him locked away from the world so that she can convince him that he should resurrect her favorite character "Misery" Chastaine. As a nurse, her intentions are to help him get better, so that he can see how wrong he was to kill off Misery. She sees herself as a savior, not an executioner by protecting Paul from ruining his best creation.

In *Gone Baby Gone*, police Captain Doyle (Morgan Freeman) is ultimately exposed as the one who had the girl kidnapped in order to get her away from her junkie mother. Doyle's intentions are good—to give the girl a better life—but he's still a kidnapper in the eyes of the law. Kenzie (Casey Affleck) discovers the truth and is morally conflicted about whether to take the girl away from him.

In *Fight Club*, Tyler Durden (Brad Pitt) believes he's saving the Nameless Protagonist (Edward Norton) from a horrible, miserable, wimpy existence. But he goes too far and essentially becomes a domestic terrorist. In a surprising twist, Tyler proves to be the repressed dark side of the protagonist—existing only in his own mind.

Traditionally, the antagonist and protagonist face each other in direct confrontation or battle during the climax. In Joseph Campbell's *The Hero with a Thousand Faces*, good always triumphs over evil.

Think of *High Noon* or any classic Western where the hero rides into a dusty town, to face the bad guy, damn the consequences. A more recent example is *Avatar*, where Jake Sully (Sam Worthington) squares off against Col. Miles Quaritch (Stephen Lang). Quaritch is leading the assault on the planet Pandora, but Sully is standing in his way; it's man versus robotic golem in this modern sci-fi classic. *See also Chapter 14 on Climaxes.*

> On an existential level, every protagonist will also be his/her own antagonist.

INTERVIEW: Screenwriter/Director Stuart Beattie

Stuart Beattie Filmography

Best known for:

Halo (announced)
I, Frankenstein (also directing) (2013)
Pirates of the Caribbean: On Stranger Tides (characters) (2011)
Tomorrow, When the War Began (also directed) (2010)
G.I. Joe: The Rise of Cobra (2009)
Australia (2008)
Pirates of the Caribbean: At World's End (characters) (2007)
3:10 to Yuma (uncredited) (2007)
Pirates of the Caribbean: Dead Man's Chest (characters) (2006)
Derailed (2005)
Collateral (2004)
Pirates of the Caribbean: The Curse of the Black Pearl (2003) (screen story)

NL: I always say that in every movie, your protagonist is also his own antagonist because he'll have inner demons to overcome. My view is there usually also needs to be an external antagonist. What are your thoughts on that?

SB: I think that the antagonist doesn't always have to be a specific character. I think it can be external *influences*, but they have to be absolutely present in the character's story. And, the idea of the protagonist being his own antagonist, I think it can work as long as you show why he is his own worst enemy which would, I imagine, involve external forces: the world he lives in, the rules that are forced upon him or her, you know whatever those external factors are, they would have to be very, very clear. It depends what kind of film you're writing. If you're writing a big, fun, commercial movie, you're probably going to want to have a character or a very clear antagonistic force: societal rules, pressures, social mores, armies or aliens—you know the kind of larger antagonistic force that doesn't necessarily need a face or a name as long as it has a distinct presence in the story.

NL: Or something like the *Alien* movies where we have these creatures, but then ultimately it becomes mano-a-mano where it's heroine versus the most evil creature. Do you feel that an antagonist needs to be specific by the time we're entering the climax or not so much?

SB: Not necessarily. *Aliens* worked really well because it was really a story about mothers. So you had Ellen Ripley being the mother of Newt fighting the mother of the aliens. I think that was a good choice to have a boss alien figure to fight at the end. The film I just finished making, *Tomorrow, When the War Began*, did not have a chief antagonist. It was simply the invading army. It focused squarely on these eight young kids who were caught up in this conflict and never really left their point of view. I think if your story has a strong point of view, which in *Tomorrow*'s case it had because we really only saw what those characters saw, then there's no need to cut away to a boss villain because you're keeping the drama with your characters and seeing it through their eyes and seeing only what they see. They may not see the big, boss villain, ever. It's just the way your story dictates. As long as there's jeopardy and stakes and you care what your character is going through, then I think that's the most important thing. However, in saying that, I think *a hero is only as good as his antagonist*. So, the greater you can make that antagonist or antagonistic force, I think the better the story because there's that much more for your character to overcome in the course of the story. If it's an easy antagonist or antagonistic force, there's not as much of a journey and you don't get as involved as an audience.

NL: There's certainly lower conflict.

SB: Yeah, the greater the antagonist, the greater the conflict. The greater the conflict, the greater the drama. The greater the drama, the greater the story.

NL: How do you approach the grey areas of your antagonist? Because I usually feel the most interesting and memorable antagonists have both positive and negative characteristics. I'm thinking about "Collateral," for example. First of all with casting, Tom Cruise—who at that time, in particular, was Hollywood's most dependably likeable actor playing a ruthless bad guy. Do you think about, and I know it depends on the genre and the tone, but do you think about imbuing your antagonists with sympathetic traits and is it important to you that we understand their point of view and why they are doing what they're doing?

SB: Yeah, I think it's absolutely essential. I think to get into grey areas with an antagonistic force is very hard. But, if you want to get into grey areas, I do think you need a specific antagonist character, and then, yeah, I think it's absolutely essential to understand where that character is coming from and why they are doing it. The more interesting antagonists have a very well thought out, rationalized, perhaps not sympathetic, but understandable point of view. An even better antagonist actually wants the same things the hero wants only they have a more screwed up way of going about it. When you hear about the hero and the villain being two sides of the same coin, I think that's when you really get the good juicy stuff. They even have a scene about it in *Raiders* with "I'm a shadowy reflection of you"—to me that's the really great stuff.

> *If you can somehow make your antagonist the darker version of the protagonist, then I think you're onto something good and I think there will be a good story there to tell.*

Then, you can understand both sides of the same situation and I think that's really interesting.

SB: Another great one is *Schindler's List*. Goeth . . . Amon Goeth.

NL: Ralph Fiennes' character?

SB: Yes, you see that guy's pure evil, but then you see where he has it all twisted up, that they're doing this to him and making him this way. I think *why* people do things is so much more interesting than *what* they do. And, so when you start getting into the why of a guy who is killing people, I just think that is absolutely fascinating. The whole idea of *Collateral* was to have this villain [Tom Cruise] that you understood why he was doing it and the why was simply that he just doesn't care that he doesn't know who they are, that they're strangers to him; they're just names on a list. And, the whole point was to make us all think that people die every day, and we don't know who they are and we don't think anything about it because there are frankly just too many people to care about every single person who dies. And, that was his point. That's the idea that I was trying to get at with that story. That our hero, cab driver Max [Jamie Foxx], was someone who didn't know that he really didn't care about other people. It was only when someone he knew was threatened that he realized he had to do something. When he finds out that the attorney he was kind of flirting with earlier in the film is on the list, that's when he decides, "I've got to do something." When you live in a big city, and people die, do we care, should we care, why do we not care? So, I use basically the two sides of that coin to explore that notion, if that makes sense.

NL: What were the origins of *Derailed*?

SB: *Derailed* was a book that I really loved, and the studio sent it to me. They sent it to a bunch of writers, and we all went in and pitched. It was a fantastic book. I remember I read it all in one night and then I got to a point, I think three-quarters of the way through, where it just took a complete left turn, a complete *deus ex machina*, everything that you don't do, and I remember reading going, "No!"

NL: It is a great setup.

SB: I heard that all the other writers were trying to fix how you got around that, but it was one of those things that just wasn't fixable. So, what I said was, "Look, you've got the movie right here, just take the first three-quarters, and forget the last one-quarter." And, I think that's how they ended up choosing me for it. I think it was the last film out of Miramax, just in time.

NL: It always keeps you guessing and you don't know what's going on until you do, and then you're like, "Oh my God, now how is he going to get out of this?" And, it's all because this guy is tempted to have an affair.

SB: In the book, he actually gets to have the affair, but in the movie, I didn't even give him that. He didn't even get to have sex with this hot chick, even *that* got interrupted. Actually, that decision was an antagonist's decision because I didn't believe that the antagonist would let this guy have sex with his girlfriend. It felt actually more cruel as an antagonist not to let him have sex with Jennifer Aniston. Yeah, to me, he was just a really cool, creepy villain. A guy you could not escape, a guy who is always one step ahead. When Clive Owen [Charles Schine] tries to enlist help, you know Vincent Cassel's [LaRoche] one step ahead and blows the guy's head off before he can even start. That to me is really good stuff. The villain that tracks down his enemy's stuff, who's in his house, invading his personal space, threatening his family. To me, you ratchet it up and ratchet it up, until you have no other choice. You find out in the end that he is going to prison to go kill this guy because he knows this guy is not even going to stop in prison. That to me, is a really cool villain. Someone that you've got to go to extraordinary lengths to stop. That's a good story: an average person going to extraordinary lengths to stop this impossible-to-stop antagonist. You know the greatest antagonist in a way is The Terminator because he will not stop. He's programmed. He will not ease up. They put your heroes in impossible situations. And, if you can come up with good clever ways to get out of it, then you've got a good story.

NL: That brings up another interesting point which is locating the Achilles' heel of both protagonist and antagonist because in order to vanquish the antagonist, generally, the protagonist has to find that weakness, if it's a person. When you're conceiving an antagonist, and I'm sure now a lot of this is very intuitive and comes from instinct, but do you consciously think, "Alright, I need this really bad ass, incredibly smart and cunning and ruthless antagonist, especially in a thriller, and he needs a *weakness*"? Or, is it more that the protagonist, once he or she has overcome that weakness, is then able to overtake the antagonist?

SB: Yeah, I think it's more the latter, and it's more of an interesting story, too. I think to put a chink of armor into your antagonist doesn't make him that great of an antagonist. I think the key is to give your protagonist a flaw that he or she overcomes over the course of the story and that is what enables them to take down the impossible-to-take-down-antagonist. *Collateral* is like that. There was a guy in the beginning who's never been in a fight in his life who's afraid of confrontation to the point that he was stuck in a dead-end job and wouldn't achieve his dreams. To throw that person into such conflict over the course of the movie, that they grow a pair by the end, basically. And, they're grateful to stand up. It's the idea that a protagonist, who does something in the end that they never would have done in the beginning, makes sense because of everything they've gone through in between. I think that's how protagonists overcome their antagonists. If you look at *Jaws* where you make the police chief afraid of water, terrified to go out there, you throw him through that story, so that he's out there in the water with a gun. It's him or the shark. That makes a great story. I would say it's about the protagonist's failings and how he or she overcomes those failings that vanquishes the antagonist. That's what makes for a good story.

NL: The protagonist is going through some evolution.

SB: It's got to be.

NL: The antagonist doesn't necessarily, and usually, often does not change . . .

SB: Yeah, they are who they are, they're set. They almost make no apologies about who they are. I did an uncredited page 1 rewrite of *3:10 to Yuma* which is an interesting one to think about because now we have an outlaw who really wanted a quiet life and the guy with the quiet life who really wanted to be an outlaw. The way to vanquish Ben Wade [Russell Crowe] in that story was to do the right thing. To do it to the point of self-sacrifice. And, that was the thing to make him change. So, I think that was a different way to approach protagonists/antagonists. In that sense, Ben Wade was the one who changed and Dan Evans [Christian Bale] was the guy who just stayed, "I've got to do the right thing, all the way through, no matter what." And, it was that insistence, that courage, that heart, that made Ben Wade change and wipe out his entire gang and go to jail. In that case, you could say that Ben Wade was the protagonist, if you talk in terms of growth and change and maybe his gang was the antagonistic force stopping him from changing. That one plays around with these ideas a bit. The more obstacles you can throw out in front of your protagonist the better.

NL: Do you think . . . and I'm asking you some of these questions even though I have a distaste for them myself, but these are the kinds of things people like to know. How early and/or how late can you introduce your antagonist? I often say that if a writer does not want to have their antagonist come in until the middle or end of act two, it's too late.

SB: Well, what's happening for the first half? As long as you can see the *effects* of the antagonist . . .

NL: So maybe not enter the picture . . .

SB: As long as you're seeing the results of what they're doing, you can delay the entrance of the antagonist. You would need other little antagonistic forces going along which I think would help delay. But, what I think is important is as long as you see, like in *Jaws*, you see dead bodies again, you see kids get ripped in half. You're not seeing the shark physically . . .

NL: Which makes it much scarier. I feel like in *Jaws* the scariest moments are when they're just sitting in the boat and it's quiet.

SB: Or, they're on that pier.

NL: It's terrifying. Can you talk about, *I, Frankenstein* and/or *Halo*?

SB: *Halo* is an insanely popular video game that I love to death. Several video games, several books, several graphic novels. It's the new Tolkien as far as I'm concerned. That's where it all came from. Now that has an antagonistic force: a covenant of alien races that are all bent on wiping out mankind for religious reasons and you get into why they had those religious reasons. Extremists. And, they think that mankind is an affront to their religion. And, then you realize that the three guys who are controlling the covenant actually know that humankind is not an affront to their religion, but have declared them so because they are getting in the way of what they want.

Now, *I, Frankenstein* actually takes the idea that the creature that Frankenstein made in the lab survives the fight on the ice at the end of Mary Shelley's book and carries Dr. Frankenstein's body out of the ice and buries him, and that's where the second part of the story really begins. It involves this whole world of gargoyles versus demons. Gargoyles you see on the church and everything. The idea is that they've been fighting a war with the demons for centuries and the demons want Frankenstein's creature. Their whole thing is that they repossess bodies who have no souls, but usually you have to wait for someone to die. So, the idea is, "Well, since the soul leaves the body when a person dies, if we can animate corpses, we'll have these ready-made vessels and can create an army and take over the world. But, we need Frankenstein's technology, the journal that Frankenstein kept, and all that kind of stuff." The demons are led by Naberius [Bill Nighy], a real demon in Christian mythology, who uses his troops against the gargoyles. There's one particular demon named Zuriel who has been hunting the creature for 200 years. Because the story is set in present day, and the idea is that the creature just keeps on living and living and living. No one knows why—maybe because he was built in a lab? There are demons everywhere he goes and all the demons know that if they see the guy, they are to get him. Our creature is just trying to survive. He has a lot of antagonists in his life, and all he wants is a girlfriend. I thought he wanted a companion.

NL: Everyone can relate to that.

SB: Basically, he's lived 200 years. He's the loneliest creature in the world.

NL: What was the source of this?

SB: It was Kevin Grevioux who came up with the idea of having the Frankenstein creature alive and today in our world. I've always loved the Frankenstein creature. It's who you are, what makes you alive. If you're born in a lab, do you have a father or a mother? So, I took that general concept and started creating this whole world of gargoyles and demons which hadn't been done before. We've seen vampires, we've seen werewolves. Trying to get away from that and do something that we haven't seen. Gargoyles, everyone knows what gargoyles are, and everyone knows what demons are. So, it seemed to be a good place to develop a rich mythology from because we all know the entry points. We all know what those things are. Gargoyles are defending churches against demons. So, it had great religious iconography built into it.

ASSIGNMENT

Write a one-page, first person monologue in the voice of your antagonist expressing why your point of view is valid and sympathetic.

8

WHAT'S THE STRUCTURAL BLUEPRINT?

Draft the Architectural Foundation

In the old days, before we were all 'held a-Twitter' and had our attention spans splintered by YouTube, Facebook, and Xbox, movies tended to unfold in three acts: beginning, middle, end, with a straight linear narrative—nothing too elaborate or complicated. Today, audiences seem to be able to digest information (aka plot) in fragments, across multiple platforms. The universal themes of stories have remained a constant, yet the way the story is being told continues to evolve with the times. The goal is always the same: grab the audience's attention from page 1, and don't let it go until The End. Keep it suspenseful, surprising, and emotionally compelling. This is what's known as "**narrative drive.**"

As you build your screenplay from the ground up, you're going to need a solid foundation and structural supports—or else your house of cards just might implode. The two most commonly used structural paradigms are:

Linear Narrative

The story is told chronologically in the tightest time frame possible. Basically: act one: setup; act two: complication; act three: climax/resolution. No flashbacks or flash forwards.

Flashback Narrative

The story begins at the end, then flashes back to the beginning and proceeds to fill the audience in on how the story got there. When the time we spend in the (relative) "present day" is only at the very beginning and at the very end of the film, it's considered a bookend structure. Flashback-heavy movies usually originate from novels adapted for the screen. Without the context of a rich backstory, much of the original spirit of the novel would be—and frequently is—lost. This is probably why short stories almost always make better movie adaptations than lengthier tomes.

Architectural Foundation

Most film schools and screenwriting books teach some variation of the following structural paradigm, see Figure 8.1.

Not every movie has to have every element in the diagram. However, after studying hundreds of films, it is clear to me that the vast majority of successful films, i.e., those that appeal to large numbers of people and do well financially tend to have most, if not all, of these fundamentals:

Act One Elements (in Order of Appearance)

Backstory: All events that occurred in the past prior to page 1 of the script.

Setup of the "Ordinary World": This term originates from Joseph Campbell's *Hero with a Thousand Faces* and establishes in the beginning of the screenplay the usual "ordinary" life of the protagonist; the idea is to establish a "typical" day in your character's life and then to disrupt the order of his/her world with the crisis at the end of the first act. In *The Wizard of Oz*, Dorothy Gale's "ordinary world" is the farm in Kansas prior to the cyclone and her being swept off to Munchkin Land.

Inciting Incident: The initial spark (around page 10) that jumpstarts the plot; will usually come in the form of either an opportunity that goes awry, or as the first baby step the protagonist takes out of his/her usual routine (aka ordinary world). The inciting incident is often a literal or metaphorical "trap." The trap is often a three-pronged process that breaks down like this:

Page 10: a trap is set by the antagonist or via a seemingly positive opportunity.
Page 17: the hero steps into the trap.
Page 25: the trap is sprung—via circumstances beyond the hero's control.

Plot Point I: The specific incident that forces your protagonist into crisis at the end of act one (around page 25). It's a crisis point because it forces your protagonist to solve a large problem—and if he/she fails, there will be consequences (stakes). Plot Point I will spark Plan A which will (ideally) challenge the protagonist for the duration of act two.

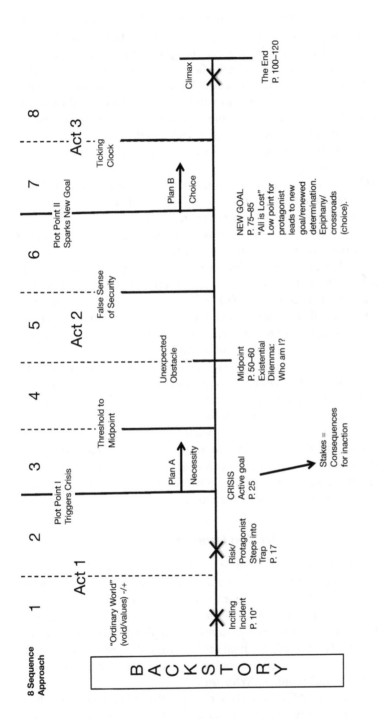

FIGURE 8.1

Act One Crisis: An event at the end of the first act that forces a protagonist to take an action or else suffer dire consequences (stakes). This crisis will spark a *proactive or positive goal* whereby the protagonist must take a dynamic action (which I refer to as Plan A) in the face of a crisis or obstacle. Ideally, the crisis will have an emotional impact on the protagonist because it's going to necessitate change—and it's human nature to resist change and to avoid the unknown. This is what defines the "reluctant hero." *Protagonists in movies will ideally have both positive and negative goals. This +/– dichotomy will generate heat. The +/– charge is the way both energy and drama work! And all goals must be active.*

Positive Goals: The protagonist's positive active goals are what we believe will lead to rewards and beneficial (positive) results and are based upon the protagonist's aspirations and/or sense of justice.

Negative Goals: The protagonist's active goals with a negative spin, usually involving something deceptive and/or immoral.

In *The Godfather*, Michael Corleone's (Al Pacino) positive goal is to marry Kay (Diane Keaton) and stay out of the family crime business. But after a second assassination attempt on his father, Don Vito's (Marlon Brando) life, Michael feels compelled to honor and defend the aging patriarch. Thus, Michael's negative goal is for revenge against the rival mafia clan—involving him in escalating violence, murder, and lies to Kay.

Stakes: Something valuable in a protagonist's life that he/she stands to lose. The higher the stakes, the better—as long as what is at risk is credible and consistent with genre and tone. Stakes are essential for drama and must continue to escalate as the story progresses.

In *The Godfather*, what's at stake for Michael is losing Kay and a chance for a law-abiding life. But equally at stake is the family's survival and legacy.

Through Line: The goals of the main character. There will be the *plot through line*: the externalized, active, physical goals; and the *emotional through line*: known as the spine of the movie.

Act Two Elements

Crisis Management: Your protagonist's main motivation for the first half of act two is to contain the crisis and resist change. He/she is dealing with the more or less *expected* complications that emerge from the crisis point.

Midpoint: An *unexpected* complication or obstacle that occurs at or near the middle of the movie. A narrative curve ball and plunges your protagonist into an "existential dilemma" in which they question their priorities, values, morals, and identity. A useful question to have your protagonist ask him/herself at the mid-point is: "Who am I?"

In *Rise of the Planet of the Apes*, Caesar's existential dilemma occurs when Will (James Franco) comes to the animal shelter to take the ape home with him. But when Caesar sees the leash in Will's hand, Caesar realizes he can never go back; he can't be a pet. He needs to be an equal. This midpoint moment has Caesar questioning whether he is man or animal.

False Sense of Security: This will usually, but not always, occur between the midpoint and the end of act two. The unexpected midpoint complication throws your protagonist for a loop—during which time he/she questions the viability of accomplishing Plan A. But after this period of recalibrating and, perhaps, some soul searching, the protagonist recovers, picks him/herself back up, brushes him/herself off, and believes that Plan A can be accomplished to solve the big central problem. It's a false sense of security because this belief is usually short-lived, and at the end of act two: Plan A is abandoned. At the end of act two, your protagonist must come to grips with the fact that Plan A was not the answer.

In *The Town*, Doug (Ben Affleck) believes he can avert suspicion from the FBI and his new love, Claire (Rebecca Hall). At this 3/4 point in act two, Doug asks Claire to run away with him and she accepts. They plan to leave together in the coming days.

But then, at the end of act two, when Claire discovers Doug's true identity as one of the robbers who kidnapped her, Doug's new goal (Plan B) becomes: help the crime boss (aka The Florist) pull off one more heist—or else Claire will be killed.

Plot Point II: The *specific incident* at the end of act two (around page 85) that causes your protagonist to abandon Plan A (which was based upon *necessity*) in favor of a new Plan B (which will, ideally, be based upon *choice*). This is also known as the "All Is Lost" or "Low Point" for your protagonist. Plan A is usually abandoned for one of two reasons: It's deemed untenable; or it's achieved but has made everything worse.

By the end of act two, in *The Devil Wears Prada*, Andy (Anne Hathaway) has succeeded at her Plan A—won the approval of her boss, Miranda Priestly (Meryl Streep), when she scores an invitation to Fashion Week in Paris. But, it comes at the expense of Miranda's former first assistant, Emily (Emily Blunt), who had become Andy's confidante, and her sweet boyfriend, Nate (Adrian Grenier). When Andy becomes more miserable than ever, her Plan B becomes finding a way to get her life back and to protect Miranda from a hostile takeover at *Runway* magazine. When she quits at the end, she has earned both Miranda's respect—and that coveted job reference for a more suitable job in journalism.

In *Se7en*, the end of act two occurs after Detectives Somerset and Mills have continually failed to find the notorious serial killer, John Doe (Kevin Spacey)—but then John Doe walks into the police station and turns himself in. The detectives' Plan A—to find and arrest John Doe—is abandoned because it's achieved. The detectives' new goal is to follow John Doe's lead in order to stop the final two deadly sins from occurring and to prevent more bloodshed.

At the end of act two in *Rise of the Planet of the Apes*, Caesar rejects his humanity and ascends as the rebel leader to the apes.

In some alternative structures, such as *No Country for Old Men* and *Shattered Glass*, the role of the protagonist shifts to another character at the end of act two. In *No Country for Old Men*, the protagonist/antihero, Llewelyn Moss (Josh Brolin), absconds with $2 million he finds at a crime scene, but is subsequently hunted down by the villainous bounty hunter, Anton Chigurh (Javier Bardem), and ends up dead at the end of act two. And then it is revealed that the narrator of the story, the laconic Sheriff Ed Tom Bell (Tommy Lee Jones), is actually the true protagonist. This was his life story. Chigurh manages to evade capture and limps off into the sunset without retrieving the $2 million. Leaving Sheriff Bell finally ready for retirement—his only alternative in this morally bankrupt world.

In *Shattered Glass*, Stephen Glass (Hayden Christensen) holds the role of protagonist through the first half of the film, but then writer-director Billy Ray expertly switches these roles in the middle so that Glass becomes the antagonist and his editor, Chuck Lane (Peter Sarsgaard), becomes the true protagonist in the end. Do these two examples break the so-called "rules"? Absolutely. Do they work? Totally. Why? Because it's unexpected yet inevitable.

Act Three Elements

Epiphany: This term comes from James Joyce and is defined as a "sudden realization" about what is truly important in one's life. The protagonist's epiphany will ideally come at the end of the second act and provide the dramatic heat and intensity to fuel the climax. An epiphany will always place a protagonist at a *symbolic crossroads* wherein he/she must now make a *choice*. An epiphany must be dramatically "earned" throughout the second act! While it may be a "sudden" realization, it is actually the outgrowth and sum of the second act events. An epiphany can be either positive or negative— or both. What's significant is that it launches the protagonist's new goal with greater determination than ever. It's like a Phoenix emerging from the ashes.

Ticking Clock: A symbolic or sometimes literal *deadline* that the protagonist must beat in act three to add more dramatic heat and intensity to the climax.

Climax: The highest level of conflict in the story. This moment will occur near the very end of the screenplay. This is usually a showdown between protagonist and antagonist and will lead to an ultimate catharsis for the protagonist and the audience. But more importantly: the climax = the truth at not only the external (plot) level, but also at the point where the protagonist is finally able to face his/her internal demons and the "true self" can emerge.

And in order for an audience to undergo collective catharsis, the protagonist must face his/her own (worst) fears.

Some films will have a two-part climax: the *emotional climax* and the *plot climax*.

In most films, these two will intersect within the same scene, but in other movies (*see* examples below in "8 Sequence Approach Breakdowns"), the emotional and plot climax may occur in different scenes.

Payoffs: The events in act two and primarily in act three that are a dramatic resolution to the setup events of act one. All payoffs must grow out of events set up earlier in the script. Payoffs that seem to just come "out of the blue" tend to feel contrived and unsatisfying. If you come up with great payoffs in the course of writing, by all means go back and reverse engineer set-ups earlier in your script.

Resonant Ending: A satisfying ending of the script that is at once inevitable, emotional, unpredictable, thematically accessible, and honest.

Navigating the Diagram

This three-act method begins with a flawed protagonist in his/her ordinary world. Something is missing or lacking in their lives or there are problems that need fixing. They may or may not be aware of them, until someone or something comes along and "incites" them into action. They usually resist, but circumstances compel them into action. They come up with a plan (consciously or, more often than not, unconsciously) to try to get what they want without risking or changing too much. Things might go well for a little while—they often do—then they meet a few unexpected obstacles. They are thrown into a dilemma. While they fight to hold on to who they were and what they had, they would probably rather just give up, but they can't due to external and/or psychological factors.

So, they have reached a decision point: take a major risk and go all in on a new plan, usually with an uncertain outcome and plenty of danger, or give up and try to go back to what they had or who they were. Inevitably, they risk all and go for it. Things get rocky and the outcome is uncertain, but after a great struggle they pull through to some degree and there is a final, satisfactory ending. Maybe they get what they wanted all along, maybe they don't. In either case, they have grown in either minute or transformative ways over the course of their journey.

The 8 Sequence Approach

Some screenwriters are daunted by the prospect of 50–60 scene cards or even the rigidity of the three-act structural paradigm—which may not suit the genre, style, or form of their intended story. An alternative approach is very simply to break the overall protagonist(s)' journey(s) into eight chapter headings—like a novel—and to tag each intended chapter with a subtitle (*Inglorious Basterds* and *Hannah and Her Sisters* employed these chapter headings *on-screen* as a stylistic, cinematic element). Eight chapters is a suggested number to target, and for a two-hour, 120-page screenplay, the structural form corresponds to the three-act paradigm like this: act one contains two sequences, act two contains four sequences, and act three contains two sequences.

For examples of the "8 Sequence Approach," see the following breakdowns of *Little Miss Sunshine, The Hurt Locker,* and *Up in the Air.* I also recommend Paul Joseph Gulino's book, *Screenwriting: The Sequence Approach* (Continuum, 2004).

Little Miss Sunshine (2006)

Jonathan Dayton and Valerie Faris (Directors)
Michael Arndt (Screenplay)

ACT ONE

Sequence 1

Sheryl (Toni Colette) picks up her brother Frank (Steve Carell) from the hospital after his failed suicide attempt. She brings him back to the family house in Albuquerque for dinner with her son, Dwayne (Paul Dano), who has stopped talking; her seven-year-old daughter, Olive (Abigail Breslin), who wants to be a beauty queen; her husband, Richard (Greg Kinnear), a struggling motivational speaker trying to sell his book and presentation, but is playing to less-than-sold-out crowds; and her father-in-law, Edwin (Alan Arkin), who's just been kicked out of his retirement home.

Inciting Incident: (10:04) Over a bucket of fried chicken, Frank admits he tried to kill himself because he lost his lover to a rival professor. Olive changes the topic to the beauty pageant routine that she and Grandpa are working on.

Sequence 2

(17:30) There's a message on the answering machine that a girl had to forfeit and Olive has a place in the Little Miss Sunshine contest in Redondo Beach, California. The family is thrown into crisis because the contest is Sunday and Sheryl's sister can't help. They can't leave Frank by himself because of his condition and loose-cannon Grandpa has to go to coach

Olive. Sheryl says she will give aspiring pilot Dwayne permission for flight school if the recalcitrant Dwayne agrees to come with them.

(21:40) Richard seriously asks Olive if she thinks she can win Little Miss Sunshine. She looks at the family and says yes. Richard says, "We're going to California!"

ACT TWO

Sequence 3

Positive Goal: Richard is going to be a winner by having his book deal happen. Olive is going to go win Little Miss Sunshine.

Negative Goal: Lie, cheat, steal: succeed by any means necessary.

Stakes: Richard needs his book deal on the Nine Steps to move forward to save the family, which is in bad financial shape. At (30:00) Richard calls his agent, Stan Grossman, trying to check in, but there is no answer. Then at (39:30) Richard gets a hold of his agent at the gas station and says he could swing by Scottsdale to see him to make it work.

Trap: Richard's agent told him back in the day that the book was a sure thing. Richard put too much faith into counting on it to support his family. Each of the other family members is trapped in his/her own way: Grandpa was kicked out of his retirement home and has no place else to go; Dwayne is desperate to become a pilot but needs his parents' approval and money for flight lessons, and we'll find out later he's color blind and ineligible; Frank has a broken heart and is too depressed to take care of himself; Olive is stuck in Albuquerque but yearns for national fame and a tiara.

Central Mystery: Olive continuously practices her routine without the rest of her family or the audience knowing what she is doing. While there are subtle hints, the performance remains a surprise until the end.

Central Question: Will Olive win? And, by extension, will the Hoover family finally feel like "winners"?

Sequence 4

Midpoint: (45:00) At the motel, Dwayne smiles in bed upon listening to his parents argue in the next room and his mother scream, "I never want to hear about the Nine Steps again!"

(45:47) Olive asks Grandpa if she is pretty.

(46:15) Olive cries. She doesn't want to be a loser. Grandpa says a loser is somebody who doesn't try. Richard leaves the motel to go "fix this." He rides 25 miles on a bike to Scottsdale.

Sequence 5

(51:15) Stan tells Richard that the book is not happening. "You're not going to win this one."

Midpoint: (53:38) The Doctor tells Richard that his father is dead.

(55:00) Richard is given the forms to handle his father's death. Problems arise because they can't cross the state. Richard says they have to get to the Little Miss Sunshine contest.

(57:58) Richard says, "We have come seven hundred miles and I'll be damned if I'm not making that contest, Sheryl." They steal the body.

Sequence 6

False sense of security: (1:15:15) The family is four minutes late to the contest and not allowed in. Then at (1:15:50) Richard gets on his knees and begs. They are put in the system, and Olive will be able to compete.

ACT THREE

Sequence 7

Richard no longer cares about Olive winning. He just wants Olive to be able to perform and supports her for who she is.

Emotional Climax: (1:29:55) With the family concerned that Olive is going to humiliate herself, Sheryl tells Olive that she doesn't have to go on. Olive gets up and goes to do her performance.

Sequence 8

(1:31) Olive dedicates the performance to her grandpa and starts to dance.

Central mystery resolved as . . .

(1:32:00) Olive starts stripping. People in the audience boo Olive.

(1:32:42) Richard stands to show his support for Olive. So do Sheryl and Dwayne.

(1:37:15) When a representative asks Richard, "What is your daughter doing?" Richard replies, "She's kicking ass."

Plot Climax: (1:33:45) Richard goes on stage and tackles the MC for trying to chase Olive off stage. When told to get her off the stage at (1:34:30), Richard joins her in dancing. Frank, Dwayne, and Sheryl then join.

(1:36:00) The family is released and not charged as long as they never enter their daughter in another California pageant again.

(1:36:35) The family opens the back of the van. Grandpa's body is gone. They tell Olive that he would have been proud.

(1:37:15) The family takes off back to Albuquerque in the yellow van.

The Hurt Locker (2008)

Kathryn Bigelow (Director/Producer)
Mark Boal (Screenplay/Producer)

ACT ONE

Sequence 1

Introduction of Sgt. Thompson, team leader, (Guy Pearce), Sgt. Sanborn (Anthony Mackie), and Specialist Eldridge (Brian Geraghty), an elite bomb disposal unit in Baghdad in 2004.

Inciting incident: (9:30) A street bomb goes off in Baghdad killing Sergeant Sanborn's team leader Thompson. Their team tech is dead.

(11:30) Sanborn meets the new team leader tech, Sergeant First Class William James (Jeremy Renner).

Sequence 2

(24:36) The first day on the job with James and the new team. James thinks he deactivated a street bomb, but . . .

(25:20) James finds another wire. When he pulls it and as the dust clears the team realizes there are six more bombs. A wake-up call for the team as to what they are up against.

ACT TWO

Sequence 3

Positive Goal: For adrenaline junkie protagonist William James: to deactivate improvised explosive devices.

Negative Goal: For James to defy orders from his superiors, putting himself and his crew in greater jeopardy than they already are.

Stakes: Death.

Trap: (27:00) For James to succeed despite his daredevil ways, he needs to be flawless or else be dishonorably discharged.

(42:35) After throwing his headset on the ground to deactivate a car trunk bomb, James says they are done.

(43:23) The team is pissed with how James handled the situation. Sanborn tells James, "Never turn your headset off again."

Central mystery: why is James so reckless? Will he self-destruct?

Sequence 4

Midpoint: (44:30) Colonel Reed (David Morse) approaches the team, impressed with James. He calls James a "wild man" and asks how many bombs James has handled. James replies with 873. Sanborn and the team think that their leader will get them killed.

(54:45) Helping a contractor (Ralph Fiennes) with a flat tire, the two teams are ambushed.

(55:45) Two terrorists that the contractor was transporting escape.

Midpoint: (57:40) Contractor Ralph Fiennes is killed. Three have been killed in action, including Sanborn's and James's team member, Chris.

(1:01) Team member Specialist Eldridge begins freaking out. James helps him through it by making him focus on cleaning blood off the ammo.

Sequence 5

False sense of security: (1:10:00) James tells Sanborn that he has a wife and young son at home. Maybe he can still make this family thing work?

(1:11:30) Sanborn tells James that his girlfriend back home wants babies but that he's not ready. Sanborn just wants to make it out alive.

(1:14:30) Messing around and play fighting, things get tense when Sanborn holds a knife to James's throat.

(1:15:40) Sanborn asks James if he has what it takes to put on the suit. James says, "No."

(1:21:15) The team finds a body-bomb in a child. James thinks it is Beckham, the kid he had earlier befriended and bought DVDs from. James deactivates the bomb, saves the kid's body for burial.

(1:27:50) On a ride-along to get out of the office, Colonel Cambridge strays from the truck and is blown up. Eldridge freaks out.

Sequence 6

(1:29:30) James calls home to his wife and baby, but doesn't say anything.

(1:35) James searches Beckham's house, but finds no answers. He wanders through the night streets of Baghdad.

(1:37:00) The team gets in the truck to respond to a tank explosion.

(1:40:30) The hole from the explosion of the oil tanker is huge.

(1:42:20) James thinks the bombers are hiding nearby and wants to go after them. Sanborn and team argue that it is not their job, but James leads them anyway.

(1:45:55) Two men drag Eldridge off in the night down an alley.

ACT THREE

Sequence 7

(1:46:50) James and Sanborn kill the two men dragging off Eldridge, but Eldridge is shot.

(1:48:15) Breaking down, James takes a shower with his clothes on.

(1:48:40) James sees Beckham. The kid is alive, but James can't have an emotional relationship with him anymore and blows him off.

(1:49:15) James and Sanborn say goodbye to Eldridge who was shot in the femur and will be recovering for six months. James apologizes, but Eldridge tells him to fuck off, unwilling to forgive his unnecessary adrenaline rush.

(1:50:15) There is a guy on the street with a time bomb locked onto his chest. Sanborn tells James they can't do it in time. He knows they've had their differences, but this is suicide. James tries anyway, but realizes Sanborn is right and has to run away from the bomb without deactivating it.

Plot Climax: (1:56:30) The bomb explodes, but James and Sanborn are alive.

(1:57:45) Sanborn says he "hates this place," and that he is not ready to die.

(1:58:40) "Who would care if I die? I don't even have a son. I'm done." Sanborn tells James that he wants a son. Sanborn asks James how he does it. James replies that he doesn't know. He doesn't think about it. He doesn't know why he does it.

Sequence 8

(2:01) Back home, James stands in the cereal aisle in the fluorescent-lit grocery store. He looks at all the different boxes and can't find a place for himself in his own town. He doesn't fit in and is not happy.

Emotional Climax: (2:02:30) James cleans gutters and then tells his estranged wife that in the news he heard that 59 people died from a bomb that wasn't deactivated in time. "They need more bomb techs." James plays with his son and says, "The older you get the fewer things you really love."

Central mystery resolved: James isn't afraid of death; he's afraid of life.

(2:04:40) James goes back to the Middle East with the Delta Company.

(2:05:30) The last image is James back in the suit with a 365-day tour ahead of him in the Delta Company.

Up In The Air (2009)

Jason Reitman (Director/Writer (Screenplay)/Producer)
Sheldon Turner (Screenplay)
Walter Kirn (Novel)

ACT ONE

Sequence 1

Introduction of Ryan Bingham's (George Clooney) world via V.O. "What's in your backpack?" presentations. On the verge of collecting his lifetime goal of 10 million frequent flyer miles. He loves to always be on the move.

(10:20) Ryan learns that he got the gig to speak at the upcoming GoalQuest in Vegas.

Inciting incident: (10:50) Ryan gets a call from his boss, Craig (Jason Bateman). He needs Ryan back at the Omaha office by the end of the week for a "game changer."

(11:25) Ryan meets Alex (Vera Farmiga) at a hotel bar in Dallas.

(15:15) Ryan and Alex sleep together. "We've got to do this again."

Sequence 2

(20:30) Craig introduces Natalie (Anna Kendrick) to the company and she presents her remote firing "Glocal" idea that will change the way the company does business (and Ryan's life).

(26:00) Craig says he wants Ryan to show Natalie the ropes. Ryan has no choice but to do this if he wants to keep his job.

ACT TWO

Sequence 3

Positive Goal: to continue his freewheeling lifestyle/career track on his own terms.

Negative Goal: to sabotage and thwart Natalie's agenda.

(23:30) Ryan tells Craig that firing over a computer won't work, but Craig says Ryan has no case and that it's happening.

Stakes: If Glocal takes hold and is a success, Ryan will lose the life he loves on the road. The unencumbered and mobile life of advantage points, miles, airports, and hotels that shields him from all those messy emotional attachments.

Trap: Two women: Natalie and the new company policy; and Alex—who appears to be his equal. Ryan and Alex have an understanding with no strings attached. But despite Ryan's better judgment, he's falling for Alex.

Central mystery: Why is Ryan the way he is? What happened in his backstory re: his parents?

(34:10) Alex calls Ryan while he is in St. Louis asking why he didn't call. He says he wasn't sure what was appropriate. She responds with, "I am the woman you don't have to worry about." Ryan responds with, "Sounds like a trap."

(44:05) In Tulsa, Ryan enters a room with Alex. The affair continues. Right after . . .

(45:15) Ryan lands in Miami and gives his speech about having as few people as possible in your life's "backpack." He asks his audience to feel the weight of those people and says that he doesn't like the burden.

(49:00) Natalie says her boyfriend broke up with her in a text. Natalie meets Alex and the three get a drink.

Sequence 4

Midpoint: (56:30) Ryan gives Alex a key to his apartment.

(58:00) Ryan tells Alex that he had to empty his backpack to know what to put back in it and then kisses her.

(59:40) Ryan tells Alex, "Hey, I really like you," as she leaves the hotel to catch a plane.

(1:02) Natalie fights with Ryan, trying to open his eyes to how special Alex is and calls him a "12-year-old."

(1:03:40) Natalie has to do lay-offs from a computer to the tough guys in Detroit.

Sequence 5

(1:10) Ryan asks Alex to go to his sister's wedding with him. He wants a "plus one" and would like it to be her.

(1:21:20) Ryan talks to his sister's fiancé, Jim, about cold feet. Jim articulates his worries, hitting all the major fears that Ryan has. Ryan comes through and tells Jim that, "Life is better with company. You need a co-pilot."

False sense of security: (1:26:00) Julie's wedding. Happy together, Ryan sits with Alex.

Sequence 6

(1:31:35) At Goal Quest in Las Vegas, Ryan starts his speech but walks off stage. He can't do it. He can't buy into his own bullshit anymore and goes to catch a flight to Chicago to get Alex.

ACT THREE

Sequence 7

(1:33) Ryan knocks on Alex's door in Chicago. She has a husband and children. She turns him away. She has a family, and he's all alone.

Sequence 8

Emotional Climax: (1:34:45) Alex calls Ryan while he is sitting in a parking lot. She is pissed. "You could have seriously screwed up things for me. That's my family. That's my real life." She thought their relationship was clear. He's a break from her real life . . . a parenthesis. He's an escape. Ryan is hurt.

(1:36) In-flight, Ryan is awarded his 10 million miles club member moment. He's #7 and the youngest to make the club. It is nothing like what he imagined it would be.

(1:38) Ryan calls and has 1 million miles transferred to Julie and Jim for their honeymoon.

Plot Climax: (1:39:30) Ryan learns Natalie quit after a woman she fired committed suicide.

(1:40) Craig wants Ryan back in the air. Videoconferencing lay-offs are being put on hold. Ryan gets his old job back like he wanted.

(1:41:20) Natalie gets the job she originally wanted in San Francisco because of a letter of recommendation that Ryan wrote for her.

(1:42) A montage of some of the people who were fired and how they are more positively coping with the support of their family.

(1:43) A free man, Ryan looks at the arrivals/departures board at the airport. Like Natalie said she would do, he's going to just pick somewhere and go. But as he stands in front of that board, he's got nowhere to go. He's been everywhere and never touched anything or anyone. He's a wraith. And there's not a place in the country that has any genuine personal meaning for him. He has this very lost empty look on his face as he takes his hand off the handle of his suitcase, lowering his eyes from the board and looking straight into camera in a really haunting way. Of course it's intended to be enigmatic, but I think he goes back to his old life but now it's a curse instead of a blessing.

Now that we've examined the plot points and eight sequence breakdowns according to time codes, let's take a closer look at how each of these structural elements can be articulated as A and B stories (main plot and main subplot) in the blockbuster comedy, *Bridesmaids*.

CASE STUDY: *Bridesmaids*

(Screenplay by Kristin Wiig and Annie Mumolo; Directed by Paul Feig)
Structure Type: Linear

Structural Summary—A and B Stories.

Bridesmaids uses a classic Hollywood setup: one main dominant protagonist, and a linear timeline. It has two primary stories, both of which unfold sequentially and are intercut until they come together for the final act.

Setup: The first act is a structurally simple setup to a traditional linear story. We see Annie (Kristin Wiig) having naughty, sometimes painful and decidedly platonic sex with the Ted character (Jon Hamm)—the worst kind of guy—he doesn't care at all about her. The first thing he does the morning after is to throw her out. She does the "walk of shame," tries to climb over his mansion gate, and gets stuck on top of it as it opens to let the housekeeper in. This is an opening that tells us a lot about where this character is—she has low self-esteem and is in a really bad quasi-relationship.

The film continues, setting up her ordinary world in the classic Hollywood way and piling on things that need fixing. Annie and her best friend, Lillian (Maya Rudolph), sneak into an outdoor exercise class to avoid paying but end up embarrassing themselves, getting chased away by the angry drill sergeant instructor. We then rapidly learn that Annie's cake business failed and that she now has a dead-end sales job that her mother got her from someone she met at A.A.—even though she's not an alcoholic. Her mom wants Annie to move in with her, but Annie's pride precludes the move; for now, she's staying put with her two crazy roommates. So, her self-image is shot, her love life stinks, and her job and housing situation are all bad.

Then the story kicks into drive with the *Inciting Incident.* It's right around page 10.

Lillian is getting married and wants Annie to be her Maid of Honor. From this point forward, with the setup out of the way, we basically follow the two parallel stories as they unfold chronologically.

The A story involves Annie's increasingly inept and comical attempts to be the best Maid of Honor possible. She hates the elegant, rich and apparently super successful Helen (Rose Byrne) who is vying to be Lillian's new best friend and take over as Maid of Honor. We follow Annie on this journey and watch as she tries and fails in increasingly fantastic ways, until she may very well lose her best friend—the only piece of solidity she had at the film's beginning.

The B story follows Annie's romantic adventures with the good-looking, but soulless Ted and the ordinary, but kind Officer Rhodes (Chris O'Dowd), the "guy she should really be with." The B story jumps into gear right around Plot Point I, or page 30, when she first meets Rhodes and it pulls us through the pain of her evolving love interests. Again, this is classic three-act structure.

Officer Rhodes really likes Annie, but demands that she grow, take responsibility for her life, and treat him right.

At around pages 67–70, Annie has gotten all the bridesmaids thrown off the plane on their way to Las Vegas, and Lillian tells her that she wants Helen to take over as the Maid of Honor. It looks like Annie is a total screw-up in a major existential dilemma—which is classic *Mid-point*.

By page 85, Lillian has told Annie not to come to the wedding—and Annie has also lost her apartment, her job and apparently any shot she had with Officer Rhodes. This is her lowest point, and from here she formulates a new plan and begins to take action.

Both of these stories eventually intertwine in act three, where we witness Annie's growth as a character when she tries to take control of her life. She dumps Ted, gets her car fixed and tries to make amends with Officer Rhodes. She gets to be the hero who actively saves Lillian's wedding (the ticking clock is the run-up to the ceremony) after practically ruining every event leading up to it. By the end, she still has the same crappy living situation, she's lost her job, has no money and is living with her mom. But after a violent pep talk from the ballsy, irreverent Megan (Melissa McCarthy), Annie decides to buck up and finds new self-esteem, friends and possibly a guy. And we somehow feel that she's going to be OK.

Alternative Structuring

Apart from the linear narratives detailed above, there are infinite ways to structure and sequence a film. One such example is **bookend**: where we begin at the end, jump back and fill the audience in on how the story got there (*Water for Elephants*, *Saving Private Ryan*, and *American Beauty*). We can also start in the middle and **zigzag** backward and then forward (*Out of Sight*); or **hopscotch** or loop de loop (*500 Days of Summer* and *Pulp Fiction*). There is also ensemble structure, such as *Traffic*, *Crash*, and *Love, Actually*— with a unifying thematic (*See Chapter 18 on Theme*).

It is up to you to determine the best structure for maintaining tension and suspense for *your* story. However, recognize that if you deviate too much from the linear basics, you might lose your audience. It is therefore important to be even more careful and diligent with planning, outlining, prep work, and structuring. *See* more examples of alternative structures at the end of this chapter.

Where to Begin

Regardless of structure type, I frequently tell my students to start the story at some point of disequilibrium, tension, or jeopardy for the main character(s). Introduce a desperate protagonist, and we're immediately drawn in. Find the structure that involves us in the protagonist's problems from page 1. Don't make the audience wait.

CASE STUDY: *The Girl with the Dragon Tattoo*

(Screenplay by Steven Zaillian; Directed by David Fincher)
Structure Type: Dual Protagonists

Setup: We first meet Mikael Blomkvist (Daniel Craig), co-owner of *Millennium* magazine, in the midst of a professional crisis—having just lost a high-level libel suit against Hans-Erik Wennerström, a corrupt corporate businessman. With Blomkvist's reputation and livelihood hanging by a slender thread, he decides to resign from the magazine. In desperate straits, Blomkvist accepts an unusual offer: to officially write a biography on retired industrial tycoon, Henrik Vanger (Christopher Plummer), but *unofficially* to investigate the unsolved mystery of Henrik's niece, Harriet—who disappeared 40 years ago and whose body was never recovered.

Stakes for Blomkvist: If Blomkvist successfully solves the case, Henrik will provide him with incriminating evidence against Wennerström that will restore Blomkvist's professional reputation. But this is an incendiary, scandalous case, and if Harriet Vanger was, indeed, murdered (as Henrik believes she was), Blomkvist could become another target and end up dead.

Central Mystery (concerning the past): What happened to Harriet? Was she abducted? Killed? Did she run away? Was it an "inside" job by someone in the family? Was there a conspiracy that's still being perpetuated?

Central Question for Blomkvist (concerning the future): Is Harriet still alive? And then the corollaries: Is Henrik telling Blomkvist the full truth or deceiving and setting him up? Is Henrik the actual murderer? Was this the work of a serial killer and could he still be active today? The secondary question for Blomkvist is will he save his professional reputation and at what cost? Will he and Lisbeth Salander (Rooney Mara) fall in love and stay together, or will he resume his relationship with his more age appropriate business partner at *Millennium*, Erika (Robin Wright)?

Equally Important, Dual Protagonist: Lisbeth Salander. In order for Henrik to trust Blomkvist with the investigation—which necessitates an extended stay at the cloistered Vanger family estate on Hedeby Island in Hedestad—Henrik asks his attorney to conduct a classified background check on Blomkvist. Enter Lisbeth, the heavily pierced, tattooed titular girl and the very best researcher and computer hacker in the security business. Although she's 23, Lisbeth is still a ward of the state deemed mentally and legally incompetent owing to a murky past that is only hinted at in the film. Lisbeth is a misanthropic social pariah, abused as a child, and sexually promiscuous.

Stakes for Lisbeth: We will later learn that she murdered her molester father and that she was abandoned and left for dead. Lisbeth takes her job very seriously and always excavates the truth. When Blomkvist discovers that she hacked into his emails and confronts her about it, his interest is actually to recruit her for his investigative assignment. And for Lisbeth, the case of a young girl, Harriet Vanger, who was possibly molested and murdered, the stakes could not be more personal.

Central Mystery for Lisbeth (concerning the past): How did Lisbeth end up this "wounded bird" with razor sharp talons?

Central Questions for Lisbeth (concerning the future): Will she overcome the predatory attorney who abuses his power over her as her new legal guardian, and will she crack the case with Blomkvist? Can she learn to trust Blomkvist, and are her romantic feelings for him requited?

Intersection: At midpoint, Blomkvist and Lisbeth cross the line into an intimate relationship. We know she's bisexual and that he's involved with Erika; Lisbeth is also young enough to be his daughter, so their romantic entanglement is fraught with issues, but they also share an intense connection. He wants to take care of her and she needs to trust somebody in the world. Despite their odd couple differences, they're a great team with complementary strengths and weaknesses. He's methodical, diplomatic, and analytical; she's impulsive, furious, and sadistically vengeful.

Payoff: In the last third of the movie, it's Lisbeth who comes to Blomkvist's rescue—flipping the bird to the outdated "damsel in distress" formula. She also manages to professionally and financially destroy Hans-Erik Wennerström —vindicating Blomkvist and enriching herself in the process.

Divergent Paths (redux): Lisbeth buys Blomkvist an expensive leather motorcycle jacket, hopeful that they can ride off together into the Swedish sunset. She has fallen in love and learned to trust a good man. But her spirit is crushed when she realizes that Blomkvist intends to resume his relationship with Erika. Lisbeth hurls the leather jacket into the dumpster, re-armors herself as a rogue, and takes off alone on her motorcycle.

CASE STUDY: *Slumdog Millionaire*

(Screenplay by Simon Beaufoy; Directed by Danny Boyle and Loveleen Tandan)
Structure Type: Midpoint-Flashback-Catchup

Strategy for Laying Out this Alternative Structural Model:

Step 1. State the Main Story in a Linear Form

Slumdog Millionaire is primarily a love story. The protagonist is Jamal (Dev Patel as Older Jamal). He is one of two untouchable brothers from the slums of India. He is pure of heart. His brother, Salim (Madhur Matel as Older

Salim), is more vindictive and driven by money and survival. Jamal falls in love with a girl named Latika (Frieda Pinto as Older Latika). Salim only sees her as an obstacle to making it, an object of pleasure, or something to sell. Jamal never loses his desire to be with her, but his life is hard. This quest eventually lands him on the nationally televised game show—*Who Wants to be a Millionaire?* The show's host, Prem (Anil Kapoor), was also from the slums. He has now grown rich and famous and is jealous of Jamal. He tries to get him to cheat, but when that fails, he simply accuses him and has the police pick him up for interrogation. When Jamal gets to the final question, he uses his lifeline and calls a friend, Salim. Unfortunately, Salim has shot himself, and Latika, having escaped from the man who was essentially pimping her, answers the phone. Jamal wins the $1,000,000—and Latika. Jamal, the brother who stayed true and chased love with all his heart, has won both love and money, but Salim, the brother who chased money, has just been killed by Javed's henchman and died in a bathtub full of it.

Step 2. Disentangle the Primary Stories into Storylines

The Jamal, Latika Love Story. Over more than ten years, Jamal continually seeks out Latika and tries to be with her. Their paths continue to cross in various cities and times and frequently it is Salim who pulls them apart. Latika is forced into prostitution. Her face is cut with a knife. She asks him to forget her many times, but he will not. This pursuit to win her back leads him to the game show, to endure beatings, all for a chance to win enough money to free her. He is doing all he can to stay on the show in the hopes that she will see and find him. This story plays out in episodes with great time lapses in between. Ultimately he doesn't know the final answer. He calls his lifeline, which is Salim's mobile number, the only one he knows. Only Salim has shot himself, and it is Latika who answers the phone. Who is the third musketeer? She has no idea. So he takes the leap of faith and guesses: A. Aramis. "Just because." And he wins the money, and they win each other.

The Game Show. Over several days or weeks, it is not entirely clear, Jamal progresses on the game show. This story line gives us the structural spine of the ten game show questions that we hear Jamal successfully answer. Each game show question is used to launch an episode of the past (Storyline 1) and show us about Jamal's life and struggles with both Salim and Latika.

The Game show host Prem begins by making fun of Jamal. As the 18-year-old "boy-man" gets more and more questions right, the audience's like for Jamal grows as does Prem's dislike for him. He does not want to be upstaged by him. He tries to feed him a wrong answer. On the eve of the final question, Prem gets Jamal arrested and accuses him of cheating. The police interrogate and beat Jamal, but he ultimately wins the money and the girl. Prem loses his job and status.

The Interrogation. This story plays out over roughly one night (about 12 hours). The Inspector's investigation of Jamal is also its own storyline. This occurs during the night between him winning 500,000 rupees and going back on the show for a chance at 20 million rupees. They try to break him through interrogation and questioning to learn how he did it. It is a given that he must have cheated. No one believes that a slumdog could possibly know all the answers. This surfaces the inherent "guilty until proven innocent" standard of India's caste system. It also plays into the "It is written" and fate themes behind Jamal's final triumph.

The Tale of Two Brothers. This story plays out roughly over nine or ten years, from the time we first meet the brothers, when Jamal is nine to when he is 18 on the show. It does not play out linearly, but rather it is structured around episodes inspired by the game show questions.

Salim and Jamal have nearly identical backgrounds. Both have lived through the same horrific events. But, Salim loses his soul to money, bitterness, and materialism, while Jamal remains romantic, faithful, and pure. Jamal is the one thing that keeps Salim human. Salim turns down the gangster's offer to become rich by turning Jamal into a blind beggar. He continually hurts Latika and Jamal, but part of him loves his brother. Salim ends up dead, shot by Javed's guards . . . right before Jamal wins the 20 million rupees.

Step 3: Pay Attention to Openings and Setting the Tone

The opening of the film begins with an introduction of the three primary stories. Our first image is the gangster Javed's (Mahesh Manjrekar) safe house. Salim is in the rupee-filled bathtub. We cut to Jamal and Prem as he is just beginning on the game show. Prem and the audience laugh at him and treat him with disrespect. Back in Javed's safe house, a gun is loaded, pressed to a head and shot. We don't know who yet. We cut back to applause and Jamal beginning on *Who Wants to be a Millionaire?* and then a hard-cut forward in time to Storyline 3, in which Jamal is strung to the ceiling and being brutally interrogated by the police on the night before the final question. This pattern continues, getting the audience used to both the cutting style and structural rhythm of the film.

Planning Before You Write: The Outline/ the Board

I always outline my screenplays before I start writing. I like to use good, old-fashioned index cards that I can lay out all over the dining-room table, allowing me to view the entire plot from start to finish. You can also use a word processing or screenwriting program. If you have an office, you can put up giant white boards. Whatever system you choose, you need to be able to erase pieces, move them around and to allow for a significant amount of trial and error.

Remember, It's All a Work-in-Progress and Not a Museum Piece.

This initial idea generation and sifting process can take days, weeks or even months to complete. Once I have about 60 cards, I'll stack them in order and type up the outline. In typing up the outline, I'll continue to add connective tissue and start to develop a sense of what needs to stay and what needs to be omitted. I weed out repetitive beats wherever they've cropped up. If you can take a scene out and the film still stands, cut it. Audiences are much smarter than you think.

By and Large, Every Scene Needs to Have Its Own Conflict, Offer Up a Significant New Piece of Information About Plot or Character, and Entertain Along the Way.

No matter how diligently you work out the structural blueprint for your script in advance, you will find that potent, often unexpected, discoveries are made during the *writing* process. In fact, if you throw away, reorder, or rewrite big chunks of the whole story that almost certainly means you are doing it right. *Creating a world takes time—so relax and have fun with it.*

Ideally, the Final Goal Here is to Make the Structure Invisible.

You want your audience absorbed in your story, not dissecting structure. However, just as the best basketball players or musicians put in thousands of hours drilling the fundamentals, beginning with extensive brainstorming and a sound structural template gives you the best chance of consistently writing page-turning material.

Initial Structure Process

1. Draft several versions of compelling loglines for ideas you feel passionate about and love enough to spend a year or more of your life on.
2. Pick one.
3. Draft simple, short linear storylines in basic prose to get a strong sense of the narrative roadmap you will possibly follow. No matter how you want to slice it up later, start here.

   a. Someone wants something. They try to get it. Obstacles and complications occur. They get it or they don't.
   b. Keep these early story spines in simple narrative linear prose to start.

4. Brainstorm scenes and ideas. Begin to jot down notes on index cards, napkins, the computer, iPads, or notepads. Do not edit yet. Just let yourself go.

5. Look for connections and potential larger pieces that can be combined into sequences.

6. Decide how many stories to include, and their relative importance in the first draft outline. Look at intersection points. Think about how the multiple stories relate and where and how they can intersect.

7. Go through the "21 Questions" in this book.

8. Find and analyze similar movies, books, plays, stories, and other reference models.

9. Give each story a letter. The primary story is your A Story. The secondary story is your B Story. Outline each story separately. They may have different structures. Then interweave the chosen stories into an initial full outline. For a feature this will usually be anywhere from 40 to 80 scenes or cards. Each card should, at this point, probably include a slugline with the Location Heading, as well as some basic information about who is present, what happens and what the key conflicts and/or story points are. I like to label them with their story as well— A story, B story, etc.

10. Sit with, examine, tighten, and strengthen the underlying stories, the scenes, and the entire outline for a period of time.

11. Start writing. Write the current version or draft.

12. Refer to Chapter 21 on Rewrites.

The happy truth is that the entire process is iterative and messy and no two people really do it the same. Some people outline for months and create ironclad models. Others do rough outlines, dive into writing, go back to outlining and jump around. Find the system that's right for you.

How to Choose: A Few Final Factors to Consider

If you are not sure, or don't feel strongly about the need for an alternative structure—go with the classic three-act structure. It has worked for decades in films and centuries in theatre. If you do feel like you want to do something different, or the size, scope, or nature of the material compels it, here are some questions to ask:

1. What is the length of time covered in the story? The longer the period over which the story occurs, the more you will have to get creative with structure.

2. Are there pieces of information from widely disparate time periods that we ideally want the audience to know for the story to work? For example, does the story take place when the protagonist is 60, but we need to know things that happened when they were 9, 11, 18 and 35? These types of structures lend themselves well to parallel stories and/or flashbacks.
3. Would presenting the story elements out of order heighten tension, comedy, drama, or suspense by changing audience expectations in helpful ways?
4. Is the story for a Hollywood or independent film audience? There are no hard rules, but as a general principle, Hollywood big budget films tend more toward linear, cohesive timelines, and fewer storylines. Indie films are much more likely to consider and/or require fractured narratives, non-linear time, reversals of time and more complex temporal and story structures.
5. Does the story start more slowly than is typical for the genre, and/or can you add significant tension or layers of meaning if the audience knows a key fact in advance? For example, in *Titanic*, it changes the movie-going experience significantly to know that Rose has survived the tragic sinking of the "Unsinkable Ship" as she narrates the love story.
6. Does the choice of structure best relate to the underlying experience of the story to be told? *The Hangover* is a good example here, as the gaps in the narrative structure seem to relate to the experience of taking drugs, blacking out, and losing big chunks of memory.
7. Do you feel really, really passionate about trying it in a new way? That's always a good sign to forge ahead.

Additional Web Resources

On the companion website to this book, you will find examples of additional types of film structure and breakdowns for some of your favorite films.

> Determine the best structure for maintaining tension and suspense for *your* story. Always begin the story as late as possible. Introduce a desperate protagonist and we're immediately drawn in. Find the structure that involves us in the protagonist's problems from page 1. Why should an audience wait for the good stuff to kick in?

INTERVIEW: Academy Award-Nominated Screenwriter/Director Richard LaGravenese

Richard LaGravenese Filmography

Best known for:

Beautiful Creatures (also directing) (2013)
Behind the Candelabra (2013)
Water for Elephants (2011)
P.S. I Love You (also directed) (2007)
Freedom Writers (also directed) (2007)
Paris, je t'aime—segment Pigalle (also directed) (2006)
Living Out Loud (also directed) (1998)
The Horse Whisperer (1998)
The Bridges of Madison County (1995)
A Little Princess (1995)
The Ref (1994)
The Fisher King (1991)
    Academy Award Nominee
    WGA Award Nominee

NL: To tell your story, how much freedom do you have when you're approaching an adaptation—especially when a book like *Water For Elephants* is such a best seller and people have expectations?

RL: The first thing is that content dictates style. Always. You can't superimpose some arbitrary style onto anything, any story. You have to respect what the content is, what the story is about, what it's thematically about, and have that dictate how you structure and how you style it. I think with every adaptation I've done, it's absolutely important to come in with a strong point of view about how you would do it. Because if it's not agreed upon, you can't write something you don't agree with. You are not applying for a job that you don't want to do. If they ask you, please read this book that we'd love to adapt into a movie. The first thing I do is read it and ask myself: Do I like it? Do I like the story? Number two, do I see a movie in it? Number three, do I see a movie in it that I feel compelled to write? Because I've read beautiful books, I'm a big reader, and some of them I actually love so much as books that I don't want to touch them as movies because they are literary experiences for me. So I read the book and as I'm reading it, I start to see a movie in my head, like this little mini-plex with a screen. I put myself in the audience as much as possible when I create because that's how I started loving films. I didn't go to film school, so everything I do is sort of based on what I've learned through osmosis, through watching films all through my childhood. Once I start to see scenes play, then I have a point of view of how to initially structure it. In this business, after they've submitted the book to you and you say you're interested, then you have to go back to them and say how you would do it. For instance, in *The Bridges of Madison County* they already had two drafts from two writers and for some reason the movie still wasn't green lit. When I was brought in, I didn't like the book, but I actually asked my older sister what she thought about it, and she absolutely loved it. I realized that although I was being a little bit of a literary snob about it, there was something in it that was appealing and touching, especially to the large female audience out there. So I went in to Amblin, to Steven [Spielberg] and Kathleen [Kennedy] and said, "This is how I would do it—I would only do it from her [Meryl Streep's] point of view. I would cut out the scenes of the back and forth between him and her—just her point of view and I listed about four things. One of which I remember saying is that there has to be an argument. Everyone is too complacent in the book. I come from an Italian American family, and Italian American women don't have great sex for four days and then all of a sudden say, "Yes, I know you must leave because you are spiritual." And they agreed with that take, and I got to do it.

NL: What about your approach to *Water for Elephants*?

RL: With *Water*, I read it thinking that the beginning was a really clever literary trick where she starts with the stampede and you're supposed to not know who killed the lead character because she only uses a pronoun. You're led to suspect that possibly the female protagonist did the murder, but I didn't believe it and I also didn't think it would work cinematically. It just felt contrived. To me, you could do an entire film about a man in an old age home, and I remember thinking about *Fried Green Tomatoes*. I remember that I loved Kathy Bates [Evelyn Couch] and Jessica Tandy [Ninny Threadgoode]—you can't get two better actresses—and thank God they were the story that interrupted the other story, but I was so into the other story that I always felt it was a bit of an interruption when I was being pulled back and forth. I felt the same way actually in *Bridges* because I would have cut down even more. Every time you interrupted Meryl and Clint to go to the children it felt like an interruption to me. Because you're cutting away from fucking Meryl Streep and Clint Eastwood. It must be something really strong to take me away from these two amazing, iconic actors.

I did go through drafts of doing the old age home at the beginning, but I was never going to cut back and forth between it. I had decided that right away. In the book at the end, he escapes from the old age home, meets the circus manager and tells him the story even though you've already read the entire story. So I decided to take that and put it at the beginning. The initial drafts of books are very respectful of the book, and it's really just getting it from one medium to another. Getting it in screenplay format, all the scenes I love, and not worrying how long it is and how fat it is, knowing that it's all going to get condensed and reinvented. I have to take all the material out of the book that I like and start to dramatically structure it. So as I'm reading it a second time, I write notes literally in the book in the margins, titling where things happen and then at each chapter head, I create a menu or a reference guide, so I can always go back and find that scene where they kissed for the first time, or the scene where August loses his shit for the first time. It's like an encyclopedia then, with everything in the margins of scenes that I want and need. I transfer that into screenplay form, and then I put away the book and I start to create the screenplay and reinvent as I find the movie. The characters start to talk a bit more to me and what might work in the pages of the book in terms of a dramatic motor might not in a film when you make it literal. When you have real people speaking real lines, you have to have an audience believe that it's real instead of in their imaginations. You can then start to see which characters need to be a bit more aggressive and proactive.

NL: I liked the way you approached the August [Christoph Waltz] character because he could have been very two-dimensional. It very much related to the times we are in now, economically, because he really had a strong point of view on why he did what he did.

RL: Water For Elephants is a special case because Francis [Lawrence] was attached as director. He was on first and he came to me with the book. So we worked together on the script as a partnership. I'd do the writing, and he would review. He has this great instinct about bumps in the story, and by "bump" I mean it reads, it's moving, the energy is right and then all of a sudden something feels unearned or pops out at you. It's just an instinctual feeling, and that comes from knowing how to tell a story. We both came to the conclusion that we wanted audiences to feel that August had a point, that he wasn't just a psychotic. The triangle in the book reminded us a bit of *Sophie's Choice*, and we wanted to move away from that and have him be a more fully dimensional character, where even though he acts abusive, at times you're going, "Yeah, but I understand that. He's got a point there—and he does love her." There's humanity to him, which makes it also tragic instead of one-sided. Plus in every draft, except for a few first drafts when we had both characters (the owner of the circus and August), August kept disappearing in the third act. As he does, in my opinion, in the book. He loses his shit and then it all becomes about Marlena separating from him, and then Jacob has to get Marlena back into the circus because Uncle Al needs her back because he's the owner of the circus. Suddenly the stakes, the motor of the thing got stalled and August disappeared a little bit and got a bit weaker, so it just strengthened the whole motor of the movie, the engine, to combine those two characters.

NL: So structurally with adaptations you are starting with the book as a template, and what's really remarkable about your adaptations is that they work so well. You always hear people say, "You know it's a good book, but it's going to be a bad movie because in literary fiction, in particular, there is so much that has to be taken out that it gets watered down." A lot of times people say short stories make the best movie adaptations—from *Brokeback Mountain* to *Shawshank Redemption*. How do you decide what stays, what goes, what needs to change in service of the movie version?

RL: When you're reading a book and enjoying it, you're not looking at it analytically. When you start to break it apart, you start to see there is repetition, that there's a yo-yo effect, and in a movie, you have to keep the train moving forward because you only have two hours. You have to invent off of the foundation and that's when you know you have to be original.

NL: Combining those two characters [August and the circus owner from the book]—that's a great example of a way to actually strengthen the material.

RL: And in writing their histories and recreating who they are as characters, sometimes you have to do that as well, but you maintain the spirit of the book and the spirit of the characters. Like Marlena in the book was a girl who married a Jewish man and her family disowned her. Whereas in our version, especially when Reese came on board, we wanted to make her culpable in what happened so that everybody had their reasons. No one is completely innocent in all this. She grew up and had a really hard life as an abandoned and abused foster child, but she's found a place in the world where she is safe and can survive and that is more important to her than love. In that way, when the young lover comes in, it's a threat to her because her world is solid right now. She knows she has an abusive husband, but she can deal with him. Love or feeling anything again is actually more dangerous for her.

NL: When you are doing a spec script like *The Fisher King* or *The Ref*, do you outline? How do you approach it when you're not coming from source material?

RL: I wish I outlined. I'm one of those people who just doesn't. I start to and then I get too itchy. I have to go into the screenplay to find things, but then sometimes I go back and forth because I'll hit a wall and then I'll go back and maybe outline a bit more, just to clear my head to come up with ideas. I tend to like to jump into originals not knowing how I'm going to get there, but I have my ending. I know where I want to go, so I decide what the movie is about thematically and I build from there.

NL: That's a very controversial subject in MFA screenwriting programs.

RL: I know. I taught a master screenwriting class at Emerson [College] and I made them outline. Then, at the end of the course after 14 weeks, I admitted to them that I don't, but that I think it is better if you do. The funny thing is though when I write television, because of how television works, you *have* to. I usually have a partner with that, and there is something wonderful about jumping into the writing of a teleplay when you know you've mapped out every scene. It may just be something that because I didn't go to film school, I didn't have the training for. I do support it. I think it's a great idea if you're good at it. I have friends who outline for three months and then write the script in three weeks because they've worked all this stuff out. I'm still developing and still learning.

The script I'm working on now, I'm thinking about all the time, and whenever ideas pop into my head, I have a file of notes and ideas that are on my desktop or in my pad. For *The Fisher King*, I did three or four different drafts over a period of a year and a half with about five or six months in between not writing at all because I wasn't making a living as a screenwriter yet. I was working with a partner on something else and I was doing this on my own. All I had was just a one-line idea that came from how I felt at the time, which was that I wanted to show a narcissistic man who performs a selfless act and that was pretty much all I had. And then literally things started to come to me like the myth, but the three different drafts before he was ever a DJ are completely different stories. One was really pretentious and heavy and very much like *Rain Man* accidentally, which was happening at the same time, and I knew nothing about it because I was living in New York and that was happening in LA. Another one was like a sitcom, but with each one of them I found a different aspect. I found a character in one, I found a little bit of structure in the other, and then one day it all clicked together.

NL: So originally Parry [Robin Williams] was like an autistic savant?

RL: A while ago, I saw two men walking across Third Avenue after I'd gone to the movies. One was a very handsome young man and the other man, he was the same age, but it was like George and Lennie from *Of Mice and Men*, and it just stuck with me. So in the first draft, Jack [Jeff Bridges] was a bitter cab driver, who was a philosopher cab driver, and Parry was a street guy who was incredible and at some point in the movie he takes him to Las Vegas. I wrote the whole draft and then one day I'm reading in *The New York Times* that this movie got green lit about a savant who goes to Las Vegas with his brother. I could not believe it. I wasn't in the business, I had no agent and I didn't know anything about that. So I threw it away and started with a different tone and that tone was too light, it was too sitcomy for me, but in that one, I found the idea of having to pair him up with a woman. And then I threw that one away too. I realize with me that I need my originals to simmer for them to really be the closest to an original voice that they can be, otherwise they can be too derivative.

NL: It seems like there's a recurring theme on grief and loss in your work. People recovering from either a death or very traumatic event and the process of going through the bereavement. The other really controversial subject that comes up a lot is how to approach theme. There are people like David Koepp who say, "Don't even think about theme. It will be pretentious and totally pull you off track. Let the audience decide what the theme is, just focus on the goals and desires." Then there's someone like Gary Ross who says,

"Theme is everything, you have to start with theme. Your characters are actually just in service of theme and the only reason there is a movie is to support the theme and that is everything." Where do you stand on the subject?

RL: There is truth in what they both say. I personally need to know why I'm writing it or what it's about. Not what the story is but what it's about, and that means theme for me. But David's right in saying that if you make it too much about that you can come up with something that is pretentious and heavy-handed. There's a balance between having a theme inside of you as an artist, and then finding a way to tell a story that engages and allows for an audience to participate in it.

NL: Right, because that's what makes it universal.

RL: Exactly. So yes, I agree. I need to have a theme to start, but I don't need that thing to be the one that everybody gets. The perfect thing is to have a theme, but then allow for interpretation. I think [François] Truffaut said that it's not about what you tell, but what you leave out. And it is in those things, in those ellipses, where an audience can engage and interpret. When I was a teenager, the movies that were the top grossing films were *Taxi Driver*, and *Network*, *All The President's Men*, and *Dog Day Afternoon* which nowadays would be art films, so now there is more of a stimulus feeling that people want. I think if you hit theme too much, audiences sit back in their seats and are ahead of you.

> *The basic thing when you are telling a story is that you don't want the audience to be ahead of you. If they know where you are going or if they think you're trying to teach them something, my image is that their backs go back into the seat instead of forward.*

However, if you keep them stimulated, but you know where you are going, you are choosing what to tell them and what not to tell them, then thematically they can decide or figure things out for themselves. The greatest feeling is that they actually do get what you mean. Critics often don't because they make a lot of assumptions, what they think you mean. You can't believe it sometimes. I don't read reviews anymore, but in the past I used to say to myself, "What movie did they see? Because that was not mine." They added all of these things that were not there.

NL: Some of the screenwriters I have admired the most have naturally transformed into directing. How has directing transformed your screen-writing? What would you say are the most valuable things you've learned from directing your own work?

RL: How much I overwrite. I write from a theatrical background for performance. I love words and I love great performances and I tend to overwrite. My style actually is more suited for theatre. What directing has taught me—and I am still learning—is the language of cinema, the language of image. It's very liberating and it's a constant challenge for me. Because I love words and I love actors saying great words. Some of my favorite films are adaptations of plays. But some of my other favorite films are pure cinema, and that's something that at this stage of my life and work, I'm looking to reinvent myself with and challenge myself to try to do more, to write with the language of cinema, the language of image.

NL: Are you finding when you get into the editing room now, having directed many times, that the idea of post-production is the final rewrite?

RL: Editing is the best because it's the other side of the coin to writing. It is my favorite process because you get to rewrite the script. And then what happens is that you know the first cuts are whatever they are and that the more honest you are and the more open you are to reinvention, you actually wind up with the film that, in essence, was the closest thing to the idea that you started out with. I've seen that happen a great deal, and it's a great process. I'm one of those writers who when I'm on set, like for instance in *Water For Elephants*, I'm completely supportive of less. I'd rewrite on the set, and there was one scene that was maybe two pages long that I got down to five lines. I was thrilled by that. Content dictates style. If you look at something like *Network*, that deserved to be literary—full of incredible speeches because of what the world was at that time with those characters. It's compelling, it's an amazing movie.

NL: Can tell me about *Behind the Candelabra*—aka the Liberace picture?

RL: Steven [Soderbergh] emailed me in 2008 saying, "I have this Liberace biography. Do you want to adapt it? I'm not kidding." That was it. I was laughing because I went, "Really, Liberace?" and then I read the book and I just loved it. It was sort of like *Sunset Boulevard* told from the viewpoint of this man [Scott Thorson] who was his lover from 1977 to 1982. It was Thorson's palimony suit that brought Liberace out in public because he had always denied being homosexual.

I think that Soderbergh is one of the great filmmakers, so working with him is always just a great opportunity. So I wrote a draft of it in 2008, and then last September, I did a quick rewrite on it. Michael Douglas and Matt Damon are playing Liberace and Scott Thorson. I'm very excited about this one. Steven's decided to make it for HBO where we'll have a lot more freedom to tell the story. I just did another little rewrite based on deposition transcripts from the palimony suit. Fascinating stuff. Steven and I did a similar thing with the *Erin Brockovich* rewrite, going back to court transcripts and finding great material.

NL: So it was based on a biography. Did you approach it in the same way that you do a novel?

RL: Yes. But the thing is that this was someone, it was their point of view, so I had to also add to it what I thought was between the lines. A one-line reference to something piqued my interest and opened up an idea for a scene that said a great deal about the character and the relationship, so I used the book structurally and for information as well. I again added layers that made it thematically what I thought I could do with it. But everything that happens, happens. There was this one reference to Lee [Liberace's nickname] that took Scott to Germany to the castle of King Ludwig II. Liberace thought he was the King's reincarnation. So I look up King Ludwig II who was actually this repressed homosexual king who used to build castles that he decorated over and over and over, which is exactly what Liberace did. I felt that would be a really interesting scene to have Thorson bring him there and have Liberace deliver what I call my "Patton" monologue, like when George C. Scott talks about Alexander the Great, and he tells us how he felt that now, through King Ludwig, he could be who he was and wouldn't be punished for it. Which was a lot of rationalization in Lee's mind for his sexual promiscuity. It was just ironic that he went through this liberation of sexual freedom that resulted in him losing his life. So structurally, those are things you add, again in terms of my own experience and my place in history right now, in bringing a story that happened 30 years ago to now.

ASSIGNMENT

Chart out three different structural approaches to your screenplay. You might discover that what you had conceived as the "middle" is actually a more powerful and compelling way to *start*.

THE MANY VARIATIONS OF STORY STRUCTURE

TYPE	EXAMPLE	NOTE
1 Linear / Flashback	Bridges of Madison County, Milk, Titanic	Live primarily in the present, with flashbacks to reveal key past events.
2 Linear / Flashforward	Mystic Pizza, You Can Count on Me, Rise of the Planet of the Apes	Start in past to show key events, then jump forward to future and stay there.
3 Flashcut	Shutter Island	Use very brief flashbacks with no dialogue for key information reveals.
4 Bookends	American Beauty, The Hangover, Sunset Blvd.	Start in present, to past for most of movie, return to present to end.
5 Parallel Stories - Same Time	Sliding Doors, Run Lola Run, Adaptation, Stranger than Fiction	Two stories unfolding at the same time, both in the same "world" and time.
6 Parallel Stories - Different times	The Social Network, Midnight in Paris, The Lorax	Two stories occurring simultaneously, but in different time periods.
	Eternal Sunshine of the Spotless Mind	
7 Ensemble Stories - Unified by Theme	Crash, Traffic, Love Actually, War Horse, The Big Chill	Multiple points of view on a large issue.
8 Ensemble - Unified by Team	Ocean's Eleven, The Italian Job, Inglorious Basterds, X-Men,	Multiple points of view held together by a Mission.
	Saving Private Ryan	
9 Ensemble - Unified by Family	Parenthood, Little Miss Sunshine	Multiple points of view held together by "family" bonds.
10 Ensemble - Unified by Special Circumstances	Cloverfield, Dead Poets Society, Zombieland, The Breakfast Club	Multiple points of view held together by "special circumstance."
11 The Roadtrip	Rain Man, Planes, Trains and Automobiles, Due Date, About Schmidt	The Journey is the story.
12 Midpoint-Flashback-Catchup	Reservoir Dogs, Slumdog Millionaire, Mission Impossible	Start in middle at crisis point, catch us up through past events, finish story.
13 Reverse Chronology	Memento, Irreversible	Time runs in reverse.
14 Zig-Zag/Hopscotch	500 Days of Summer, Duplicity	Move backwards and forwards in time, nearly "random."
15 Tryptic	The Hours, Amores Perros, 21 Grams	Telling three interwoven stories.
16 Parallel Universe	Harry Potter Series, The Narnia Films, Inception	Dual story engines in parallel realms.
17 Deja-Vu	Groundhog Day, Source Code	Keep returning characters to same time or moment, until they "fix something."
19 Voiceover - Reliable Narrator	Shawshank Redemption, Jerry Maguire	Narrator is straightforward, honest and reliable.
20 Voiceover - Unreliable Narrator	Fightclub, The Usual Suspects, Notes on a Scandal	Narrator toys with our expectations, misleads us, etc.
	The Opposite of Sex	
21 Exceptions	Tree of Life, Pulp Fiction	

FIGURE 8.2

9

WHAT'S THE SPARK?

Hook Your Audience with an "Inciting Incident"

Most agents, producers, and studio executives will only read the first ten pages of your script before deciding to "pass"—so getting the plot jumpstarted as soon as possible is strongly advised. Page 10 is the common benchmark. In *The Shawshank Redemption*, page 10 is when Andy arrives at Shawshank Penitentiary. This event is known as the **inciting incident**.

Can this incident happen a bit later than that? Absolutely. In *127 Hours*, the boulder doesn't trap Aron Ralston's (James Franco) arm until page 24. Can it happen way sooner? Sure. It can be argued that the inciting incident in *The Descendants* happens on page 1 when Matt's (George Clooney) wife, Elizabeth, gets in her near-fatal boating accident—and it works beautifully. But most screenplays require about ten pages to set up and steep us in the **"ordinary world"** of your protagonist(s). Joseph Campbell tagged it the ordinary world because it sets up some form of regular routine or a more-or-less "typical" day in your main character's life—so that you can disrupt that routine with the so-called inciting incident.

I wouldn't get too hung up on hitting the *exact* page 10 target and I urge you not to become slavishly devoted to any one rigid paradigm. If there was an absolute formula, every screenplay would be brilliant—and we all know that's not the case. If it works, it works. If the script *isn't* working (according to you and a consensus of your trusted advisers), then page number benchmarks can be a highly useful diagnostic exercise. The bottom line to ask yourself at the bottom of page 10 is this: Will my reader be compelled to turn the pages and continue reading?

In some movies, the inciting incident is something that just happens either directly or indirectly to the protagonist, and then he/she is forced to react.

For example, Erin Brockovich (Julia Roberts) gets blindsided in an intersection and seeks legal assistance for her whiplash. This initial misfortune leads to her eventual fortune.

In *A History of Violence*, the *indirect* inciting incident focuses on two ruthless henchmen, Billy (Greg Bryk) and Leland (Stephen McHattie), who go on a killing spree and then go on the lam. Later, Billy and Leland enter a sleepy, idyllic small town. Billy sneers, says he's tired of Podunk towns. And they need money. This puts these lowlifes on a collision course with our hero, Tom Stall (Viggo Mortensen), a retired hit man who's now a peaceful, law-abiding citizen, with a wife and son. But he's been living under an assumed name, and he's going to be compelled to "out" his dangerous side at the end of act one (around page 24).

In *American Beauty*, the inciting incident occurs around page 10: The new neighbors move in next door to the Burnhams, and the creepy neighbor kid, Ricky Fitts (Wes Bentley), videotapes Lester. But it's not until page 16 that Lester first sees Angela Hayes (Mena Suvari) dancing in the gymnasium—and it rocks his world and cracks it wide open.

The inciting incident in *The Kids Are All Right* occurs when the cryo bank calls Paul (Mark Ruffalo) to confirm he was the sperm donor, and Paul tells them it's okay for them to release his contact info to the recipient requesting it. By page 13, Paul's biological daughter and son, Joni and Laser, agree to meet Paul. Note that the kids' moms (Annette Bening and Julianne Moore) don't discover any of this until page 25.

The inciting incident will (usually) lead to a full-blown crisis point at the end of act one (around page 25).

In *The Pursuit of Happyness*, the "inciting incident" occurs when Chris Gardner (Will Smith) sees a successful businessman getting out of a Ferrari—and Chris asks the guy what he does. He's a stockbroker. This seemingly innocuous encounter plants the seeds of hope for financially-strapped Chris to later pursue an unpaid internship at Dean Witter for a chance to become a stockbroker. During the training, Chris will struggle as a newly single dad, who must find the strength to remain optimistic for his young son and must show up in a suit and tie every day for his unpaid job—all despite the fact that they are homeless. His risk pays off as he is awarded the job as a paid stockbroker.

In *The Social Network*, the inciting incident (on page 10) occurs when a cast off, inebriated Mark Zuckerberg (Jesse Eisenberg) starts a website allowing users to compare and rank college girls. It's not until page 24 that twin brothers Cameron and Tyler Winklevoss (both played by Armie Hammer) introduce themselves to Mark and say they have an idea they would like to talk to him about. Between pages 10 and 24, we flash forward to a Deposition Room, foretelling the inevitability of a colossal legal battle. The Mark in the deposition is much more guarded and combative than the insecure but brilliant college student we've been observing. The deposition scenes provide counterpoint, irony, and subtext to every scene in the past.

In *Gone Baby Gone*, the inciting incident occurs when private investigators, Angie and Patrick (Michelle Monaghan and Casey Affleck), reluctantly agree to take on the case of the missing little girl. In *The Town*, the inciting incident is when bank robber Doug (Ben Affleck) goes to keep an eye on Claire (Rebecca Hall) at the Laundromat.

In *Little Miss Sunshine*, the first 16 pages establish the ordinary world of the struggling Hoover family in Albuquerque, as Sheryl (Toni Collette) brings them all together for a bucket of chicken. The inciting incident comes on page 17 in the form of an answering machine message from Sheryl's sister with the news that a girl had to forfeit and runner-up Olive (Abigail Breslin) now has a place in the Little Miss Sunshine contest in Redondo Beach, California. Every family member reacts differently: from ecstatic to "Hell, no." The end of act one crisis point arrives on page 27 when Richard (Greg Kinnear) realizes that Olive's quest might be this family of losers' only chance for success. Richard also sees this as a chance to road test his "winner" strategies, so when Olive convinces her dad that she can and will win the pageant, Richard proclaims: "We're going to California!" It's a crisis because nobody gets along, they're totally broke, and their VW bus is supremely unreliable. It's an impossible but necessary journey. The answering machine message *incites* them with the *opportunity* to break out of their mundane routines. The end of act one is when they actually hit the road paved with comedic misfortunes.

I often cite the wonderful quote from the late author, Stanley Elkin, that goes: "I would never want to write about a man who is not at the end of his rope." So don't just use the first ten pages to "lay pipe" and write heavy-handed exposition. Start with a character already *desperate* in some way. If our goal, as screenwriters, is to find the dramatic heat in a story, then inject as much credible conflict as possible—in any genre—from page 1.

In some movies, the inciting incident is brought on by an *active choice* (or risk) made by the character to take a *step out of his/her ordinary world* and make a change in his/her life. Get us invested in his/her plight. Make us worry about your protagonist at every turn because without our emotional investment, there is no suspense. Stories without a dynamic through-line will most likely just flatline.

INTERVIEW: Screenwriter/Director Ed Solomon

Ed Solomon Filmography

Best known for:

Now You See Me (2013)
Imagine That (2009)
The In-Laws (2003)
Levity (also directed) (2003)
Charlie's Angels (2000)
Men in Black (1997)
Leaving Normal (1992)
Bill & Ted's Bogus Journey (1991)
Bill & Ted's Excellent Adventure (1989)

NL: I wanted to talk to you about so-called inciting incidents, which a lot of screenwriting gurus say are supposed to happen by page 10. How important is this to you when you're starting a script?

ES: I know we have to have a visceral sense of who our characters are and then something really needs to happen to make this story worth seeing. I can say honestly in my entire life, I've never once thought in terms of an inciting incident nor have I ever used the phrase with the exception of using it in the question, "Wait, what is an inciting incident?" I've never really considered it. I want people to be interested in the story. I don't want to wait too long until they are interested in the story, but my experience is that if the story is well-written, then people are pretty interested. They give it a break while it's getting started, but they know intuitively if they're in good hands really quickly. It's that feeling that allows you to sit back and take the leaps of faith needed to get into the movie. Until the filmmaker or screenwriter breaks that contract with you, you give them the benefit of the doubt.

Almost every time what I think needs twenty-five pages, needs seven pages. There's this winnowing down and winnowing down and what you realize is that people grasp a lot more, a lot faster than you think. Not because modern audiences are used to more, but because the human brain is capable of more.

> *B*ecause the human brain is able to project into your story all kinds of meaning, you realize that you need far, far, far less setup than you originally thought you did.

I took a writing class from a woman named Cathy Colman, a fiction writing class, and we used to do these exercises at the beginning of class. I think you'd write a sentence and then you'd fold it and hand the paper to the person next to you, and then they'd write a sentence. What was fascinating about the class was that what you think is utter nonsense, just by the fact that one thing happens right after the next ended up, creating meaning because your brain makes all these leaps like, "This person must be this way." You just make all these assumptions and you bring all of your experience into the meaning of it or if you're watching something, into the viewing of it. What I realized in this exercise is that meaning is half. So where you think you need a scene to setup something about a person, what you really need is just a line or a look. What I feel should be happening on page 20 usually ends up needing to happen much earlier, so that gradually my script starts to look like it has an inciting incident around page 10. But, it's not because I'm saying, "I need an inciting incident," it's because after a few minutes, I'm starting to feel like something needs to start happening.

NL: A lot of it is intuitive for you and so two things: One, I was talking to Scott Burns who wrote *Contagion*, and he said that [Steven] Soderbergh talked so much about the importance of transitions and how telling the story in the cut is what creates the narrative drive of the story. It sounds a lot like that exercise you did with Colman. Each time the paper was folded and everyone wrote something else, it was like a new "Cut to:" If you're in this new place then the audience says, "Alright, then I have to fill in what might have happened to get us to this point and if the leap is too great then we lose them." If it's logical or even a little mysterious at first, we'll kind of go with it for a while because we're on the ride.

ES: I absolutely believe that. Somehow we think when we're writing that everything needs to be contained within the scene and what you realize is that it's actually the sequence or the sequence of sequences. That meaning is created as you move through it. It's this, combined with that, combined with the next thing that imparts a deeper sense of meaning, creates what really is going on in your piece. You get lost within your scenes thinking, "Well, now, he needs to say this, and then she needs to respond with this because the audience is really going to be listening to what my characters are saying here." The truth is that what the characters are saying is such a minor piece of the whole thing that they're picking up. What happens is so much more important and somehow superior for me. I tend to wallow within the mood or within the tone or within the sound of the voices—the little minutiae. I would agree with what I'm understanding Scott [Burns] to have said.

NL: Especially in something like, *Contagion* or even *Traffic*, where you're cutting back and forth between lots of characters and lots of locations, the audience is able to pick up where they left off even if when you jump to the next sequence it's days or weeks or months later. The audience can fill a lot in as long as they're invested in the characters. It's less about overexplaining exactly how they got to this spot, it's more about what their goal is, what they're trying to accomplish, and why. Do you consciously think about stakes? For example, in *Men in Black* when Edwards [Will Smith] decides he's going to become one of the Men in Black. He's basically saying goodbye to his life. It's a one-way ticket. One of the screenwriter's dilemmas is, of course, motivating that. In *Men in Black*, he seemed to be motivated by a couple of things: one, he saw this supernatural thing happen with the guy on the roof of the parking structure, and the other is that the guy says the world is going to end. I guess he feels that it's up to him to help stop that from happening. Is that what your thinking was? How much should you think about both the goal and the stakes should they not accomplish the goal?

ES: People always believe that the fate of the world is going to raise the stakes for the characters in the movie and for the audience, but it never does. It's a completely cerebral thing. Therefore, my character's going to try harder? It doesn't work that way. First of all, people really only care about more personal things in movies like that. But, specifically in terms of *Men in Black*, a lot was made early on in my first ideas for the movie about what the James [Edwards—Will Smith] character had to give up and I really spent a lot of time with that in his past life. Initially, it was a small town that he gave up and then no one knew him anymore when he had to return to this town— that was part of the original story. Then, we changed it and moved it to New York. Then, there were these conversations about why he would give up everything. What it ended up being was that he gave it up because it's cool and because nobody ever asked, "What was he before that?" "What did he give up?" Nobody ever asked. It literally never came up. You're right, he gave up everything. But, nobody cared. So, to me, those two things that you mentioned, they were simply about creating the emotional pull to go, "Wait, we want to see what's on the other side." Because we didn't know anything about his past dramatically, we didn't meet anyone from his past, and the only people you did meet were asshole policemen that you didn't care about anyway. For the relative scope of what we knew about him which was that he was a New York cop, you didn't care about him leaving, you just wanted to see where he was taking you next which was into this world. The realm where the real and the mundane are juxtaposed.

NL: It's a function of tone because you establish a really playful tone that's comedic and science fiction at the same time. To me, that's a big part of the movie's success. The humor works so beautifully because we're having so much fun. It's not a totally gritty realistic story, so you go along with it. It almost feels like it's a graphic novel or even a much more nuanced comic book kind of story—like a fable.

ES: The tone was a big thing that was discussed a lot. I always felt on *Men in Black* that I had an innate sense of what the tone should be. It's fun and playful and generous, meaning the attitude of the film is, "Hey, everybody come check this out. Let's all go in and play in this place together." So, that was the first place—that one needed to create a playful mood. Then, you were willing to take some leaps of faith. The discussion over how much of this is comedy and how much is science fiction was one early on that did not always go well. I remember Tommy Lee Jones being livid with me saying, "You've got to decide whether this is science fiction or comedy. It's got to be one or the other." And, I remember saying, "It's not good enough science fiction to be a drama." You need some kind of leap of faith that comedy provides. You need to feel like this is a comedy, so you're willing to buy into the ridiculousness that we're positing here. To me, the whole thing is a comedic premise, but it's a playful comedic premise that behind this sign could be lurking someone from another dimension and these totally straight-laced guys have access to it. Point of view—that became a big question early on. Is it J's point of view, the Will Smith character, or is it Tommy Lee Jones' point of view? Before the movie was cast with both actors, Tommy Lee Jones had just gotten an Oscar for *The Fugitive*, and he was the first person cast to play Agent K, so I was instructed to rewrite the movie from K's point of view. My strong suspicion was that doing that would actually deflate the comedy, which I felt was needed. The movie had to be from that point of view to bring the audience into the premise.

NL: Right, then you can have those great set pieces where he's causing problems in the lab because he doesn't know better.

ES: I was thinking he, like the audience, believes that this world is the only world we know, and then suddenly something happens that says, "No, the world is a little bit different than you think it is." As he starts to get his equilibrium, he sees how his entire world is different—things within that world start changing. He has to start to deal with it and get his sea legs as he goes. But, the Tommy Lee Jones character doesn't change in that movie. Will Smith's character does the full arc. Tommy Lee Jones has a little arc.

NL: Tommy Lee Jones has that ability that he can break the rule that's set up earlier where he's able to communicate with his wife and he ends up retiring and going back.

ES: Yes, that's right.

NL: Do you outline or use any kind of planning document before you start writing?

ES: Most of the time, I outline. I find that with every script a different amount and style of outlining is required. Sometimes at every stage within a script, a different process is required. Part of my job now is to understand what is appropriate for which stage in that script. Sometimes I outline in incredible detail. Sometimes I outline in broad strokes. Sometimes I'll have a vague outline and then I'll throw the outline out ahead of me, like a tracker lining up as I'm going. I have found that in general it's usually better to know more than less. I usually find that there's so much discovery to be had anyway. I would be more than happy to send you examples of outlines or my boards. Every wall in my office is covered with metallic dry erase boards so that I can both attach things with a magnet and I can write. [My new] race car movie I outlined in incredible detail on the same boards, and then never looked at the outline again from the board. It was on my wall for a year like patterned wallpaper that I paid no attention to. Then, I did a series of typed outlines. I'll do beat sheets quite often because I find the process of writing through my fingers helps me think and add new things. What I feel with my own writing is that every different type of expression seems to emanate from different parts of the brain and every expression seems to inform what I'm working on in a different way. So that sometimes sitting someone across from me and talking about what I'm trying to write can be really helpful, and then sometimes typing up and writing—and I've often found that writing to somebody makes it easier for me to outline than just writing an outline with Page 1, Scene 1, etc. But, sometimes if I write to the producer or director or my friend: "Dear Neil—what I'm trying to accomplish is a way to set up an interesting opening that lets me know that . . ." And, as I'm doing that images will come to me—some way to describe the part of so-and-so as he . . . and then I start writing and stuff actually formulates. Sometimes I find that it's best to write up on a board and look at it as an overview. I find that all these different things when utilized in the right proportions really help me. So, going to one spot seems to help in one particular phase. Whereas, I might need to be in a different place because I need different visual clues. I don't know what it is, but to keep looking at it freshly, I can't be doing it all from the same spot. If I'm only sitting behind the same desk, looking at the same wall, it's almost like I memorize a rut and I'm not aware anymore of what I've got there.

NL: Whenever you look at something with a different perspective, it opens you up to a whole other discovery process which I do think is really useful. How important is it to have a central question or central mystery? The metaphor that I often use in classes is that as the screenwriter you're holding all the power because only you know what cards you have. Do you think about holding back something that you don't reveal until the third act?

ES: It depends on the story you're telling and how you want to do it. Every story's different, but absolutely part of the craft or art or whatever it is that we do is trying to figure out the most meaningful way, the most interesting way to tell your story and a lot of that is what you withhold and what you offer forward. Right around halfway through the script, the characters are getting to a place where I'm personally uncomfortable. Sometimes I find my own psychological barriers going up against really pushing the characters to a place where I might not be entirely comfortable going. So, sometimes that's the problem and then sometimes I'm a little too expulsive and I want everything to be said early. And, I realize, "No, no, no—just hold that back and reveal that later." It's a dance that you're constantly doing.

NL: I guess another way to say that is creating in the audience the need to know more because that's where you want them. You want them to be filled with anticipation and you want them to want to know more. It's what makes a page-turner.

ES: Those things can happen in a linear fashion and they can also happen when several things are happening at the same time. There are all sorts of ways that you can create the need to find out what's happening next. One is you have a character fascinated to see where this is headed. Another is one character happens to know something that the other character doesn't know. So, you're trying to figure out what's in store. Are they going to find this out?

NL: So, creating some kind of urgency for the information. In *Men in Black*, he's faced with what could be the most important decision of his life, whether he should join or not. We're interested because we all think, "What if this happened to me?" How much of yourself do you put in a story that way? Do you think, "What would I do?" Or, do you think about the audience putting themselves in that situation? Or, are you less concerned with the audience than with the story?

ES: I try to look at the story, the audience, and me as all being part of one shared event. Having said that, it's very, very hard for me to write a character that I don't understand or can't see myself in. With my story about three teenagers in the minor leagues of auto racing, the main character's a girl. I'm not a 17-year-old girl from Indianapolis, so I was really struggling with writing her, until I suddenly understood myself in her—and that doesn't mean that the character is at all like me because on paper, she's so different from me: her rhythm, her cadence, everything about her. However, once I was able to hook into a part of her which was also hooked into a part of me, I was able to understand her on a deep level. Now I know everything she'll do at every turn. I'm open to her surprising me too, in a way that is true to her character and doesn't feel contrived. A character starts to then come to life. It's almost like by understanding the character on some visceral level, the character was suddenly free of me.

NL: How much of you is in the characters in *Men in Black*? Did you try to imagine if someone would come up to you and ask if you'd be willing to leave your life behind?

ES: I didn't really think about that for *Men in Black*. It was more as if I was sitting in my own life, and I wanted to sort of project forward a really cool version of my own life. What would I do? What would be fun? This makes me laugh, this makes me smile, I think this would be really, really cool. Initially, Will Smith's character was in the Secret Service. If you're in the Secret Service, you're at the apotheosis of your career because you're going to guard the most important human being in the world and that's the president of the United States. And, then you find out that that is nothing compared to what's really going on. And, what would happen if that shit was happening, but you didn't have access to it, but someone did and that person invited you in? That's what got me hooked. That's not me, there's no version of Will Smith that's even remotely like me. Now, maybe to a degree, the initial character was a bit like me, but not really. And, the character of K, the Tommy Lee Jones character—those guys are very different from me—they're very different from each other.

NL: How did you craft them? Where did they come from? Are they based on anyone you know? Research?

ES: They were just made up. It's funny because *Men in Black*, I guess it's the most successful thing I've done, but it was also probably the least personal in a way. But, I worked on it for years and years. So, it's not like I just dashed it off. It was hard. There were a lot of really good people working on it too. Other talented collaborators, director, producers, all sorts of key craft people. There was a tremendous amount of really talented people working at the top of their game, so I was really lucky to have that kind of help.

NL: Last question: Is your new race car project based on something? Is there source material? Is it an original?

ES: Dreamworks optioned a beautiful, wonderful documentary about 12-year-olds in the go-karting world called *Racing Dreams* by [writer/director] Marshall Curry. But, the movie isn't that story because there are different characters. How do I tell the story of three people in the course of a season? What is the thing that binds them together? What is the thing that is interesting? And, then I realized, they all want to win. So, I did a little more research and I discovered that there can be a prize offered to the points champion at the end of the season, in that way, you can theoretically construct a movie where it all comes down to the final race and the winner of that race gets to become a professional. Finding the point of view and the angle took a while for me, but then once you've got it, it all makes sense. Up until that moment, it just feels confusing and disorienting and you're wondering if you even know how to write it. I knew it was from the point of view of this girl, but it was also three characters. Do I cut away to each? Do I give them their own setups? Do I need to give all three their own setups? What ended up working was to give the first boy his own introduction and then give the second boy his introduction through her point of view.

NL: It's actually very comforting to all screenwriters, but particularly to newer ones because I think everybody thinks it's just them struggling and grappling and trying to find the story. It's just something that everybody goes through. One of the things that experience gives you is that maybe you don't panic quite as much because you've been through it before.

ES: Or, you just recognize the panic as panic that you experience all the time. Although, I think at every stage the fear is there and it feels very real. And the fear is: "Oh my God, will I make it as a writer? "Will I ever sustain my career as a writer or can I still make it as a writer? Or, have I lost it as a writer?" The fear feels real at every stage. I think managing it is a big deal. I think the main difference between me as a writer now and me as a writer 20 years ago is I know a little bit better when to stop and when to keep going. But, the difference is I know now how to read my own pages and know approximately how long it will take me to revise those. I know just how many drafts it will actually take me till I actually think it's good. I know also when to stop applying paint to the canvas. And, I know that feeling I feel when I finish something, which is kind of elation, is not to be trusted. It's not to be trusted as an actual indicator of how good it is. I know it's easier to trust it when I've had some time off and re-read it, or I've given it to four or five people and have gotten some feedback.

NL: I'll leave you with this. There was a great interview with Andrew Stanton of Pixar in the October 17, 2011 issue of *The New Yorker*, where he said: "Be wrong fast or fail early. It's like every movie is a kid, and no kid avoids puberty. Just dive through it—get that outline that should take three months done in one, so you get the inevitable bad stuff out of the way and have more time to plus the good stuff." Everybody sees the finished Pixar product, which looks so brilliant and perfect, but they go through so much trial and error. They throw so much stuff out and they don't release movies until they're just right. It's always comforting to hear people say that they go through this trial and error period, which is what you're saying too.

ASSIGNMENT

Examine the backstory of your protagonist and make a hierarchal list of his/her top ten priorities on page 1. What are the routines in his/her life? If he buys a cup of coffee every morning from the same Starbucks and always boards the same train, the "inciting incident" might be the day his wallet gets stolen, setting into motion a chain reaction of events that spirals down into a full-blown crisis at the end of act one. Chart the expected course of your protagonist's intended or expected journey, and then throw in some interference—with an unexpected opportunity. This opportunity will often initially feel like something positive, but devolve into a situation beyond his/her control. See if you can articulate this situation as a three-pronged "trap."

10

WHAT'S THE TRAP?

Plunge Your Protagonist into Crisis at the End of Act One

This crisis point will effectively ensnare your protagonist in a literal or figurative "trap" that compels him/her into action—and often quite reluctantly. Think of this active goal as "Plan A"—which needs to be an urgent, challenging quest. And, the more difficult it is to accomplish this challenge, the better. Ideally, Plan A will sustain the entire second act of the movie.

Ideally, Plan A motivates your protagonist's need to regain control of his/her destiny and will be based upon necessity versus desire.

When you're in crisis, you **must** do something—or else. Stakes are your protagonist's consequences for inaction. If Plan A is accomplished, he/she will gain or win. If Plan A fails, then he/she has something of value to lose. This +/– polarity is the source of dramatic heat.

In *Knocked Up*, 23-year-old slacker, pothead, Ben Stone (Seth Rogen) gets lucky one night out at a club and hooks up with beautiful, type-A career woman, Alison Scott (Katherine Heigl). They chat, laugh, dance, and have sex by page 22. The morning after, even in their foggy hung-over haze, they immediately realize that they have nothing in common. She's out of his league and finds him disgusting. No problem—she'll just be on her way. No harm, no foul. He's disappointed; she's relieved . . . until page 28 when we cut to "Eight Weeks Later," and she's horrified to discover that she's pregnant with Ben's baby. This is Alison's crisis point, but Ben remains happily oblivious . . . until page 37 when he gets a call from her. They go for dinner, and he's stoked to see her again . . . until she drops the bomb that she's pregnant and he's the father. Ben is stunned and blames her for not being responsible. They argue. She agonizes over whether or not to keep the baby; what's best for her career, her lifestyle, and the baby. When she reveals to Ben that she's decided to keep the baby, he's thrilled and delighted. This unplanned pregnancy with this gorgeous, successful stranger could be the best thing that ever happened to him. What's significant to point out here is that Ben's crisis point continues to evolve in stages—very much in accordance to Elisabeth Kübler-Ross' Five Stages of Grief: denial, anger, bargaining, depression, and acceptance. The final stage is Ben's true crisis point because once he intellectually accepts that he's going to become a father, he needs to come to terms with his immaturity. In order not to lose Alison, Ben *must* grow up—and he's only got seven months to do it.

In *Up in the Air*, Ryan Bingham's (George Clooney) crisis point comes when he's introduced to young, brash Natalie (Anna Kendrick) and the buzzword "Glocal." Natalie is an efficiency expert brought in by Ryan's boss to streamline operations and keep the crew of corporate terminators grounded—so they can fire people remotely via the internet instead of flying all over the country. Given that Ryan's whole purpose in life is his nomadic, unencumbered lifestyle—and his desire to accumulate frequent flyer mileage and hotel loyalty points—Natalie is his worst nightmare. Feeling trapped in company policy, Ryan spends the bulk of the second act determined to protect his territory. He *must* sabotage Natalie's new protocol in order to return to his comfort zone—up in the air. During the process of road testing the new program, Ryan succeeds at dismantling Natalie and sends her packing, but he also comes unmoored when he meets the beautiful traveling executive, Alex (Vera Farmiga) who is his perfect match in virtually every way. Smart, sexy, funny, charming, impulsive—and married. In the end, Ryan gets his corporate life back on track, but the void in his personal life has come to life, and where he goes next is a destination unknown.

The setup in act one is often a literal or metaphorical "trap."

The trap is often a three-pronged process that breaks down like this:

Page 10: a trap is set by the antagonist or via a (seemingly positive) opportunity.
Page 17: the hero steps into the trap.
Page 25: the trap is sprung—via circumstances beyond the hero's control.

In *Thelma and Louise*, first the two friends (Geena Davis and Susan Sarandon) depart on the fishing trip (trap is set); second, they stop at the roadside tavern for some drinks and fun (they step into the trap); third, a strange man flirts with Thelma, tries to rape her in the parking lot, and Louise ends up shooting and killing the rapist (trap is sprung). Now they must escape arrest due to Louise's complicated backstory.

In *The Dark Knight*, the inciting incident occurs when Batman visits Commissioner Gordon (Gary Oldman) in the bank vault and discovers that the notorious Joker (Heath Ledger) is back in action stealing mob money (trap is set by Joker). This compels Batman to prioritize his super-heroism and move in on all the mob banks at once. Gordon asks what about the Joker? Batman says, "One man or the entire mob? He [Joker] can wait." And wait he will. But we know the Joker is baiting Batman into a trap that's going to test the limits of Batman's invincibility. The mob can be leveraged because they're greedy and power hungry; but Joker doesn't care about money at all, and his only goal is to obliterate Gotham—which Joker deems as beyond salvation. Batman's crisis point is Joker's wrath. All Joker is concerned with is to annihilate Batman. But Batman is compelled not only to vanquish Joker, but also to protect the good citizens of Gotham. Joker exploits Batman's "handicap": his heroism. And the trap is sprung.

Failure is not an option.

A strong crisis point forces protagonists to be proactive. They *must* formulate a plan. There is no going backward; either they've burned their own bridges back to normalcy or the bridges back have been erased by others.

In *The Hunger Games*, it's clear that Katniss (Jennifer Lawrence) has no alternative to winning the game. She's put her life on the line to protect her little sister, and winning the game will also help save her family and her entire district. Her crisis point is the start of the games.

In *Rise of the Planet of the Apes*, the crisis point comes when protagonist Caesar is wrested away from his human "dad" Will (James Franco) and sent to live in an animal shelter. Now the formerly coddled Caesar must fend for himself—first, against the other apes in the shelter, and later against the sadistic human handler in charge of the shelter.

In the documentary-style, sci-fi thriller *District 9*, Wikus van de Merwe (Sharlto Copley), is the operations manager for the munitions corporation Multi-National United. The genial Wikus is tasked with evicting a burgeoning alien population (known as "Prawns") from their refugee camp outside Johannesburg. The camp has become a slum, and the local human community wants them relocated to a new internment camp. But the aliens are resistant to leaving their homes and protest this blatant discrimination against them as third class citizens. The movie is an allegory to the apartheid era in South Africa. Wikus performs his eviction duties as dispassionately as possible, trying to think of the aliens as less than human. At the same time, we follow our dual protagonist, alien Christopher Johnson's (Jason Cope) POV, by meeting his alien son and alien best friend, and experiencing their humanity and emotional need. Their dilemma is to either remain in District 9 or to utilize a covert alien technology—a chemical fluid they keep hidden in a canister—

to return to their planet. Subsequently, Wikus raids the shack of Christopher's friend and seizes the canister. But in the scuffle, Wikus gets sprayed in the face with the mysterious fluid. Alien Christopher's crisis point comes when his friend is killed, and the canister containing his only hope for salvation is taken away.

Wikus' crisis point arrives soon thereafter when, having been infected by the fluid, he becomes gravely ill . . . and begins to metamorphose into an alien Prawn. Wikus is not only facing the loss of his human identity, but he's also being transformed into what his government has deemed a disposable species. Wikus has become a prime specimen for experimentation, so now the predator has become the prey. Wikus must escape and fight for his life. His only ally is the alien, Christopher, and they unite in a common cause against the oppressive government. The stakes could not be higher for both men. Wikus is desperate to find an antidote and return to his wife and family. Christopher is equally desperate to locate the missing mother ship and return to his home planet with his son.

The crisis point at the end of act one will usually feel like a loss of destiny for your protagonist, and act two is all about his/her struggle to regain control—or some sense of normalcy.

In *Juno*, the inciting incident is when 16-year-old Juno MacGuff (Ellen Page) discovers that she's pregnant, but she's still in high school and totally unprepared for parenthood. Detached from the true gravitas of the situation, Juno calls the women's clinic (on her hamburger-shaped phone) and inquires about her need to "procure a hasty abortion." Simple, easy, no problem. Except as Juno sits in the waiting room of the abortion clinic, she freaks out and can't go through with it. She bolts, and must find another alternative—and fast. This is her crisis point: she doesn't want to be a parent, but she doesn't want to have an abortion either. So, the whole second act of the movie is about her efforts to find the right foster parents to adopt the baby once she carries it to term.

Your protagonist's secrets (and lies) fuel the crisis.

In *A History of Violence*, congenial family man Tom Stall (Viggo Mortensen) is living a quiet life in the small town of Millbrook, Indiana. Tom's crisis point comes at page 25 when two murderous thugs enter his diner looking for trouble. Tom instinctively fights back—but with the agility and prowess of an assassin. It's a surprising, graphic scene that changes our perspective of Tom in a flash. The victimized diners are shocked and awed by Tom's burst of killer heroism. And, we immediately suspect that Tom has a secret past—the film's central mystery.

Tom's Plan A is to keep his secret hidden and preserve his family and idyllic lifestyle. But he's now a reluctant media hero, and back on the radar of his former enemies. Tom's biggest fear was having his past come out, and now he has no choice but to deal with it. Mild-mannered husband and father will gradually reconnect to his past identity as a mob hit man. The side effects of unleashing his repressed dark side will transform every aspect of his family life: from increased sexual aggression adding danger and spark to his marriage, to motivating his bullied son to stand up for himself and fight back.

In *The Graduate*, Benjamin Braddock's (Dustin Hoffman) initial crisis point at the end of act one is that he can't resist the seduction of the sultry, aggressive, middle-aged alcoholic Mrs. Robinson—and he needs her because she's the one thing in his life (at this point) that makes him feel alive. This launches his secret—which will also become his kryptonite. His proactive goal is to feed his libido and keep his affair with Mrs. Robinson a secret; if he alienates Mrs. Robinson, he loses his sex partner. If his secret gets out, he'd suffer the scorn and lose the financial and emotional support of his devoted parents. He's trapped in a perilous situation that's not about life and death, but is entirely fueled on Benjamin's need not to disappoint anyone. He's a pleaser with low self-esteem. If Benjamin had the wherewithal to speak up and tell everybody the truth, there would be no movie. It's a story about a lost boy who finds his manhood by owning up to his Truth.

Human nature is to take the path of least resistance. If there is an easier escape route available to your protagonist and he/she doesn't take it, the audience will groan: "Why doesn't he just do ———?" If it's that easy to get out of trouble or overcome the problem, then it's not a viable crisis.

INTERVIEW: Screenwriter Carl Ellsworth

Carl Ellsworth Filmography

Best known for:

Red Dawn (2012)
The Last House on the Left (2009)
Disturbia (2007)
Red Eye (2005)

NL: In reading a lot of scripts, especially from students, I find that one of the most common weaknesses is that the stakes aren't high enough and the goals of the protagonist are not clearly defined. What strikes me about your work is you plunge your protagonists into situations where they're literally trapped.

CE: Hearing you say that, another word just popped into my head, as I look over the movies I've done, and that is that they're all survival movies and that's a pretty clear goal. One of the biggest movies that has influenced me was the original *Die Hard*. It's such a classic and such a perfect script structurally because the end of act one is clear. Terrorists take over the building and John McClane [Bruce Willis] escapes, but he's got a big problem.

NL: And, he's the only one who can solve it.

CE: Yes, against incredible odds, and we're with him through the entire rest of the movie, mostly from his point of view. Plunging a character into crisis has, for me, been instantly relatable. I love these, what I call "situational thrillers," where you force your characters to react to the crisis that visits them—that they had really no say in. It's just a situation that they've got to get out of, and when I look back, it's those types of movies that really turn me on. I think that is because it is the most clear cut way of doing it—an instant motor for the rest of the script. I realize looking over *Red Eye*, *Disturbia*, *The Last House on the Left*, and now *Red Dawn*—that they're all essentially *Die Hard* movies. You have a central protagonist, usually an Everyman/Everywoman character in an extraordinary situation fighting for his or her survival and trying to figure a way out of it.

NL: There's a sense that McClane is an Everyman, and yet, he's obviously a trained policeman.

CE: He is that, but I would also say he's this blue collar every-guy. Even though he's a trained policeman, we're also given the Everyman problems that he has. He's going through a divorce, he's been estranged from his wife, and he's also got this biting sense of humor—he's a smart ass. And what that movie is so efficient at doing, if you look at just the first eight minutes: the plane arrives at the airport, his hand is gripping the armrest, so you know he's not comfortable with flying, and the guy sitting next to him notices and gives him advice on how to relax. Obviously, I've studied this movie, I have it in my head with every single shot because it's such an exercise in economy, and the most important thing, definitely one of the top three or four most important things in a script, is you have to care about this person. You have to be with them, you have to get who they are very economically—otherwise why am I sitting in the theater for two hours?

NL: I can definitely see the influences in *Red Eye* because of the relationship with her father and the phone calls, but then also how you use the loved ones as stakes later in the movie. The whole first ten pages of *Red Eye* is incredibly relatable for her vulnerability.

CE: It's all on purpose. And the more I look at movies lately, something that's struck me is that one of the things you learn about your protagonist in the first few minutes is that they're dealing with some kind of loss. Many times, it's a death. Lisa Reisert [Rachel McAdams] is dealing with the death of her grandmother. Again, it's a tool that works. Some writers might say it's the easiest. And, we learn later that she's been dealing with the divorce of her parents after many years of marriage.

NL: With time frame, the loss, in *Red Eye* is very immediate in that she's flying back for her grandmother's funeral. You also contain your time. It's basically the duration of the flight. In *Disturbia*, he's got his ankle monitoring bracelet on, so he's trapped and confined for a certain period of time. I often tell my students to compress the time frame as much as they can to tell the story. How conscious are you of time when you're structuring? Are you doing it hour by hour, minute by minute, day by day? How much do you think about that?

CE: Are we talking about ticking clocks in a way? In the course of writing *Red Eye*, I found that I love having the villain on his own ticking clock. It makes for more interesting villains if they are also under stress. I love those elements: it just makes the characters much more fascinating and much more potentially dangerous.

So, in *Red Eye*, we were on Jackson Rippner's [Cillian Murphy] time. It just so happened that the circumstances fell into place that he had to pull this job off by this particular time. I consciously worked backwards from that: so, this guy shows up at 5:30 a.m. at the hotel. Lisa is the manager and the key to his success, and she just happens to be here, in Texas, at the time he needs her. Obviously going into it, I knew I wanted it to take place all on a red eye flight, but I had to think about where she was taking off from. At one point, it was California. Well, that flight lasts three or four hours, but Texas to Florida is shorter. So there were adjustments made there, but the situation dictated the amount of time. In *Disturbia*, I would say that we eventually get to a ticking clock in the third act, but it's more nebulous up front, because he's trapped in his house certainly, but we play with time and have the montage. Days are passing. We wanted to convey that the poor kid is out of his mind because he can't get out of the house, and he starts off with the video games, but that kind of wears off, and then the girl moves in.

NL: The girl is everything.

CE: And the girl captures his interest. But for me I don't enter into something necessarily thinking about time immediately, I usually rely on the situation to sort of give me an idea of what kind of time we're looking at.

NL: Since *Red Eye* was a spec script, was the original threat of the guy at the hotel always there and were you just not going to show it?

CE: Yes, it was always there. It was always about Cillian Murphy's character needing Rachel McAdams' character to help him pull off the murder. In the original spec, I thought it didn't matter who he was. I never named who he was. It was a guy that she knew very well, and I even implied that she might have hooked up with the guy at some point because, in the original spec, I wanted no one else to be aware of the situation happening at the back of the plane. I was fascinated by the idea that there's a hostage situation going on an airplane and no one knows about it.

But ultimately what made us break the movie out was Dreamworks and Steven Spielberg, and they were very smart in saying that. In the original spec, I had her basically stab Jackson while the plane was still in flight, but I struggled with that for a while. I knew that she had to take matters into her own hands and fight for survival by doing something extreme. I remember thinking about the movie *Cast Away*, and why that movie works. It's because Tom Hanks has to save himself. That's the analogy I drew from that movie, so I remember thinking, "Yes, Rachel McAdams' character has to save herself." In the spec script, she stabs him while still on the plane, and so to follow, what would happen in the real world after such an event happened on a commercial airliner? Enter the FBI. Enter the questioning. The proverbial interrogation.

NL: But then it enlarges and gets out of her hands, so that she no longer controls her own destiny.

CE: Then, Spielberg said it had to be about Lisa saving her father. That was huge—it was this element that didn't exist before. We just had to wait until the plane got to the gate, and she had to stab him there. In order to stay with these two characters, that's the only way it could happen and still have her maintain control of the situation. Sometimes people say, "Why didn't she just throw him to the cops?" Well, she couldn't. Can you imagine the red tape she would have run into immediately? And she would not have been able to save the day. So, that's what got us into that third act romp through the house.

NL: And she's still trapped even when she gets off the plane. She's trapped the whole way. It's very organic the way he finds her there. It turns into a monster movie, but in a really smart, credible way.

CE: There were some discussions even as we were shooting the final sequence of the house, where we were asking ourselves, "Why does everything happen the way that it does?" And they were asking, "Why does Jackson even go back to the house? Why does he even go there to potentially expose himself?" And I think it was Wes Craven who looked at me very calmly and said, "Because he's pissed."

NL: You made this an extremely personal battle. It comes out of character—not just from the situation. It's from who he is.

CE: It's because of what Wes was able to get out of Cillian's performance. I realized after the experience of *Red Eye* that I love seeing villains in distress. You can see that the more the phones don't work on the plane and the more that Rachel fights back, the more pissed off he gets. He's losing it because it's more than likely that if he screws up, he's going to get killed because whoever he's working for—they're not going to be happy with him.

NL: Now, with *Disturbia*, you have a smart ass guy (Shia LeBeouf) who is so humorous and likeable even though he's privileged and rebellious. I remember that the actual murder, or what may or may not have been going on with the neighbor, comes in pretty late. It seems like a very long first act with a lot of humor around his obsession with the girl and how he keeps being thwarted by trying to push the boundaries.

CE: To this day, I remain very happy that we were actually able to do that. I think what bought us the time was that incredible opening sequence with the death of his father. It's the scene where they're fishing at the pond and we get who they are. Again we have this horrible accident, and the way D.J. [Caruso] directed it, I think that people's expectations of what they thought the movie was going to be instantly changed. It was a gritty, realistic, horrible accident. Again, that's a situation where the tone of the movie was quickly conveyed. We also do the one year later where Shia's in the classroom with the hoodie over his head, and the reason why we're sympathetic to him is that we totally understand why he's a smart ass and screwed up at this point. And then he smacks the teacher, and now he's got the ankle bracelet on, plus he's getting shit from his mother with, "Clean up your room"—again very relatable situations. But then where I was really happy, where D.J. and I always saw eye to eye, was in utilizing that great house. There's this slightly haunted feeling, as he walks through the house. Silences for me also work. Like when he opens the door to his dad's office, and he doesn't step over. Again, I wish that studios had a little more faith in audiences that they want to get involved in the scenario that you're setting up—to not be in such a rush.

You could say that scene represents that he's still not done dealing with the loss of his father and that he still feels responsible for it. And then, once he's able to go into the office, it's because he's spying on the girl from there. Those moments again go to character. We're caring more and more about this kid, so we're going to be rooting for him the rest of the way and we don't want to see his life get any more screwed up than it is.

All those characteristics informing the character, hopefully you'll be able to pull those off within the first 20 or 30 pages, so that by the time you get to the crisis that will come upon them—you're with them. You do not want this crisis to be thrust upon these people that you are now invested in. And that's the basic kind of set up in all the movies that I've had a chance to get made. I saw *Die Hard* when I was 15 or 16, and I have never seen a movie affect an audience like that one did. People were cheering, clapping, rooting, and jumping up from their seats. It was an audience participation movie in every way, and I've never forgotten it, and I've always tried to pull that off.

D*isturbia was one of those where people were going nuts, especially by the end of the movie. They're just going crazy, yelling and screaming, but why are they doing that? Because they care, they love this kid.*

NL: Can you talk about the crisis point in *Red Dawn*, and why only that character could save the world?

CE: Ultimately, this movie is about two brothers, and how the younger, immature brother finally steps up and becomes a man or a leader which gave us a reason to tell the story from this particular group of kids' perspective.

NL: They're compelled to act. In a lot of your work, and I talk about this too, it's usually more effective for the second act, if you actually remove choice and force the characters to take action.

CE: In *Red Dawn*, one might naturally think, "Well, the end of act one is the biggest crisis you could possibly throw at anyone which is the invasion: the North Korean paratroopers dropping down and you're trying to escape." But actually, that is not the end of the first act because that scene happens around page 10 or 12.

NL: It's like the inciting incident, like in *War of the Worlds*.

CE: Yes. Then, 15 pages later, our kids have escaped to the mountains, and then their father is murdered in front of them.

NL: Now they have to act.

CE: Not necessarily, but they choose to. As they go deeper into the mountains, the Chris Hemsworth character turns around, and says, "I'm going to fight."

NL: What would his alternative have been?

CE: To wait it out, but we've also trapped him. He plays the Patrick Swayze character [from the 1984 version], and we've made him a marine in this one. He's come home on leave, and he's trained. He's John McClane again. The end of act one is the choice he makes based upon the loss of a father. *Red Dawn* is a coming-of-age story. We've painted the younger brother character, played by Josh Peck, as a kid who is very much into doing his own thing. He has a lot to learn over the course of the movie, and ultimately he learns it in the hardest way. He grows up and leads the wolverines to continue the fight.

NL: What have you learned from the directors that you have worked with about your writing? How has it influenced you?

CE: One thing that was great about working with Wes Craven on *Red Eye* and D.J. Caruso on *Disturbia* was to see just how visual they are. Sometimes in your mind's eye when you're writing a screenplay, you're completely envisioning how you think the movie should look, but more often than not, they have called me out on my own lack of vision. Actually, there was a moment in the final sequence in *Red Eye* where Rachel is being chased through the house by Cillian Murphy, and I remember Rachel McAdams came up to me very concerned. She basically said, "Wes just had me head-butt Cillian Murphy on the stairs." And I said, "What? No, that's not your character." And I had this little panic about it, but it got the biggest cheer from the audience when she did that. There is Wes Craven knowing his audience and knowing what works visually in a movie like this. It was a brilliant choice.

NL: So, you had the advantage of being on set in the physical space of the house, which is so incredibly valuable for production rewrites.

CE: Absolutely. I don't understand why you hear about writers not being on the sets or being banished from the sets. Writers don't need to be there every step of the way, but you do need somebody because the situation is constantly fluid. I wrote many versions of the final chase through the house, but you never know for sure until you have a location. So finally, after many months they found the house, and it was a matter of walking through it with Wes and dreaming stuff up as we did. Like: "Okay, she can go through here, and this bathroom connects to this bedroom—oh, wouldn't this be cool?" So that's how it finally evolved, and not too long before it was filmed.

NL: That was the scene when I was hiding behind my pillow: when she's in that bedroom and there's a door that's opening, and you're not sure if he's going to be behind it. That house is like a house of mirrors where you're not sure what's hiding behind what. On the plane, I felt safer. I had a moment of calm every time we could see where he was in relation to her. As soon as he wasn't in his seat and she didn't know where he was, that's when I got scared.

CE: It was also very Wes Craven. Rachel McAdams' character is out of her element on the plane, but it's all about her standing her ground. But, once we get to the house, obviously she knows the geography. She finally has a tactical advantage, which is great.

NL: In terms of genre, *Red Eye* and *Disturbia* seem to be thrillers, and *The Last House on the Left* was much more of a horror movie. It turns into something much more graphic. I remember when the movie came out there was a lot of controversy about it, and I think at one point, it might have been veering into an X rating. Could you talk about some of your experiences writing that movie, or some of the differences as a writer working on a horror movie versus a thriller?

CE: It was difficult for me. It was my first attempt at a hardcore Rated R, ultra-violent story. It was a rewrite situation. The way that it came about was Wes Craven's producer, Marianne Maddalena, approached me. I was very reluctant because I watched the original and couldn't believe what I was seeing. It is so brutal, so graphic, so twisted, and on top of it, you have these three horribly evil, totally irredeemable people. Then you have these two girls who they cross paths with, and they're dropped into this crisis situation where they're taken into the woods, raped and murdered. But the great irony is that the killers end up seeking refuge in the house that happens to be occupied by one of the girls' parents, who then end up finding out about what's happened and exact revenge on the killers. I was fascinated by that moment, the irony of that. However, my biggest concern and problem was: why am I watching this? This is not satisfying for me personally as a movie-going experience. A lot of people looked at the original movie as a statement on

Vietnam or revenge. I didn't look at it like that. There was no enjoyment for me. I get what it is, and at the end of the movie, the parents have killed the bad guys, but look where the parents are. Personally, it should be pretty clear that I like to go to the movies to cheer on the characters and hopefully know that they are in a better space at the end. So *The Last House on the Left* was very tricky because where do those parents go from there? They're screwed. So I went back to Marianne and told her that's how I feel about this, and in order for me to even approach it, I have to have a rooting interest in it. And, what was my rooting interest? The only thing I could come up with was one of those girls had to survive.

They actually said that Wes had shot a version like that, but they opted not to do it for whatever reasons. And so they were totally on board with it, and that really opened it up for me. Now I could bring in classic thriller and suspense elements. I call it a horror-thriller or a suspense-thriller. Yes, there are horror elements, but we can have incredible suspense too. Yes, you can say that the parents do exact revenge, but now it's born out of circumstance. It's born out of having to save their daughter's life and to protect her from this ticking clock of the killers in the guest house. No one in the audience wants all of this for the family, they're like, "Oh my God, are you kidding me?" They're piling misery upon misery and it's just like, "No!" While working on *Disturbia*, I heard another Spielbergism: you have to make your stories continually unfair—the worse your protagonist is treated, the better. So the situation in *The Last House on the Left* is the most unfair thing that can happen for a family.

ASSIGNMENT

Make a list of three potential actions that your protagonist must accomplish—or else face the consequences. Make a list of all potentially dire consequences should this goal not be achieved. What's the worst case scenario? What is the best possible outcome should Plan A be achieved?

11

WHAT'S THE CURVEBALL?

Ratchet Up the Stakes at the Midpoint of Act Two

Act two is generally twice the length of acts one and three. As a result, it's not uncommon for the plot to sag at the midpoint. But an effective midpoint will provide a surprising plot twist—or *reversal of fortune*—that will increase dramatic tension and intensify our anticipation.

Must the midpoint of your screenplay occur precisely at the halfway point? Not necessarily. There are no absolute formulas or benchmarks. But many screenwriters like to structure their scripts into four parts: act one, act two (a), act two (b), and act three. In this configuration, the midpoint would occur at the end of act two (a). This affords the writer with a built-in midpoint event to avoid the potential monotony of sustaining one central event that lacks a central complication.

At the midpoint, the plot thickens.

In the first half of act two, your protagonist is in "crisis management" mode. He/she is in the midst of the crisis and forges a plan based on the known variables. For example, let's say your house is on fire. Definitely a crisis. What to do? Prioritize—and quickly. Call the fire department. Get your loved ones to safety. Turn off the gas. Grab an extinguisher or garden hose or buckets of water and start dousing the flames. You're facing the expected obstacles of the crisis.

The midpoint is when an *unexpected* obstacle arises—usually something your protagonist (and the audience) did not see coming. It throws us for a loop. The crisis has complicated things, so that now the second act goal is going to be much more difficult or downright impossible to accomplish. This is known as a "reversal of fortune" because whatever fortunate advances your protagonist has made, he/she has now reached a setback. To continue our fire analogy, despite your desperate best efforts to extinguish the blazing house, you didn't realize that there were explosives hidden under the floorboards—or that the fire was set by an arsonist in your own family. There could be any number of other possible extenuating and inconvenient circumstances that undermine an easy solution.

In *Drive*, after Driver (Ryan Gosling) discovers Irene's (Carey Mulligan) ex-con husband, Standard, has been attacked in the apartment building's underground garage, Standard confides that he owes $40K protection money to a prison gang. It's a midpoint/"curveball" moment because Standard's release from prison came earlier than anticipated, and has driven a wedge between Driver's blossoming romantic feelings for Irene. As a rogue, Driver had started to distance himself from Irene and her son, Benicio, but now Driver is being pulled back into her orbit. Out of necessity and concern for Irene, Driver agrees to help Standard repay the blood money—a fateful decision that will have tragic consequences for Standard, and tear Driver and Irene apart.

An effective midpoint usually hinges on a "pivotal character."

A pivotal character is neither protagonist nor antagonist—and yet is the vital missing link between them. If a midpoint plunges your protagonist into a major or minor "existential dilemma," then that becomes a pivotal moment in his/her character development. This essentially plants the seeds to a protagonist's eventual epiphany and/or evolution.

The pivotal character is the *agent of change* who provokes growth in the protagonist and pushes him/her to be his/her best self. The protagonist may see this person as an antagonist for early parts of the story, but he/she is not. The pivotal character invariably clashes with the protagonist by not allowing him/her to go back to living a life of quiet desperation. The pivotal character might be the intermediary between worlds—such as Oda Mae Brown (Whoopi Goldberg) as the psychic medium character in *Ghost*—or is often a mentor, confidant, or love interest. At the midpoint in *Ghost*, Sam Wheat (Patrick Swayze) urges Oda Mae to find his killer. She's reluctant to get further involved in his life after death. But she becomes the ultimate link in the final climactic kiss between Sam and his beloved, Molly (Demi Moore).

At the midpoint of *The Hunger Games*, Katniss (Jennifer Lawrence) discovers that pivotal character, Peeta (Josh Hutcherson), is conspiring against her—he's seemingly aligned with the splinter group lead by Cato (Alexander Ludwig). Understandably, Katniss feels betrayed by Peeta whom she'd believed was her ally. On the plot level, this is her reversal of fortune; she's running and fighting for her life. The stakes could not be higher. If she manages to survive, she'll be able to return to her family and district and provide them with a bounty of food. We know from the setup that Katniss is a loyal daughter and loving sister. We're emotionally invested, so this fuels the stakes. On the emotional/story level, there is a subsequent midpoint scene between Katniss and Peeta that digs deeper into their relationship and psyches. Katniss confronts Peeta about his actions and he explains that he had not abandoned her, and had only appeared to join Cato and company, but his allegiance has and always will remain with Katniss. Although she's a tough girl, his sincerity looks genuine, and she chooses to believe him.

What's most significant in their scene is how Peeta is adamant that he'd rather die than allow the Hunger Games to fundamentally change who he is; of all the sweet talking and equivocating he could ever possibly conjure up, it's these words that cinch it and win Katniss' heart. Without saying a word, we instantly know that they share the same conviction to remain true to themselves no matter what happens. This midpoint moment bonds them and helps them transcend the conspiratorial rules of the game. It also solidifies the theme: that love and hope can rise above fear.

In *Up in the Air*, the midpoint occurs when Ryan (George Clooney) and Alex (Vera Farmiga) are on a corporate yacht, and he tells her about his near-death childhood accident; how he'd been rescued by helicopter and how it changed his perspective on the world and even his belief in miracles. This heartfelt, confessional scene is when Alex falls in love with him, and Ryan admits that his unburdened backpack lectures are really just empty rhetoric. When they kiss in this scene, it's now a much more soulful connection, and is a decisive moment for Ryan who begins to dedicate himself to pursuing a committed relationship with Alex.

The pivotal character is embodied in the theory of "Six Degrees of Separation."

This principle is the belief that there is a trail of six people between each one of us and every other person on the planet. You just have to connect with the right six people. In movies, Six Degrees of Separation adheres to the laws of synchronicity. Everyone your protagonists need to meet, they will meet. And every person they encounter has the potential not only to open up a new door to a new world for your protagonist, but also to facilitate a protagonist's ability to open a new door to a dormant or repressed side to Self. The pivotal character plays this role. He or she might be a stranger who comes into town, or a new neighbor or coworker, or perhaps an already known but distant acquaintance.

In the provocative film *Six Degrees of Separation* (screenplay by John Guare based upon his play), an imposter comes into the life of well-to-do, Upper East Side New Yorkers, Flan and Ouisa Kittredge (Donald Sutherland and

Stockard Channing); this stranger, whose name may or may not be Paul (Will Smith in the film version), claims to be friends with their children at boarding school and also the son of the movie legend Sidney Poitier. This is a story about reinvention and illusions, and we bear witness as the sycophantic Paul seduces his way into people's lives by telling them what they want to hear . . . until the midpoint of the movie when his fictional identity is exposed (Poitier only had daughters).

The irony of the movie is the lingering impact—or side effects—that Paul has on Ouisa. It's astonishing to watch as she evolves from materialistic, subservient wife into a liberated woman who walks away from status and her marriage to pursue an uncertain future on her own terms. The fiction of Paul has unlocked the truth in Ouisa. The visual parallel in the film is a masterpiece supposedly by Wassily Kandinsky that's painted on both sides of the canvas. On one side you see Kandinsky's *Black Lines*, and on the other you see *Several Circles*; it's the Kittredges' prized possession. In one key scene, Ouisa spins it around as she chants to an interested collector: "Chaos, control, chaos control. You like? You like?" Indeed, the (fictitious) painting represents both sides of Ouisa Kittredge. It turns out that "Paul" wasn't the only imposter, living a lie. In the end, Ouisa's repressed, wild side is finally set free, and the pivotal character was the key. And, it was Flan, not Paul, who emerged as her true antagonist.

In *The Social Network*, the turning point in the evolution of Facebook comes courtesy of pivotal character Sean Parker (Justin Timberlake). Mark Zuckerberg (Jesse Eisenberg) runs into his ex-girlfriend, Erica (Rooney Mara) at a club (on page 76 of the 168-page original screenplay by Aaron Sorkin); upset by yet again being blown off by her, Mark tells his best friend Eduardo (Andrew Garfield) that they have to expand the website into more universities on the west coast. Shortly thereafter, we cut to Stanford and meet Sean Parker, post-coital, as he logs into a pretty coed's "The Facebook" page. It's Sean's stoked curiosity and business savvy that soon lead us to that fateful exchange (on page 97) over *appletinis* at a tony New York City restaurant when Sean tells Mark his idea is worth billions. Ironically, for all his computer geek-ness and alleged grandiosity, Mark Zuckerberg probably wasn't driven by greed or power. He was trying to impress a girl. But then Sean Parker swept into his life and changed its course—along with history.

Structurally, the midpoint is often when a platonic, fraught, and/or forbidden relationship crosses the line into romance (often with the pivotal character).

In *The Departed*, the midpoint occurs when undercover cop, Billy (Leonardo DiCaprio) begins to develop an emotional attachment toward his mandatorily assigned police psychiatrist Madolyn (Vera Farmiga); she also happens to be the girlfriend of and is about to move in with crooked cop/mob informant

Colin (Matt Damon). In the 163-page screenplay, the actual midpoint of the plot is when Billy and Madolyn become friends outside the professional boundaries of her office. One night, he shows up at the door of her apartment. If she truly loves Colin, why is she still living here by herself? She admits she's stalling her move-in with Colin. By page 104, they're kissing passionately, a taboo for both of them. They're both aware that this is a dangerous, high-stakes love triangle. And it directly motivates Billy to step up his efforts to bring Colin down. In the end, inevitably, both men are killed. If there's a moral to be learned from taboo movie romances, it's usually this: you play with fire and you get burned.

In *Juno*, the midpoint scene is when Mark Loring (Jason Bateman) and Juno MacGuff (Ellen Page) bond over cheesy slasher flicks and retro music. Mark misconstrues Juno's interest and seems to want more than friendship—which she rebuffs. But their intense (platonic) connection motivates him to leave his wife, Vanessa (Jennifer Garner); he realizes he's not ready for fatherhood. And Juno's idealistic bubble about this "perfect" couple is burst. Both Mark and Juno have a lot of growing up to do.

Midpoint complications compel your protagonist to look within.

Generally, the unexpected midpoint obstacle will force your protagonist not only to face the external antagonistic forces, but also to soul search and begin to contemplate his/her inner demons. This will plant the seeds to your protagonist's inevitable epiphany by placing him/her into an *existential dilemma*. Depending on genre, some crises will be life threatening, and others will be significant challenges to the natural order of things—the sense for your protagonist is: This Shouldn't Be Happening! And the accompanying questions: Why is this happening? And if your protagonist is introspective (and/or narcissistic): Why is this happening to *me*? In the face of any major crisis, I believe that it's human nature to question one's priorities, values, morals, and identity. In some cases, this initial question will lead to a significant epiphany at the end of act two or by the end of the movie. In other cases, this introspection will root a protagonist more firmly into his/her sense of self.

> If you find yourself slogging through the vast wasteland of act two, instead of adding more and more plot, try digging deeper into your characters' psyches. A valuable question for protagonists to ask themselves at the midpoint is: Who am I?

INTERVIEW: Screenwriters Rick Jaffa and Amanda Silver

Rick Jaffa and Amanda Silver Filmography

Best known for:

Rise of the Planet of the Apes (2011)
The Relic (1997)
Eye for an Eye (1996)
The Hand That Rocks the Cradle (1992) (Amanda Silver, writer; Rick Jaffa, executive producer)

NL: How do you begin? I'm assuming there's a lot of research involved just in choosing an idea. How do you decide, "Okay, this is something we want to spend the next six months to several years of our lives on?" Do you outline? What's your creative process?

AS: We always have a theme, but we don't always begin with it. The egress into a film depends on the project, but before we start writing, we always outline pretty extensively. We need to know what the theme is before we begin writing because it guides us.

RJ: We work hard on the outline, and yet, don't always follow it once we get started. We follow it closely, but not carefully, if you know what I mean. I spend a lot of time just coming up with flashes of ideas or moments—that interest me or that would be cool in a script. We keep legal pads of paper and as we talk—we spend a lot of time just talking about the project—we take copious notes. It could be ideas about anything. It could be structure or an idea for a character or a moment in the movie.

AS: If a character has to have a pivotal moment or change, we'll talk about what that will look like—how to make that dramatic. How to, as much as possible, show rather than tell. We usually know what those moments are because the character's journey is so tied to the theme.

RJ: With *Rise of the Planet of the Apes*, we also read a lot. We did an enormous amount of research. I guess I'd say that we talk a lot, we read a lot, and we write a lot before we even start doing an outline. Then, we work very hard on the outline before we start the actual writing of the script.

NL: Do you use index cards or do you have a process where you physically lay it out visually?

AS: We tried doing index cards because we read that other writers use index cards, but it never worked out for us.

RJ: Honestly, we keep legal pads and have tons and tons and tons of notes. Several pads . . . they just fill up. Amanda's got this knack for remembering which pad has a certain note in it.

AS: I have a photographic memory where I can picture an idea in the middle of the pad. We outline in sequences. Sometimes we'll know what a sequence is generally, but the scenes within the sequences are not necessarily figured out ahead of time. Scenes will be laid out in the outline, but usually by the time we get to them, they need adjusting.

RJ: We'll ask ourselves "What's the tension of this sequence?" "Will the good guys arrive in time?" "Will the guy get the girl?" Then, as we're outlining it, we can use those tensions for the sequences. We'll try to build the structure that way.

NL: In *Rise of the Planet of the Apes*, you have that first action sequence, which sets the tone and gets our hearts pumping. After which, you go to the laboratory and introduce Will [James Franco]. I know it can be different with each project, but with *Rise of the Planet of the Apes*, did you start with the idea of Caesar or with this Alzheimer's medical testing idea? Or, did you start with the character of Will and decide that his father [John Lithgow] had Alzheimer's? It's overwhelming to a lot of young screenwriters because all they see are finished movies. What's so great about your movie is that you make it look easy. The work is so strong that they just think, "Well, of course, that's what it always should have been."

AS: Rick had been collecting articles. He collects articles that are interesting to him in general. He had collected a series of articles about chimps who are raised as babies—human babies—in homes and how that often goes awry. Many times it ends tragically for the chimps, who get sent to horrible facilities. So Rick went away for a weekend to try to come up with an idea.

RJ: I took a ton of files and folders and all kinds of ideas. I had them all laid out on the floor of this hotel room. I just kept going back to those articles about the chimps and thinking there's got to be a great movie here. What could it be? I had those articles for about three years to be honest. I never really got past, "Well, it must be a horror film," and that wasn't really appealing. As it worked out, I also had articles about genetic engineering and other thriller ideas laid out in front of me. My eyes went back and forth between the piles a couple times. Finally, I looked back at the articles about those chimps and a little voice in my head said, "It's *Planet of the Apes*." And, immediately, Caesar was born. I knew enough about the mythology of *The Planet of the Apes* series that I knew the revolution was never completely explained, but hinted at. I remembered from *Conquest of the Planet of the Apes* that it was a chimp named Caesar who led the revolution, but the reality was that none of those movies specifically came to mind. It was just that I instantly knew, "You know, this is how apes really could take over the world." So, I came home and presented it to Amanda.

AS: At first, I had that fake supportive smile that you get with your partner when you have to say, "Oh, yeah, that's a great idea, honey."

RJ: Imagine coming home and saying, "Honey, good news, we're going to reinvent *Planet of the Apes.*" The response was like, "Yeah, but how are we going to pay our bills?"

AS: But when he started talking about the character of Caesar, very quickly, the shape of the movie, the entire movie . . . and this does not always happen . . . became clear. Because what we were talking about was a character piece with an ape as a protagonist. Although I think to this day, the studio would still say that Will is the protagonist.

NL: That was actually one of my first questions—who is the protagonist? Because you can fashion it from both points.

AS: It does have that Frankenstein story edge to it, and you can make the argument that Will is the protagonist. But we always saw Caesar as the protagonist because he's discovering his identity through crisis, and that discovery leads him to the revelation of who he was meant to be—born to be: a mighty leader. In an earlier draft, Caesar had an ape father in the beginning. He was a great warrior, with the same birthmark, and leads a rebellion to fight off human poachers.

RJ: Caesar's ape father is the de facto leader of a family of chimps. When the poachers come, he tries to wage a battle against them. Of course, they are not equipped to fight humans, especially humans with guns. He loses and he gets killed. So when Caesar's born and John asks, "What's that?" And James says, "It's a birthmark," our intention was that it sets a bomb under the table for the audience: "Oh my God, this chimp is going to grow up to be a great leader."

AS: Yes. It gives you a sense at the top of the movie about Caesar's destiny. Because it's a Moses story. He was born to lead his people, his ape people, to freedom.

NL: When my students ask, "How do you decide who the protagonist is?" I tell them it's generally three things: (1) it's the character with the most active goals, (2) it's the character with the most at stake, and (3) it's the character who changes the most. Unless it's an ensemble, you might not have to make this decision. With that definition, Will and Caesar are both on parallel tracks because they both do change, but Caesar does change the most. He has the most at stake because he could be killed. He's not going to do very well at that shelter facility. He has very active goals. You could make a case either way.

RJ: He was always the protagonist in our minds.

AS: We sold the idea in 2006, so there were many, many drafts. We didn't write all of them. There were a couple times we were fired and then brought back on. But Caesar's story remained the same from the beginning. In fact, many of the beats, like those at the ape facility, haven't changed.

RJ: I'd say from once Caesar attacks the neighbor through the end of the second act, that about 80 percent of the scenes have stayed the same from the very first draft. The majority of the rewrites were about human characters.

AS: It was always our weakness. The hardest part was when the two protagonists' storylines diverged. You have to maintain their separate stories as well as their connection to each other. We had a lot of clarity about Caesar's goal, but the Will character has to fail in what he's trying to do, which is to free Caesar. We had to find ways to keep his character active and organic, so that it would feel like Will's goals were coming from a place of true desire.

NL: Did you have the Alzheimer's treatment medical trials as a part of the original story as well?

RJ: No, the Alzheimer's idea came in the third draft, I think. The facility's original goal was to create a drug that made people smarter. We were really into that for a long time because it matched what we felt was the theme of the original 1968 *Planet of the Apes*. Man's hubris will be his downfall. We had pointed out to the studio that apes didn't put Colonel Taylor on the beach; humans put Colonel Taylor [Charlton Heston] on the beach. We thought then, as a Frankenstein story, if Will's goal was to do something that man is not intended to do—it's going to come home to roost.

AS: It's interesting, too, because in the rewriting process something that was bald and blatant evolved into something more nuanced, once we brought in the desire for a cure for Alzheimer's. It challenges the audience not to blame Will necessarily, but to have empathy. A lot of things came together for us in that draft.

RJ: Although, we were concerned about whether people would think that we were trying to say that curing Alzheimer's was a bad thing. Even if the intention of the drug was well meaning, he still had to cross the line at some point and he does. He has to cross a moral line.

NL: It gives him a secret. The potential of being discovered. I truly admire how you introduce the Alzheimer's subplot when Will comes home from the lab and you think he's talking to the nanny about his kid. Then, his father is revealed and you get to show the progress of the drug through the music—it's emotional. If we look at Caesar as the protagonist, the midpoint of the movie is when he's in the animal shelter. He starts to bond with the other apes and the orangutan who also have very distinct characteristics, which is great. It seems like the key moment at the middle of the movie is when Will can finally get him out, but Caesar doesn't want to go. Screenwriter Gary Ross thinks of the midpoint as the moment when you place your protagonist in an existential dilemma. I tell my students that a good question to ask of your protagonist at the midpoint is "who am I"? It's where the characters are literally questioning values, ideas, identities, and priorities.

On the one hand, Caesar wants to go with Will and on the other hand, he wants to stay because he's bonded and he wonders, "Am I an animal or a human being?" Certainly with Caesar as the protagonist, it hits that definition pretty well. It's also a place where everything deepens in the story because it's so much more than we think. It makes the ending unpredictable because in the middle the character isn't even sure who he is. Do you think consciously at the midpoint that you really need a moment where Will is questioning his motivations? For example, "Am I bringing him home because I want him or do I now want him to be who he is?" How conscious are you of that kind of character evolution when you start outlining and arcing your characters? How conscious are you of the middle of that journey when you begin?

AS: If we're not conscious of the character arc when we outline or write, then we're very nervous. That's when we have to stop and take a step back. If we don't know why the character "needs the movie"—how they transform —then we're lost at sea. We have to know exactly what the character's transformation is going to be and how that will play out.

RJ: We will certainly know where the character starts and ends, so sometimes the journey for us is to find the journey in between. We'll ask ourselves: "What six steps can the character go through to get from here to there?"

AS: And, sometimes, it's two steps forward and one step back.

RJ: Exactly, it'll be a reversal. So, we try to identify what the idea of the scene is: is it a scene of betrayal? Is it a scene of sacrifice in order to change? We spend a lot of time doing that. It's interesting that Caesar asks who he is, but it's certainly not the midway point. It's a long first act because it ends when he is sent to the facility. He asks, "What am I?"—which is answered when he stays with the apes.

AS: But there's a series of scenes that lead up to that change. It's an epiphany that's earned, which begins when Caesar's dropped off and betrayed. A few scenes later, he begs to be taken home. He doesn't feel like he belongs there, but they can't take him home. Then, two things happen: one is that Caesar begins to find his footing in this new place by becoming the alpha male, and the other is that Will has deserted him. There's a moment in that scene when Caesar looks down and sees that Will's carrying a leash— and he makes a decision in that moment. It's that moment when you can't go back. You've got to go forward. He's tempted, as we all are, to run into daddy's arms and be with him—to forget he's an ape. We all want to go back to what's familiar, even if it's wrong. The key to Caesar is that he had to be relatable. Ironically, as Caesar is discovering he's an ape, he is going through a very human journey of self-discovery. At that moment, he could say goodbye to Maurice [his new orangutan friend] and go back to the familiar, but he knows he can't do that. Andy Serkis, the actor [who played adult Caesar], did a great job of portraying this, because when he turns around there's pain in his decision. It's not like he's banging his chest and kicking James out. It's hard for him.

RJ: We wanted anybody who was a teenager or will ever be a teenager to be able to relate to Caesar. The facility is almost like a very brutal summer camp. Everyone else has been there for a while and your parents are off on vacation, so you feel screwed and abandoned. What happens on your very first day is that you get your ass kicked. And, you've got to figure it out. The scene where Rocket beats him up is his first day at a new school. We did that very intentionally. Then, he does get his footing and he becomes a man, in the broad sense of the change.

AS: Structurally, the scene you're talking about is earned in the first act, which was extremely important. We really fought to keep the bonding scenes with the family, which may seem boring or without action. But they build the foundation for the audience's feeling that Caesar needs both his grandfather and his father and that they need him. You have to spend time earning that. If you want the audience to feel something, you have to do your homework at the top. In early drafts, Caesar wasn't taken to the facility until page 60 because we overdid it and there were too many of those scenes!

RJ: We had a great time writing those scenes.

NL: They are great scenes. It's very important to create the emotional connection over time. He starts when he's a little newborn baby and very quickly and visually grows up before our eyes.

AS: People will intuitively understand things that are short-handed correctly. One of the big challenges in this script was to show the movement of time. With John Lithgow's character getting sick, getting well, and getting sick again, we had a lot of awkward, jerky things to dramatize. We had to keep the story moving forward while planting exposition and plot points.

RJ: Laying the pipe.

NL: How do you externalize all of that internal psychology? It's one of the reasons I admire the script so much because you're able to shorthand so many things and create emotional links with the audiences through tangible things, like the window in the attic.

AS: My writing teacher at USC used to call it "visualization of the idea." It's hard to come up with, but it's worth forcing yourself to do it. In *Apes*, we had a moment when John Lithgow gets better and has this long conversation about what he can see and what he can feel, but in the end, it was much better to use the music.

RJ: To get back to your question about the midpoint, we do work hard at knowing what the midpoint will be. It's just I don't believe we've ever asked ourselves the question: Will the protagonist wonder who he is at that point or not? Never consciously anyway.

AS: It's a salient question though.

RJ: It's a great question. We always have a real firm idea of what the midpoint will be, but we're not slaves to where it comes—meaning, it can be late. If the script's 120 pages, it certainly doesn't have to be on page 60.

NL: When Caesar's released to Will, but refuses to go, it's 63 minutes into a 103-minute film.

AS: The reason it had to be late is because once that happens, Will doesn't have much to do.

NL: Right—until they break out.

RJ: And then it's actually about Caesar, who is leading the breakout, which is fun and exciting. It almost plays like the end of the second act.

NL: You also get the benefit of when Caesar breaks back into the house to steal the remaining serum, so even though Will's not there, he's integral to keep the story engine running. One of the things that impressed me so much about the movie is that you have your human audience rooting against themselves. You have multiple antagonists in this film. You have the love story with the veterinarian at the zoo with her philosophy that some things aren't meant to be changed. You have Jacobs [David Oyelowo] at the lab who is a greedy, corporate guy. And, you have the animal shelter with Brian Cox [as the guy in charge] who's trying to do his job. I went back and forth with him since he's pretty benevolent, but it's the son who's the real sadistic jerk. Are you asking early on "who's our main antagonist"? Often I'll say to my students to go to the climax to see who the main antagonist is because sometimes that's not even revealed until the climax. What kind of creative process do you have around injecting antagonists and antagonistic forces into your work and this script?

RJ: I think the irony with *Rise of the Planet of the Apes* is that usually we go by the edict: the bigger the antagonist, the better the protagonist.

AS: Especially in a thriller.

RJ: With *Apes*, we kept arguing that we didn't really need a central antagonist. Many rewrites were spent building up the Jacobs character to be the antagonist. What's interesting is that a lot of people really love the movie because it has several antagonists.

AS: At one point, we had a "monkey in the middle" scene where the neighbor's kid—who's a little jerk—makes fun of Caesar. It gives the first act more of a Pinocchio feeling.

RJ: We loved that scene. In the script Caesar wants to play with the kid, so he sneaks out and they have a game of catch. One of the kids throws the ball over Caesar's head, not intentionally at first, and then the other kid throws it back, and almost immediately, they realize, "Hey, isn't this funny? It's literally monkey in the middle." The kids start chanting it, and Caesar realizes he's being made fun of. The scene presented our first glimpse of threat and danger because Caesar's like, "Hey, that's not so funny." He gets up in one of the kid's faces, and you get the idea, "Oh no, this could go south."

AS: You could say that the antagonist in that earlier draft of the script was more intangible. It could be described as a way of looking at the world, embodied in a few different characters. And that's what Caesar, and to some extent, Will, are fighting against. It's not racism, but perhaps a stunted nature that fears differences and accepts only similarities. An intolerance, a cruelty. This is embodied in all the movie's antagonists who deny that other animals—apes—have souls.

RJ: Certainly, you can read Dodge, Tom Felton's character, in this way. When he says, "Stupid monkey," we wanted the audience to consider "monkey" like the "m" word. It was peppered throughout the script. When very early on, Will says, "I can't take care of a monkey," and Franklin [Tyler Labine] says, "He's not a monkey, he's an ape." That was to say a number of things. In some ways, it was to say the theme that Amanda is talking about: differences and the fears that people have about being different.

NL: One of the other aspects of midpoints and pivotal characters is that it takes you to this moral grey area. I think everyone can take the fact that Jacobs plunged to his death because he's just a greedy person. He was only after the bottom line. At the same time, I think everybody feels that great cathartic sense when Caesar says to Will in the last line of the movie, "No, I am home." Because it feels like he's going back to nature. As they evolve further, it's probably going to get closer to the *Planet of the Apes* that I remember where it's going to start to be a power struggle. I wonder if the audience is going to have an easier time of knowing who to root for.

RJ: One of the other things that we always start off with is not only why does the protagonist need the movie, but what does the protagonist want? If you create a character who wants something desperately, then the audience is going to root for that character and it doesn't matter if it's an ape or a human or a demon.

AS: Often too, what a character wants is not what they need. Many times the audience can be ahead or discover that with the character.

RJ: Which are choices, by the way, that we very specifically make in the outline before we start writing.

AS: What we are realizing, or maybe re-realizing, in constructing the sequel is that we can control who the audience roots for and that mastering this type of manipulation is a huge part of our craft. Once when we were watching Roger Federer play tennis, the announcers said that he never takes his eye off the ball—that's Federer's deal. I would say that when we're doing what we need to be doing, we never take our eyes off the audience.

We have to know on every page what the audience is feeling and to maximize what those feelings are.

We need to know if they're worried or upset or hoping for something or fearing that something is going to happen. In terms of the human characters and the ape characters, I think that they come in all shapes, sizes, and rootability. There are good humans and bad humans and good and bad apes. And always, if we've done our job correctly, the audience is going to feel strongly about them—no matter the species.

NL: Right, that's the key to not having to really pick sides because sides are made up of so many different points of view and attitudes and beliefs. To me, the strongest moment of *Rise of Planet of the Apes* is when Caesar says, "No," because he speaks. For me, I was sitting there thinking I just want him to say, "Go screw yourselves." And, then when he says the thing you want, you just feel this collective rush in the audience. It took that much time for him to say no. I really liked how it unfolded in a gradual, nuanced way.

AS: It's all about character. If you take Will and Caesar, it's a father and son story with a clear beginning, middle, and end. At the end, Will takes responsibility and apologizes and Caesar forgives him, so that there's a sense of closure. We got incredibly lucky because Fox let it be what it was. Nabokov has this term that he uses called, "fondling the details." They let us do that.

NL: It's not just an action movie of apes versus humans. It goes much deeper because you focus on a core group of characters.

RJ: The thing about the *Planet of the Apes* series is that they're all contained. If you think about it, the first movie took place in and around what used to be Manhattan. All the other ones take place in the same area. We were lucky and naïve in some ways. I think also one of the things that helped us is that the visual effects were really expensive, so to put it on a bigger canvas would have been prohibitive. I think from the beginning everyone involved was really compelled by Caesar's story and really moved by his journey, and so if that hadn't been the case, we would have really gotten into trouble with the script. The studio really supported it. They pushed us hard. The Golden Gate Bridge was not in the first several drafts. There was always, though, a rush to freedom, an escape.

AS: That's the inevitable ending of the story.

RJ: There was always that. It took place in different ways, but the Golden Gate Bridge didn't really happen until just before [director] Rupert Wyatt and Chernin Entertainment came on board.

AS: The whole movie is leading to that moment. From the moment that Will found that baby and took him home. From the moment they plucked Bright Eyes from the jungle. It was inevitably going to end up with Caesar in those woods—and the fun is watching it unfold. It's not about the destruction of the human race. It's about the liberation of these animals, who we've treated with hubris and the human need to dominate. The decimation of the human race is a by-product. I think people want to feel. They want to spend time with characters and feel all the different range of emotions, including heartbreak and triumph.

ASSIGNMENT

Make a list of your protagonist's three highest priorities at the beginning of the movie. Examine how these priorities start to shift as a result of your protagonist's active "crisis management" from the end of act one to the midpoint. Do we get a glimpse of your protagonist's dormant (repressed) side at the pivotal midpoint? Who/what motivates this partial revelation?

12

WHAT'S THE "AHA" MOMENT?

Position Your Protagonist at a Crossroads at the End of Act Two

The end of the second act is often referred to as the "all is lost" moment. It might seem like the Worst Thing That Could Happen—but things are actually going to get even worse (*see Chapter 14 on Climaxes*).

After spending the bulk of the second act trying to accomplish a major goal, your protagonist has arrived at a crucial make it or break it moment. It's a low point because they're losing hope that their Plan A goal can actually be accomplished. Your protagonist's early rumblings of existential introspection at the midpoint—the "Who Am I?" introspection—is now being forced to the forefront and will require active soul searching. In act three, often your protagonist isn't the same person he/she was in acts one and two. The challenges of the second act have necessitated character growth. So now what? It's decision time.

If the end of act one is based upon a crisis point and necessity, I like to think that the narrative drive of act three is based upon a choice.

A choice is about passion—which will fuel the heat of the climax. A choice means that your protagonist has reached the point in his life where he/she's calling the shots. An apt metaphor might be how sometimes a firefighter's best tool is to set a "controlled blaze" in order to put out a fire. Act two is about throwing water on the dramatic flames to get them under control—but that didn't work. The fire is still out of control. And so, act three is about *fighting fire with fire*. In many great films, the protagonist's decision point comes in the form of an epiphany.

The epiphany at or near the end of the second act will (ideally) hoist your hero onto the horns of a dilemma—a metaphorical or literal fork in the road.

While a true "epiphany" is a sudden realization of what is most important in one's life, in a movie, character epiphanies usually grow out of the mid-point. Screenplays are all about setups and payoffs. Cause and effect. So, ideally, your protagonist's epiphany shouldn't feel to the audience like it's coming-out-of-the-blue. Instead, weave in the threads that will situate your protagonist at a crossroads at the end of act two.

If it's going to be a moment of epiphany, it's going to grow out of deep desperation—and will require great courage to activate. Frequently, the two choices are the possibility of returning to the relative safety of his/her familiar "ordinary world," or moving on in a courageous new direction. The more challenging choice is always the most dramatic, so that's the road your main character must endure to find release from pity and fear (aka catharsis). *And in order for an audience to undergo collective catharsis, the protagonist must face his/her own (worst) fears.*

By choosing the road less traveled, your protagonist's main quest (Plan A) will usually be superseded by a new goal (Plan B) in act three.

At this juncture, Plan A gets abandoned because either: (1) it's deemed untenable, or (2) it's achieved—but has in some way made your protagonist's journey even more difficult.

In *Se7en*, detectives Somerset and Mills (Morgan Freeman and Brad Pitt) spend the entire second act searching for the mysterious John Doe serial killer. At the end of act two, John Doe (Kevin Spacey) walks into the police precinct of his own volition. Plan A is abandoned because it's been attained. They got him. John Doe is immediately apprehended. But the story isn't over. There are still two more deadly sins that he's already set in motion, and unless the detectives follow his request, two more people will be dead by the end of the week—the 7th day. The detectives don't have an epiphany, but they are at a **crossroads**. Their decision to take the bait and follow John Doe's lead is rooted deeply within their characters. Somerset, who had been defined as the cynic, has now found a glimmer of idealism and is hoping he can save some lives. Mills, who was the idealist, has become a nihilist and doesn't believe any good can come from John Doe's final request.

The "aha" moment in *Se7en* is the resolution of the central mystery. And it just happens to be 7:00 p.m. when the mysterious box is delivered to the rendezvous point. We never actually see what's inside the box, but Somerset's face, when he sees it, says it all. The last two sins—Envy and Wrath—are played out between Mills and John Doe. John Doe's self-proclaimed jealousy of Mills' well-adjusted and loving home life motivates his final act. And David Mills' homicidal rage when he discovers his wife's murder and the pregnancy she had kept from him. Mills gets arrested for the vengeful murder of John Doe. In the end, Somerset's quasi-epiphany is that he's still tethered to the chaos of the city, the hunt; it's in his blood, so it's inferred that retirement will have to wait. With the sun setting over the desert, Somerset's voiceover quotes Ernest Hemingway's *For Whom the Bell Tolls*: "'The world is a fine place and worth fighting for.' I agree with the second part."

In *Little Miss Sunshine*, the Hoover family's Plan A is to get to California for the kids' beauty pageant. At the end of act two, this goal is accomplished—they've arrived. Unfortunately, the contest organizer is now standing in their way, and Richard (Greg Kinnear) has a crisis of conscience about whether or not he should allow his daughter, Olive (Abigail Breslin) to compete after all. He's afraid of humiliation and defeat. But his "aha" moment comes when his wife, Sheryl (Toni Colette) convinces him that love and dedication are more important than winning. The family's new goal is for Olive to realize her dream and compete—regardless of the outcome. Richard has given up the hubris of thinking he can control everything or even should. By the climax, this formerly miserable family is finally set free. And they're able to revel in being outcasts because they have each other.

At the end of the second act of *Rise of the Planet of the Apes*, Caesar escapes from the animal shelter. Armed with a stolen supply of the serum that can imbue him with super strength and heightened intelligence, Caesar is seemingly invincible. Furthering his "existential dilemma" at the midpoint—his struggle to define himself as human or ape—Caesar now fully embraces his identity as ape. But his "aha" moment comes in the form of becoming the leader of the apes. During act two, Caesar's quest or Plan A was to assimilate with his human family. As act three begins, he has the opportunity to reunite and join forces with the man who raised him, Will (James Franco). But Caesar rejects this path, and his Plan B is his choice to rebel against the human race. Will loves him, but can't stop him. Caesar is now a force of nature and knows his true destiny. The pithy tagline for this film foretells Caesar's journey, to be further explored in the sequel: *From Evolution to Revolution*. (*See* my interview with screenwriters Amanda Silver and Rick Jaffa in Chapter 11).

The primary difference between the two plans is that Plan A is based upon necessity: you've effectively trapped your protagonist in the crisis and either he/she has no choice but to take an action—or he/she has something of value to lose. Plan B, on the other hand, is often (but not always) based on choice, as your protagonist has become stronger and more decisive during the second act.

INTERVIEW: Academy Award-Nominated Screenwriter Jose Rivera

Jose Rivera Filmography

Best known for:

Celestina (also directing) (2013)
On the Road (2012)
Letters to Juliet (2010)
Trade (screenplay/story) (2007)
The Motorcycle Diaries (2004)
    Academy Award Nominee
    Writers Guild Award Nominee

NL: I wanted to mainly focus our conversation on *The Motorcycle Diaries* because it's a literal journey, but also a journey inward for the characters. The movie is untraditional, in terms of American story structure, because their initial journey isn't compelled by any huge crisis. They simply set off on this journey because they wanted to explore a part of the world they weren't familiar with. In fact, your protagonist doesn't start to become passionate about his goal until later in the story when he gets to the leper colony. I know there was also source material and that you were basing it on true events. Did you map out the structure before you started in any kind of linear way?

JR: When I wrote the script, the end of act one was the two guys finally getting on the road. I generally pay very strict attention to where the act breaks fall, even though I don't subscribe to certain terms like inciting incidents because I find them to be a little clinical and not particularly organic. I do, however, follow the act breaks religiously: at page 30, the main hero has accepted the adventure, at page 90, the hero is at his or her worst moment, and at page 120, we end the story. In that way, I have a very formulaic approach. What's interesting about *The Motorcycle Diaries* is that when [director] Walter Salles was cutting the film, he realized that all the act one material that I had written and he had filmed, as interesting as it was, was not nearly as interesting as the road fiction. So, instead of the 30 minutes that we had originally, we ended up dispatching with act one in about a minute and a half. We watched the movie and realized it was way too long at the beginning, so I wrote a new voiceover, and Walter cut act one down. The idea is very much what you said: there wasn't a compelling reason to hit the road. They weren't in a war-torn country, they weren't looking for gold, and they weren't compelled by huge external forces. A lot of the film was conceived as a coming-of-age story, and in a coming-of-age story, the central character is looking for knowledge and a place in the world—that was really the internal motivation. It's the moment where Alberto Granado [Rodrigo De la Serna] says, "Che, you don't want to end up like that old guy over there." A creepy, chubby old guy sitting all alone—and of course no one wants to end up like that. So that was about the extent of their inner motivation. A lot of it was just for fun. And the irony, and what's interesting in the film, is that those kicks turn into something significant, life changing, and surprising because they didn't expect to really change, they just expected to see things.

And there were many steps along the way in which Ernesto [aka "Che" Guevara; played by Gael García Bernal] confronted poverty, misery, or sickness and had to take action. It's the accumulation of small moments that lead to the climax of the film, which is his swim across the Amazon River.

A nd when we talk about epiphany, that was his moment because he's literally facing a world in which the poor and dispossessed are on one side of the river and the healthy are on the other side, and his internal question is: "On what side of the river will you belong?"

He realizes he belongs on the other side where the poor and dispossessed are, so he literally swims there. The very physical manifestation of a very abstract theme, but it definitely works. Walter and I realized that that scene was our climax because it answered the thematic question, so the entire film was structured to lead up to that moment.

NL: And what helped infuse that moment too with such suspense was his Achilles' heel, which is his asthma. That long swim across the river could literally kill him. You're really worried about him. It's dark, and he's breathing heavily, so he also has to overcome his own physical limitations to get to the other side. I felt like it was such a true epiphany because the moments leading up to that are really what set the course for him to become a revolutionary and go to Cuba. The sum of all those events turns him into the man he is meant to be. I wondered about the first act because it's so economical, and the only other clue was when the father said, "If I were a few years younger, I'd be doing this." You get the sense of: do this while you're young and while you can. Did you have a voiceover in your original draft?

JR: No, there was no voiceover in the beginning, we just saw their life unfolding. We saw them playing rugby, we saw him at medical school, we saw Granado's life, and we saw a lot of Che's family. The feeling that he had that life wasn't fulfilling, but routine and stale. So when we decided to compress all that, I wrote the voiceover to cover that information and to give a sense of excitement.

NL: Did you know starting out that you wanted to cover this specific road trip during this particular time? Basically where Granado wants to finish this road trip by his thirtieth birthday?

JR: That was invented, and at the end I revealed it, when Ernesto says, "I know this is not really your birthday." And Granado says, "Yeah, I know. I just said that to motivate you." There's also a running motif about having five dollars that they were going to spend on a bathing suit for Ernesto's girlfriend, which was also invented. It actually really occurred, but it doesn't occur in *The Motorcycle Diaries* itself. It was a biographical detail I discovered in my research. One of the structural things about adapting that particular book was that the diaries themselves were very picaresque and episodic. They also tended to meander with millions and zillions of moments. They lacked structure. So one of the things we had to do was to create some running motifs that linked the different scenes of the film, so it didn't feel that episodic.

NL: There's voiceover of the letters home to mother. But with the girlfriend, there's a scene where he gets a letter from Chichina [Mía Maestro], and he's devastated because she's not going to wait for him. And then pretty much right after that, he meets the migrant workers who have been kicked off their land, and it restores his belief in humanity. So thematically, he certainly doesn't want to take the easy road. He could have just gotten married and finished med school. Was that a part of his original biography? Was there one specific woman that he could have ended up with that you ended up turning into a compilation?

JR: I worked from two sources: one was Ernesto's book and one was Granado's book. They were both about the same journey, but the points of view were very different. One book would include incidents that the other book didn't have. Granado tended to make Ernesto into a hero, whereas Ernesto's point of view was basically very interior and not about what he was doing. The interesting thing about Chichina's letter is that it severs him from the last thing that was connecting him to home. And that's one of the turning points in the film because that's when he really starts to embrace the road and starts getting involved with people. Until then, he was just a tourist.

NL: After working on *The Motorcycle Diaries* and the adaptation of *On the Road*, can you speak to the similarities and challenges that came from two very different road movies? The road movie itself is one of the toughest screenplays to write because they can be inherently episodic—and the challenge is to get it to build and keep intensifying.

JR: The differences were huge in terms of the source material. Ernesto never imagined that his diaries would be published. They were written really for himself to record the events of his life and were published posthumously, whereas [Jack] Kerouac obviously wrote for national consumption, and he had a very novelistic structure. *On the Road* was, in a way, a much tougher one to crack.

NL: It's such a beloved text, and people would have expectations which would be very different than those for *The Motorcycle Diaries*.

JR: Especially in this country. In South America, obviously, *The Motorcycle Diaries* resonates in a different way than it does here. But here, *On the Road* resonates for so many generations, and there's a lot of baggage, including the fact that many people are still alive who were part of the events of the book. My approach with both books was to leave the baggage at the door and not assume the weight of that responsibility because I don't think I could have written either one that way. To me, it started as an academic challenge in structuring this sprawling massive book into a tight, three-act film structure. That was really the first challenge. And then, it was to find the incidents that contributed to that structure and to delete the ones that didn't.

NL: You obviously know the source material very well. Did you put the book aside and try to approach it with what was indelible, or did you go through and highlight, using the book as a living text?

JR: I felt I had to honor the book. I didn't feel I was going to reinvent the wheel with Kerouac. And there's so much great material that it's a crime not to use it. I highlighted very carefully and underlined the scenes that I thought were filmic and the dialogue that I thought was useable in terms of the screenplay. Usually, I would X-out pages that didn't fit at all. There was a lot of material in there that I loved and wanted to include. It's interesting too because one of the things that I find in adapting books is that, in some ways, one of the jobs of the screenwriter is to fix the flaws of the book. And even a great book will have flaws. So one of the flaws of *On the Road* was its lack of a compelling female character.

NL: Yes—Marylou [Kristen Stewart] and Camille [Kirsten Dunst].

JR: So those two characters have certain scenes in the movie that are not in the book which are there to give them some backstory and more dimension. In some cases, I had to reset the dialogue. Carolyn Cassady, who was the model for the character of Camille, is still alive and dislikes the book because all she does is cry. So we worked extra hard to give her character a real backbone and a greater humanity, so that she's not just a victim. That's one of the things that I approached the book with.

NL: Do you actually do a formal outline or do you have a certain method that you use to approach the planning stages before you start writing the script?

JR: I don't have a super formal outline. As I said, I'm very conscious of where the act breaks fall, and I usually create a list of interesting scenes in more or less the order that seems most organic, and I tend to follow that list and incorporate three acts. I don't like to write a detailed treatment or outline of the film because then I feel like most of the fun is over, and I like to be surprised as I go and discover things as I write.

NL: I think that's where most of the magic really happens—in the discovery process. And a lot of times, if you're too slavish to an outline, you can short circuit that process. Are you writing toward a specific theme?

JR: I don't stress about a theme. I'm much more obsessive about tone and story. The tone of the storytelling is very important to me, and obviously the story is important. In terms of the theme, I like to think that themes will emerge and that people will project a theme onto the story without having the story telegraph a theme. And there aren't that many great themes. And they've been used so very often, that you're not going to get very original in that area. But we do have to get original with our story and with our characters. I think that's the idea behind "On what side of the river will you be?" as the theme that Walter and I came up with, but you don't really feel the heaviness of it until the movie's over. And then you go, "Oh, that's what it's about." But, that's not what was really on my mind. What was on my mind was: "How do I propel the story forward, and how do I keep the audience consistently off balance, so they can't see where we're going?" To me that was really important. I do think that the writer and the central characters share very strong points of view on life and can't be neutral. And maybe the writers who think theme is very important are really thinking about that: that our points of view on the world should be very strong and interesting, and our central characters should be very clear in a way that relates to theme. Because you could ask yourself: what is a point of view? Well, a point of view is our theme.

NL: I think that's actually very well put because to me theme is a universal truth that all people can relate to on some level, and a point of view is, especially with a character like Che Guevara, the character's truth. It becomes more apparent to both him and the audience who he is, and what really matters to him. His perspective links to the thematic. That he can't just allow people to suffer and turn his back on anyone. That everyone is equal. There's the thing with the gloves where he refuses to wear them because it's the first layer of separation and, of course, the water separates them too. That scene becomes where he wants to cross the divide which defines him and is so powerful.

I know that you originally started as a playwright, and I'm wondering what are the main differences for you between playwriting and screenwriting? And, as a corollary to that question, I see that you're directing the feature *Celestina*, what have you learned from screenwriting and directing, and/or from working with talented directors?

JR: The theater requires language, and the medium of the theater is symmetry. To be a good playwright, you have to hear very well, and you have to be able to paint pictures with words, whereas in film, you create those pictures with a camera. Right off the bat—that's an extremely different way to tell a story. I've been doing both for many years, so my theater writing has helped my screenwriting, and my screenwriting has helped my theater writing. My theater writing has become more visual and more sweeping in a way, and I've been able to incorporate skills I've learned writing dialogue as a playwright to my screenwriting. As a director, I've directed some short material so far, but I've been on set many times with Walter and have loved watching him work. I learned a great deal sitting in editing and learning that the cuts I never would have made on the page are, sometimes, essential on screen. Things that seemed so vital in the writing, I realized are secondary to other things. So that's been a real education to watch those pictures be rearranged, cut, and spliced up, in a way to tell a story that you never would have attempted on the page.

NL: Despite all the planning and storyboarding and outlines and drafts, filmmaking is always a process of experimentation because so much gets revised on the page, and then shot, and then cut out in the editing room, and you don't really know what works until you see it all put together.

JR: It's a very organic exercise. It's all intuitive ultimately. I've cut short films that I've done, and it's all intuition: this feels right or doesn't feel right. And the master plan really gets thrown out the window.

ASSIGNMENT

Make a list of all possible choices or directions your protagonist might choose for his/her life at the end of act two. Order this list hierarchically from most valuable to least important. Has your protagonist's perspective shifted from act one to this point? Did the stakes intensify as a result of acting upon this epiphany?

13

WHAT'S THE RUSH?

Set the Clock Ticking

In the phenomenal 24-hour film, *The Clock*, artist/collagist Christian Marclay visually chronicles ticking clocks in movies (and some from television) by cutting together thousands of film clips, each snippet marking the exact minute or even second that featured a shot of a watch or clock, or a snatch of time-related dialogue. What's even more remarkable about the film is that it plays in *real time*, so if you happen to be watching the film at 2:05 p.m. in Los Angeles, the clips on screen will correspond to precisely the same time. The film itself is a clock and drives home one of the few absolutes in this book:

Movies encompass many different genres, stories, and characters, but on the plot level: all movies are about time.

In *Shame, American Psycho, Somewhere, Natural Born Killers*, and *About a Boy*, the protagonists have way too much time on their hands. In *Groundhog Day, Source Code*, and *127 Hours*, they're going nowhere fast. And films such as *Beginners, Up, The Curious Case of Benjamin Button, Extremely Loud & Incredibly Close, Y Tu Mamá También*, and *The Descendants* all poignantly demonstrate that we never have enough time with the people we love most.

Organically impose a deadline ASAP—no later than the middle of act three.

Once the plot crosses over the threshold into act three and your protagonist has come to terms with who he/she truly is and what he/she *really* wants: increase the urgency by turning up the heat with a time lock. The most common deadlines imposed in movies tend to be rites of passage: births, deaths, weddings, graduations—and New Year's Eve. Tests are also used to great effect: the game show in *Slumdog Millionaire*, the championship game in *The Longest Yard*, and the big match in *The Fighter*. And, of course, there's often the rush to the airport or the wedding altar—which have become timeworn movie clichés. Although all of the above examples can be effective to create a sense of urgency en route to the climax, all deadlines need to emerge from specific character needs and not arbitrarily assigned merely to service the plot.

Ticking clocks in movies can be literal or figurative.

Some filmmakers choose to use a *chyron* (time code on screen) or subtitle to let us see the countdown. This can create an even greater sense of urgency.

In these films, the countdown begins within the first five pages: *The Hangover* (four hours before the wedding and the best man is MIA); *Run Lola Run* (she's got 20 minutes to obtain 100,000 German marks to save her boyfriend's life); *Phone Booth* (an arrogant publicist is held hostage in a phone booth by an extortionist sniper); *Crank* (he's been poisoned and urgently seeks an antidote).

In other movies, the clock starts ticking at the end of act one (around page 25): *Red Eye, 127 Hours,* and *Contagion*.

A ticking clock can traverse over days: two in *Weekend*, three in *Three Days of the Condor*, four in *Michael Clayton*, five in *Titanic*, six in *Apollo 13*, and precisely one week in *Se7en*.

In *Toy Story*, the ticking clock is established when Woody alerts the toys to moving day in the first act, and we know then that Woody and Buzz must get back before the family moves—or face being lost forever.

A story might take place over one or more weeks: *My Week with Marilyn*, in which an eager young film student is held in thrall by Marilyn Monroe for the most memorable week in his life; *28 Days Later*, in which a handful of survivors try to find sanctuary after a mysterious, incurable virus spreads throughout the UK; and the twisted, erotic cult classic *9 1/2 Weeks* about a complex and engrossing, yet impersonal affair that made Mickey Rourke a star.

Movies can also take place over many months: birth in about nine months in *Juno* and death in less than 12 months in *American Beauty*. Or, they might cover a quantified timeframe: the baseball season in *Moneyball*; the upcoming fashion week in *The Devil Wears Prada*; and the election cycle in *The Ides of March*.

Or, perhaps the story spans years or even decades—but with an acute sense of a history, such as in *Milk, The Curious Case of Benjamin Button, Forrest Gump,* and *War Horse*.

In many films, the countdown is palpable, but less tangible.

Lost in Translation captures the profound sense of isolation, connection, and insomnia of two strangers: movie star Bob Harris (Bill Murray) and young newlywed, Charlotte (Scarlett Johansson), over the course of a few days in an upscale Tokyo hotel. As the clock ticks away in *Eternal Sunshine of the Spotless Mind*, Joel Barish's (Jim Carrey) new memories are replacing painful, yet cherished past memories of beloved Clementine (Kate Winslet).

> As time evaporates, push your protagonist closer and closer to the edge. In movies, a watched pot *always* boils.

INTERVIEW: Screenwriter/Director David Koepp

David Koepp Filmography

Best known for:

Premium Rush (also directed) (2012)
Ghost Town (also directed) (2008)
War of the Worlds (2005)
Spider-Man (2002)
Panic Room (2002)
Stir of Echoes (also directed) (1999)
The Lost World: Jurassic Park (1997)
Mission: Impossible (1996)
The Paper (1994)
Carlito's Way (1993)
Jurassic Park (1993)
Death Becomes Her (1992)

NL: Your scripts are known for ticking clocks, urgency, deadlines, and ratcheting up conflict and stakes.

DK: Yes, I do have urgency issues.

NL: How conscious are you of the timeline and chronology at every point in the script? From the outlining stage forward?

DK: It varies depending on the nature of the story. Some stories are highly dependent on time and, in fact, adopt a rigid overall movie structure. I've always enjoyed those "bottle" films. It doesn't have to be just time, but it's the container into which, hopefully, your tasty wine is poured. An example would be *The Paper* which was incredibly rigid—24 hours to be exact. In the beginning of the movie, you see the inner workings of a clock in the title sequence and the clock turns over to 7:00 a.m., then it's 24 hours until the last shot of the movie which is a clock turning over to 7:00 a.m.

NL: I remember that very clearly. It stays with you too because that's also generally when people's newspapers hit their front stoop.

DK: We knew we wanted to do this movie about a tabloid in New York and a producer, Fred Zollo, said, "Why not make it 24 hours?" Which is good for a number of different stories, but particularly good for a newspaper story since that is the cycle. As a result, the movie adopted a morning, noon, and night structure, which is also perfectly suited to first, second, and third acts, so 24 hours works very well. John Kamps and I just finished *Premium Rush*, which is coming out this year. The film follows a time structure of 90 minutes with clocks used as references throughout. The idea behind the time structure was that this messenger has to get a message from Columbia University which is way on the upper west side of town, down to Chinatown which is way on the lower east side of town, and he's got 90 minutes to do it. We use flashbacks throughout, but the 90 minutes is the bottle, which also happens to be the duration of the movie. I heard an interesting essay once on a *High Noon* commentary track that the reason stories, movies, and plays tend to be 90 minutes to 2 hours is because our dreams tend to change every 90 minutes to 2 hours, so it feels like the right cycle for a story.

NL: In *The Trigger Effect*, you're very aware of time because of the power going out, and the longer it lasts, the more urgent the situation becomes.

DK: I purposely set that film over a weekend because it also follows a structure of: Friday, Saturday, and Sunday along with the different feelings associated with those days. Friday's the liberation, a little bit of party; Saturday is your long second act in which the bulk of the activity happens; and Sunday is the feeling of dread and remorse.

NL: In *Panic Room*, you're ratcheting up conflict and stakes exponentially because they're trapped. The situation keeps getting more and more dire because of the basic necessities of being trapped in that panic room. At what point in the process, did it occur to you to make her daughter insulin dependent?

DK: That came in over the course of the writing. I knew I wanted to flip the problem about halfway through the movie. Instead of her being in the room, and not letting anyone in, I made it so there had to be a real good reason to get her out of the room. It was a little bit cheap as a device perhaps, but super effective.

NL: I thought it worked well actually because it also showed how fiercely maternal Jodie Foster's character was. I often use *Panic Room* in my classes because I find that with my students, there's almost never enough conflict or urgency in their scripts and people seem very resistant to add more conflict. I usually tell them to put in more than you are comfortable with and then you can always dial it back. If you're playing it safe or trying to be too subtle, a lot of times it doesn't even register, but when you watch a movie like *Panic Room* the problems just keep getting more and more intensified and her options just keep running out. It may be instinct for you, but can you speak to strategies for ratcheting up conflict in terms of all forms of urgency?

DK: Absolutely. First, I just want to say that *Panic Room* uses place as a bottle. I gave myself the limitation that the whole movie had to take place in this room that's only 17-feet wide, and as the movie was developed and made, the space got wider and we had a scene outside at the beginning and the end, but still it was pretty close to my original strict rule. This idea goes back to Aristotle and the unities of time, place, and character. He was the strictest of all. He said that it should take place over no more than 24 hours. It had to be in the same place, following the same character. That's cool, but nobody can live like Aristotle, it's too hard. But, it's a good point and it does help unify stories to observe those rules. In terms of ratcheting up conflict, stories tend to be boring without it, and not just boring to watch, but boring to write.

If you take, for example, a scene where a guy has to come home and tell his wife that he's been fired. If he comes home and says, "This horrible thing happened at work: this guy told a lie and I got fired. It was awful, and I'm upset about it. I'm going to hire a lawyer." And, she says, "Honey, that's the worst thing I've ever heard, you should absolutely hire a lawyer. This guy who went to school with me is an excellent lawyer." "Great, let's hire him." That dialogue can set up an interesting movie about litigation, but what if we know he's just gotten fired and he comes home and she says, "How was work?" and he says, "Fine." They start talking about something else, and then it comes out that he was fired, but he doesn't want to do anything about it. She gets mad at him, saying, "How could you not want to do anything? What has happened to you is an injustice." He says, "Look, I just want to leave it alone." We don't know why, and now they're fighting about it. It's way more fun for the writer to write that scene. It's way more fun for the actors to play it. And, it's way more fun for the audience to watch it.

NL: And, if he looks outside the window and sees that the pool contractor has just started digging and that they're about to go further into debt . . .

DK: Absolutely. Because it's drama and without it, it's flat. Certainly there can be things that are just observational, but they're not the stories I like to watch or help write.

NL: I think that most of those things you end up cutting out. Sometimes they're helpful just in early drafts because you're trying to find the story and you're trying to figure out who the characters are. What I've learned most from you is that it has to be lean and keep moving, and that the larger tent pole big studio movies you've worked on are like rides. They're just great fun to read. They're like rides with special effects. The pace is consistently moving really, really quickly. For those larger movies, how do you deal with the willing suspension of disbelief because one of the ways urgency can work in a movie like *Premium Rush* or *Panic Room* is it's because you're in a realistic situation, but when you're in a fantastical film like *Spider-Man* or *Jurassic Park*, is it more difficult? *War of the Worlds* feels very realistic, but when there are special effects and supernatural elements, do you worry about how realistic to make it within the tone of the movie?

DK: It's a constant struggle. I mean one of the first times I had to deal with that was on the first *Jurassic Park* which was the first time I'd written stuff with gigantic effects. *Death Becomes Her* had big effects, but it was written with the assumption that it would be a simpler effect. *Jurassic Park* was weird because people were running and screaming from rampaging dinosaurs. Now, you have to create their reality that seems to be on a level of fantasy that's equal to that, but you still want to care about them as characters, so they can't be cartoons. So, what you end up trying to do in those movies is to just jam in as much interesting character stuff as you can in the first 20 minutes because once the Brontosaurus shows up, you're screwed. Because nobody in the world is going to say, "Let's talk about our relationship," when there's dinosaurs running around. They would talk only about the dinosaurs and sometimes that's the right choice. Don't try to do any personal stuff, just leave it aside and have them be human beings who are reacting to the situation around them. Different characters would react in different ways, so you tend to be writing only to their reactions and you're not able to tell or settle a personal story. It's very hard.

Every movie has its own level of fantasy and everybody has to match that. For *Jurassic Park*, the dinosaurs were fantastic elements, but everything else had to be real. It's a very tricky balance. *War of the Worlds* was much easier. The decision from the beginning on that movie was to give it this working class background with a very specific guy in a very specific place. We even shot it in the place I wrote it for, which is very unusual, you usually don't get that. It looked great. It was a friendly place to shoot. It was a survival story that had more in common with *The Trigger Effect* than anything else I'd written because it was about what would happen in our real world. It wasn't on *Fantasy Island* where dinosaurs were running around. Because it was in your neighborhood, we got to be much more realistic and give the characters much more prosaic concerns. It was also just a few years after 9/11, so there were very specific emotional echoes from that incident that came into play.

NL: Both *War of the Worlds* and *Jurassic Park* absolutely terrified me. Honestly, like wanting to hide under my seat. Even though I knew it was fantasy and special effects, I think it's a testament to you that the characters and situation felt so real that I fully believed that these people were in danger and was worried about them. It seems to me that suspense comes from our emotional investment in the characters because the dinosaurs appearing with characters who had less realistic needs and attitudes might have disengaged me. You're extremely good at creating characters that we connect to and care about very early in the movie, very economically, and with spare dialogue, but you get us to connect, it's a real goal. You make what you do look easy because we see it all done and we come along for the ride. So, along with creating characters we connect with and we emotionally invest in, how important is it for you that they're likeable versus flawed?

DK: I don't think likeable is terribly important. I think understandable, recognizable, and relatable is very important. Cruise's character in *War of the Worlds* came off much more likeable than I intended him on the page. I think that he's very good and effective in the movie and I think it's a fine interpretation. But he's not a great guy. He's a pretty bad father, he was strangely competitive with his own kid, and he's inattentive. He has a lot of flaws, but I thought that those made him more interesting. Maybe just because Cruise is inherently likeable on screen, he came off more so. Recognizing actual people we might know or traits from ourselves is what counts.

NL: If they're flawed, it also gives you some place to take them.

DK: Exactly.

NL: So that while they're running and trying to survive, they're also growing up or overcoming someone.

DK: You can't redeem a saint.

NL: I wanted to ask you about the role of the antagonist in terms of time and deadline. I remember reading something that William Goldman wrote years ago that, in order to write a thriller, he needed to plot it from the point of view of the antagonist first. He figured out their agenda, and then worked backwards in terms of who should be ensnared in it. At what point, do you start thinking, who is my main antagonist or what is my antagonistic force?

DK: That's a good point you make. I hadn't thought about it that way, but the antagonist in most movies is usually the one who has a stronger agenda, something they shouldn't be doing. It's rather nefarious, and the protagonist, especially in a thriller, is just fighting for the status quo. He wants to get his life back and keep the antagonist from achieving his goal. In *Premium Rush*, all the deadlines are set by the bad guy. He needs what he needs by a certain time.

In general, even if a movie doesn't have a rigid time structure, it's still incredibly helpful to know early on what needs to happen by when.

For instance, "We've got to have this wrapped up by Wednesday, otherwise you're not going to get the job," or "We have to get to California by such and such time." You can get away with a lot more lackadaisically, if you just give the audience a hint up front, because then everybody can relax, knowing that you are going to have something happen at a certain time. It's going to be a regular story.

NL: Right, it's the agreement you make with the audience.

DK: And, it doesn't have to be based on time or the calendar either. I'm thinking of *Raiders of the Lost Ark*, and what I think is one of the best expositional scenes ever: the scene in the classroom where the army intelligence guys come to see him and say, "What's Hitler after?" and he says, "Oh, the Ark of the Covenant, and here's what you do: first, you get this thing, and you put it in this place and the light shines through and tells you where to dig, then you go there and you dig, and you get the Ark of the Covenant." Then, they ask, "When do we have to get it by?" and Indy says, "Before Hitler does because it's powerful." It's everything you need to know for the rest of the movie. So, the deadline doesn't necessarily have to be Wednesday, the deadline is before Hitler.

NL: You're speaking now to stakes . . .

DK: Right, the "or else" is "or else Hitler will be undefeatable." Which even though we know he wasn't, they still didn't know. Your heroes need to *not* know that everything's going to work out okay. The audience, of course, knows that nine times out of ten things are going to be all right because that's how most stories end.

NL: They just don't know how or at what price.

DK: But, the hero can't know.

NL: Do you feel in general a hero needs to make some sacrifice in the course of the story or be faced with a moral dilemma? Do you think about those things or do they just occur organically?

DK: I think what happens is that it either occurs organically or it doesn't. As you're telling the story, you might think, "Gee, it feels like things are awfully easy for him," so you often give him a difficult choice. He can do this, but then he can't do that or he can do this, but it will be misunderstood by this person he cares about who will then not like him, and they'll have to deal with that. As to whether it specifically has to be a sacrifice? Probably—because otherwise things are just happening too easily for him.

NL: Generally, you see characters or heroes who are flawed in a way that they are a little bit selfish, and usually in the course of the story, they evolve to care. Like in *Jurassic Park*, he had a problem with kids and then he becomes more paternal over time.

DK: He's forced into a situation that he can't handle in that regard.

NL: I often think that almost every movie is a coming-of-age story on a certain level because characters have to mature or evolve in order to move to the next step in their life. Even if they're senior citizens in the story, it seems like there's something they have to get and the movie forces them to examine that.

DK: Most stories are about change just because change is interesting. What's fun about that rule is that when you see it broken, it's memorable. I always think of the end of the *War of the Roses* when they're lying on the ground dying and he reaches out to take her hand and she slaps it away. It's fantastic because you're like, "Oh, I get it, this is not a growth and change story." This is different. This is a morality tale. They should have grown and changed, but they didn't, so now they're dead.

NL: That's what makes it a tragedy because it had the potential to go another way. I define stakes generally as consequences for inaction: if they don't do something, they're going to lose something. I also interviewed Jose Rivera who did *Motorcycle Diaries*, and, of course, it's a very different narrative than a typical hero's journey because it's showing us the origins of how Che Guevara became a revolutionary. However, there's no impetus for them to go on the road trip at the beginning. He said that originally, for example, there was this 25–30-page first act that established why they needed to go, and they ended up cutting it all and deciding that they're just going to go because they wanted to.

DK: That works great in that case because they're young and they feel like it.

NL: They're young, they feel like it, and he's in his final year or semester in medical school before he becomes a doctor. He needs to see a part of the world he's never seen, and that, of course, changes him.

DK: It's an incredibly liberating feeling when you're working on a story, and you find that you're laboring very hard to explain or motivate something, which does not, in fact, really need it.

NL: Do video games, social media, and online videos have an impact on your screenwriting? Do you think about them?

DK: No, I don't because I think that you just can't lead the parade if you have to chase it. I think also the stories you're interested in telling are imprinted on you at a fairly young age. You can try to branch out, try different kinds of stories, try genres you haven't done before which is very good for you, but if you want to change your approach to storytelling, it's tricky and it's also, I think, dangerous because you're trying to imitate something that is natural to someone else—not you.

If your kids decide to go into storytelling, I think these new media forms will affect the way they tell the kinds of stories they're interested in and the way they tell them. But, I don't think you can consciously think about that stuff. I think if it happens to get inside you and change you without your knowledge, fine. I also think that these worries come and go. I remember in the mid-90s, we were all uptight that everything was going to be interactive because interactive CD-ROM's were hot. It was like people just weren't interested in having stories told to them anymore. They wanted choice in the matter, and all movies were going to have choices every ten minutes, so you were going to have to write 18 different story lines. This was a big thing for a year or two, and then everybody got bored with it because people *do* like to have stories told to them and they have for thousands of years. The kinds of stories they're interested in will change with the times, but I think the fundamental nature of watching someone tell their story doesn't change. You want them to tell their story. You don't want to do work. You want to watch their story because if you wanted to make your own story, you would.

NL: The technology is moving so quickly that it's created limitations for the dramatist by giving people more choices for survival and how they communicate.

DK: I think scenes are very interesting when people go talk to each other. It used to be that you could come up with reasons like he's out running, so he would stop by another character's house. Now, he would call him, or he wouldn't even call him, he would text him. Great, so now we all have texting screens in our films. You have to constantly think of ways to get around the cell phone. If you're doing any spy movie—I was just working on the new Jack Ryan movie—you've got to incorporate cell phones. It's like a central part of a field agent's life, how he uses cell phones both to help himself and to mess with other people. The problem is some poor director has to shoot a hand, holding a cell phone, which is just terribly dull. Nobody wants to read screens. It's the movies; you want to see things happen. So, cell phones are a scourge, but it's the way it goes.

NL: Do you think movies and scenes are getting shorter? Do you believe an "inciting incident" needs to happen by page 10 or is that arbitrary? Should you necessarily think about benchmarks and page numbers?

DK: I think, conversely, that movies are getting longer. I'd love to see some numbers on it because it feels to me that if you're going to get somebody out of the house, you've got to make them feel they got their money's worth. I'm a big fan of short movies. I love films that are shorter. *Premium Rush* is only 88 minutes.

NL: I almost always think they should be shorter too.

DK: I've never walked out of a movie theatre and said, "That was good, but it was just too short, if only they'd padded out the middle a little bit." And, of course, there's much talk about how people's levels of apprehension are increasing because things are moving faster. That's true. You don't have to lay stuff out quite the way you had to 20 years ago.

As for inciting incidents—yes, whatever one wants to call them, I do think it's important that incident begins to kick in by page 10—or ideally, long before—so that we have some idea of where the story is going, or at least who seems to be in opposition to whom. The *Chinatown* reference that Syd Field makes is still a great example, but then, the inherent structure of a private eye movie makes that a lot easier. Somebody's gotta show up with a case and lay out the parameters. I only think about benchmarks and page numbers in the sense of making sure things are happening and things are progressing and shit is getting done, in an attempt to avoid a very boring movie.

NL: What are your thoughts about consciously writing to theme as you're writing versus not?

DK: I think your themes are something that are best pointed out to you by someone else later. If you're going in and saying this is a story about man's inhumanity to man, then you're going to be didactic and dull. If you're going in because this story about a bully just speaks to you on some personal level, then you're telling a story about man's inhumanity to man without it being conscious or overt. Sometimes you end up writing without any powerful theme underneath it, but you find that out because your story's not working. Not because you didn't articulate a theme, it's just that your story doesn't feel right yet. One of the first things they try to make you do in meetings is articulate the theme, and I think that's wrong. They should just let you articulate the story and then draw their own themes.

NL: At the same time, it's hard to imagine *Spider-Man* without: "With great power, comes great responsibility." Is that because the source material is embedded in there?

DK: Somebody else had already written that. That was just a good line. I don't think the guy said when he was writing the comic book, "I'm going to write a comic book story, and the theme of it is going to be 'with great power, comes great responsibility.'" I think he wanted to tell a story about this kid and his uncle and his terrible guilt. I'm sure the line just came out as he was writing the comic book. It was a powerful story with elemental building blocks, but I doubt very much that he went in saying this is my theme.

NL: What advice would you have for people who are trying to break into the business now? What should they write?

DK: What they would love to watch. I think the absolutely best thing to do is pretend you are suddenly given the afternoon off of work and you decide to go to the movies—what would you love to see? What would you be very excited is playing?

ASSIGNMENT

Chronologically graph the final 12 hours (or less) of your protagonist's journey at the end of act three—hour by hour. Where does he/she go? Who does he/she see? What does he/she do? Which events are vital to the plot and which are extraneous? Now edit and think elliptically: which events could you weed out to increase dramatic tension? In addition, select an existing movie similar to your screenplay in spirit or structure and compare the final hours or its timeline to your own screenplay-in-progress.

14

WHAT'S THE WORST THING THAT COULD HAPPEN?

Push Your Protagonist to the Edge at the Climax

The climax is the ultimate test. The protagonist's facing his/her ultimate fear, and usually requires a final challenge of the character's growth or change. A deep understanding of the needs, wants, and fears that drive the hero allows for the creation of an "ultimate" test, action or crucial symbolic "graduation" that is the best fit for that particular protagonist, genre, and film. Choose wisely.

I believe that all movies are, on some level, coming-of-age stories—no matter the age of the protagonist. For it is this test that shows us, the audience, if the hero has, in fact, grown. After the climax, there are usually only one or two scenes of resolution, reaffirming that the hero has really changed, and then the film is over. Sometimes the change is substantial. Sometimes the change is almost imperceptible. What matters most is that we care.

Heighten the climax.

The anticlimactic ending is predictable and lacks dramatic heat. A potent climax will be surprising and even explosive. Some touchstones for an effective climax can include making the protagonist: (a) confront the *true* antagonist; (b) overcome character flaws; (c) come-of-age (a rite of passage); (d) deliver the truth; (e) face an ultimate moral dilemma; and (f) emerge as a freer and/or truer self (aka **catharsis**—more on this below).

In *Jerry Maguire*, Jerry (Tom Cruise) is great at friendship, but terrible at intimacy. In the climax, he puts himself completely out there for love. His audience is a bitter group of divorced women. He tells Dorothy (Renée Zellweger) that she completes him and then waits. He is emotionally naked, raw and vulnerable. Will she love him back?

In *127 Hours*, Aron Ralston's (James Franco) lowest point at the end of act two is when he finally gives up hope and resigns himself to death. But then he wills himself to live—intentionally snapping the bone in his arm and cutting off his own limb with a small, dull blade. After he extricates himself, he's still not home free; Aron must hike back to civilization for medical attention and sustenance. The worst thing that could happen at the climax would be for him to have come this far and still not survive. His subsequent rescue is the resolution. The marvel of this unconventional film is how our expectation of his self-amputation is not even his ultimate test.

In *50/50*, Adam (Joseph Gordon-Levitt), our mid-20s protagonist, gets diagnosed with life-threatening cancer, which he fights through chemotherapy and counseling. In the end, he finds a deeper connection with his best friend, Kyle (Seth Rogen), the spark of real love with his mid-20s therapist, Katherine (Anna Kendrick), and a more grown-up relationship with his mother (Anjelica Huston). The "worst thing" that could happen after all that growth is for him to die before he has a chance to really live. The emotional climax is when he says his goodbyes before the potentially deadly surgery, knowing that whether he lives or dies is out of his hands.

In the comedy, *There's Something About Mary*, Ted (Ben Stiller) has dreamed about Mary (Cameron Diaz) for decades since his unfortunate prom night zipper accident in high school. Twenty years later, he goes through hell to reconnect with her, they hit it off, and are beginning to fall in love. The "worst thing" that could happen at this point is that she would find out that he set one or more dangerous "stalkers" loose on her in his quest to find her—and Ted could lose Mary forever.

What's the source of the "catharsis" and how can we make it more deeply specific to our character?

Catharsis, from Aristotle, literally means *cleansing or purging of pity and fear*. In crafting great climaxes, the universal emerges from the particular. In a great story, we strongly identify with the protagonist and his/her quest. We know both their dreams and fears and are strongly rooting for a specific, uplifting outcome for them. When they break through, or fail to, we feel and experience that pure moment of "raw life" with them. In *Good Will Hunting*, Will Hunting (Matt Damon) finally breaks down and cries in his therapist's (Robin Williams) arms. He has let down his emotional walls and is capable of intimacy, love, and happiness. When he drives off west to "see about a girl," we know he's going to be all right. *See Chapter 6 on Character Flaws.*

In *Dead Poets Society*, Todd Anderson (Ethan Hawke) starts the film as the most quiet and reserved student in an elite boarding school. On the first day of class, he is terrified to be noticed, to speak publicly or to stand out. By the film's end, he has been transformed by Mr. Keating (Robin Williams), a daring poetry teacher. In the closing scene and climax, Todd defies the administration, stands on his desk and leads the members of Mr. Keating's class in saying a stirring goodbye to their teacher. This instructor has changed his life forever.

In *A Few Good Men*, Lieutenant Kaffee (Tom Cruise) confronts his fear over never living up to his father's reputation when he risks his career and jail to pursue justice and answers. When Colonel Jessup (Jack Nicholson) confesses on the stand, Kaffee finally gets the truth.

In *Seabiscuit*, we end on a race. However, there is no external antagonist because Seabiscuit has already beaten the great horse, War Admiral, an hour into the film. Instead, the end of the film is an internal confrontation. The undersized Seabiscuit and the overlooked jockey "Red" (Tobey Maguire) have dropped back to dead last in what was considered a "comeback" race for them both. We root for them to at least finish respectably without getting hurt. As they pass horse after horse, we hope that both Red's and Seabiscuit's injured legs will hold. Then we celebrate with them as they cross the finish line first. A big part of the power in this story comes from the fact that they are not just riding for themselves. The filmmakers have created a connection where we see that this group—horse, jockey, owner, and trainer—all stand for Great Depression Era people, who were bowed, but not broken, representing all underdogs across time.

There is often a difference between the emotional (story) climax and the physical (plot) climax of the movie.

In *Juno*, the **emotional climax** occurs when the cynical, too-clever-for-her-own-good Juno (Ellen Page) discovers that Vanessa and Mark Loring (Jennifer Garner and Jason Bateman) are splitting up and not planning to offer her baby the idyllic, two-parent home Juno had hoped for. This is a major rite of passage for Juno—her loss of innocence. Juno rushes out of the Lorings' house, gets into her vehicle, and takes off. The snarky, happy-go-lucky Juno's bottled-up emotions get the best of her. She pulls over to the side of the road and starts bawling, like a baby. Her protective, maternal instincts are kicking in—and the ordinarily insouciant Juno feels lost, vulnerable, and scared. She's a high school girl and can't handle all of this right now. She comes home and reaches out to her meddling stepmom and dad for emotional support and guidance.

On the plot level, the **physical climax** of the film is when her water breaks and she goes into labor. This is the highest level of conflict in the plot, but Juno is less vulnerable here because she's evolved into a more balanced, mature young woman. And even though she decides to go through with placing the newborn baby up for adoption—with the soon-to-be-single mother, Vanessa —Juno is now ready to admit her true feelings for Paulie Bleeker (Michael Cera). She emerges at the end more authentic. It's an unpredictable, bitter-sweet, and emotionally satisfying ending, offering no easy solutions. The gravitas of what begins as a superficial response to her pregnancy is impacted by morality, irony, truth, and consequences.

Climactic Case Studies

1. *UP* (2009) is an animated film produced by Pixar. Like the best animated movies, *Up* is a *family* film appealing not just to kids, but to parents and people of all ages and cultures.

Protagonist

The protagonist of *Up* is Carl (voiced by Ed Asner), a senior citizen and widower. For most of the film, Carl is unable to embrace life because he is holding on to the past.

Fear

Initial: Carl's greatest fear is that he will not get to Paradise Falls to honor his late wife. And that he will die having never been on a great adventure. Final: Carl's final fear is that his blind pursuit of this dream will cause the death of Russell, the young boy who has stowed away on his journey.

Setup

Carl always dreamed of being a great explorer, like his hero Charles Muntz (voiced by Christopher Plummer). As a child, Carl met Ellie. They grew up together, fell in love and married—all the while dreaming of shared adventures, but they were never able to have kids or travel and the decades raced by. Then, she got sick and passed away, leaving Carl alone. To make matters worse (and always make them worse, if you can), his neighborhood and their home is now being taken over by a greedy developer. A judge has sentenced Carl to a retirement home. This is literally his last chance.

Antagonist

Carl's long-vanished childhood hero, Charles Muntz, is the film's antagonist. Muntz was an explorer of great fame who was accused of faking a giant bird skeleton. He vowed to clear his name, and for decades he has been searching the island, determined to capture one of the giant birds, return to society, and restore his reputation. His inability to let go of the past twists him and transforms him from hero to villain. In Muntz and Carl, we have two parallel characters, two old men initially unable and unwilling to let go of their pasts and their regrets.

Showdown

In the climax, Carl and Muntz have a series of fun, action-packed showdowns —from old man swashbuckling sword fights to races across flying dirigibles. Carl saves Russell and the day. Muntz ultimately falls to his death as his unwillingness to let go of the past dooms him.

Catharsis

Carl risks all to save Russell, but loses the house he shared with Ellie in the process. Only, it doesn't matter to him anymore.

Truth

We can't live life while holding on to the past.

2. *SHAKESPEARE IN LOVE* (1998) recreates the central themes of Romeo and Juliet by putting us through the fictional journey of Will Shakespeare as he discovers true love and the inspiration for this timeless story.

Protagonist

Will Shakespeare (Joseph Fiennes) is a playwright of passion and emotion who throws real life risks and concerns to the wind.

Fear

Initial: Will's greatest fear as the story opens is that he will not find his Muse and will be a failure as a playwright.
Final: Will's greatest fear at the end of the film is that he will lose the true love of his life, Viola De Lesseps (Gwyneth Paltrow).

Setup

Will has been commissioned to write a play, to be called *Romeo and Ethyl, the Pirate's Daughter*. However, he lacks a Muse and can't find inspiration until it appears in the form of Viola De Lesseps. Viola is the passionate, play-loving daughter of a newly wealthy family. She loves the theatre and longs to join in, but her family plans to marry her to Lord Wessex (Colin Firth).

Antagonist

Lord Wessex is a penniless, soulless, pompous nobleman of "true blood and royal pedigree." He does not love Viola and knows that she does not love him. He will blithely deny her happiness in the service of his claim to her father's wealth.

Showdown

The big showdown occurs between Will and Wessex in a sword fight at the theatre. Although Wessex is determined to kill him, Will wins the fight (even though his attempt to stab Wessex fails because he is using a prop sword). Will is powerless against his social class and the rules of the world in which he lives.

Catharsis

After many hardships, the renamed and now finished play of *Romeo and Juliet* opens. Viola has married Lord Wessex, but appears at the playhouse and the two star-crossed lovers perform a play unlike any before. They finish to a great silence, then thunderous applause. The Queen herself says that it is the first play to capture the true spirit of real love, but this story must end as all stories do when love is denied—with tears and a long journey.

Will and Viola say their goodbyes in a passionate, tender, funny scene that is heart wrenching and upbeat at the same time. He vows to never write again. She tells him she will be the saddest person on this planet if that vow is carried out. She loves him. He has earned 50 pounds and is a hired player no more. The queen wants a comedy from him for the upcoming twelfth night holiday. He says he could never write one. His hero would be the saddest wretch in all the land. She tells him it's a start. Both have been transformed. Viola will carry Will in her heart forever and Will has found a Muse, forevermore.

Truth

True love is eternal and the best art captures the essence of this emotion.

3. *THE 40 YEAR OLD VIRGIN* (2005) is a comedy that redefines masculinity through the eyes of a man who is afraid to be physically and emotionally intimate with women. He's moved past the threshold of "late bloomer" into ashamed and embarrassed.

Protagonist

The protagonist in this film is Andy (Steve Carrell), a 40-year-old virgin. He has more hobbies than nearly anyone in the world, is closed off emotionally, and is terrified of women or physical contact.

Fear

Initial: As the movie starts, Andy's surface fear is that his co-workers will find out he's a virgin. He has constructed an elaborate façade to appear to be "just one of the guys," but this is keeping him from finding real love, happiness, and friendship.

Final: As the film progresses, Andy's deepest fear is that he will lose Trish (Catherine Keener) because of his virginal blemish.

Setup

Andy works at an electronics store in the back to avoid customers. He cannot even talk to women. He works with a group of mostly male players who love to chase women.

In the inciting incident, his co-workers find out that he's a virgin. This leads to their quest to make him normal and get him laid, so that he can get on with his life. This is our A-story. As the movie unfolds, these attempts at putting a notch on Andy's belt backfire in ever more comical ways. In a parallel B-story, Andy begins to have real feelings for, and an adult relationship with, Trish—a divorced mother his own age. This backdrop sets up the third act and dramatic climax of the film.

Antagonist

This film is a great example of an internal antagonist. Andy fights his own internal fears and insecurities. He also fights society's expectations. His friends want him to have meaningless hook-up sex. His internal moral compass tells him that his first time should be with a person he loves.

Showdown

Andy turns down the opportunity to have sex with the promiscuous Beth (Elizabeth Banks), for whom he has no real feelings. He returns to his apartment to find Trish waiting. She's never been inside his place before and has found all the porn tapes, speed dating cards, and sex books that have been given to him by his work friends. She immediately thinks he's a deviant or pervert, maybe even a murderer. When he tells her he loves her, his worst fear happens—she runs out and drives away. As our hero, Andy must chase her on his only mode of transportation—his bicycle.

Catharsis

In the middle of a busy road, with traffic backed up and in front of a huge audience, he tells her that he loves her and that he's a virgin. It's the only way he can win her back. He admits that he was embarrassed to tell her before. She loves him back.

Truth

True love conquers all.

> Keep the audience at the edge of their seats by pushing your protagonist to the edge of vulnerability. We go to movies to escape from our lives, to be entertained, and to vicariously watch "strangers we care about" (i.e., great characters) face their (and our) greatest fears. The #1 goal for a screenwriter is to provoke an audience into a powerful emotional release (i.e., undergo catharsis).

INTERVIEW: Screenwriter/Director David S. Goyer

David S. Goyer Filmography

Best known for:

Man of Steel (2013)
The Dark Knight Rises (story) (2012)
Ghost Rider: Spirit of Vengeance (2011)
Flash Forward (television series) (2009)
The Unborn (also directed) (2009)
The Dark Knight (story) (2008)
    WGA Award Nominee
Jumper (2008)
Batman Begins (2005)
Blade: Trinity (also directed) (2004)
Blade II (2002)
ZigZag (also directed) (2002)
Blade (1998)
Dark City (1998)
Death Warrant (1990)

NL: My first question is about your creative process. Where do you begin? Do you outline? Do you start with plot or character?

DG: I've been writing professionally for about 24 years now. I'm not even sure how many scripts I've written, probably over 50 at least. I have definitely evolved a style of working over the years. I start first with a blue-sky period where I tend to write anything that comes to mind. I'll start researching, and then on a legal pad or computer, I'll write down everything in no particular order: cool ideas, snippets, or dialogue. After a week or so, I'll sit down and look at what I've got and then start writing an outline, which is normally for myself. I almost never give an outline to a studio.

NL: Do you work off of index cards or some kind of process?

DG: I've done both. I do tend to use index cards, particularly all the times I've worked with Chris Nolan. I find it's a good way of actually forcing you to get your ideas out and re-order things, so I'll tend to write an outline which will be anywhere from 10–20 pages, fairly extensive. The worst part of writing is always actually figuring out the mechanics of how you get from A to B to C. The first 40 percent is always the easiest because it's all setup, and then you get into the middle, and it's a pain. There's the impulse to just start writing without having completely figured everything out, but I never do that now. The couple of times I've done that, I've gotten lost in the middle of the project, so now I don't go to script without an outline. I tend to write chronologically and during my first pass, I try not to put on my editor's cap, I just try to write and get it done. Finally, I put it in a drawer for one to two weeks and then I'll spend a couple weeks rewriting. After all that, I will have my first draft. That's my process.

NL: You write chronologically once you have the outline, but when you're outlining and figuring out the structure, do you ever start with the climax and think this is how far I can push it? This is how far I'm going to push the protagonist to the edge—and then work backwards? In other words, do you outline chronologically?

DG: Most of the time, but every once in a while, I will have an idea for how it will end. I won't reveal what it is, but in *The Dark Knight Rises*, the upcoming Batman film, I had the idea for the end first. In that case, I did the story with Chris Nolan and we ended up writing an expanded outline, a 25–30 page treatment. The ending just came to me, so everything was working toward it, which is sometimes a more gratifying way of working. It just depends. I'm working on a new television show now, and we recently wrote the second episode which was another situation where I knew the ending and wrote toward that.

NL: Do you believe in three-act structure?

DG: Generally, it's nice to have structure and rules to fall back on as a guideline. Although Chris and I have always, probably much to Warner Brothers' horror, beaten out the stories for the Batman films and the upcoming Superman films in four acts. Those films tend to be longer than your average movie because of it: 2 hours and 20–25 minutes long. It is not something I would recommend a neophyte do. I think it's the old adage that it's good to start from the basics and then when you know what you're doing, branch out from there.

NL: Is that act one, act two (a), act two (b), and act 3?

DG: No, it's act one, act two, act three, and act four.

NL: What about theme?

DG: You asked about plot, character and theme. I am of the mind that most writers tend to be more plot-based writers than character-based writers. I think both are perfectly acceptable ways to approach writing. I tend to come up with my plots first, and then create my characters, and then inevitably what happens is—and this is when I feel like I'm on to something—a theme emerges and it's probably something that's been unconscious the whole time. When I look back, it becomes fairly obvious and a bit easier to manipulate as I begin rewriting. The other thing that starts to happen is that the final version of my screenplay ends up diverging from my outline anywhere from 20–30 percent, maybe 40 percent. When that happens sometimes I come up with better ideas, and even more exciting, the character comes to life, and you realize that the character wouldn't do what you had plotted. So, in order to stay true to the character, the plot has to change. It's always thrilling when the character does something that makes sense for them specifically because it feels like they're more alive then.

NL: If you have to force them to do something, it's not growing out of who they are. Thematically, would you say what emerged with *Batman Begins* was the advice from his father, "Why do we fall, Bruce? So we can pick ourselves back up" or is it something else? In *The Dark Knight*, there's the motif of "you make your own luck," but there's also the theme of "You either die a hero, or wait to become a villain." Were there other themes that you intended?

DG: Batman Begins is a story principally about Bruce trying to live up to the long shadow cast by his father. He meets Ra's al Ghul who is a paternal figure. He is looking for another father and ends up feeling betrayed by this character. We very deliberately had in one of the initial climaxes of the movie that Wayne Manor gets burned down. It is literally the house that his father built. The scene was meant to be the moment that he was trying to do all these things to live up to this shadow cast by his father, but then he ends up potentially destroying them all and having to rebuild from those ashes. *Batman Begins* is really about him grappling with trying to live up to his legacy and ultimately, hopefully, finding his own way.

NL: Batman has a code of conduct in that he won't kill, so he ends up saving Ra's al Ghul. At the end, however, he's back in the same position: is he going to save him or not? He chooses not to with that amazing line, "I don't have to kill you, but I won't save you." It's the idea of transcending a limitation. Does that also feed into the theme and main challenge for him?

DG: The third and final film in Chris's trilogy, our trilogy, will come out next summer, *The Dark Knight Rises.* I think it will become pretty apparent by the end of that film what we've been working toward with all of these movies, but principally, it's again about Bruce trying to live up to this ideal that was espoused by his father. He's trying to help Gotham, but in helping Gotham is he just making it worse? Is he really just being selfish in using Gotham as the canvas in which he's trying to deal with his own demons? Does he have to burn the city down to save it?

NL: Was it always planned as a trilogy? Because *Batman Begins* has a very open-ended conclusion.

DG: It wasn't planned as a trilogy in that Chris very much believes in throwing everything you have into each movie and not doing what he calls "sequel bait." With each successive film we started, it was not a foregone conclusion that he would agree to do another one. We always sit down for a while and talk. He needs to decide for himself that it's a film worthy of being made. He was really hesitant before *The Dark Knight Rises,* but when I told him my idea for the end, he started to respond. You could see that spark in his eye that we might be onto something.

NL: You two seem to be completely redefining the superhero genre, and I think that's what people are responding to. There's a real moral complexity to him.

DG: There's a lot in the final one. I'm really interested in seeing people's reactions.

NL: The more typical superhero genre is that the superhero does not change, but changes the world around him. What's different with *The Dark Knight* is that he is changing, he's evolving, and at the end of *The Dark Knight,* he makes a sacrifice. He's willing to sacrifice what people think of him for the common good. Are you completely off the comic books at this point and just reinventing the genre? In what other ways might you be reinventing this type of film?

DG: You mean with the Batman films?

NL: Yes, and with *Man of Steel.*

DG: With the Batman films, and this is taking nothing away from the source material which is great, I do feel that we legitimately have some real ownership over those movies in terms of where we took the story and the complexity. Even if you were into the first movie, we were charting a significant amount of new territory, and certainly by the time we got to *The Dark Knight,* we included The Joker to be sure, but the rest of the plot was not any plot that had been in any of the comic books. Although there are some tangential elements in the final film, the plot does not exist in any real story arc from the comic books.

NL: Do you think the evolution of the superhero genre, and the Batman and possibly Superman characters, is because the audiences are becoming more sophisticated? Is it also the influence of Xbox and other games because that's such a big part of the audience now?

DG: I think it's both. Part of what happened is that I think it took a long time for the movie depiction of comic book characters to catch up to the moral complexities that were in the comic books because when *Batman Begins* had come out, the moviegoing audience had never seen a complex Batman movie before. Their conception of Batman was the Tim Burton Batman, which was very cool, but still cartoonish with a lot of garish colors and things like that, or the 1960s TV show. Whereas, dating from the 1980s, the comic book depiction of Batman had been markedly more sophisticated than the film depiction was. So, I think with *Batman Begins*, we brought the film depiction of Batman up to speed with how he had been portrayed in the comic books. For the moviegoing audience that was a real revelation and subsequently *Batman Begins* influenced most of the comic book movies that came after it, and a lot of movies that weren't comic book films. I think the *Casino Royale* reboot owes a lot to *Batman Begins* as does the *Star Trek* reboot. A lot of film reviewers have agreed. It sounds simple, but the biggest thing we did was to treat the Batman mythology as if it was "real" and not a comic book. We always said on this movie that we were never going to do anything in this movie just because it was a comic book, and to a certain extent we've applied that same methodology to Superman in the *Man of Steel*.

NL: Are you reinventing the mythology? Like the *Seven Years in Tibet* kind of mythology for Batman, was that invented?

DG: To an extent. Some people have said Superman is not a dark character, so why are they making Superman dark? We're not making Superman dark; we're just making it more real. It would be ridiculous to apply the same darkness and grimness that the Batman stories have. I agree it wouldn't fit.

NL: The mythology seems to be the touchstone of the new Superman/superhero genre, but also in terms of fueling the climax to push it so much further. It seems to me that in more standard superhero movies, it would basically be the hero versus the one main villain who would get pushed to triumph over that villain and then move on to a new villain in the next movie.

DG: One of the big differences in the way we chose to approach these films, as opposed to the original films, is that when those people sat down to write, they thought, "what villain will we use?" We've always resisted that. We think about the story we want to tell for the hero first, and then ask, "who would be the thorniest adversary or adversaries to use in order to tell that story?" We look at the rogues' gallery of those characters and say this is the one that makes the most sense if the hero has this problem. That's how we arrived at Ra's al Ghul because we knew we wanted to tell a story about Bruce who is trying to live up to his father's legacy, and Ra's al Ghul made the most sense in terms of being a villain that could be a paternal mirror to his father. Everyone at first was like, "you're not going to use The Joker?" No, we picked a villain who had not been used in the movies before and who was the only villain with the qualities of a father figure. It was a very holistic way of approaching the villain. Most people don't think of themselves as villains; most people are the heroes in their own story. So, we've tried very hard with our villains to articulate their points of view and to give their points of view validity.

NL: And, a lot of complexity. They're as complex as your protagonists if not more.

DG: Yes, a lot of the things that The Joker, even though he's kind of crazy, and Ra's al Ghul say are right. If you take them in the abstract, you can completely understand their point of view.

NL: Let's talk about set pieces for a minute because when you think about the climax in any action movie, you have these huge visually, mind-blowing action sequences, and I would imagine there's pressure to keep topping yourself, so that by the climax, that sequence has to be even more spectacular in some ways than the ones you start with because I feel like your fanbase is waiting for the next one to be bigger, cooler, and louder. How do you come up with all these gadgets and weapons and action sequences we haven't seen before? How do you keep expanding and building on them or is that even a consideration?

DG: Yes, it's a consideration. Action sequences are really hard to do and really hard to write. We've all seen a lot of movies where there's just wall-to-wall action and your eyes glaze over because you either don't understand the stakes or you're not really invested in what's happening with the character. An action sequence is only as good as your emotional investment in the character.

NL: I say that all the time.

DG: It's true. I was just involved in filming a fairly large one for *Superman*, which evolved over the course of many, many drafts, where there was absolutely something emotional at stake for Superman. One of the things I love to do when I'm plotting out a story is we'll be in the middle of an action sequence, particularly near the end of the second act where traditionally things are always the darkest before the dawn, and I'll say . . .

NL: In *The Dark Knight*, he says, "I wanted to save Gotham. I failed."

DG: Right. So what I love to do, and I say this all the time even when I'm working with other writers and working on TV shows, is say, "Okay, that's cool, but on top of that,

*W*hat's the worst possible thing that could happen to our hero right now? Just the worst thing."

And, it's fine sometimes as an exercise to say, "His girlfriend dies." "Oh, but it's a superhero movie, you can't kill his girlfriend." Well, that's how Rachel ended up dying in *The Dark Knight* which a lot of people were shocked that we did. I think it's the first comic book movie where the woman in peril actually dies. It doesn't happen very often. So, I always like to say what's the worst possible thing that can happen and then if you can figure out a way to make it happen, that's fantastic. The other thing I like to say, and I picked this up from someone, is that it's always bad if you have a coincidence that works in favor of your hero, but it's fine if you have a coincidence that works in favor of the villain because then it becomes yet another obstacle. At the end of the day, the more obstacles you can throw in a hero's path the better, and the more of a hero that he or she will be if they can overcome those obstacles. Although sometimes you come up with an obstacle that you can't write your way out of and occasionally you have to abandon it.

NL: Right, but it's always exciting as a writer if you write yourself into a corner and then you solve it because the audience can never get ahead of you.

DG: Inevitably, I'll be plotting something and I'll have written myself into a corner, and I'll struggle with it and struggle with it, and then I'll jump ahead and then it will come to me. I would say nine times out of ten that I'll figure something out.

NL: One of the things I tell students is the climax is the truth. It's almost like you're playing poker and you're holding back one card, so you have something to reveal. Is that something that you're consciously aware of when you're plotting? As Walter Mosley says, "Plot is revelation." Does central mystery figure into your creative process at all?

DG: As you're plotting, it's great if you can come up with reveals and twists. After I'm done with my first draft, I then go backwards and say, "Okay, I've told this in a linear fashion in terms of letting the protagonist in on various things, but where can I justifiably restrict that information without making it seem contrived?" Sometimes it's cool to let the audience know about it, but not let the protagonist know about it, which is another fun way of plotting. If you can justifiably withhold information, you should absolutely do it. Having said that, there's no excuse for being in a situation where the character absolutely would tell the protagonist something, but they don't. If the character's about to tell the protagonist something, but then the house blows up, that's fair game. But, there's a lot of lazy plotting where I pull my hair out and say, "Why didn't they just say what was going on there? Any normal person would."

NL: Right, it feels like you're being manipulative with the audience instead of just letting it be organic to the story.

DG: I will say again with regards to character that it is the best feeling in the world when the character does something that doesn't logically make sense. Recently on television, we've seen Tony Soprano do things that were self-destructive. In *Breaking Bad*, Walter White's allegiance to his former student is completely self-destructive. However, you absolutely understand why these characters are doing it because of their backstory. It's really exciting for me, and a lot of audience members, when they see a character doing something like that. In the real world, people do things that make no sense objectively or things that are self-destructive all the time because we're primarily inspired by these internal motivations and not really by logic. That's really the human condition. When that happens, that's a really interesting way to have the plot pivot in an unexpected way. You can have this perfectly plotted beautiful story and everything can pivot on a dime, but if suddenly one of the characters decides to do something for an emotional reason as opposed to a logical reason, that's the best way to have climax happen. I think that's happened in a lot of the best movies, and hopefully people will see that in the final Batman film.

NL: Do you think it would be fair to say there's an emotional climax and then there's the plot climax?

DG: Sure, sometimes you can make them work hand-in-hand, but they don't always have to. There are many movies where they don't. That happened in *The Dark Knight* where he defeats The Joker, but the emotional climax has to do with how he deals with Two-Face at the end of the movie. The decision to brand himself an outlaw is based on an emotional decision that he, Bruce, thinks it's better for the city that they believe Harvey Dent to have been a good man than for him to believe that he, Batman, is a bad man which is absolutely an emotional climax. He saved Gordon's son, he stopped The Joker, and he didn't have to do that final act at the end.

NL: Most superheroes, and Batman and Superman are certainly part of this, have an Achilles' heel. They have a very well-known weakness that the villain exploits. Would you say at the climax that they're going to have to overcome that weakness and is that also one of the conventions of the genre?

DG: I think that it's definitely a convention of the genre—an overused convention of the genre—that a character has an Achilles' heel that will appear at a crucial juncture of the movie—like Indiana Jones with his fear of snakes. If you're wearing your character's Achilles' heel on his sleeve, then I think you're doing a bad job of writing it. I think it's much better if you can look back at it thematically, and then say, "Oh, yeah, he was pushed into that place over the course of this half an hour as opposed to it being forced on him."

ASSIGNMENT

Break down your own screenplay concept into your protagonist's:

a. initial fear
b. void in ordinary world

c. tension with antagonistic person or force
d. showdown with antagonist
e. cathartic moment
f. revelation of some kind of truth in the final payoff.

15

WHERE ARE WE GOING WITH ALL THIS?

Pay Off the Setups

Screenplays are all about setups and payoffs. What's obscured in the setup will now come to light in the payoff. This will also include resolving the central mystery (*see Chapter 17*), providing the punch line to the running gag, and capping off the leitmotif in an ironic, meaningful, resonant way. Many of these larger plot payoffs will occur at the climax. But there are also smaller, yet significant payoffs that accumulate along the way. For a brilliant examination of this, check out the Academy Award-winning film *Slumdog Millionaire*, in which the entirety of the protagonist's life provides the answers to the multi-million-rupee question on India's version of *Who Wants to Be a Millionaire?* The kid is arrested on suspicion of cheating because, after all, how could a teenaged orphan from the slums of Mumbai know so much? As we witness his police testimony, his life story unfolds through flashback—and every detail of every sequence pays off on the game show.

The Usual Suspects, Fight Club, Shutter Island, and *Extremely Loud & Incredibly Close,* deliver similar *cumulative* payoffs. Nothing is random. Each subtle detail in setup correlates to the eventual big payoff at the climax. This is a kind of narrative and cinematic sleight of hand that works on us almost subliminally. In M. Night Shyamalan's *The Sixth Sense,* Cole Sear (Haley Joel Osment) sees dead people, but both Dr. Malcolm Crowe (Bruce Willis) and the audience don't comprehend the full context until the end.

Foreshadowing is another example of setup and payoff.

Foreshadowing is the setup of events and scenes so that the audience is prepared to some degree for what occurs later in the story (the payoff). This can be part of the general atmosphere, or it can be a specific line of dialogue or object that gives a clue or hint as to a later development of the plot.

In screenplays, there's virtually no room for extraneous expository elements. Everything counts.

In an early scene in *The Kids Are All Right*, lesbian moms, Nic (Annette Bening) and Jules (Julianne Moore) are in their master bathroom trying to figure out how to handle the news that their kids have tracked down and met their sperm donor father, Paul (Mark Ruffalo). As they brush their teeth and get ready for bed, the moms discuss their discomfort with the situation, and how they would have preferred that Paul's identity had remained anonymous. As Jules exits the bathroom, *Nic finds a clump of Jules' red hair in the drain of the sink* and admonishes her for being so sloppy: "The plumber was just here. Ew . . . gross." End of scene. This seemingly innocuous line later pays off in a big way. As Nic bristles over Paul's infringement into *her* family, Jules continually seems to take Paul's side . . . to the point where Nic starts to sense a certain connection between Jules and Paul. Nic tries to shrug off her jealous concerns, but when moms and kids all gather at Paul's place for a family dinner, Nic inadvertently discovers *strands of Jules' red hair in Paul's bedroom and bathroom*. The affair between Jules and Paul comes to light; the clump of hair in the drain erupts into a full-blown scandal, and the future of Nic and Jules' relationship is gravely threatened.

Another example of foreshadowing occurs in *Little Miss Sunshine*. Grandpa Edwin (Alan Arkin) coaches his granddaughter, Olive (Abigail Breslin) for the talent portion of the upcoming beauty pageant. But their rehearsals are all off-screen, and we're not privy to the choreography until the climactic scene. In between, we're teased with Olive practicing dance moves—including a feral animal's growl—but we have no idea what she and Grandpa are planning. We do know that Grandpa Erwin is a curmudgeonly heroin addict who got kicked out of his retirement home; we know he's got a filthy mouth, likes "really nasty" porn, and offers lewd sex advice to his teenaged grandson. We know he's not exactly an appropriate role model for this innocent little girl, but Olive seems to be the one person the misanthropic Grandpa Edwin truly cherishes, so we trust he has only good intentions when he tells Olive, "You're gonna blow 'em out of the water. I guarantee it." Upon the harried family's late arrival at the pageant (sans the deceased Grandpa Edwin), Olive is disqualified. Olive's father, Richard (Greg Kinnear), begs and pleads with the unsympathetic contest organizer to let his daughter per-form. At this point, we are so preoccupied with whether or not Olive will be allowed into the competition that we're distracted from predicting the *content* of her dance routine. When the mean contest organizer finally relents and Olive comes out on stage, she dedicates her performance to her Grandpa, and proceeds to perform a raunchy stripper routine, shocking her family and outraging the prissy judges. It's a hilarious, provocative payoff, surprising, and completely organic to everything that led up to it.

In *Fight Club*, there is a quick, subtle hint early on that Tyler Durden (Brad Pitt) isn't real. When the Narrator's (Edward Norton) condo blows up, he calls Tyler from a payphone, with no answer. Then, a few seconds later, the phone rings. As the Narrator goes to answer it, the camera zooms in on some text on the payphone that reads, "No incoming calls accepted." In other words—Tyler could not have called him back because this phone cannot ring. It should be noted, however, that there is a difference between setup-payoff and a final plot twist. The ends of both *Fight Club* and *The Sixth Sense* turn the story in a different direction, whereas a payoff doesn't have to carry that kind of weight.

In the paranoia thriller *Rosemary's Baby*, Rosemary (Mia Farrow) is given an amulet necklace by her nosy neighbor Minnie (Ruth Gordon) filled with a mysterious, strange-smelling herb ("tanas root") and told that it's for her good luck. But it's all downhill for Rosemary once she succumbs to the scent. This is subtle foreshadowing—eventually unscrambled when Rosemary spills out Scrabble tiles and realizes that TANAS is an anagram for SATAN. We're treated to a similar word scramble in *The Shining* when we realize that the "redrum" the boy keeps muttering in the hotel hallways is actually "murder" spelled backwards.

We are also surprised by the payoff in *The Shawshank Redemption* when Andy Dufresne (Tim Robbins) manages to escape through the tunnel in his prison cell—concealed by a poster of Raquel Welch. Even with the emphasis on *The Count of Monte Cristo* in the prison library scenes, we didn't realize he'd been planning his escape all along. The best payoffs are the ones we should have seen coming—but didn't. We saw a Rita Hayworth poster arrive earlier in the film (which might have tipped us off). Ultimately, Andy faked us out too.

In *Up in the Air*, when Ryan Bingham (George Clooney) finally reaches his once-coveted Million Mile frequent flyer status he seems to be just as surprised as we are. His obsession with travel bonuses had been set up so emphatically in act one. But, by the end of the movie, after he's been on such an emotional rollercoaster, he finds that when he gets the ultimate travel reward, it's virtually meaningless. Which brings us to . . .

The MacGuffin.

"MacGuffin" is a term coined by Alfred Hitchcock to refer to an object, event, or piece of knowledge that both the good guys and the bad guys consider to be extremely important, thus serving to set and keep the plot in motion. But the twist is that a true MacGuffin (as Hitchcock defined it) turns out to be essentially worthless: the black bird in *The Maltese Falcon*; the engine plans in *The 39 Steps*; the mysterious contents of the briefcase in *Pulp Fiction*; the lock to the mysterious key that young Oskar finds in his late father's closet in *Extremely Loud & Incredibly Close*. Over time, MacGuffin has become movie plotting shorthand for any object of desire—which may or may not turn out to be valuable: the diamond in *Blood Diamond*; the microcassette in *Enemy of the State*; the briefcase in *No Country for Old Men*, the gold bricks in *The Italian Job*. In the looser interpretation of MacGuffin, sometimes the valued object is paid off and revelatory, and sometimes (as in *Pulp Fiction*) the actual value and contents of the briefcase remain a mystery.

The best setups and payoffs require that the writer track both plot and character progress.

There are two primary types of tracking: logistical and emotional.

Logistical tracking is plot continuity to ensure that events set up in dialogue or as signposts are not haphazardly forgotten or illogical; these are known as plot holes. Show, don't tell, how your main characters attain all-important clues and information. Avoid coincidental, easy solutions to problems that are author-convenient. All payoffs must be authentically and dramatically earned. Logistical tracking also includes being consistent with the rules of a sci-fi or supernatural world (the simpler, the better).

Emotional tracking is making sure that your characters' psychological and emotional lives are consistent throughout the story; this does *not* necessarily mean that their emotions are neat and controlled. But it *does* mean that you, as the author, need to be meticulously mindful of their state of mind from scene to scene. Aristotle rightly proclaimed that characters are defined by their actions; as screenwriters, we must understand not only how our characters *feel* at every plot point, but also find visual ways to express their feelings via their actions and the nuanced subtext of dialogue.

There are the logistics of the plot (external events) and the emotions of the story (internal journey). As plot and story intersect in each and every scene, place an emphasis on the cause and effect, *setup and payoff*, of: truth and consequences; authenticity and posturing; acceptance and judgment; forgiveness and grudges; atonement and punishment; healing and wounds. Every life is sacred and has value. And so, even in a horror movie: make the body count—*count*. Logistical and emotional tracking will reveal the trouble spots of sloppy plotting and missed opportunities for character development.

**INTERVIEW: Screenwriter/Executive Producer
Laeta Kalogridis**

Laeta Kalogridis Filmography

Best known for:

Altered Carbon (2014)
Battle Angel (TBA)
Shutter Island (also executive producer) (2010)
Avatar (executive producer) (2009)
Pathfinder (2007)
Alexander (2004)
Night Watch (2004)

NL: What sort of challenges did you face in doing the adaptation of *Shutter Island* [the novel by Dennis Lehane]? I would imagine that the biggest challenge is what can you leave in and what can you take out because the book is always more substantive. You have to make decisions from the get-go.

LK: I would say they probably fall into three categories. The first one is the obvious one with a book this dense. It's what you keep in and what you leave out. And, that's presupposing you're dealing with an adaptation where you want to keep the plot, characters, and themes substantively intact. Some adaptations are much looser than that. It depends on the source material. In this particular case, I felt that the book was already extremely cinematic and that it had a profoundly filmic structure. I didn't feel like I needed to rework things as much as I needed to pare things away. In that respect, I feel that it was similar to *Silence of the Lambs* which as a novel, structurally, is very, very similar to the movie. The novel is very dense—*Shutter Island* is a very dense story—a lot of characters, a lot of things happened. So, the first item was what to keep and what to leave out, but primarily what to leave out because, otherwise, it would have been a 10-hour movie.

The second challenge was the interior quality of the main character. Teddy thinks constantly—one of the great advantages of a novel is you can be literally in the character's head with a constant, running voiceover. The novel is written from Teddy's point of view, so everything is experienced through his perspective. Essentially, you are experiencing it in first person even though it's not written that way. Consequently, one of the big challenges is translating what is more or less a massive interior dialogue into something that the audience can partake in without having a continuous voiceover. The challenge was finding a way to collapse down or rework certain story elements, so that I could stay true to the themes of the book. I really, really loved the book, but I think one of the dangers of adaptation is that you can fall in love with the source text and then try to very faithfully reproduce it and end up losing the spirit of the text entirely.

I would say the third challenge for me was trying to find a way to maintain what I felt was the emotional core of the book which has to do with what we believe is a descent into insanity, but is actually an ascent into sanity. The book makes you think that you're watching someone losing his mind when actually what you are watching is someone regaining his mind. The little girl at Dachau, for example, is a creation that's not in the book because I needed a way to tie together the disparate elements of his experience at the liberation at Krakow along with his relationship with his daughter, Rachel. I needed a signifier that would explain why those two things were linked in his mind. In the book, there's an emotional/theoretical assumption that what happened to him when he was part of the liberation of Dachau was that he was fundamentally damaged, and it had an effect on how he reacted to his wife's illness. You get the sense of that in the book through a great many flashbacks of Dolores that become increasingly more and more disturbing as the story goes forward which I chose not to do. A little girl does appear in one dream in the book when she calls him a bad sailor. I liked the idea of having a girl who appears to be one thing, which is a victim of the camp, but is actually another thing, a victim of Dolores, who went as far as she did because he was unable to stop her due to his experiences in the camp. I'm oversimplifying, but his post-traumatic stress disorder (PTSD) affects both the choices that he makes in his marriage and as a father. Those choices turn out to be horrifically wrong. So, in order to connect those things together, I had to create a character who didn't exist in the book and then I had to give her a through line in the dream sequences, so that she would then pay off at the end.

There were a couple of other choices like that; probably the most significant one would be the ending. The ending of the book is different in that Teddy does actually reset, he goes back to being Andrew Laeddis from being Teddy. He literally relapses, and you see at the end that they are going to lobotomize him. When I was adapting the book, my feeling was that although it was a phenomenal ending for the novel, I wanted to have gone on a journey for a larger reason. I wanted it to be about the real expiation of his guilt. His active choice to be lobotomized, or as Marty [director Martin Scorsese] called it during rehearsal "a suicided soul," was very important to me, and a departure from the book altogether.

NL: Your decision also became the overriding theme in that the choice at the end becomes knowing you can live and be crazy or die and regain your sanity.

LK: I would qualify it a little bit more. He's essentially saying, "I am sane now and I can't go back to being insane. If I stay alive, I am the man who allowed his children to die. Whereas if I am lobotomized as Teddy, then I die as this U.S. Marshall who is here trying to do the right thing." It's a more honorable place to be and is an expiation for the guilt that he very reasonably feels for what he did and didn't do.

In this case, I knew what I wanted to re-create was the experience I had when reading the novel, but the question was, using these characters and this structure, how can I re-create that experience because the enemy of that re-creation is a slavish devotion to the novel. When you just try to transcribe what's in the book, you'll lose it. You'll lose the magic of what you felt because the experience of being an audience member versus the experience of being a reader—they are completely different.

I tend to do a more traditional break with an act one, an act two (a), act two (b), and an act three. I look at the novel and see where the places are that fit narratively into what I consider to be a more traditional cinematic structure. Again, the book was already cinematic. It had a five-act structure. There was just more in it than it was possible to translate. I don't normally have a set way of doing it. Sometimes I'll do cards within that structure, but I'll always start from what happens at the beginning of the first act, what happens at the bottom of the first act, what happens at the top of the second act, what happens in the middle of the second act which is your transition from two (a) to two (b), what happens at the bottom of the second act which is a very, very important moment, and then what's at both the top of act three and the end of act three. I look at the skeleton of the story and then I will start looking at how to start draping the muscles and the ligaments, and the other connective tissue onto that skeleton.

NL: How much did Scorsese's vision influence the project? He is such a virtuoso storyteller. One of the things I love about the movie is when they first arrive on the island. The symphonic score, how the camera pulls back and makes everything have such an ominous feeling, and the grandeur of it really makes it such a cinematic experience.

LK: Those are things that aren't in a script that can never be in a script which is why the version of the movie that would have been made by any other director would have looked radically different, felt radically different, been radically different even if you had not changed a word, even if the script had stayed exactly the same. "Did his vision guide the writing of the script?" No, but his vision guided the *movie*. The script is a departure point as far as I'm concerned. It's a blueprint for a house, but it is not anywhere near a house. And, if you've ever built a house, a blueprint is a lovely thing to have, but you can't live in it.

NL: Shutter Island is all built around what happened in the past and how it impacts and pays off in the present. When you approach projects, is central mystery something that you think is essential to every screenplay or is it situational?

LK: In terms of the idea of a central mystery, I feel like there is always a series of questions that you are trying to ask and they may be more overt about plot or they may be more covert about character, but I do think that is the case with every great story. There are several questions in it, but at a micro level within scenes and at a macro level within the whole thing. There's usually some kind of larger question that you're trying to answer. Even if it is as simple a question as "what will this person do?" because that can be a mystery too.

NL: As a screenwriter and a storyteller, what are the major things you learned from working with Scorsese, James Cameron, Oliver Stone, and Timur Bekmambetov?

LK: I tend to gravitate toward directors who have a fierceness and singularity to their vision, a certain uncompromising quality to what they do. All of the directors I've worked with are also their own best editors. From a writing perspective, I do tend to gravitate toward writing directors. Certainly, Marty writes dialogue all the time and he's an incredibly gifted writer. Jim is obviously Jim, Oliver is Oliver. I find that people who write and direct and edit realize that the process is the same in its own way. Jim always says, "You make a movie three times," you write it, you direct it, you edit it, and each time, you're making the film again, and each process is in its own way a writing process. It's hard to encapsulate what I've learned, but I certainly feel I have been very, very, lucky to watch the process of people taking something from script form and making it into a fully realized film without losing track of what it is they set out to do. One thing that I see happen a lot in our business now is that people start making one movie and then somewhere midstream, because of all the myriad, insane pressures, they start to make another movie, oftentimes one they're not necessarily happy with.

NL: I think that's very common. It's generally why there's not a lot of great movies because studios are worried about how to market films and who they're going to offend. Since some of these things are not necessarily artistic decisions, but business decisions, I can see where having a fierce general at the helm can be protective.

LK: No amount of second guessing for "marketability" can ever match the way in which a great filmmaker can make something that people don't anticipate and therefore want to see. The problem with the idea of making everything non-offensive and marketable is that the blander you create things, the less interesting they are to the audience. The idea of the four-quadrant movie, while it seems very sound as a concept, doesn't work. There is a reason that you can't replace artists with computer programs. We can't be replaced with a computer program that plugs in ideas in a certain way. Whenever you start trying to apply those certain formulas, you get a product that people don't want to see which to my mind defeats the purpose. If you can market it really well, but nobody wants to go because the product itself isn't good, then I would say it's time to revisit the idea that everything needs to be as inoffensive as possible.

NL: Where do you stand on the subject of a unifying theme as umbrella to setups and payoffs?

LK: First off, I think there's a difference, of which I'm sure no one would disagree, between theme and polemics. It's possible to be in service of the theme without having it override everything to the point where you have characters behaving in a way that feels unreal and therefore off-putting. I would say, honestly, that I don't have a strong opinion. I write with consideration to theme. The themes that were already in *Shutter Island* about personal responsibility and guilt, both societal and individual, were palpable to me. I was interested in seeing them be made into a movie. I tend to start with character and then theme. I would never create a character in service to the theme because then the character is not going to be human— they are going to be polemical. People don't live that way.

> *Characters, real characters, are surprising, and I think that's the reason I create the characters first. I want some time for them to do things that I am surprised by because that is the way life is.*

You're surprised by what people do around you. I wouldn't say don't think about theme, but I wouldn't say constantly think about it either. I do think people confuse theme with polemic, and I do think polemic, in my mind anyways, is the enemy of good storytelling because it's so inflexible.

NL: I agree with that. When I talked to Jose Rivera about *Motorcycle Diaries*, he said that he doesn't think about theme, but he does think about point of view. He needs to know each character's point of view which could be political, moral, immoral, or amoral. Last question, what makes a satisfying ending? How important is it for you to pay things off?

LK: I would say that satisfying endings are a necessary part of drama. From the time Aristotle wrote *Ars Poetica*, there has been a lot of discussion about what qualifies as a satisfying ending. In a comedy, usually it's a marriage or a birth. In a tragedy, it's some sort of cathartic death. The question for me is, "What is the ending specific to the narrative you are telling that makes it satisfying for the story?" The story is its own entity. I've been working on a big, thriller horror piece, and we've been discussing the ending of *Poltergeist* which was atypical in that most horror movies, almost all horror movies, have an ending that undercuts the triumph that you think you've just seen. If you think about *Nightmare on Elm Street*, when you think everybody is okay, and then they all essentially die.

That's the very definition of a satisfying ending in a horror movie. If you take a look at something like *Poltergeist*, it's a horror movie, but it doesn't have that kind of ending, so it becomes a horror/adventure film. The ending of *Poltergeist* is unbelievably satisfying, so each movie makes its own rules.

It's one of the reasons why when you try and impose some kind of widget-making/marketing process, it just never works well and it doesn't work consistently. I think in the case of *Shutter Island*, that particular story had a different ending in the book than it had in the movie, and I would say they're both satisfying even though they are radically different. They just say different things about the character and about the journey you've been on with him. So, how important is the ending? It's as important as any other part. If not more so. But, is there a right ending? I don't know if I would say that.

NL: The big challenge for screenwriters and all filmmakers is this predictable versus inevitable concept because I find that if the ending is too predictable, it usually feels unsatisfying because the audience gets ahead of you.

LK: An ending is the contract that you've made with the audience that they expect you to give them something, so they're waiting for that. Likewise, if the ending is something different or unearned, they may get very upset.

NL: It's almost like they want you to give it to them, but not in the way they think. With *Shutter Island*, your ending was surprising for me because you created a moral dilemma and two choices which were both positive and negative in their own ways.

LK: Thank you, thank you. I hope so. I felt given the kind of story we were telling that it was the sort of catharsis, or emotional release, I wanted to see as an audience member. And catharsis, whether it's laughter, tears, or fear, is the ultimate payoff.

ASSIGNMENT

Isolate and *track* each main character's journey (or arc) from start to finish. Watch *Shutter Island* and identify all the specific clues that lead to the inevitable conclusion.

16

HOW DID WE END UP HERE?

Crafting the Inevitable Conclusion

To entice a buyer, you need a great opening sequence. To close the deal, you need a killer ending. *Don't Tell Mom the Babysitter's Dead* (co-written by yours truly and my former writing partner, Tara Ison) began as a spec screenplay that—as luck would have it—we sold to 20th Century Fox. It was our "big break" into the biz, not only because it snagged us an agent and big bucks, but also because *it got made* (by HBO and Warner Bros.—but that's another long story . . .). We had a blast writing it, but I'm under no illusions that it's a brilliant screenplay. At best, it was a dark comedy with some edgy macabre scenes and a few memorable one-liners and set pieces. A popcorn flick for teenagers that's somehow *gained* in popularity since its release and (many of my students tell me) has attained "cult status," but I have no idea if that's true. At this writing, Dreamworks is developing a remake. Not too shabby for a little movie we dreamt up in my apartment. We outlined it extensively before we started writing. And the one thing that never changed—from inception to finished movie—is the *ending*. We'd outlined using scene cards, and the last card was always:

MOM

```
One more thing, where's the babysitter?
```

Our plotting strategy was to kill off the old sitter by page 10 (our "inciting incident") and then have so much chaos swirling all around our protagonist, Sue Ellen "Swell" Crandell (Christina Applegate), that the audience would forget the dead babysitter. What was always funny to me was that Swell had also forgotten about her, so we had that deer-in-the-headlights moment—and then an abrupt CUT TO BLACK. To this day, I still believe that we sold the script because of that final payoff. The movie was a semi-clever, kind of fun ride. But that ending was our trump card because it was inevitable but surprising.

A satisfying ending feels *inevitable* without being *predictable;* there's a big difference. A thoroughly predictable ending is a disappointment because it lacks surprise—and surprise is the lifeblood of your screenplay. Even if the audience can predict the ultimate outcome, be sure to throw in some interference so the audience can't predict *how* you'll get there. Be forewarned: This chapter contains many **spoilers** and endings are dissected and revealed. A great ending is sacred to an audience.

Consider the following as you map out your own surprising yet inevitable conclusion:

How and when you dole out information is your power over the audience.

Determine the final revelation of your story. I like to use a poker metaphor. Your power in a poker game is that only *you* know which cards you have in your hand. The same holds true for a storyteller. You get to choose which cards to reveal to the audience and which cards to hold back. The screenwriter that effectively controls the payoffs about plot and character owns the game. What is your final trump card?

There is no need to tie up every loose end of the plot into a neat little bow.

A *suggestion* of where the main character(s) is/are heading is almost always better than telling us everything. One of my favorite movie endings is from *Sideways* when Miles (Paul Giamatti) walks up the stairs to Maya's (Virginia Madsen) apartment and knocks on the door. We don't need to see her open it; what matters most is the courage it took for Miles to show up.

A satisfying ending must be earned by your protagonist, and emerge from deep within his/her psyche.

Avoid *deus ex machina* (from the classical Greek: "God from the machine") in which the gods were literally suspended above the stage and improbably solved everybody's problems. Instead: *Let your characters actively solve their own problems.* And it's usually more emotionally satisfying for the audience when the protagonist is compelled to make the more difficult choice.

In *The Descendants*, attorney Matthew King (George Clooney) struggles to make the right decision about his wife Elizabeth's (Patricia Hastie) life support and an important land deal. He avoids both decisions for as long as he can, but the more he seeks clarity, the more conflicted he becomes. Can he forgive his wife for her infidelity? Can he forgive himself for being a deadbeat dad? Can he accept the recommendations of his relatives and sell the estate land to their choice of buyer, or does he make the shrewd business move and dispassionately sell the land to the highest bidder? Eventually, Matty is compelled to take a stand. He forgives his wife and lets her go, and decides not to sell the estate land to *anyone*. Throughout the movie, he'd been a flip-flopping attorney (in flip-flops). By the end, he knows what feels right. He roots himself in his family and the sacred beauty of the island. And there is no greater representation of this than he and his daughters scattering his late wife Elizabeth's ashes at sea. The final scene is Matt and his daughters all watching a movie together at home, lying side-by-side on the sofa under the same quilt that had once covered Elizabeth in the hospital. It's a parting shot filled with warmth, comfort, and love.

After the climax, get out fast.

In some cases, the climax *is* the ending: *Thelma and Louise* (Geena Davis and Susan Sarandon) transcend oppression and drive off the cliff. The ill-fated, sexually-frustrated *Bonnie and Clyde* (Faye Dunaway and Warren Beatty) are annihilated in their getaway car in an almost orgasmic barrage of bullets. The Bolivian army fires at the fleeing *Butch Cassidy and the Sundance Kid* (Paul Newman and Robert Redford), and we continue to hear the gunfire over the doomed bandits in freeze frame. In *Iron Man*, Tony Stark (Robert Downey, Jr.) faces the glare of the media and brazenly lets that whole world know the truth: "I *am* Iron Man."

Don't just show us a happy ending. Make us feel it.

When the Oakland Athletics win the division in *Moneyball* and Billy Beane (Brad Pitt) feels vindicated, it feels like *our* victory, too. It's a shared experience. A classic Hollywood "happy ending" leaves the audience with a sense of hope and wonder, lifting our spirits and inspiring us in our own lives. At the end of *Billy Elliott*, we not only get to experience young Billy's (Jamie Bell) jubilant acceptance to the Royal Ballet School, but also get a glimpse into his future when adult Billy does his gravity defying leap across the expansive stage. It's exhilarating and makes our hearts leap too. Billy and his family have pulled through tough times against nearly impossible odds—and prospered. A happy ending tends to work best when it's in defiance of conventional wisdom. After all, as Osgood Fielding III (Joe E. Brown) points out at the end of *Some Like It Hot*: "Nobody's perfect."

Satisfying endings are most cathartic when they require your protagonists to embrace their vulnerability.

They drop their pretense and their metaphorical (or literal) masks, and allow themselves to be authentic. In romantic-comedies, this occurs when the two lovers finally stop their decidedly tentative mating dance (avoiding their fears of commitment and abandonment) and admit their love for one another. *See: When Harry Met Sally* and *Bridesmaids* for hilarious and touching examples.

Keep other possible outcomes viable until the end.

Another touchstone of the rom-com is the love triangle—with two choices, and the more viable *both* choices remain until the end, the better. In one of the very best of this genre, *The Philadelphia Story*, we have no idea who socialite Tracy Lords (Katharine Hepburn) is going to marry until she walks down the aisle. Spoiler alert: her cynical yet charming cad of an ex-husband C.K. Dexter Haven (Cary Grant) graciously and ultimately wins out.

Defy the formulaic.

In the dark romantic-comedy, *My Best Friend's Wedding*, Jules (Julia Roberts) ends up losing out on her beloved (the groom, played by Dermot Mulroney), but rebounds in the platonic friendship of her gay best friend (Rupert Everett). It's not the storybook ending she'd been seeking, but it is a *satisfying* ending befitting the home-wrecker she tried and failed to be, so she gets her comeuppance and the consolation prize. In *Broadcast News*, control freak network news producer Jane Craig (Holly Hunter) rejects both special men in her life (the handsome but dim anchorman played by William Hurt, and the too-smart-for-his-own-good reporter, played by Albert Brooks), but stays true to her integrity. It's a satisfying conclusion, just not an especially happy one.

The most satisfying endings, like life, are bittersweet.

At the end of *Rise of the Planet of the Apes*, Caesar is finally home in the Muir Woods, but there is also the sadness of being separated from his human father figure, Will (James Franco).

At the end of *Beginners*, Oliver (Ewan McGregor) finds true love—which goes hand-in-hand with experiencing profound grief over losing his father, Hal (Christopher Plummer).

In *The Social Network*, Mark Zuckerberg (Jesse Eisenberg) has earned billions of dollars, but at the expense of friendship and love.

At the end of *Schindler's List*, Oskar Schindler (Liam Neeson) laments that he wasn't able to do more to prevent the millions of atrocities. He knows his good intentions weren't nearly good enough. Oskar survives, but the infinite tragedy of the Holocaust overwhelms him with guilt and shame. He was one man who managed to make a difference against impossible odds, yet he's bereft.

Classic love stories are usually bittersweet—and virtually never work out in the end.

This subgenre of drama shows us that a great, passionate romance is ephemeral, but *true love lasts forever*. It transcends the laws of time and space. The form of the relationship might change over time, but the love endures—even in death. The classic dramatic love story ends with the two star-crossed lovers torn apart. Their love burns so intensely that it flames out due to a combination of internal and/or external circumstances: *Romeo and Juliet* (warring families/suicide pact gone wrong); *Gone With the Wind* (miscalculation/apathy); *Casablanca* (war/sacrifice); *Out of Africa* (geography/diametrically opposed views of love); *The Way We Were* (politics/irreconcilable differences); *Doctor Zhivago* (revolution/infidelity/heart attack); *Brokeback Mountain* (taboo love/prejudice); *The Curious Case of Benjamin Button* (bad timing on steroids); *The Bridges of Madison County* (fidelity/sacrifice); *Titanic* (class clash/iceberg); *500 Days of Summer* (rogue/irreconcilable differences); and *The Verdict* (femme fatale/betrayal). In each example, there was the *potential* for a positive outcome, and therein lies the emotional tug on the audience's heartstrings. We yearn for the two lovers to overcome their troubles, and despair when they can't or won't do so. At the end of *Shakespeare in Love*, Will and Viola are forced to go their separate ways, but she remains his Muse as he sits down to write *Twelfth Night*; her spirit infuses his work. Their love is immortalized.

Satisfying endings usually require some form of personal sacrifice for a greater good.

Protagonists can't always get what they want, but will often discover what they truly need. Rocky Balboa (Sylvester Stallone) doesn't win the championship fight against Apollo Creed (actually, it's a split decision), but he does manage to win Adrian's (Talia Shire) heart. Elliott must say good-bye to his alien pal, but he gets the exhilaration of flying on his bike, and heroically, helps E.T. evade capture and go home. Elliot cannot have his family back, but he can give that to E.T.—he can reunite him with his family. This is also a good example of a movie that doesn't go past the climax. E.T. go home—THE END.

In *The Artist*, silent movie star George (Jean Dujardin) can't accept the changing tides at the dawn of talkies, but he *can* acquiesce to the sweet charms of the devoted starlet, Peppy (Bérénice Bejo). He went to bat for her against the studio boss (played by John Goodman) when he was at the top of his game. Years later, when Peppy becomes a bona fide star and George has hit rock bottom, she returns that kindness—and helps restore his dignity. She still believes in him, even when he's lost all faith in himself. He loses the battle but wins her heart. There's a sense of *karmic justice* at play here. He doesn't get what he thought he wanted all along (to be a silent star again), but now he's ready for change.

In *The Dark Knight*, we experience a superhero compelled to sacrifice his own heroism in order to override the Joker's victory, making Christopher Nolan's iteration of Batman a notable exception to the superhero rubric. The Joker (Heath Ledger) had succeeded at corrupting D.A. Harvey Dent (Aaron

Eckhart) and turning him into a murderer. But if the good people of Gotham discovered the truth about Dent, they would lose the symbol of hope and faith Dent had given them; the prisoners Dent helped put back in jail would be let out, and chaos would erupt. Batman (Christian Bale) rationalizes to Commissioner Gordon that Gotham can never find out about Dent's evil deeds, and he (Batman) takes the blame for the murders. Gordon tells his son that while Harvey Dent was the hero Gotham needed, Batman is the hero that Gotham deserved. The bat-signal is destroyed and a manhunt is issued for Batman. As Batman gets on his Batpod and speeds away, Gordon asserts: "He's a silent Guardian. A watchful protector. A Dark Knight."

A satisfying ending usually demonstrates a character's growth, as he/she overcomes a vital flaw.

A protagonist's evolution can range from definitive and transformational. Erin Brockovich (Julia Roberts) progresses from a bitter single mom who blames everyone but herself for her misfortunes, to a formidable legal advocate and champion of the disenfranchised.

In *The King's Speech*, Prince Albert, Duke of York aka Bertie (Colin Firth), desperately yet begrudgingly recruits an unorthodox speech therapist, Lionel Logue (Geoffrey Rush) in order to overcome his debilitating stutter. Their gradual bonding helps Bertie find his voice, embrace his role as King George VI, and boldly lead his country through war.

In *Greenberg*, the emotionally stunted antihero musician, Roger Greenberg (Ben Stiller) does everything he can to sabotage a blossoming romance with the lovely Florence (Greta Gerwig) . . . until she can't take it anymore. "Hurt people hurt people," she tells him. It's her insight into his psyche that simultaneously attracts and terrifies him. But, in the end, Greenberg is forced to outgrow his self-destructive patterns and let her in.

In *Precious*, abused teenager (Gabourey Sidibe) evolves from passive victim to empowered woman and mom.

In each example, our satisfaction is derived from each protagonist's unique ability to evolve: from oppression to liberation; from the burden of deceit to the relief of authenticity; from hubris to humility; from selfish disconnection to (tenuous) connection; from breakdown of communication to greater understanding; from physically and/or emotionally wounded to potentially healed.

Not all protagonists are required to change.

Forrest Gump (Tom Hanks) doesn't change at all, but he does have a profound influence on others and several significant historical events. Danny Ocean (George Clooney) in the *Ocean's Eleven* films doesn't change; heists and capers are in his blood. Indiana Jones (Harrison Ford) doesn't change; his adventures do.

Superheroes tend not to change, but do heroically manage to *change the world around them*. They battle against evil in its many villainous forms, seek truth and justice, and juggle secret dual identities. James Bond 007 doesn't change; he's always a cad who lands on his feet, virtually unscathed. We revel in his Bond-ness. He always wins. However, the latest Bond (Daniel Craig) and Bruce Wayne/Batman (Christian Bale) offer greater moral complexity than ever before. Maybe it's just audience superhero burnout, but there appears to be a new wave of character evolution for superheroes to exceed the audience's expectations.

Or, this may have something to do with needing to see our heroes be more vulnerable. They are no longer in control, unflappable, and invincible. Perhaps this is what we need to see in a post-9/11 world in order for a superhero story to hold any meaning for us now. It's much more satisfying to watch our heroes take a hit and fall . . . and learn how to stand again. We as an audience need that desperately. The character complexity and evolution are a consequence of this vulnerability. It's also why it's been so challenging to bring *Superman* back to the screen—he's invincible. How do you make a man of steel vulnerable? Kryptonite seems too simplistic now. *See* interview with David Goyer on writing the new *Superman* film in Chapter 14.

Some protagonists resist change with a vengeance, and actually become more entrenched or committed to being Who They Are.

Think of the Woody Allen *kvetch*. Despite decades of psychotherapy, this character (in myriad films) pretty much stays the same neurotic, noble loser. In *Annie Hall*, Alvy Singer (Woody Allen) *wants* to be with Annie (Diane Keaton), but she can't live with his relentless pessimism—and he can't live without it. Alvy doesn't change; Annie does. She wants to enjoy life. He's incapable. (The movie's original title was *Anhedonia*—a psychoanalytic term for the inability to experience pleasure from normally pleasurable events.)

At the conclusion of *The Hurt Locker*, seemingly fearless, adrenaline-junkie, Sergeant First Class William James (Jeremy Renner) has come home from Iraq to reunite with his wife and baby son. As a soldier, he wasn't afraid of anything. As a civilian, the quotidian details of suburban life—grocery shopping, cleaning out the rain gutters, and helping his wife in the kitchen— are anathema to him. The endless rows of cereal boxes at the supermarket have become the enemy. And we realize that he is, indeed, not afraid of death; he's afraid of *life*.

Talking to his son in the nursery, he offers words of advice to his boy; the words are spoken to his son, but he's mainly telling himself that he only truly feels alive while situated on the razor's edge between life and death. When James pops open the jack-in-the-box for the wonderment of his baby, the toy isn't merely set dressing; it's emblematic of James' love for his job as a bomb dismantler. At war, he's a specialist, a savior; there's no one quite like him. At home, he feels ordinary and numb. He can't handle it. As much as he loves his wife and kid and wants to stay at home, he needs the danger more.

The title card at the beginning of the film, a quote from Chris Hedges, has prepared us for this inevitability: "The rush of battle is often a potent and lethal addiction, for war is a drug." James' transport back to Iraq happens in the cut. Inevitably, he's back for another 365-day rotation in Delta Company, and, per the final action line in the screenplay: "we watch him go down the unnamed road until he disappears."

In the action-thriller *Drive*, the nameless Driver (Ryan Gosling) leaves the tainted cache of money, the corpse of his defeated nemesis (Albert Brooks), and the woman he loves (Carey Mulligan) behind . . . and drives off alone. He's helped rescue her and her young son from danger—an act of mercy. He flirts with personal transformation, and we even believe that he might change. But, in the final analysis, he doesn't change at all. Inevitably, he's a rogue, and only trusts himself. He sacrifices love for freedom, beholden to no one but the open road.

In addition to these archetypes, there are many, many other examples of protagonists who don't change from start to finish—but these tend to be the exceptions in Hollywood films. There's almost a tacit understanding for an audience with the price of admission that the protagonist's journey is going to lead him/her someplace new and unexpected.

The intentionally ambiguous ending offers the moral complexity of the grey areas in life, with no definitive solution.

Just what does Hollywood movie star Bob Harris (Bill Murray) whisper into Charlotte's (Scarlett Johansson) ear at the end of *Lost in Translation*? Her Mona Lisa smile is equally enigmatic. The audience is left to ponder what happens next. At the end of *Up in the Air*, Ryan Bingham (George Clooney) studies the flight arrivals and departures board at the airport, and we have no idea where he's going. He narrates: "Tonight, most people will be home with their families. I'll be on a plane. And if you look up at the sky, one of the stars shining more brightly than the rest will be my wingtip, passing over." Ryan's future is literally left up in the air.

At the end of *Doubt*, the devout Sister Aloysius Beauvier (Meryl Streep), the truth-seeking principal at the Bronx parochial school, will have to live with not being able to prove her suspicion that the priest is guilty or innocent of molesting the boy. The central mystery of the story remains unresolved. And, for the first time in her life, Sister Aloysius is plagued by doubts about her personal faith in God.

At the end of the powerfully provocative Iranian film, *A Separation*, the battle-weary married couple is situated on either side of a glass partition outside the Judge's office. They silently wait for their daughter's gut-wrenching decision as to which parent she's chosen in this bitter custody dispute. But rather than delivering the definitive answer, the screenwriter/director, Asghar Farhadi, has the daughter just walk right past them, and makes us draw our own conclusions.

The key ingredient to a tragic ending is wasted potential.

Tragic heroes have flaws that cannot be overcome—leading to the character's unfortunate demise. But tragic endings only resonate when we see there was another more positive alternative—the road not taken.

At the end of *American Beauty*, that final moment of resonance comes when a distraught Caroline (Annette Bening) opens the closet door and throws her arms around all of her just-deceased husband, Lester's (Kevin Spacey) clothes. Indeed, she loved him all along, but now, tragically, it's too late.

In *Black Swan*, a ballerina's (Natalie Portman) obsessive quest for perfection leads her into the downward spiral of madness and a spectacular plunge to death.

The antihero, Salieri (F. Murray Abraham) in *Amadeus*, meets a similar fate: his overwhelming envy for his musical prodigy rival, Wolfgang Amadeus Mozart, drives him to insanity. If only Salieri could have accepted being second tier, he could have avoided losing his mind.

The antihero, Daniel Plainview (Daniel Day-Lewis) in *There Will Be Blood*, is a greedy, deceitful, vindictive oil tycoon who yearns for a familial connection, but destroys every relationship in his life and devolves into a faithless, paranoid, murderous loner.

The Perfect Storm ended tragically because the captain (George Clooney) of the ship had several chances to turn around, but his hubris compelled his crew forward—into the eye of the storm. All resonant tragic endings are tinged with the regret of "If only . . ."

An inevitable ending offers an audience the satisfying feeling that they should have seen it coming all along—but didn't. The effective ending is the sum of all the pieces of the movie, but the entire puzzle doesn't coalesce until the final moments, leaving us with an indelible, resonant, lasting impression.

INTERVIEW: Screenwriter/Director Billy Ray

Billy Ray Filmography

Best known for:

The Hunger Games (2012)
State of Play (2009)
Breach (also directed) (2007)
Flightplan (2005)
Shattered Glass (also directed) (2003)
Hart's War (2002)
Volcano (1997)

NL: Since both *Shattered Glass* and *Breach* were stories based on real people, what kind of challenges did you face in crafting the inevitable conclusion, but maintaining as much suspense as you did? Particularly in the case of *Breach*, since we know from the beginning what the conclusion is.

BR: What makes conclusions so difficult is that you want them to be inevitable, and yet, you don't want them to be obvious. In other words, you want people at the end of the movie to say that it could not have ended in any other way or that, in no other way, would it have been this satisfying. You don't want to have laid so much pipe for your ending that people say, "Well, I saw that coming the whole entire time."

When I think about truly great endings, I always start with *The Godfather* which, for me, is the greatest movie ever made. Completely inevitable and yet completely unexpected. So, the question is if you know that's where you're going—how do you lay tracks in the first and second act of your movie so that it is earned? So that your ending can be as resonant as it can possibly be. In the case of *The Godfather*, you take a guy who states very clearly from the beginning, "That's my family, that's not me." He looks different. He's in a uniform; everyone else is in a tuxedo at the wedding. He talks to Kay differently. He responds to everyone in the family differently than anybody else does. He keeps on saying over and over again, "This is not what I want, this is not what I'm going to be." He promises Kay later on, even after he's committed a murder, that the Corleone family is going to be completely legitimate. So, to see him turn into a more violent expression of his father is unbelievably satisfying, haunting, and great. I think they were crafting that ending through the entire development of that movie. It's a great model.

However, when I was working on *Shattered Glass*, I found that *All the President's Men* was a better template for me since everybody knew the ending in that case, too. You know that Woodward and Bernstein get Nixon in the end. So, how did William Goldman and Alan Pakula figure out how to make that the most satisfying movie possible? First of all, they set up a gigantic canvas. They set up a real bad guy at the beginning. Nixon at the peak of his power. You've got the majesty of Air Force One and congress, and everyone is standing and cheering. It doesn't seem like there's any way these two dummies can take down this guy. Great, great setup. But then, you find out that these guys are just grinders. They are not going to stop until they piece this thing together. They have enormous hurdles placed in front of them.

I think the best choice that Goldman made when he was writing the first draft of that movie was that he ended on their biggest screw up. They go after Haldeman, Nixon's Chief of Staff. They don't totally have the goods on him yet. They aim too high and they tumble which makes Woodward go to Deep Throat and say, "I'm tired of your chicken shit games, I need to know what you know," which is the point where he learns that their lives are in danger. He goes to tell Bernstein and together they tell their editor, Ben Bradlee, who rips into them. So, you actually end the movie at the moment they are at their lowest. Because what Goldman is trading on is your knowledge that they are going to succeed, which you see with a Teletype and a great double focus shot. Spectacular stuff. I had all of this in mind when I sat down to write *Shattered Glass*. Also, I knew I had a hook that I could hang a character on because when Buzz Bissinger wrote the article, he planted in there that Stephen Glass kept saying, "Are you mad at me? Are you mad at me?"

But, the question was: if we get too caught up in the world of Stephen Glass and then reveal him to be a liar, will the audience come out feeling horrible? I thought the answer would be "yes," so I tried something, which I would not suggest, because it's tricky. The first half of that movie has one protagonist, Stephen Glass [Hayden Christensen], and the second half of that movie has a different protagonist, Chuck Lane [Peter Sarsgaard]. By the end, you shouldn't know as an audience, where we've transitioned from one story to another, but I can tell you the exact point in the movie where it does happen.

If you can transition to make the movie more about Peter Sarsgaard's character, people will be happy in the end that he got the bad guy. However, you just can't start with him because he's not dynamic enough at the beginning of the movie. Ultimately, the movie is about what would happen if the least popular kid in high school had to take down the most popular kid in high school. So, you've got to start with the most popular kid because he's the dynamic rock star that is going to suck us into the movie. Then, as you thread Chuck Lane into that story, you gradually let him take over. For me, the transitional moment of that movie is the conference call that they have with the guys from Forbes Digital. At that point, truth starts to take over and the bullshit starts to fade. I think it was Mandy Walker, my Director of Photography, who suggested that we have a visual signature that changed halfway through the movie so that subliminally you were telling the audience that something has just shifted here. During the first half of the movie whenever you're in the offices of the New Republic, all the shots were handheld. Then, from the moment of that conference call, you're on sticks [slang for a tripod].

NL: So it's grounded.

BR: Right. The movie stopped shaking. No one has ever asked me about that change.

NL: It's very subliminal. I honestly never noticed it.

BR: Which means it's successful, but it's a transition which sets up your conclusion and tells your audience that something has shifted here. The rules of the game have now changed in a subtle, but fundamental way. Stephen Glass is no longer in charge. It's now Chuck Lane's story and therefore Chuck Lane's movie. That is how we tried to craft the inevitable conclusion. It was very, very tricky.

Breach was a different animal because it was a better-known case. People came into that movie knowing that Hanssen had done it. In fact, even if they didn't know, we tell them in the first frame of the movie because there's John Ashcroft, the Attorney General, talking about the arrest of Robert Hanssen and what it means. By the way, that Ashcroft piece came in after the first screening of the movie because people felt that there weren't enough stakes. In a post-9/11 world, does it matter that someone was giving secrets to the Russians? So, by having John Ashcroft tell us what a big deal it is at the beginning of the movie, the tension gets heightened.

NL: It gives you the gravitas.

BR: And, it did. No one ever asked again about the stakes of the movie. I first read the draft of what was then called, *The Eleventh Hour,* which was written by a team of writers named Adam Mazer and William Rotko. They had told a more straightforward story about Eric O'Neill and Robert Hanssen in which you knew from the beginning that Robert Hanssen was a spy and that Eric O'Neill was going to catch him. There was nothing wrong with it, but it was just that there were no big reveals left in the movie. There was nowhere for the movie to go.

*S*ince we've got an inevitable conclusion, how can we get there in a way that no one expects?

What if O'Neill was duped by the bureau? What if he was told this case was about a sexual deviant? And then, in that way, he gets drawn into the story of Robert Hanssen. Once he comes to the conclusion that this sexual deviant stuff is nonsense, he is so drawn in by Hanssen that when the FBI says, "Well, he's a spy," O'Neill has nowhere to go. He's stuck in that room with that guy.

Breach didn't wind up being what I thought it would be about on a thematic level, and this took hold more in the cutting of the movie than in the development of the script. The difference was a subtle shade. As I was writing the script, I thought about how our mentors fail us, even if they're teaching us. It turns out that the movie we made actually said something slightly different. Being stuck in a room with Robert Hanssen [Chris Cooper] forces Eric O'Neill [Ryan Phillippe] to reevaluate how he feels about his career, his marriage, and his religion. He comes up with different answers at the end of the movie than he would have given at the beginning of the movie. Hanssen actually arced the character of Eric O'Neill and the movie traces that. Which is why it ends with Hanssen in the elevator saying, "Pray for me." And, O'Neill saying, "I will." He actually will. So, those are two movies where there was an inevitable conclusion, and the fun was going to be how we got there.

NL: I think there's a willing suspension of disbelief with *Breach* in particular. You think that Hanssen is so meticulous about everything that he's not going to slip up. You think that he's just going to stay one step ahead. So, it's the cat and mouse game. Even though you know intellectually that he gets busted, there's that part of you as a moviegoer that thinks maybe somehow there will be a different result this time. I felt the same way about the doomed Apollo 13 mission.

BR: It's part of your job when you're writing that script and you're shooting that movie to make a case for an alternate ending. In other words, you're trying as you're making *Breach*, to present evidence that would support some other way for that story to resolve itself. In that way, your ending can feel a little bit like a surprise. What people didn't know going into that movie was who O'Neill and Laura Linney were, and what the complications of their relationship would be.

NL: At the climax, when Hanssen pulls out that gun and he's drunk, you do wonder, does he kill O'Neill? You definitely kept a lot of that tension going. Was the gun in the trunk of the car documented?

BR: Yes, that's all real, but I took dramatic license with the guns in the climactic park sequence.

NL: How much of the script was based on the true story?

BR: I didn't put anything in there that was not true to the spirit of the event. However, the bar was higher for *Shattered Glass* because you're telling a story about fraud in journalism. If you tell it in a fraudulent way, then shame on you. That's just not acceptable. We had to tell the facts exactly as we knew them, and I didn't put anything in there that I couldn't double source. In fact, the only thing I made up was the idea that Stephen Glass was speaking to his high school class.

As a framing device, it was pretty good. In fact, that came about after I cut the movie together. I needed a framing device that I thought would elevate it. I called a meeting with everyone from Lionsgate who financed the movie. I said, "We've got a cut of the movie. It's good, but I don't think it's great. I don't think it's going to blow anyone's doors off. I don't know what to say other than I'm sorry, I tried to get it there and I didn't. I apologize. But, I have this idea for some new material and if you'll let me go reshoot for three days, I think we can make the movie materially better." And, they could have said go jump in the lake, but they didn't. I got really lucky.

NL: What was the budget of each movie?

BR: The budget of *Shattered Glass* was $5.8 [million] and the budget of *Breach* was $25 [million].

NL: A lot of above the line [actors, director, producer, salaries], I would imagine?

BR: Yes, above the line went up on *Breach*. It was the difference of shooting 50 days instead of shooting 28. And Toronto instead of Montreal. Plus, we had ten days in D.C. on *Breach*."

NL: Gorgeous, incredible movie.

BR: Thank you. I had to have the real corner where Hanssen was arrested at the real time of year and the real time of day. I was going to spend more for that.

NL: Structurally, one of the things which plagues screenwriters the most, is act two and the midpoint. Gary Ross talks about the midpoint as being an existential dilemma for a character. I tell my students that it's a good time for the protagonist to ask himself, "Who am I?" It's a soul-searching moment. In *Breach*, there's the scene when he goes to talk to his father at the house, which felt like such a great midpoint moment.

BR: I don't know if it's exactly the midpoint or not. I never think in terms of "Oh, boy, act one better be over by page 25 or oh boy, we better have a turn on page 60." I never think of it that way. I think most scripts kind of wind up being there because there's a certain sort of storytelling that's just hard-wired into our brains and we wind up landing near those points. But, I never ever think of it that way and I never ever cut a movie in that way. Breach has sort of a normal act one ending, and it definitely has a turn, but the turn I'm sure came before page 60. It's the moment where Laura Linney tells him what's really going on and I think his reaction is to sit down with his father and ask.

NL: A lot of new screenwriters are told that readers only look at the first ten pages, so something pretty explosive better start to happen by page 10.

BR: I don't buy that either. I know that there's a temptation to ramp something up really fast in a screenplay because you're afraid that it's just going to get tossed across the room in its competition with 11 other scripts that someone is reading that weekend. My belief about screenplays is that the purpose of page 1 is to intrigue someone enough to read page 2 and that's it. I don't think anything has to happen by page 10, but I can tell you within half a page, if that writer has a voice. I know if they have something interesting to say and I know if they don't. I know if I'm engaged and I know if I'm not. And, that takes a lot less than ten pages to figure out.

NL: What kinds of things engage you in those first ten pages?

BR: A world that's accurately depicted. Either because I know it to be as it's being described or it intrigues me like, "Oh, wow, I didn't know about that. That's interesting." Or, a character who is just unique and yet recognizably human in their idiosyncrasies. Sometimes, very rarely, it's an action set piece that I've just never seen before, but I usually have a knee-jerk resentment of that too early. And, very, very rarely, it's a piece of dialogue that crackles within a page, but that is tough to do.

NL: So, it's character.

BR: It's character, tone, or world.

NL: Your work is so real—there's no heightened sense of tone. It's where you feel like you're there.

BR: The trick, however, is if you're writing something that is heightened, can you make that feel just as real? Recently, with *The Hunger Games*, my draft was very heightened, but had to feel real—and that's a tonal challenge. Gary Ross has done his own draft now and is also directing.

NL: Do you have a process for writing? Do you outline? Do you use notes and cards?

BR: The first thing to consider is: how do you choose what it is you're going to write? I don't think writers spend enough time thinking about this. I'm very happily in a position right now where people are offering stuff to me and I'm trying to evaluate what's the right thing to invest my time in. The simplest litmus test that I can apply also happens to be the best, which is: "Do I wake up thinking about it?" If I don't wake up thinking about it, it doesn't matter who the director is, who the star is, or what the auspices of the project are, if it's not living in me, I'm not going to do my best work. It's not right for me.

If I do wake up thinking about it, it means that subconsciously something was eating at me about this idea. Problem solving was happening while I was asleep. So, that's the first big thing: choose something that is going to bring out your best work. Writers, particularly as they are trying to break in, are so mercenary in terms of thinking about, "Oh, this is an idea that I should write because this is an idea I can sell."

NL: It's almost always a mistake.

BR: It is almost always a mistake. The easiest test is: don't write a movie you wouldn't pay to see. It's that's simple. But, even if it is a movie that you would pay to see, if it's not a movie that's obsessing you, you're not going to do great work. You just can't. So, the first thing is: choose the right project.

NL: Do you think that in the current Hollywood climate that *Shattered Glass* and *Breach* could still get made today?

BR: No. I got out just before the door slammed behind me. I was very lucky.

NL: Smart drama, smart political thriller.

BR: Very. A $25 million dollar Chris Cooper movie? Forget it. It's just not happening.

NL: Is that affecting your choices?

BR: Sure. There was something that came my way the other day which was very much in the tone of *Shattered Glass* or *Breach* that I would love to do that I said no to because I just don't believe that that particular project is going to get made. And, it's too heartbreaking to dive in, do the research, to know the true story, meet the people, take the notes, and then go kill yourself over it. It's just not worth it.

So, when you have chosen the film that is the right movie for you to write, the next question is: what is the tone? What does it feel like? Once I know what that tone is, I like to drive around listening to a soundtrack from a movie which has a similar tone. *The Thin Red Line*—I'm big on that soundtrack. The HBO movie, *And the Band Played On*—I'm very big on that soundtrack, too. If it's a movie with action in it, I'll listen to the soundtrack from Speed. And, if you drive around listening to those soundtracks that are right for the tone of your movie—and I'll listen to *The Thin Red Line* over and over and over again—the movie starts to follow in your head.

You need a notepad with you at all times. You need it by your bed. Your work-in-progress should be the last thing you think about before you go to sleep and the first thing you think about when you wake up. I always have something to write on in the car. Always. I drive around just making random notes. The process takes a couple weeks. Where you're just making notes on napkins or whatever.

Once I have a stack of them, I go into the office and actually open a computer file where I start to assemble those ideas. I have big headlines with general thematic ideas—where I'm just thinking in the broadest sense about what I'm talking about. Ideas for a character, such as Stephen Glass walking around in his socks. Okay, that idea's going in somewhere. I don't know where yet, but it will. Then, big headlines with: first act ideas, second act ideas, and third act ideas. Then, I take those notes that I wrote in a very haphazard way and start putting them under possible act headlines. Once the ideas are in the acts, sequences start to emerge. At this point, you shouldn't be editing yourself at all.

Once you have this gigantic document—and for me it's about 40–50 pages—you go back to the idea of knowing how to sculpt an elephant. You start with a block of granite and you chip away everything that is not the elephant. You now have your block of granite. You start to chip away everything that is not the story you want to tell. By the time you're done with that, your treatment is pretty long. Usually when I sit down to write a script, my treatments are about 50 pages. And, basically, no one's paid you. This is all on spec. Even if I were going to go pitch an idea at a studio, I would do this much work. If it were an idea that a studio had offered me, and they were just waiting to see what I thought of the idea, I would do this much work. For two reasons: firstly, because I want to walk into the studio and communicate to them that if they hire anyone else, they're insane. No one's going to outwork me; no one's going to outprepare me. And, I don't care if they're 25 and hungry—they're still not going to outwork me. I work harder now than I did when I was 25.

But, secondly, I don't want to take their money until I know I'm going to be worth it. When I walk in there with a 50-page treatment, I know that I know how to craft this movie. I know how to start it, I know what goes on in the middle and I know how I'm going to end it, so I'm never going to be in terror as I sit down to actually write "Fade In." There are no blank pages because I've got 50-some pages written already. I just have to fill them in. That's how I do it.

NL: Theme has become a polarizing question in this book. Some people say theme is everything that you have to start with theme. And, others say don't ever think about theme because it will get pretentious. It'll be pedantic. Just tell the story and let the audience figure it out. It sounds like you need to know what it's really about.

BR: I need to know what it's saying, but I'm very open to the idea that it might be saying something different by the time I'm done. Even by the time I'm done with the draft, it may be saying something different than I thought it was going to be saying. You're trying to be a steady hand guiding it, but it may lead you somewhere and you have to be open to that experience.

NL: How important is the role of central mystery in terms of generating suspense and the idea of inevitability? Because some of your films start with foregone conclusions: we know at the end that they get Hanssen and Stephen Glass. As a result, are there things you need to hide? Do you consciously think about holding things back or do they just emerge organically?

BR: I don't think every movie needs a mystery, but it does need to reveal how far a character is willing to go. There's no mystery to *Jaws* which I think is one of the best-crafted screenplays ever. I mean it's staggering, particularly when you place it in context with the book which is also great, but the changes Carl Gottlieb and Spielberg made to transition it from book to screen were so smart and just so on the money. In the book, Brody grew up on Amity Island and he's an islander, but in the movie, he's a New York cop spending his first summer on Amity Island. They did that so that they could make him afraid of the water. If Brody was told at the beginning of the movie that he'd have to kill a shark on the balustrade of a sinking whaler, he would have said get someone else. That's not a mystery—that's just a character evolving.

For me, in *Shattered Glass* and in *Breach*, the mysteries were all about the characters. Who are these guys actually? Stephen Glass and Robert Hanssen are both men who are just clearly lying about who they really are. When are we as the audience going to figure it out? When is our protagonist going to figure it out and what's the cost? Those are the mysteries of those films.

ASSIGNMENT

Determine all possible outcomes for your ending. Make a hierarchical list of which ending is most probable and which one is most unexpected (happy, bittersweet, tragic, ambiguous?). Steer clear from the path of predictability. Satisfying endings involve an active choice made by your protagonist, so quantify the different choices available from his/her POV. List all significant characters' corresponding plotlines, and prioritize which subplots need to be definitively tied up and which ones are best left dangling in the minds of the audience.

17

WHAT'S THE MISSING PIECE?

Infuse Your Story with a Central Mystery

The exceptional screenwriter/director/executive producer J.J. Abrams did a TED Talk several years ago called "The Mystery Box." If you haven't seen it yet, it's only about 20 minutes long and definitely worth checking out. Basically, when Abrams was a kid, his grandfather bought him a "Mystery Box" at a magic store. The packaging on the sealed box promised: "Fifteen dollars for fifty bucks worth of magic!" Abrams explains to the rapt TED Talk audience that he still has this box today; it sits on a shelf in his office—for inspiration. But what's most remarkable about the story is *Abrams has never opened it*. Because he knows it will be disappointing. He talks about how the *expectation* of what's inside the box is its true magic. As soon as he opens the box, the suspense and anticipation—the mystery—vanishes.

When we go to the movies, it's like we're being handed our very own mystery box. The setup introduces us to characters in their world, then wrests them out of their usual routine and challenges them. At this point, if the movie is good, it's arousing our curiosity, our need to know more. What protagonists don't know *can* hurt them.

What audiences don't know will always—for the time being—be more interesting than what they do know.

Great storytellers are always dangling a new plot development in front of our eyes, instilling in us the need to know more. When you're telling a story to kids, this will compel them to ask you: "*Then* what happens?" Audiences don't outgrow these anticipatory instincts. It's as if there is another smaller mystery box inside, and then another one inside that one, and so on. And as we open and discover more layers of mystery, the storyteller is creating momentum for the audience to keep unwrapping and exploring. This momentum is called narrative drive. The fuel for narrative drive is the audience's curiosity.

I recently heard Matt Stone and Trey Parker (the creators of *South Park* and Broadway's smash hit, *The Book of Mormon*) speaking to a screenwriting class at NYU Tisch School of the Arts. I'm paraphrasing, but the gist of their remarks on plotting was that if the connective tissue of the scenes in your screenplay is "and then . . ."—you're totally screwed (but they used the F-word). Instead, Parker and Stone suggested—and I wholeheartedly agree—that the connective tissue needs to be either, "but then . . ." or, "therefore." Their point, as I see it, cannot be underscored enough. "But then . . ." invigorates us. "And then . . ." lulls us.

A central mystery usually concerns the past; a central question is about the future.

A central mystery makes us wonder *what happened* in the past that is affecting the present—and usually has us asking why and/or how? A central question makes us wonder *what's going to happen* next.

Not all mysteries deal with deep, dark secrets. Many mysteries are less about what's completely hidden, and more about something that's masked or partially obscured. As long as the characters keep trying to figure things out in their lives, and as long as they keep trying to solve the why/how/when/where of their problems, then you have narrative drive. But the big caveat is we have to *care* about them. They don't have to be likeable, but they do need to have sympathetic goals and/or some kind of vulnerability. We need to recognize their humanity—warts and all. If they *must* solve their problems, if they *need* answers, and if we care about them, then the audience is listening.

If they don't care, we won't care.

Characters are defined by their actions more than their words. They might *say* that they don't give a damn about anything, but the subtext might be exactly the opposite. In *Shame*, Brandon (Michael Fassbender) doesn't *seem* to care about anybody or anything but his own libidinous desires, but as the story progresses it becomes abundantly clear that he loves and wants to protect his kid sister, Sissy (Carey Mulligan). We wonder if they're both going to self-destruct or manage to save one another. This is the *central question* in the movie. The *central mystery* is why are these two siblings so profoundly screwed up? Was it incest? Childhood sexual abuse? We never learn why they left Ireland, or why they're both incapable of sustaining healthy, stable relationships. For me, this felt satisfying because of the immediacy of the story; I cared more about their futures than about the past that damaged them. In *Shame*, the mystery box remains sealed.

Good plotting will encompass an overarching central mystery or question.

The audience and the protagonist need to know more. And they actively try to reach a positive solution to their central dilemma, but they keep

encountering greater internal and external obstacles. This is the "but then
. . ." that Parker and Stone were talking about. After all, movies are about
people with problems, and as the movie progresses, their problems intensify.
I'm not encouraging you to write a bad soap opera where things just happen.
I am, however, heeding the advice of a very wise old man named Aristotle
that stuff needs to happen on the plot level based upon cause and effect—
the absence of which leads to ". . . and then." Satisfying movie plotting is
surprising, emotional, and each new scene is impacted by the scene(s) that
preceded it. In a mystery, this is the accumulation of clues—usually
concerning the past. In a central question-driven film, the plot progression
involves the outcome of the present trouble.

An aimless story is lethally dull.

I have a perfectly delightful friend who happens to be a hopelessly bad
storyteller—plagued by "and then" to the point where it feels like a story is
never going to end, and I want to jump out the window to escape. In the
hands of great storytellers, you trust that they're taking you on a journey to
someplace you want to go or can't resist its lure. Because there are escalating
stakes and a sense of mystery—not just a barrage of information and
extraneous details. And if you know a person like my bad storyteller friend,
he/she is probably incapable of telling just *one* story at a time; they keep going
off on tangents and losing the narrative thread.

The gradual, suspenseful unfolding of a story's principal conflicts can be the crucial difference between intrigue and apathy.

When a storyteller loses us, it's usually because the story isn't moving forward
fast enough—due to convoluted plotting, too much exposition, too many
flashbacks and jump-forwards, too many characters, and/or overly
complicated subplots—so we get bored. Conversely, when a story gets too
far ahead of us, our patience tends to run out. Lost and hopelessly confused,
we tune out. The trick—and this is very hard to accomplish, mind you—is
for the screenwriter to be just about half a step ahead of the audience.

There are generally two kinds of mysteries: closed and open.

Most movies in the psychological thriller and drama genres are *closed*
mysteries (aka "whodunits") in which solving a puzzle in the present is
predicated by finding a missing piece from the past. And the ultimate solution
isn't revealed to the audience—and/or protagonist—until the climax of the
movie.

In a "closed mystery," the protagonist is usually just as much in the dark as the audience until the moment when—and if—we all discover the truth.

In the *closed* mystery dramedy *American Beauty*, Lester (Kevin Spacey)
tells us from the very beginning—via voiceover—that he'll be dead in less

than a year. We're not sure if he's telling us the truth, but he does have an omniscient POV, so I believed him. And then, sure enough, at the climax, Lester is shot in the back of the head and killed. In the case of *American Beauty*, there are two closed mysteries at play: (1) if he's actually going to be dead by the end of the movie, and (2) who killed him. The brilliant part of this climax is that virtually every character in Lester's orbit could have done it, so we get to see what each one of them is doing seconds before, during, and almost immediately after the murder. Everyone has motive and opportunity. Lester's wife, Carolyn (Annette Bening) even has a loaded gun. His aloof, rebellious daughter (Thora Birch) has even discussed killing her dad with the kid next door, Ricky (Wes Bentley)—her new boyfriend—on page 1. Was she kidding? Or was it foreshadowing? In the end, it's revealed that it was Ricky's homophobic, ex-marine dad, Colonel Frank Fitts (Chris Cooper)—who had fallen in love with Lester and couldn't accept his own sexual identity nor being rejected by Lester. It's a closed mystery because we don't discover whodunit until the climax.

In the political thriller, *The Contender*, Senator Lane Hanson (Joan Allen) is the sitting President Evans' (Jeff Bridges) #1 choice to fill the vacant seat of the retiring Vice President. But she's a liberal Democrat, and the Republican Senate Confirmation Committee is chaired by her hard-line conservative nemesis, Senator Shelley Runyon (Gary Oldman), who will do anything to torpedo her nomination; Shelley manages to dredge up a sex scandal, alleging that Lane participated in an orgy back in her college days. Shelley's henchmen produce sordid photos of said orgy, featuring blurry photos of a college girl who may or not be Lane.

Lane is outraged, and we get the sense that she wasn't the party girl in the photos. But she defiantly refuses to comment on the scandal despite the media glare and all of her political advisors urging her to refute the accusations. Lane's explanation is that commenting on the accusations is "simply beneath my dignity." Throughout the movie she sticks to the courage of her convictions. The revelation about Lane's past doesn't come until late in act three—when Lane confides to the President that she was not the party girl in the scandalous photos. The closed mystery is solved for the audience. However, no one but President Evans, Lane's husband, and the actual girl in the photos will ever know the truth.

The severed ear that Jeffrey Beaumont (Kyle MacLachlan) finds in the grass near the beginning of *Blue Velvet* ignites the classic cult film's closed central mystery. Who did the ear belong to? What happened? Who is responsible? The ear is like a tiny crack in the veneer of this seemingly idyllic slice of 1950s Americana. In this small town of secrets and lies, repression and perversion, the ear portends a dangerous underworld that's going to be uprooted. It's as if the earth has been *listening*.

In *Winter's Bone*, Ree (Jennifer Lawrence) must locate her delinquent dad—and fast—or she and her little brothers and sisters will be evicted from their home. But the audience, just like Ree, has no idea if he's dead or alive. It's not a whodunit; it's a "who knows (the truth)?"

The subgenre, the paranoia thriller, usually focuses on a closed central mystery that hinges on a protagonist's (in)sanity.

This provides the audience with a limited, subjective first person point of view. In *Black Swan*, is Nina Sayers going crazy or is she undergoing a real metamorphosis into a black swan? Or is there a new nefarious ballerina out to seduce and destroy her? *See also*: *Rosemary's Baby*, *Shutter Island*, and *Fight Club*.

In an "open mystery," the audience knows upfront whodunit, but the question remains: will they get caught and brought to justice—or get away with it?

In *Breach*, we know from page 1 that FBI veteran Robert Hanssen (Chris Cooper) was convicted on charges of spying and selling U.S. government secrets to the Soviet Union. It's an open mystery because the end result is a foregone conclusion. The film's protagonist, young FBI operative Eric O'Neill (Ryan Phillippe), is tasked with working undercover as Hanssen's assistant. *How* Eric incrementally manages to get the obsessively vigilant, suspicious, and meticulously private Hanssen to let his guard down is the core mystery of the film. Their working relationship is rife with subtext and fuels the central conflict.

In Woody Allen's *Match Point* and *Crimes and Misdemeanors*, the audience knows who orchestrated the murders of their mistresses Nola and Dolores (respectively played by Scarlett Johansson and Angelica Huston), but just about every other character is oblivious. The precursor to these films was *Rope*, directed by Alfred Hitchcock, in which two geniuses plan the "perfect" murder and then get their intellectual jollies playing a game with the victim's family and their shrewd professor (Jimmy Stewart). *Rope* was based upon the notorious true crime case of Leopold and Loeb.

In *Murder by Numbers*, hardboiled homicide detective, Cassie Mayweather (Sandra Bullock), investigates a mysterious murder—ostensibly a "perfect crime." The audience knows from the get-go who, why, how, where, when, and what happened, but the creepy, scary fun is watching Cassie try to beat the genius killers, Richard and Justin (Ryan Gosling and Michael Pitt), at their own game.

Other examples of open mysteries:

In *Fargo*, we know who's guilty, who's lying, and who's killed whom—then we watch as the seemingly innocuous, very pregnant, and incredibly shrewd cop, Marge (Frances McDormand) outsmarts the band of misfits, murderers, and degenerates.

In *The Departed*, we know up front who's corrupt and who's dutiful. The mystery is which side will be exposed and killed first, and who—if anyone—will leave unscathed and/or be brought to justice.

In *Apollo 13*, we know before we enter the movie theater that the mission was dangerously compromised. But we don't know exactly how it felt to be part of that fateful space mission—or exactly how they managed to survive. We know the ending at the beginning, but we're compelled to know *more*.

Central questions are less about solving a puzzle or uncovering a secret, and more about sustaining our investment in the outcome of the story.

There's not much of a central mystery in *Rocky*, for example, but we're filled with the anticipation of whether underdog Rocky Balboa (Sylvester Stallone) will win the big fight at the end—or not. And will his new girlfriend, Adrian (Talia Shire) show up and cheer him on, too?

In *Jaws*, again, there's no central mystery. We know from the beginning that there's a hungry, menacing Great White shark on the prowl on Amity Island. There's no mystery as to why. The central question that keeps our pulse pounding is *when* and *where* the shark will strike again—and *how* our ragtag trio of shark hunters will stop it before they become shark bait.

In *50/50*, we have no idea *why* 27-year-old Adam (Joseph Gordon-Leavitt) has contracted a rare form of spinal cancer. The central question is whether Adam will live or die. But this isn't a "murder mystery" or thriller. If this were a film about finding the miraculous cure for cancer—the race against time to decode the DNA of the disease—then it would be a mystery. But *50/50* explores how Adam deals with his life threatening circumstance. We're more emotionally invested in his relationships with family, friends, and his pretty new therapist than we are with solving anything. We hope for the best but prepare for the worst, just like Adam.

In *Toy Story 3*, the central question is: will Woody and the gang make it home in time to go away to college with Andy—or not?

In *The 40 Year Old Virgin*, we wonder if Andy will get laid and by whom, but the biggest question of all is: will he find true love?

In *The Artist*, will George Valentin (Jean Dujardin) overcome his insecurity and hubris and embrace both technological progress and his true love?

In *Moneyball*, will the Oakland A's win or lose based on their unorthodox general manager's new strategy? The "how" and "why" are not mysterious. The "when" and "if" keep us riveted until the end result is revealed. Effective scenes in a screenplay will have dramatic tension running under them—aka conflict between the characters—as relationships unfold, unravel, regroup, disconnect, and reconnect.

Writer versus moviegoer.

Every writer I know is a control freak. We like to describe how people look and what they wear and what they say. We like to manipulate the plot to serve our storytelling agendas—and this can't help but spill into our real lives.

In real life, I normally hate unexpected complications and surprises. I hate being kept in the dark. But in reel life, I love to be on the edge of my seat and out of control. In the hands of a skillful filmmaker, I want to shield my eyes at the scary parts and cringe at the protagonist's excruciating vulnerability. I don't want to know everything right away. I want to participate. I want the wheels of my brain to be calculating possible outcomes. Or, even if I can predict what happens, I'm still desperately hoping that I don't know how, when, and where it happens.

> What do audiences want? They want to be surprised.

INTERVIEW: Screenwriter Andrew Kevin Walker

Andrew Kevin Walker Filmography

Best known for:

Sleepy Hollow (1999)
Fight Club (uncredited) (1999)
The Game (uncredited) (1997)
Se7en (1995)

NL: I thought of you for this particular subject because *Se7en* is so intricate and layered. I was wondering about your process with that since it was a spec script—what you started with in that particular story. Did you think it would be interesting to write about a serial killer with that type of profile?

AKW: I was working for low budget production companies in New York City at the time, and my thought process, when it came to writing, was in high concept exploitation mode. So the film started with the idea of seven deadly sin murders. I don't remember how that specific thought came about, but it started with the conceit of what if someone's committing these murders based on the seven deadly sins, and it grew from there playing with what order would the sins be in. The storytelling started with the ending. Very early on, I knew that one of the cops, one of the good guys was going to become Wrath, and I built it backwards from that. So in a way, my thinking had to be what John Doe's thinking was, which was how do I, as a screenwriter or serial killer, ensure that what happens, what transpires, ends up with this bastion of goodness becoming the seventh sin as it were. The company I was working for in NYC was making things like *Blood Rush*, which was a slasher movie in a fraternity house. I remember one concept they had was *Abusement Park*. So being able to say to somebody in one sentence a description of these murders which would take place based on the seven deadly sins was a valuable starting point.

NL: And then you raised the bar with your literary allusions—Milton, *Paradise Lost*, and Hemingway, so there's a really smart sensibility to this that we haven't seen before in these slasher movies.

AKW: Again, I intended to write what would have been essentially a slasher movie or a straight horror movie, and it just became a little bit more. The idea expressed a lot of my frustration with New York City because I was from a suburban existence living in an in-your-face city. Looking back, New York, at the time I lived there, was at the height of the crack epidemic. It was also the time of the central park jogger and even Robert Chambers. It was a strange time, not as burdened by crime as the seventies necessarily, but it was a real culture shock for me. So the screenplay spoke to some of my frustrations about living in a big city, and it just grew into a little more than your standard old cop/rookie cop concept. A lot of the literary cultural references came from research, and I'm sure you probably have a chapter about research. Research is an incredibly valuable thing. It informs, I think, every aspect of the investigation from research in forensic science to the idea of the literary religious origins of the seven deadly sins. It was as simple as picking up *Benét's Reader's Encyclopedia* and just poring through from encyclopedia reference to reference and connecting the dots from the seven deadly sins to St. Thomas Aquinas to *Paradise Lost*. As I have said many times, I am much more the Mills [Brad Pitt] character with the CliffsNotes than the Somerset character who already had that kind of knowledge. I'm a big believer in research because you can read an entire book, come out with one great idea that springs from that, and it was worth it, obviously.

NL: And the number seven, you started with seven deadly sins, Somerset's retiring in seven days, so you have the countdown day to day.

AKW: The ticking clock.

NL: The ticking clock at the end, as they're getting closer and closer to that power line field, John Doe says, "What time is it?" And it's 7:01.

AKW: I was trying to obtain a certain kind of symmetry and perfection to it, and that's, I think, a big part of knowing your ending when you start something. I am a believer in that. If you don't know what the ending is going to be, I don't think you can really lay in as much subtext or whatever you want to call it. Symbolism. Foreboding. You can be as high-brow or as low-brow as you want to be about it. For something like the seven deadly sins, it made sense to be ticking off the days, ticking off the victims, and ticking off the hours.

NL: And you have built-in stakes because by the end of act one, they know there's a pattern, and they know there are going to be five more murders committed.

AKW: "They" being the detectives, and the audience.

NL: Structurally, do you outline before you start writing?

AKW: I outline incredibly extensively. For my own sanity, I need the outline. I do it on one page, I divide the page into three columns, and I do little tiny sentences for every single scene basically in the movie. Now, I do that knowing that it will all change as I'm writing, but I need that as a lifeline to know that I can go back to that outline if I feel like I'm getting stuck in the writing. I'm a big structuralist; I'm a big believer in three-act structure. I adhere, to a certain extent, to the teachings of Syd Field. His textbook, *Screenplay*, was one of the best screenwriting books that I ever encountered, and I read a lot of books about screenwriting when I was living in New York City. But yes, I outline extensively, and I can only speak toward the script for *8MM*, I can't talk about the film because I've never seen it. In the script for *8MM*, I had a full specific third act structure outlined with three people having to be dispatched by the lead character, and I realized at a certain point in the writing that the third act was going to be too long. It was right when I had one character pointing the gun at another character, and so I decided right then, as I wrote, to have the gun go off, and I suddenly and drastically changed my structure. So you've got to be flexible, but I do believe in structure.

NL: Very often, the outline will tell you where your structure is off. One thing that I find people do not discuss as much is the middle of the film. Do you have a specific approach or a way that you think about the midpoint? Because in *Se7en*, from what I was able to analyze, it seemed like the midpoint is actually when Tracy (Gwyneth Paltrow) calls Somerset (Morgan Freeman) and says, "I need to talk to you," and he meets her at the diner and he discovers she's pregnant.

AKW: I'm trying to remember myself whether that was before or after. I don't know what the midpoint of *Se7en* would be—I would have to take a look at it. It was interesting because *my* end of the first act of *Se7en*, I think would be different than what a lot of people think it is. In my mind the end of the first act of *Se7en* comes when Somerset says, "You know what, I quit, go ahead, do this without me." Because I see his character making a decision that turns everything in a different direction, and then he has to be drawn back into it. And obviously then the end of the second act, for me, is when the John Doe character turns himself in. That's a good place to discuss a little bit of your chapter's topic, which is mystery. A big reason why I feel that *Se7en* works is because there was a really strong awareness of the audience's expectations. One of the things that I had in mind from the beginning was how this cop was going to become Wrath, as I said. Frustration has to play a part in that, and there has to be absolutely no other choice for the character in the story but to dispatch John Doe personally. Part of creating the frustration I'm talking about was a conscious decision to essentially say, "Let's have the satisfying moment that the audience is waiting for, when the cops get the bad guy and capture him … let's just take that away from the audience." They're going to be sitting there waiting for that moment, craving it, the characters are craving that moment also, and instead of giving them that moment, John Doe just comes in and says, "Here I am." And it's indisputable, "I'm the one who's victorious." The reason that I hope it was powerful is that it's a slap in the face. It's so the opposite of what you as an audience member wanted. It takes the formula of: almost anything you're writing is going to fall into a certain genre, and there are certain expectations specific to each genre, and the real trick when it comes to plotting a satisfying story, in my opinion, is turning some of those expectations on their head; in this case so that you're heading into the third act thinking, "I now have no idea what's going to happen."

It's another trick altogether to satisfyingly and artfully fulfill that expectation of what is going to happen. That's one of the most valuable things in writing genre stuff; mystery stuff, suspense stuff. I don't think it's underrated, but I don't think that it's valued as much as it should be—trying honestly to be clever in the storytelling. In other words, attempting to lead the audience into thinking one thing story-wise without it being completely, like in almost every movie, nonsensical. Too often, I believe stories may seem to be clever, but it's at the expense of logic, or disregarding logic altogether. Meaning, in the end, the plot just doesn't tie together in any way.

NL: But *Se7en* exceeds whatever the expectation is going to be for a couple of significant reasons, in my opinion, which can also tie back into the topic of mystery. Foreshadowing: there's actually a lot of foreshadowing if you see what the result is, and I wonder how deliberate these things were. If these were choices that David Fincher (director) made? These were just a few things I noticed: One, when he's in the library, I noticed when they were looking through the books there's a shot of a woman with a severed head, in the book, very fast.

AKW: I'm sure that was Fincher's foreshadowing.

NL: In that scene, around what I'm calling the midpoint, when they talk about the pregnancy, when Somerset tells his story about his love, and they were pregnant, and he convinced her not to have the baby. And Tracy adamantly says, "No, no, I'm going to definitely have the baby, I wouldn't even consider it," which is another little piece of foreshadowing. My question is, and I know you worked on *The Game* and *Fight Club*, there are hints dropped in these films, are some of them subliminal?

AKW: The use of foreshadowing, in each of those examples, goes right back to my point about knowing your ending. Somerset says, for example, "This is not going to have a happy ending," and that was directly trying to prepare the audience to a certain extent. There was always a lot of concern about how would this test and what would audiences think, and my argument was always that if people can make it through the Lust murder, which is so heinous, no matter how little you see of it, then they will survive and make it to the end of the movie. They've already been bludgeoned enough, so they'll survive. In regard to that pivotal scene, where Somerset sits with Tracy. For that character, Somerset, it's an incredibly huge kind of secret that he keeps, because then he knows that his partner's wife is pregnant before the partner knows, and that's a real burden. It's been a little while since I've watched the movie, but I think you have to assume that other than John Doe, only Somerset knows this even at the end. And John Doe's the one who reveals it to Mills. And Somerset's heart is breaking into another couple of pieces, because he knew. And again, that speaks to outlining your story beforehand. You think to yourself: "God, wouldn't it just be shattering if this one guy knew this secret about the wife . . . John Doe discovered it and saved it for when he most needed it?" There's all this stuff that John Doe keeps, and because of the endgame he's planning, he's saying to himself: "If this happens I'll use this. Or I want to push this guy until he kills me, so if it doesn't seem to be working, at least I've got this ace in the hole . . . that she was pregnant." And Brad's character, Mills, is going to know that it's the truth, because he'll see it in Somerset's face.

NL: It's Shakespearian, it's inevitable. There's a shot early on—I don't even know if this is in the screenplay or not—one of the first opening shots of the movie and we see a chess game in Somerset's apartment. And the end of the movie is the last move, like checkmate.

AKW: That may have been a Fincher touch. It's that kind of stuff that can be satisfying when you're watching it the second time, hopefully. This next example comes specifically from the novel that Chuck Palahniuk wrote, but watching *Fight Club* the second time is obviously an entirely different experience than watching it the first time. And in a way, you as an audience member watching it the second time can go back and see for yourself . . . did Fincher cheat? And he absolutely did not. For anyone who hasn't seen it or read the book, I won't say any more, but . . . so often in *The Game, Se7en,* or *Fight Club,* the foreshadowing is just Fincher at work.

NL: When you do rewrites, whether in *Fight Club* or *The Game,* do you find that there are common weaknesses, or anything that you are able to bring to the table?

AKW: Not really. Again, in those cases, much of it comes down to Fincher. He is extremely specific. This is one reason it is a joy to write for him. Also, he is incredibly inclusive, so that he reads and perceives stuff in a way that many other people don't, so you, the writer, are actually welcomed into the process in a way that with other people . . . it just doesn't always work. One of the things that I read before I wrote the straightforward horror spec screenplay, *Psycho Killer*, was the book, *Danse Macabre*, a Stephen King nonfiction book. It talks to a certain extent about Stephen King's passion for horror movies and obviously about his writing. He goes into great detail about the allegorical "monster behind the door," and the viewer or reader's expectation always being so much stronger than once you actually open the door and show the monster. You know, that inevitable disappointment, which is interesting to me. In the script for *8MM*, the character of the Machine is masked, and I specifically wrote in the script at the end, after the Machine is defeated, that the main character, Welles, reaches down and takes the mask off, and I said, "We in the audience do not see his face, and we never will." They went a different way with the movie, from what I'm told. Again, there are many reasons why I never saw the movie, but to me that ending as originally written played into that whole idea of, there's nothing you can show the audience that will ever live up to what evil they imagine lies under that mask. Now, because *8MM* for me was kind of a wash, almost like a do-over, I've definitely gone through and extracted little thematic things from it, and said, "I deserve to re-explore that." So one of the core conceits of *Psycho Killer* is the classic masked slasher character, but what I laid into that script was this notion of whether or not you should ever see his face. I love the idea, which I seem to deal with often—almost as frequently as my having beheadings in nearly everything I write, it seems—of withholding horrors from the audience. For obvious reasons. Like we never do actually see inside the box at the end of *Se7en*, although many people believe they did. And I'm aware that some may believe the idea of taking an audience through an experience like *8MM* and then withholding actually seeing the killer's face is a cop out, but I embrace the pretentiousness of that.

NL: I don't think it's a cop out at all, and it's also kind of an achievement saying that these kinds of people, you could walk right past them. They're anonymous.

AKW: Well, that was the whole point of John Doe. The whole point of John Doe is that he would pass you on the street and you wouldn't think twice about it.

NL: And they even do.

AKW: It's not like, "Oh, look at that scary, lumbering guy, steer clear of him."

Trying to have a well-earned mystery be either central to the story or a really nice piece of the background . . . the ability to achieve that suspension of disbelief, to attain the payoff of that mystery in a satisfying way without cheating the audience, without the entire story being nonsensical—that's an amazing thing to strive for.

I think it's equally amazing to try and keep the monster behind that door for as long as you can, and then opening the door and still having as much of a sense of satisfaction as you can possibly achieve. There are images of horror that you can see in the paintings of Hieronymus Bosch or in a movie like *Häxan*. Effective, terrifying depictions; I don't know whether some of them would be considered taboo, they're almost too realistic, you know what I mean? Too much for people to handle if they were fully utilized in modern horror filmmaking, maybe, I don't know. But there are certain envelopes that I think could still be pushed when it comes to horror, and these days anything, of course, can be attained with special effects. I think it's important sometimes to open that door as wide as possible, and really strive to pay that off and face that difficulty. I think it's a brave thing to do. Although, I could be wrong about this, but when it comes to horror, overall I think there's much more of a PG-13 mentality, as opposed to Rated R; hardcore horror. I prefer the latter.

NL: It seems with your work that you open up the most taboo doors, like with *8MM* the idea of a snuff film, but yet it's not exploitive.

AKW: In the screenplay for *8MM*, it says, underlined and probably in bold print, "We will never see this film," meaning the snuff film. In the script, you experience the snuff film from a locked camera perspective showing only the private investigator while he's watching this thing, so that you experience the horror of it. You never see it. Again, this also speaks to what you're talking about: mystery or suspense. So that you as the viewer don't have the experience of watching the snuff film and thinking to yourself, "Oh, is this real or could it be achieved by special effects?" Within the story, I mean. So in a way, it's stronger . . . to put across the idea that this must be real, because look at the way this guy's reacting.

Mystery, as a conceit, is useful in every genre, not just horror or suspense, to state the obvious. But for example, there's the mystery of "who is this character that people are talking about?" early in the movie. In a script I'm working on right now, called *A Reliable Wife*, adapted from the novel of the same name, there's a character who appears right, in my opinion, smack dab at the perfect kind of midpoint of the story. Until that moment when the character arrives, there are others talking about this as yet unseen character. Anytime someone on screen is talking about someone that you know that you're going to meet, this in itself creates a certain amount of heightened expectation, because it becomes exciting that there's another page that's about to turn. It's just to say, "mystery" belongs in every genre, not just in horror or suspense films.

Along those lines, another spec that I worked on, a comedy called *Old Man Johnson*, is about this young girl in her early twenties who goes to visit her elderly grandfather. The grandfather just occasionally mentions this guy, Johnson, who lives down the hall. Now, you go into the story knowing, because the story is called *Old Man Johnson*, that Johnson is obviously important. But this person is talked about and mentioned a few times, with "he would be upset if he heard that," and "he would be upset if I wasn't there to play Gin Rummy with him," and there's definitely a feeling that, "Oh, Johnson must be this elderly peer of the grandfather." Then right around page 10, in walks Johnson and you see that he's the same age as the young girl . . . he's in his twenties, but he clearly thinks that he's 80 years old. So again: expectation versus the reveal. In this case, I made sure to bring that character in by page 10. You know that kind of magic first ten minutes where you as a reader or you as an audience member, are either going to buy into the story or step back from the story. When you talk about somebody off screen, it can really build a mystery in a non-mystery context. Does that make sense?

NL: Absolutely. When I was talking to Stuart Beattie about the role of the antagonist, he referenced *Se7en*, and in a lot of books people talk about how you have to introduce your antagonist in the first act. What Stuart was saying, which I agree with, is that you have to introduce the *idea* or the *presence* of an antagonist. So like in *Se7en*, you don't have any idea who the antagonist is, you see the effect of what the antagonist is doing, but then in the meantime, you need other sources of antagonism. You need to know where you're going. I think William Goldman said that in a thriller you have to start with your antagonist, like in *Marathon Man*, and then work backwards, from what the antagonist's M.O. is, and then decipher it. That's the key to the puzzle. Maybe it's not a fixed thing in your work or in your process, but how much work do you do in adding dimension to your antagonists?

AKW: Well, it's a bit of a cliché, but it's true that the antagonist is often easier and more exciting to write. I think that there are movies like *The Day of the Jackal* where the antagonist kind of is the protagonist, and it's balanced by bouncing back and forth within the story. I don't want to talk too much about *Psycho Killer*, because hopefully it will get made one day and I don't want to ruin the surprise of it, but it plays with structure and with point of view throughout. And one of the core conceits of *Psycho Killer* is that, as with any good slasher movie, you're obviously going to be looking through the eyes of the antagonist sometimes. But that may all just fall under the category of whatever the formula is, you need to try and do the opposite . . . or at least give a new gloss on the formula. Apply some reinvention.

You can sell an antagonist fairly easily by way of a brief, one scene introduction, if you feel it needs to be done early on in your story. However, I agree with you . . . I think that it doesn't matter when that person comes in, so long as their presence is felt.

There was a specific argument going on, literally, on the first day of shooting *Se7en*, where I kept resisting showing John Doe earlier. *Se7en* was a long road of resisting a lot of changes requested throughout its development, and then later, luckily, Fincher came along and saved it by going back to earlier versions. But there was discussion on the first day of shooting where producer Arnold Kopelson expressed his concern, saying essentially, "Where's the conflict? Where's the antagonist? They're just walking in upon these murders." And my argument, to a certain extent, was the conflict is that these characters are trying to maintain their sanity, and that's one of the things at stake. If there's any villain in the first part of *Se7en*, it's the oppressive feeling that there is this evil presence out there. It's just to say there are different ways of doing it. Different ways of telling a story and expressing "conflict."

Again speaking to mystery, with *Se7en*, I did not want to be omnipotent in the storytelling. We chose not to show John Doe in his laboratory making preparations. We don't show him torturing anybody. There's a whole franchise movement that I believe swung things in the other direction, which is the kind of *Saw* torture porn screenwriting/filmmaking where you *do* show. You could make a movie of *Se7en* where you do show every single person being tortured; it's just less valuable to me.

Se7en does, to be honest, cheat in a way, by jumping POV to show John Doe getting out of a taxi cab, walking across the street and turning himself in at the end of the second act. If it were really pure, we would literally be standing with Mills and Somerset and watching their point of view instead at that moment. But you as a storyteller do want that build up . . . you want that sort of necessary jump over to fudge the POV a little bit. And you've got to do that sometimes. In that instance, it's better to mine the suspense than to say, "I stuck to the rules that I set forth." But the less that you saw of John Doe—the more that you were following along with the protagonists— the more you felt their frustration, the more you wondered . . . the more powerful that scene is when you finally get into this guy's house, John Doe's, and he's long gone, but you get to look around and go, "Oh my God!"

NL: And piece it together from there. Everything was a clue.

AKW: I think that it all boils down to examining the story from every different angle, and doing this kind of thing which I have been taught is important, and that is to fully imagine what it is you're writing. So the idea of John Doe cutting off his fingertips so that there wouldn't be any fingerprints obviously arises from thinking the crime scene through! You have to think: what evidence might have been left behind? Especially nowadays, when everyone's so aware of that forensic stuff now, because it's all over the television every week.

But this concept of "fully imaging" means also thinking it through from the audience's point of view. Within the idea of mystery, I'll talk for a second about the screenplay of *The Wolfman*. My original screenplay was quite a bit different from the film. Here again, I have not seen the film, but I know some of what was rewritten. Just like in *Sleepy Hollow*, *The Wolfman* script was designed as a murder mystery. You have a quote/unquote detective in this

Benicio Del Toro character, returning to his childhood home . . . entering a situation where his brother is missing. So I know that the audience is thinking, "Okay, the brother may have been murdered by a werewolf, or the brother may actually be the werewolf." And so as you're writing it, you're trying to get a little ahead of the audience, because they're trying to get ahead of you. And that's the fun battle which takes place between you as the writer versus, or in concert with, the audience. The audience is always trying to figure out the mystery before you want them to. The most satisfying way to pay that off, for the audience, is to fool them and lead them honestly astray, and yet still eventually, and logically, guide them to the conclusion that is the true and fully earned solution to the mystery. You write with that battle in mind the whole time.

Assignment

Think of your screenplay-in-progress as eight sequences, and let's say you're playing an eight-card hand in a poker game. Which two cards get played out in act one? Which four cards get played in act two? Which two cards get played in act three? Which card is your *trump card*—revealed *last* to the audience—and why?

18

WHAT'S THE MOVIE *REALLY* ABOUT?

Illuminate the Central Thematic Question

A theme is a universal truth about life. There's the movie, and then there's what the movie is *really* about. The legendary UCLA film professor, Howard Suber, posits that "themes must be expressed, not as platitudes but as *actions*" (*The Power of Film*, Michael Wiese Productions, 2006, p. 373).

Ideally, no character should speak the theme in dialogue—which tends to feel didactic and obvious. Instead, have the *entire* screenplay—every character, every plotline—represent the theme allegorically. While different audiences will extract different themes from the same script—you must have a point of view as the author. Know what you want to say, and infuse your scenes with the DNA of this theme.

Screenwriter/director Gary Ross (*Big, Dave, Pleasantville, Seabiscuit, The Hunger Games*) once told my UCLA screenwriting class that *theme is everything*. To Gary, characters are created for one reason alone: to serve the theme. He also said that our characters are always more ignorant than we are (as screenwriters) because the character can only see what's happening right in front of him, whereas we can see his past, present and future. Armed with omniscience, Gary structures his screenplays around a central guiding theme so that *acts one and two pose a thematic question that demands an answer in act three.*

In *Big* (screenplay by Gary Ross and Anne Spielberg), the central thematic question is: Can an innocent child succeed in a cynical adult world? Can 12-year-old Josh Baskin (Tom Hanks) navigate the corporate jungle and a mature relationship without having lived the defining experiences of adolescence and young adulthood? At the end of act two, Josh finds himself at a crossroads; his childhood buddy has located the fortuneteller machine, giving Josh the ability to reverse the spell and become a kid again. But Josh has fallen in (puppy?) love with toy company executive Susan (Elizabeth Perkins) and has become a valued asset at the toy company. Susan is the crucial pivotal character in the mix and presents Josh with his biggest challenge. He may look grown up on the outside, but he's still emotionally immature. By leapfrogging over his formative years, Josh realizes there's a void in his life that his superficial age can't fill. He's missed too much. There is also a secondary theme of wish fulfillment, *"Be careful what you wish for,"* which comes full circle in his narrative arc. At the beginning of the movie when Josh feels humiliated at the carnival for not being physically big enough for a ride, his deepest desire is to be big. But, at the end, he'd rather just be a puny kid again and have fun.

In *Dave*, Gary Ross explores a similar, but more political thematic question: Can an idealistic citizen succeed in a bureaucratic political system? Can Dave (Kevin Kline), the spitting image of the fictional President of the United States, prosper in the Oval Office despite the corruption and political gamesmanship surrounding him? This is the question posed in acts one and two that demands an answer in act three. Dave starts off as a politically naïve neophyte, an innocent dupe unwittingly manipulated by his Machiavellian Chief of Staff (Frank Langella). But Dave soon begins to assert himself, leading to a power struggle. The pivotal character here is the First Lady (Sigourney Weaver) with whom Dave begins to fall in love. She encourages his good intentions, but Dave must learn that there are no easy solutions to complex political problems—one citizen's boon can be another's bane. Dave grows into a wiser, worldly faux-President, but realizes that the sitting Vice-President (Ben Kingsley) is much better qualified for the position, and so he hands over the reins. In the process, Dave stays true to his roots as an employment counselor, and integrates his political lessons into his "ordinary" world—in which one ordinary man can make a world of difference.

The Ides of March, The Devil Wears Prada, The Firm, and *Wall Street* all explore the same innocence versus cynicism and/or corruption themes, but with distinctly different settings, characters and plotlines. Their stories are unique; their themes are universal.

Pleasantville poses this thematic question: do spontaneity, free will, and imagination improve the quality of life, or would we be better off in a pre-determined, homogenously agreeable, whitewashed community of wholesome family values? Ross creates the perfect scenario to weather test his theme: teenaged brother and sister (Tobey Maguire and Reese Witherspoon) from the present—in Technicolor—inadvertently time travel through their TV set into a black and white 1950s sanitized sit-com. At first, they're horrified and just want to escape. But they're trapped in this time warp with their present consciousness, so why not exploit their advantage and milk the experience for all its worth? What's most fascinating about the movie is how the black and white world is impacted by these two new arrivals; their semi-jaded, colorful attitudes and values gradually shift the paradigm, causing the dependable fabric of the Pleasantville community to unravel. The cheerfully efficient, loyal housewife, Betty (Joan Allen), whose sole purpose in life is to make her husband and children happy, begins to seek personal fulfillment.

In a key scene, when she apprehensively shows her perpetually genial TV husband George (William H. Macy) that *color* has begun to peek through her white pallor, his reaction is, "It's fine. You'll put on some make-up . . . [and] it'll go away." And Betty's defiant response is: "I don't want it to go away." Allegorically, the theme is linked to prejudice for and discrimination against those in our society who look and think differently than the mainstream. Pleasantville is a microcosm; it's also a trenchant, political theme made accessible through exaggeration, irony, humor, and magic. In the third act, the denizens of this static 1950s Father Knows Best world are questioning why the pages in their books are blank. Progress and change are inevitable.

Gary Ross discussed his approach to theme in his adaptation of *The Hunger Games* (*Written By* magazine, April/May 2012), which explores the central question: *In a brutal society, how vulnerable can you [dare to] be*? The protagonist, Katniss Everdeen (Jennifer Lawrence) is a tough, maternal figure, behaving more like a selfless, protective parent to her little sister, Primrose, than their severely depressed, widowed mother. Growing up in the dirt poor Dystopian/Appalachian *District 12*, Katniss already possesses a stalwart survival instinct before the Hunger Games competition begins. Exacerbated by her father's tragic death in a mining accident, Katniss has been forced to live by primal, animal instincts. She's a proficient archer, not for sport, but to sustain her family. Ironically, as the games become more brutal, Katniss grows simultaneously more aggressive and more vulnerable. She's smart and resourceful enough to realize that her cunning as a solitary soldier has its limitations, so she takes the leap of faith to join forces with Peeta (Josh Hutcherson). Together, they're able to triumph. The answer to the thematic question is: love conquers all.

The poster for *Rise of the Planet of the Apes* spells out the theme in three pithy words: *Evolution Becomes Revolution*. Caesar is no ordinary ape. He's been injected with a powerful experimental drug to cure Alzheimer's—which provides him with extraordinary intelligence. Caesar eventually realizes the limitations of being an animal in a man's world and is compelled to rebel against human authority, becoming his own master. We're told up front that he's going to evolve and revolt, but the movie is still able to surprise us with the complexity of empathy. Incredibly, the filmmakers manage to actually get us to root against ourselves. In the climactic third act, there is pandemonium on the Golden Gate Bridge. It's men against apes—and we're cheering for the apes. Thematically, it seems that when science messes with Mother Nature, she always bites back. Human progress always comes at a cost. And films such as *2012*, *Jurassic Park*, and *Avatar* demonstrate the fragile balance between man and environment, between Earth and the Universe.

The science-fiction movie *District 9* is an allegory to the cruel injustices of apartheid, poverty, and racism. This cinéma vérité-style film follows government agents in Johannesburg who are tasked with forcibly evicting an extraterrestrial race (nicknamed "the Prawns") from a squalid, overpopulated urban ghetto. The Prawns are deliberately grotesque and menacing, like monsters—so we don't immediately empathize with them. But when Wikus (Sharlto Copley), the Chief Inspector overseeing the evictions is exposed to a strange toxic chemical emitted by one of the Prawns, he finds himself with no one to turn to except his new alien friend, Christopher (Jason Cope). What's worse, Wikus is not only fighting for his life, but also battling against his gradual metamorphosis into a Prawn. As the lines are blurred between hunter and hunted, warden and prisoner, friend and foe, the audience is compelled to question its allegiance. The movie makes us question our knee-jerk repulsion and condemnation of the extraterrestrials by showing us their vulnerability and humanity. Thematically, it's a film about tolerance, compassion, and empathy, as the protagonist ends up in his enemies' shoes, feeling what his enemy must feel.

War Horse offers a similar theme. The movie is set during World War I, and Joey, the titular thoroughbred, is put into compulsory service to fight for the Allies. Yet Joey lives purely on animal instinct, and remains neutral. His fierce loyalty is highly personal, yet not impacted by enemy lines or politics. When English teenager Albert (Jeremy Irvine) becomes Joey's caretaker, the horse repays the boy with unwavering devotion. It's an undeniably intense bond. Nevertheless, when Joey is separated from his commander in battle, and subsequently adopted by a French girl, Emilie, the horse becomes equally devoted to her. And when German soldiers take him away from her, Joey bonds with his new caretaker, Friedrich, until the steed is able to escape once again.

In one of the film's most powerful scenes, its theme comes into sharp focus: Joey is painfully ensnared in a mess of barbed wire, and two enemy soldiers (British and German) are compelled to work together to help free him. As Joey thrashes around in agony, the soldiers put aside their guns and pick up wire cutters to set the noble creature free. When the horse is extricated, the two men agree to flip a coin to decide ownership of Joey. The British soldier wins the coin toss; the men shake hands, and go back to their respective sides of the war. Even in the midst of horror, their mutual compassion for the vulnerable horse overrides their animosity.

In an ensemble movie, with multiple protagonists and diverging plotlines, a unifying theme will be the glue. In *Crash*, the theme is we're all connected by our humanity. In *Traffic*, the thematic through-line is how the drug trade impacts all people from every strata and city—and how it's essentially unwinnable without global cooperation. In *Love, Actually*, the theme demonstrates how we all yearn for connection and love despite the terror of rejection and loss. Ultimately, the most enduring theme remains: love conquers all.

All themes are related to the power of the human spirit: love, truth, honor, integrity, courage, redemption, faith, etc. We aspire to these virtues amidst the constant challenges of life. Characters must face their fears and struggle to transcend their limitations. Where there is struggle, there is drama. Where there is drama, there is story. Embedded in every worthwhile story, there is a compelling, universal theme.

INTERVIEW: Academy Award-Winning Screenwriter Eric Roth

Eric Roth Filmography

Best known for:

Extremely Loud & Incredibly Close (2011)
The Curious Case of Benjamin Button (2008)
    Academy Award Nominee
    WGA Award Nominee
The Good Shepherd (2006)
Munich (2005)
    Academy Award Nominee
Ali (2001)
The Insider (1999)
    Academy Award Nominee
    WGA Award Nominee
    WGA Paul Selvin Honorary Award Winner
The Horse Whisperer (1998)
Forrest Gump (1994)
    Academy Award Winner
    WGA Award Winner
WGA 2012 Laurel Award Winner for Screen (lifetime achievement)

NL: After you research, which I'm sure you do extensively, what's your first step? Do you outline? Do you start with character, plot, premise, or theme?

ER: I think my first approach to an original or an adaptation is theme. In other words, what are the bigger things that are being said in the piece? And, these may be ideas that are really there or things that I like to think I found there. In the case of adaptation, these can even be issues I felt were there even though the author may or may not have intended them. Theme becomes most important to me in that everything is in some way associated with the theme of the piece.

NL: This has been the most polarizing interview question because a lot of people have said, "No, I never think about theme because it will get preachy or heavy-handed and then it will derail the drama and the storytelling." And then, other people like you have said, "No, theme is everything."

ER: I think it's everything. I don't think it's easily definable. I don't care if it's a more subtle or subtextual version of it, which, by the way, is the best way to handle it. A director once shared with me the worst line of exposition he had ever heard which was, "Good morning, Mr. Water Commissioner." I think I'm at least experienced enough to write exposition in a clever way. In *The Insider*, the exposition was intentional and done very cleverly. We needed to bring the audience into the movie, so that they knew exactly what had to be done to increase the tension of the piece. Michael Mann and I crafted a scene in the CBS lunchroom where we intentionally had Al Pacino, playing the reporter Lowell Bergman, lay out the whole movie. "We have to get this guy a lawyer, and we have to get him out of this," and then all the other tasks were laid out for us. It was well done. It didn't feel like exposition. One of the big problems is that everybody tells you what's happening or they have characters talk to each other who both know what's happening. I'm going to give you a bad example. Having a character say, "Our sister died," when they both very well know that their sister died. It's a forced way to get the audience drawn into the story.

As a general rule, I would say my process is to write to what I think is the general theme of the piece. It may not be particularly definable, but it is my way of getting a sense of what the movie should be about. If it's about loss, forgiveness, redemption, or whatever the general notion of the piece is, I think almost every scene should relate to that. After you know what the theme is, you can get into all sorts of structural things like where you need to end up in the first and second acts and all those other very strict rules of drama. A really good writer said to me once, "What does a main character want?" You have to state that in some way, it can be heavy-handed or not, because that's what the movie should really be about. I'm writing right now, something that is very unlike anything I've done before, a space movie, a sort of adolescent film somewhere between *Star Wars* and *2001*, and I was thinking, "What does our hero want?" It's very simple: he wants to go home. And, I literally have him say just that. So, for the rest of the movie, you understand completely where he stands, what his quest is, and where things are in relation to him getting home. I think it's a valuable thing. If I talk about an overall arching quality to my work, and I've had a number of conversations with various people who have been nice enough to like my work, people like Tom Hanks, Brad Pitt, and David Fincher, they all feel like my work is about loneliness. And, I can't disagree.

L *oneliness is probably the most consistent theme of all my work.*

NL: I had the same exact conclusion after watching all of your films back to back. Each of your characters fears being left alone in the world.

ER: I think that's all true. You can, maybe, criticize my work for being one note. To be honest with you, it's probably because I've never been alone in my life. I am probably terrified of being alone, even though I'm alone all of the time. I've never even had a room of my own my whole life. Loneliness has always been a big theme, even with other authors I've adapted. When themes become moral dilemmas like you brought up earlier, I think those are more interesting films.

NL: Well, certainly, Forrest Gump doesn't end up alone because of his child, so you have a bittersweet, mostly sweet, conclusion. Benjamin dies . . .

ER: I think he dies in peace, but it may have other meanings for people. I wrote that strictly for my mother who had just died or was in the process of dying and my father who had also died while I was writing it, so that was probably about me coming to grips with being an orphan.

NL: I wondered about the choices of the present-day story, especially with Caroline losing her mother, Daisy, who is dying in the hospital, in relation to your "being orphaned/loneliness" theme. We're born alone and die alone.

ER: While we were getting ready to film it, Hurricane Katrina came through and became everybody's tragedy. We thought we would be remiss if we didn't use it in telling a story about New Orleans. It's a character on its own to a certain extent. In other words, hurricanes are going to come and go, and you're obviously going to have terrible things happen to you, but this was just another milestone in this woman's particular life. It was another event that was part of the clock of everything. I watched my mother as she was dying. How she would remember some things accurately and other things were fanciful dreams due to the morphine. I just wanted to tell the story backwards through Daisy's voice because if one wanted to be really imaginative, the whole movie could just be a morphine dream from this woman's point of view. Benjamin may never even have existed.

NL: Right, right.

ER: That's an extreme version, but I can make a case for it. I thought it would be interesting to have her potentially fabricating this fable alongside some reality to help people join the story faster because when you have a fable, you have to suspend disbelief. Some great movies have started with, "I'm going to tell you a story," from Lucas saying, "In a galaxy far, far away," to *Peter Pan* with Wendy being read to, or even *Harry Potter*. Once you're willing to sit down as an audience to listen to the story, you can go all over the place. If people believe that you are telling something from the rules of the piece, they'll stay with you.

NL: Well, structurally, it also seems to give you both a spine to tell the story and a sense of where you're headed. There's inevitability to Benjamin and Daisy's relationship. Then, Katrina kind of crescendos.

ER: On that note, I think David Fincher brilliantly had the idea to end with that clock scene because he just felt that time had washed over everything.

NL: Yes, it's gorgeous.

ER: At the warehouse where the water level goes up and just basically swallows everything. That was the reality of what happened to poor New Orleans and what happens with life. Eventually time just becomes a big watershed.

NL: On the idea of inevitability in terms of the plot, do you consciously look for some kind of central mystery? One piece of the puzzle to hold back? I often talk to students about how the climax is the truth and how, ideally, you're going to hold something back so that you're building toward a final revelation. For example, in *The Good Shepherd*, it's the reveal of what was in his father's suicide letter. And, also who is the person in the mystery film? In *Benjamin Button*, you're holding back the fact that Carolyn is his daughter. Is that something you do when you're structuring your film?

ER: I think it's sometimes easier with originals because if you want that to become part and parcel of the structure of the piece, you can build in certain things. I can give you one example of how this does and doesn't work. I just recently finished writing this film which will be out at Christmas time called, *Extremely Loud & Incredibly Close*, which has a built-in mystery to it, so that was rather simple. It's from a best-selling book about a little boy who is searching for his father who died in 9/11. Tom Hanks and Sandra Bullock star. He had a very close relationship with his father, and they would do these scavenger hunts together. The boy is supposed to have Asperger's or a form of it. He finds an envelope in his father's closet that has on the outside the word, "black," and on the inside a key after his father is gone. He assumes this is some message from his father. One of the tricks utilized in the book was to keep certain mysteries alive and then, at the end, give everything a certain kind of conclusion. The director and I added some elements to this device as well. It may not be as conclusive as solving a mystery, but will hopefully give you an emotional conclusion where you'll feel good about it and also be able to grieve with the boy. The built-in element of this book was probably what attracted me because I visually found it interesting.

Contrast this with my new space movie where I've had the idea to maybe do three movies, so that you don't have to end the first one. I mean it would have an ending, but maybe more of a cliffhanger. I'll have certain things I want to utilize in movies two and three, but not in the first one. It might be something that may never see the light of day. So, the answer is "yes," I structure the film in such a way that the audience feels they know where they're going, but they won't know how they got there. There's a mystery in that. I'm not a big comic book guy, so this will probably be a bad example, but if you knew Superman ended up on earth, and if he's telling the story, you'd be interested to know how he got here. You may not find out for three movies, but you will find out. So, if he's sitting alone in a bar, and telling the bartender, "You won't believe my story. I came from another planet and I have super powers," then, when he tells us what he is, you've established some kind of mysterious element to it. I think that where you're right about me, and I probably should get away from this because I've been doing it a lot lately, is that I've been telling stories with a voiceover from another time. Like *Benjamin Button*, *Forrest Gump* has a voiceover from the bench. *Extremely Loud* has a voiceover, because the boy's from a certain period of time in the movie, and the space movie is going to have a voiceover for a specific reason too. I have to figure out if I'm cheating or being lazy, but I find it a great way to add a whole other element to the movie—maybe it's just a way to avoid trying to tell the story in the most linear way.

NL: Well, it affords you the music of language. There's a poetry to the voiceovers which is great, and it gives us access to the character's thoughts which we normally would get in a novel and you can't usually get in a screenplay. I also think they seem very necessary in works that are so sprawling. You're covering decades or many, many years. It bridges the gap.

ER: Well, that I like. It's a major value of voiceovers but they can also be a crutch, so you have to be very careful.

NL: Right, I think in the wrong hands, but in yours, the voiceovers feel right.

ER: Well, so far, it's been okay.

NL: When you're thinking about premise, in addition to starting with theme, do you think about what the central conflict of the premise is? For example, in *Benjamin Button*, he's going to age backwards, but he's going to lose people, and in *Forrest Gump*, he's going to significantly alter or be embedded in history, but he can't really be with the woman he loves because of the differences in their intellectual capacities or in *The Insider*, he wants to just tell the truth, but at what price? He ends up losing pretty much everything, but it ends up being worth it in the end.

ER: I don't think you can compare *Benjamin Button* with *The Insider*. I don't see, except for maybe the feeling of loneliness, any relationship between those two movies.

NL: Well, not so much the relationship because they're all so different. I actually meant *Benjamin Button* and *Forrest Gump*.

ER: There are some similarities. As a matter of fact, I was criticized for it.

NL: Well, mainly just the love stories . . .

ER: Well, in *Benjamin Button*, except for obviously taking Fitzgerald's main idea of someone aging backwards, I structured his life in my own way with familiar themes. In other words, there's always a lot of water in my work and there also might be some kind of housekeeper. People found certain similarities and then made fun of them or enjoyed them. It was one of the two. It's fine either way.

NL: Well, the boarding house and the old people's home . . .

ER: Some people thought it worked and some people thought it was derivative. I didn't think it was derivative. I thought they were totally different stories. For example, Martin Scorsese's *Goodfellas* versus *Casino*—certain motifs and characters, ideas, and the way he expresses them are similar. In other words, you may like those better or worse, but you won't criticize him for being derivative. I can tell you maybe six directors who are like that who are storytellers. The good news is that people are aware of my work and have time to compare one to the other.

NL: I wasn't comparing them as being derivative. It was more particularly for newer screenwriters and screenwriting students. I've been trying to teach them to stay on story, to stay on point and to know what the movie's about and what the movie's not about.

ER: Right, that's very important.

NL: With regard to central conflict of premise, do you think consciously about this on a plot level? In other words, that this is the particular struggle of a man just trying to tell the truth, but at a great cost.

ER: I think those are very different. I don't know how to compare *Benjamin Button* to *The Insider*. *Benjamin Button* was a love story I wrote to my mother about what I thought about her time on this earth, and my time on this earth with my relationship to my children and grandchildren, as well as the more universal idea of how everybody does or doesn't have people in their lives. I was just showing a man's life and how he comes to grips with the possibility that he's going to go away or disappear while the people he has loved are going to get older. Another theme I was interested in was her ballet world and what happens when people get injured. It was a very, very predictable story in a way. It's as if I were Jack London, and the story is that of a young man going off to war, a young man coming back from war, and his adventures in between. He comes back from war, he falls in love, and he falls out of love. So, there was nothing grandly different about it, it was just this story of this particularly oddball character. *The Insider* was set to be an interesting look inside. You want to call it "the truth," and I agree with you. What are you going to have to suffer for telling the truth? This guy's a very flawed man, so he was particularly brave because he was a guy who really didn't have any axe to grind at first, he just wanted to get his fucking pension. It was really actually kind of an unlikely movie. When Michael asked me to do it, I couldn't understand how it could be a thriller, but as I got into it, I found it to be gripping, so we set it like a thriller.

NL: Yes, it's structured like a thriller.

ER: As for degree of difficulty, that was probably the hardest screenplay I ever had to write. Probably felt like it succeeded as well as anything. I've liked other ones differently. I loved *Forrest Gump* because it's close to me and was embraced in a great way across the country. I've loved other things. I wasn't as happy with the reaction to *The Good Shepherd*. I liked that it was a very intricate and interesting piece. Because it was rewritten, I wasn't happy with some of the directions that *Munich* went. Even though I think Tony Kushner is a great, great writer, and that Steven simply had some other ideas. It's all fine, it's part of what you do. I think they're all different. Each one presents a different problem, different need for solutions and the only thing that remains the same—and I really believe this for every screenplay I've ever written and I've probably written 20 movies—is that their themes have been generally different and my own theme has stayed the same. You have to apply the rules—I don't care if you stand on your head there's going to be whatever number of acts you want to attribute to a film—there's always going to be a Greek-structured drama. There's going to be three maybe four acts. The first act delineates the problem, the second act tries to both solve and complicate the problem, and the third act is going to decide the problem. And, then hopefully the film starts to take on some coherent whole. I always know the beginning and the end, but I know nothing about the middle even if it's from a book.

NL: Well, what seems to happen in the middle of most of your work is this existential dilemma where the character has to re-evaluate or starts to re-evaluate the "who am I?" question. What do I really believe in? What really matters? And, what is particularly powerful for me about *The Insider* is that it's a dual track because as Jeffrey Wigand is going through his full existential dilemma, so is Lowell Bergmann. He is questioning the power of journalism and truth within the corporate world and how things have changed.

ER: That definitely was done intentionally. There are some odd similarities between the two. He found himself an outsider in his own work which was the irony of the concept of *The Insider*. To me one of the better scenes I've ever written was the one where he's trying to get a cell phone signal and walks into the water.

NL: Me, too. I love that scene.

ER: It's him screaming, "I told the truth." There was great drama to that. That really worked well.

NL: Just two more questions. What is the significance of the man who was struck by lightning 17 times in *Benjamin Button*?

ER: I always loved The Book of Darwin and the Darwin Awards for when people have had terrible things happen to them. It's sort of ironic. They did one of them very well in the movie, *Magnolia*, where the father had a fight with his wife and fired off a shotgun, accidentally killing his son who was committing suicide as he jumped out of the window. I love these kinds of oddball facts in life. The idea behind the lightning man was that this guy would stand the test of time forever, so I just decided to put him in.

NL: I love the randomness of life, too. How you could be struck by lightning and live or you could get hit by a bus after your doctor gives you a clean bill of health.

ER: Exactly—those sort of vagaries of life.

NL: What about the ship in the bottle motif in *The Good Shepherd*?

ER: I had actually seen one or two of those up close and liked the mystery of them. How do they get in there and how do you get them out again? I liked the intricacy around them that if one thing went wrong, the whole thing was going to break apart. I play around a lot with what's fate and what's destiny and what's accident. For Jenny in *Forrest Gump*, I intentionally had this scene that we took out where she killed her father. Her father tries to rape her, and she kills him. So, she is doomed to this terrible psychological life that leads her down some bad paths. You'll find in my work that I try to make everyone feel real and that they have some inner psychological life that will naturally take them in directions that only that particular kind of psychology would do.

ASSIGNMENT

Analyze the thematic questions in three current movies, and how each one poses a thematic question in acts one and two that *demands* an answer in act three.

19

WHERE IS THE HEAT?

Fuel and Stoke the Dramatic Fire

Ideally, your protagonist will have both a primary positive and corresponding negative goal. It is this +/– polarity that will generate dramatic tension or "heat" to keep the story engine running. Heat is also generated by the friction of your main character's need to seek his/her potential destiny (+) while simultaneously not succumbing to his/her potential fate (–). According to UCLA film professor, Howard Suber:

> You seek your destiny; you succumb to your fate. Destiny originates within the self; fate comes from outside. Fate is the force that lies beyond individual will and control; it pushes you from behind. Destiny is the attracting force in front of you that acts like a magnet and that you choose to acquire.
>
> (Suber, H. *The Power of Film*, Michael Wiese
> Productions, 2006, p. 117)

Act three needs to emotionally feel like trial by fire (even in a romantic-comedy) or else the climax is going to be too tepid. In *When Harry Met Sally*, it's Harry's (Billy Crystal) fate to be alone on New Year's forever, but it turns out, at the climax, that his destiny is to marry Sally (Meg Ryan).

In *The Hurt Locker*, it is Sergeant First Class William James' (Jeremy Renner) apparent destiny to be a heroic bomb specialist who is able to dismantle explosives against the most impossible odds imaginable. We wonder if his fate is to get himself blown to smithereens, or if he'll survive to seek what might be his "true" destiny: in the role of devoted husband and father to his baby boy. In the end, his destiny is to remain a rogue thrill seeker, as he re-enlists for another tour of duty.

In *Precious*, emotionally scarred teenager Precious' (Gabrielle Sidibe) fate appears to be following in her abusive mother Mary's (Mo'Nique) miserable footsteps. But the determined Precious forges a new path, and seeks her destiny to break out of the vicious cycle, get an education, and find independence.

In *District 9*, Wikus' (Sharlto Copley) fate is duty bound: to carry out the orders of his bureaucratic superiors and evict the burgeoning population of alien "Prawns" from their refugee camp. But after Wikus is accidentally exposed to a toxic chemical and begins his metamorphosis into a Prawn himself, he teams up with alien Prawn, Christopher (Jason Cope), and seeks his destiny not as persecutor, but as savior of the displaced alien race.

Start with a protagonist who's already desperate on page 1.

In *The Girl with the Dragon Tattoo*, Mikael Blomkvist (Daniel Craig) is initially desperate to put the libel suit scandal behind him. In *Midnight in Paris*, screenwriter Gil (Owen Wilson) is desperate to finish his first novel. In *The Hunger Games*, Katniss (Jennifer Lawrence) is desperate to feed her family.

In *A Separation*, Nader's (Peyman Moadi) wife, Simin (Leila Hatami), is seeking a divorce so she can make a new life abroad, but Nader refuses. He wants to stay and raise their daughter in Iran. Simin is desperate for change; Nader desperately wants to keep things the same.

Some protagonists are aware of their desperate straits; others are hardly conscious.

The screenwriter's goal is to provoke these "stuck" characters into action. Show us the void in their lives and we'll be on the edge of our seats, waiting for the surprising, but inevitable change that's about to come.

Check out the opening sequence in *Trainspotting*—exposition via the shot-out-of-a-cannon approach. It's breathless and exhilarating, and we know these blokes are in trouble from page 1:

```
EXT. STREET. DAY

Legs run along the pavement. They are Mark Renton's
[Ewan McGregor]. Just ahead of him is Spud [Ewen
Bremner]. They are both belting along.

As they travel, various objects (pens, tapes, CDs,
toiletries, ties, sunglasses, etc.) either fall or are
discarded from inside their jackets. They are pursued by
two hard-looking Store Detectives in identical uniforms.
The men are fast, but Renton and Spud maintain their
lead.
```

>   RENTON (voiceover)
> Choose life. Choose a job.
> Choose a career. Choose a family.
> Choose a fucking big television.
> Choose washing machines, cars,
> compact disc players, and
> electrical tin openers.

Suddenly, as Renton crosses a road, a car skids to a
halt, inches from him. In a moment of detachment he
stops and looks at the shocked driver, then at Spud, who
has continued running, then at the Two Men, who are now
closing in on him. He smiles.

[And a bit later. . .]

INT. SWANNEY'S FLAT ROOM. DAY

In a bare, dingy room, Renton lies on the floor, alone,
motionless and drugged.

>   RENTON (v.o.)
> Choose good health, low cholesterol
> and dental insurance. Choose fixed-
> interest mortgage repayments. Choose
> a starter home. Choose your friends.
> Choose leisure wear and matching
> luggage. Choose a three piece suite
> on hire purchase in a range of
> fucking fabrics. Choose DIY and
> wondering who you are on a Sunday
> morning. Choose sitting on that couch
> watching mind-numbing spirit-crushing
> game shows, stuffing fucking junk food
> into your mouth. Choose rotting away
> at the end of it all, pishing you
> last in a miserable home, nothing
> more than an embarrassment to the
> selfish, fucked-up brats you have
> spawned to replace yourself. Choose
> your future. Choose life. But who
> would want to do a thing like that?

[And then we get the real kicker of Renton's rant. . .]

INT. SWANNEY'S FLAT ROOM. DAY

Renton lies on the floor. Swanney, Allison and Baby, Sick
Boy and Spud are shooting up or about to shoot up. Sick
Boy is talking to Allison as he taps up a vein on her arm.

> RENTON (v.o.)
> I chose not to choose life: I chose
> something else. And the reasons?
> There are no reasons. Who needs
> reasons when you've got heroin?

These are desperate characters, but numbed out, oblivious, and constantly desperate for their next fix. As the movie progresses, Renton's passionate goal is to kick heroin. But his potential withdrawal is thwarted by his inability to extricate himself from his junkie friends.

Initial desperation grows hotter as a protagonist becomes increasingly passionate about a personal, emotional, and tangible goal.

In *The Graduate* Benjamin Braddock (Dustin Hoffman) is, at the outset, one of the most passive protagonists in movie history. When he arrives at the L.A. airport having just graduated from college, he's on a moving sidewalk—not even required to walk for himself. Despite his upper middle class upbringing, this is a young man overwhelmed and desperately paralyzed by the uncertainty of his future. But despite his vow to cougar Mrs. Robinson (Anne Bancroft) that he will stay away from her precious daughter Elaine (Katharine Ross), Benjamin falls madly in love with her. And, his passionate goal will be to win back the woman he loves, and nothing—not even her scheming mother—will get in his way.

Up in the Air begins with several real-life interviews of recently fired people—who range from incredulous to bitter to downright enraged. All are scared of what they're supposed to do next. How are they going to pay their bills? How are they going to support their families? And then, we meet the corporate axe man, Ryan Bingham (George Clooney)—via voiceover— who tells us how his life is all about dodging these bullets of pain and uncertainty. The people he fires are grounded and miserable, but his job and peace of mind are secure—as long as he keeps moving. Initially, Ryan is desperate to retain his unencumbered, frequent flyer, bachelor lifestyle. But he's about to have the runway pulled out from under him. As the story progresses, Ryan gradually lets his guard down and begins to fall in love with a female executive traveler, Alex (Vera Farmiga), and their close bond and intimate conversations stoke the fire of his passionate goal, which becomes to sustain a long-term, intimate relationship with her. For the first half of the film corporate perquisites and career were everything to him. By the end, he yearns for family and a lasting connection.

In *Erin Brockovich*, we're introduced to Erin (Julia Roberts) at a job interview at a doctor's office, we learn that she has no actual experience in the medical field, and how she lost her last job because "my son came down with the chickenpox and 104 temperature and my ex-husband was useless." She'd always wanted to go to medical school, but then she got married and had a kid too young and that kind of blew it for her. The doctor then looks down at her resume, trying to figure out a polite rejection. All he can offer is a perfunctory, "Thanks." Followed by an awkward pause and then: "Look . . ." And by Erin's "been there, done that" exasperated expression, she knows what's coming—or rather what's *not* coming: this job.

We cut to her outside the medical building as she finishes smoking a cigarette. Her crappy old car has a parking ticket on the windshield. As she's unlocking it, she breaks one of her ridiculously long fingernails. And if that wasn't bad enough, as she drives away through the intersection, a speeding car runs the red light and Erin gets blindsided. Crash!

Later, at home, we discover she actually has three kids—one a cranky infant with the sniffles—and then there's her roach-infested kitchen and the past due bills and the broken-down plumbing. Trust me, this is a desperate woman with problems. But she's trying, so we're instantly drawn into her world. Her passionate goal evolves as she becomes the legal advocate of the sick and disenfranchised in their fight against the giant utilities conglomerate PG&E. Erin's down-to-earth, no bullshit demeanor earns the trust of the underdogs in this landmark civil lawsuit. Because their problems become her problems, Erin champions their cause with unrelenting determination.

> Great movies are about the collision between desperation and passion: something to gain and something of value to lose. Therein lies the dramatic fire in your story.

INTERVIEW: WGA Award-Nominated Screenwriter Melissa Rosenberg

Melissa Rosenberg Filmography

Best known for:

The Twilight Saga: Breaking Dawn—Part 2 (2012)
The Twilight Saga: Breaking Dawn—Part 1 (2011)
The Twilight Saga: Eclipse (2010)

The Twilight Saga: New Moon (2009)
Twilight (2008)
Step Up (2006)
Dexter (2006–2009)
    WGA Award Nominee

NL: Let's begin with the specific challenges you faced in adapting the phenomenally popular *Twilight* novels from page to screen.

MR: The trick with these books was that they were all written from the lead character's perspective, which meant that the voice was all in her head. This type of internal monologue is wonderful for a book, but doesn't necessarily work in a screenplay. The other problem was that when her thoughts were finally voiced—there was a lot of conversation and very little action. My job was to make the conversations Bella was having with both herself and Edward visual and cinematic.

NL: Can you elaborate on your use of voiceover?

ML: Voiceover is one of the hardest elements of a screenplay to write, and it was one of my main issues when writing Bella. Because she doesn't have anyone she can talk to, there has to be some exposition in order to reveal who she is. Bella is a very internal character. The voiceover is used to externalize her. But it has to be done in a way that's not blatantly expositional which is very, very difficult. Voiceover can be a real crutch. And, it's generally looked down upon. But, after trying to remove it from the third film, we realized that the voice of the movie was not right without it.

In *Dexter*, the voiceover was especially challenging because you have to be in Dexter's head. And there's a really fine balance between saying what's happening—sometimes it's used for exposition. And you have to have it. Because Dexter's not telling anybody what his plan is. So if the audience doesn't know that he's stealing this truck for a particular reason, they will be like, "What the hell is he doing?" So we need the voiceover to tell us why he's stealing it. But it has to be in his unique voice. You have to get that— deceivingly so. I think a lot of people think voiceover is easy, but it's *so not*. And that's the thing—it's the same issue for Bella. She doesn't really have anyone she can talk to either because she can't tell anyone her secret. So you have to understand some of what she's doing—there has to be some exposition, but it's also about revealing who she is. Bella and Dexter are very internal characters.

NL: What about your views on flashbacks?

NL: Flashbacks are also very tricky. I try not to use it, but sometimes it can be a fantastic visual tool. For example, when you have a secret between characters for an entire movie, and then you finally see what it is. In this way, you *earn* the flashback. When you look at great movies, you realize that the character is unfolding for the audience as they go through all of the acts. You don't have to reveal everything about them in the first act. In fact, what weighs down a first act, is thinking, "We have to know this, we have to know that." Maybe we *don't* need to know all of *that*.

NL: One of the biggest challenges with adaptation is condensing a lengthier novel into a lean and mean screenplay. So besides the central love triangle between Edward and Jacob, Bella's relationship with her father really anchors the story emotionally; he's her authority figure that she actively rebels against, and yet she lost her mother, so he's all she has. I would imagine that this relationship was a critical element to retain in the script.

MR: Yes, it was very clear from the book that the father was crucial to Bella, so that was definitely staying in. It created this amazing dramatic tension with her father because she has to hide Edward's true nature from him in order to live her own life.

NL: When writing the screenplay, did you feel constrained by the fact that you were working with a very beloved text?

MR: Yes and no. I felt I could remain faithful as long as I took the character on the same journey that they went on in the book. The actual scenes were secondary to that. I felt that if the characters went on the same emotional journey, then the audience would feel satisfied. I went through the novel and found the moments that were the touchstones for that journey, and then I used those scenes as my structure. There were also certain characters who had to be in the first movie because, as the franchise continued, they took on very important roles. For example, there was a character in the first book who had just a couple scenes—and that was Jacob. Initially, I had only read the first book, so I asked if we really needed him. And, the answer, of course, was "Yes—he's pretty important." After that, it became about combining scenes and characters in order to serve the main storyline and keep the movie going forward.

NL: Is theme important for you to nail down before you start to write?

MR: Each of the *Twilight* novels suggested a theme, which I then had to visually articulate and externalize through action. Every aspect of production was focused on the question: "What is this movie about?" I felt that the entire series was about Bella coming into her own—a coming-of-age story. When you're writing character-driven material, theme is crucial. Theme becomes less important with action movies and suspense/thrillers, where it's mostly about plot. I would argue, however, that the best of those movies are action and character driven. Some of the questions I like to ask are: Why am I telling this story? What am I trying to communicate? I think theme is everything.

NL: In terms of ratcheting up dramatic tension and forging new ground in each sequel, how did you avoid repeating yourself?

MR: It goes to Bella's choice: her examining what she wants for herself— and what she ultimately wants is to be a vampire. In every movie, the antagonist is the worst version of that vampire. She's in love with the best version of that vampire, and his family is made up of the best versions of that vampire, too.

NL: She's wrestling with an emotional and moral dilemma, as well as how to reconcile the positive and negative sides of immortality and brutality. And we're always worried about Bella. She's tough, yet vulnerable and getting more and more over her head. How consciously do you plot out the consequences or *stakes* (a more apt word for a vampire movie!) in your planning process?

MR: The stakes need to be as high as possible.

> *For a teenage girl, love is life and death. Their emotions are so heightened. I think Stephenie Meyer dramatized that and made it literal. That to love was to risk death. And, to do that, repeatedly, over five movies. It takes that experience and makes it very visual. I think that's what the universal appeal of those stories is: the passion—in loving Edward, she could lose everything.*

NL: My son is now a teenager. Every parent's worst nightmare is that their child is going to fall in love with the bad boy or girl, or the one who's going to be a bad influence, and *Twilight* just pushes this situation to extremes. But, there's an inherent universality to this taboo teen relationship. I'm wondering if your approach to Edward was "I need to write him *not* as a vampire, but instead as a mortal, edgy, sexy, 'Rebel Without a Cause' kind of guy"?

MR: Actually, for me, Edward is the Jordan Catalano of the story.

NL: Claire Danes' love interest (played by Jared Leto) in *My So-Called Life*?

MR: Oh my God—such an iconic character! Although, in this case, what makes him the outsider, the bad boy, is that he's a killer. And casting is everything. Stephenie wrote this great relationship which I could have written the hell out of, but, if you don't have that chemistry, it could still have been a disaster. The casting was perfect.

NL: Let's discuss your process on adaptation versus writing an original screenplay. In terms of outlining, how much advanced work do you do before writing?

MR: I do very detailed outlines. They're usually about 25, single-spaced pages. It's a habit I picked up in television where you're dealing with so many moving pieces, and you have to write the script quickly because you're on a very tight schedule.

NL: Do you think in numbers? Like: act one needs to end on page 30?

MR: Absolutely. I have four acts: act one, two (a), and two (b), and act three. Each act is probably 12–13 beats. The hardest part of the process is the outline. In fact, my outline is my first draft. My outline includes dialogue and other details which will probably fall away, but what usually stays the same is the structure.

NL: Once you finish a draft and receive feedback, do you ever go back and re-outline?

MR: Sometimes I'll do a little beat outline that's just a one-sentence summary of the scenes. It makes it easier to move the pieces around.

NL: I know you're a very intuitive writer, so this might be a tough question to answer, but do you have any tips on how to pump up the dramatic tension of a scene or sequence of scenes?

MR: If a scene is feeling flat, I'll go back and review what the scene needs to be about. I'll look at where the actors are situated and where they will be when they come out of the scene. I'll often add activity to the scene by having them jogging, boxing, or running for the train. I like to see what an active change adds to the energy of the scene.

NL: How do you infuse more dramatic tension into a script when you're doing a rewrite of your own work or others'? Are there any common weaknesses that you've noticed?

MR: I always end up going back to structure. If your setup is not strong enough, then there will not be enough punch to carry you through the first act and launch you into the second act. And then, there's also a common problem with hazy midpoint turnarounds.

NL: Can you elaborate on that a bit more? What do you consider a strong midpoint? Because it's probably the most neglected subject of screenwriting.

MR: It is because there's this whole idea of the three-act structure. But, I think that the second act is really two acts, and if you think of it that way, then the midpoint is what takes you into the whole second half of the movie—it's what turns the action around. Without this impetus, the movie flat-lines.

NL: Can you comment on the role of mystery in your work—and how to avoid a predictable outcome?

MR: It's a balancing act of how much to reveal and when. You need to define characters and the conflict in the first act, but it should be the least amount you need to know in order to engage the audience and create the conflict.

NL: A few wrap up questions . . . is there one film that comes to mind that has had a strong influence on your storytelling?

MR: Almost Famous has influenced my writing, partly because of the nostalgia, but also because of the relationship and that character's journey. My favorite scene to write about is realizing one's dreams, and part of realizing one's dream is realizing what that dream is in the first place. It's about knowing who you are and what your place in the world is. Once you know what you want your place in the world to be, how do you realize that? And that's really Bella over all five movies. At the end of the third movie, I included a speech that wasn't from the book. It's when Bella says to Edward, "It's not all about you." I didn't want it to just be about Bella. It is all about her falling in love, but falling in love doesn't involve losing yourself. What makes Bella a viable character is that she's actually choosing a life. In fact, the last two movies became about her realizing her dream by actively choosing to make it happen.

NL: How does this apply to the iconic television character Dexter? Does he have a dream?

MR: He has a conscious dream and an unconscious dream. I think his unconscious dream is to be human. To connect. He's always looking for connection—that which makes him human. Connection is what makes us human. So that is his unconscious dream. But he doesn't think he can have it, or every time he tries for it, something horrible happens. So I think his overall dream is that. And he keeps trying to make it happen. But he doesn't realize that little by little, he's getting closer.

NL: How has working with directors influenced your writing?

MR: Because they think so visually, they have made me a more flexible writer. At the start of your career, you often become very attached to the scenes you write. I think part of the reason is that you think, "I won't come up with a better way to do it. Or, what if I don't come up with any more ideas?" The truth is that there are 6,000 different ways to write a scene. There's a certain confidence that comes with age and experience. You learn that it's about letting go of something and trusting yourself to come up with another idea.

ASSIGNMENT

Write a prose narrative articulating what your screenplay is about first in one sentence, then in three sentences, and finally in three paragraphs. Each version should ideally encompass the beginning, middle, and end of the story with progressively more detail. In addition to simply telling the story, challenge yourself to seek out the hottest, most dynamic conflicts facing your protagonist. At every plot point in your script, continually ask yourself: *Where is the heat?*

20

HOW DOES IT MAKE YOU FEEL?

Connect to the Emotional Core of Your Characters

The crisis in a movie will usually compel protagonists to exert control over a situation that is particularly challenging to them. They've got a pressing problem that *must* be handled. This might be a life and death problem, or a more nuanced dilemma. In any case, their quest is to put out this "fire" and get on with their lives. But, in general, in trying to control, manage, and/or overcome the issue, they just might find themselves confronting their destiny. This simple sentiment is expressed beautifully in the animated film, *Kung Fu Panda*, when Grand Master Oogway says: "*One often meets his destiny on the road he takes to avoid it.*"

In *Juno*, her dilemma is how to handle her pregnancy. This is not an optional course of action. She's a minor, and the clock is ticking from the moment of conception. Is she ready to be a mother? Is she willing to invite the teenaged dad to share in the decision? She knows *how* this happened, but somehow she didn't expect this result. And yet, today is her day of reckoning. Initially, Juno believes she can just "procure a hasty abortion," but when she can't go through with it, she moves on to Plan B: finding the perfect foster parents. But as she gets to know the foster couple and dispassionately carries the baby closer to term, Juno discovers that while she can navigate the mundane issues in her life with snarky cleverness, the one thing she can't control are her *emotions*. At the core of almost every protagonist's trials and tribulations is the conflict between head (psychology/intellect) and heart (passion/emotion).

As protagonists grasp at and grapple for control in their lives, they inevitably find themselves in the unpredictable chaos of life—which often leads to emotional upheaval. Most protagonists seek swift resolution and a return to the status quo—but must face the reality that life is about compromise, mystery, wonder, and constant change. This is all good news for the screenwriter. In a great movie, the audience should feel that virtually anything could happen next.

In *Psycho*, Hitchcock famously killed off "the star," Janet Leigh as the thieving bank teller, Marion, early in the movie to make his audience feel ill at ease. In *Raiders of the Lost Ark*, Indiana Jones (Harrison Ford) immediately fails to get the idol in the opening sequence. In fact, he fails at everything in that movie. And bad news piles up pretty quickly for Grady (Michael Douglas) in *Wonder Boys*.

> These movies work by keeping us on edge. When an audience gets too comfortable, it usually translates into boredom. We want to be excited, provoked, surprised, and even shocked by movies, so be mindful that your "plot points" emerge as crises for your characters because they force your characters to contemplate change. And while each crisis presented in your screenplay should be suspenseful, your characters' emotional lives are what keeps your reader hooked—not the crisis itself.

INTERVIEW: Academy Award-Nominated Screenwriter/Director Guillermo Arriaga

Guillermo Arriaga Filmography

Best known for:

The Burning Plain (also directed) (2008)
El búfalo de la noche (novel and screenplay) (2007)
Babel (2006)
    Academy Award Nominee
    WGA Award Nominee
The Three Burials of Melquiades Estrada (2005)
21 Grams (2003)
Amores Perros (2000)
A Sweet Scent of Death (novel) (1999)

NL: Even though I'd like to focus our conversation on emotional storytelling, I'd first like to ask you about the idiosyncratic structure of your movies. You seem drawn to interconnected plotlines, and in *The Burning Plain*, you have parallel stories. Why is this structure attractive to you and how do you begin? One of the notes I wrote after looking at all of your movies is that they're structured like puzzles with missing pieces and you have to keep watching to see how it all comes together. So, how do you start to construct as an architect or a builder?

GA: I have no plan. I never write outlines. I never write the background of the characters. I have no idea of the characters. I have no idea of the ending. I have no idea of anything. I just sit down and write.

NL: Do you often start with this random tragedy and then build the plot around it? Or, do you start with character? Or, do you start with theme?

GA: Let me tell you something personal that has to do with *Amores Perros*. I had a car accident myself. I was on a hunting trip. My SUV was a Cherokee. I was sleeping in the backseat and a very small guy was sleeping on the floor. There were three kids in the back, so the guy who was driving began poking the ribs of the guy who was sleeping beneath me, so he would wake up and drive because I had been driving all night long and had only been sleeping an hour and a half. So, as he was poking him, he lost control of the truck, and we fell down a cliff. I woke up in the middle of the accident. I remember that my face crashed against a rock. After the accident, I had a vision. I can remember the accident perfectly, how I woke up in the middle of the accident saying, "I will not die," during a free fall of 30 feet. I became obsessed with the time frame of the accident. From the accident, I began reconstructing it: the image of the accident and what happened just before the accident. What happened during the accident and what happened after the accident, so that's the structure of *Amores Perros*—that's where it comes from. So, it was nothing planned. I just wanted a movie to represent my own reconstruction of the events.

NL: Certainly in *21 Grams*, we see the car accident from so many different perspectives, like a prism. What I admire so much about it is when the Naomi Watts character (Cristina Peck) goes back to the scene of the accident and she sits there, all the details with the leaf blower/gardener, you take us right back to the most excruciatingly vulnerable painful part. Did you go back to the site of where this accident was?

GA: We went back. I had to pick up the truck because it was 12 hours away from Mexico City. It was in a very remote region of Mexico in the jungle. So, yes, we went back, and I saw where we fell and everything else just like Naomi's character.

NL: How many years ago was this?

GA: 26th of December, 1985, 6:18 a.m.

NL: And, you've been exploring this in all of your works since.

GA: Yes.

NL: The American tourists (Brad Pitt and Cate Blanchett) stuck in Morocco in *Babel*—probably the sense of feeling stranded, having a medical emergency and nobody can help you. Is that where *Babel* came from?

GA: I was the only one who was hurt in the accident. I have a gash on my head, but my other scars disappeared. I don't know why. I have had several surgeries with no scars. Some bones were broken, and my nose was completely gone. I asked for a ride from a trailer. He stopped, and a friend came with me. I began puking blood and the driver said, "The guy is dying. I don't want someone to die on my trailer, so get off." So, I walked like three miles to a doctor. And, of course, there was no anesthesia or anything. He just sewed my wound and when he tried to fix my nose, he said, "There's nothing there" because all the bones had gone into my brain. So, there I had to wait for another bus to go to an emergency room which was five hours away and I arrived about 24 hours after the accident. There's that tension.

NL: It seemed like you had this personal experience because it's so immediate.

GA: But, I will tell you something, I had never been to Morocco or Japan before I wrote *Babel* and I never do any kind of research. I hate research. I just wrote the screenplay based on personal experiences. I was hoping that my experiences in the north of Mexico with the goat keepers would be almost the same as the Moroccan goat keepers and that Japanese teenagers would behave like my teenage daughter.

NL: It seems incredibly authentic. The other theme that runs through all of the movies is this idea of outsiders. Because in Morocco, obviously the American tourists are outsiders and then when the nanny, Amelia (Adriana Barraza), takes the kids to Mexico, you have this clash of cultures. Chieko, the Japanese girl (Rinko Kikuchi), always feels like she's outside because she's deaf. There are always these dual themes of disconnection and people trying to connect. So, whether it's Brad Pitt (Richard) or Cate Blanchett (Susan) in the beginning of *Babel* where they're disconnected on their vacation because of lack of forgiveness due to a problem in their marriage. Or, at the end of *Babel* when Amelia blames herself, she did something under impossible circumstances, and yet she carries so much guilt. In *The Burning Plain*, Charlize Theron's character, Sylvia, carries around all of that guilt of setting the fatal fire. It just runs through each story. You have the disconnection between people because of either internal fear and guilt because of a physical handicap or because of just cultures where they're a fish out of water. Do you also feel a particular affinity or are you drawn to feeling like an outsider culturally?

GA: I grew up in a middle class neighborhood and my parents were devoted to education. Where we were living, we were the only kids in private school. When I went to private school, there were these fancy kids who were going to Europe and blah blah blah. My parents were making an effort for this private school and then my father had a good economic situation and everything became even. But, it was like not feeling quite part of that world. It has more to do with that than traveling. I always liked the idea of people in extremes. When you go to the extremes of something, you're crossing to another territory.

NL: When you're an outsider on some level, you always feel much more vulnerable. I travel to Russia quite often and when it's not your first language, when you have trouble reading the signs, when you don't understand the customs, you're so much more vulnerable right from the beginning. In *Babel,* Chieko has so much shame about being unable to hear or to speak. She doesn't want people to realize. She just wants to blend in. There's a great scene in the café when she goes to meet her friends and when the woman asks her if she can help her, she pretends that she's not deaf and just walks past her and wants to "pass" in a way. This idea of vulnerability though is the crux of this chapter. I've been teaching now 23 years. The most common ailment that plagues most of my students is that they play it safe. I tell them there's not enough conflict, that they need to push the character to the edge. I actually say to some of them make it so bold and make the character so excruciatingly vulnerable that you, as the writer, are almost embarrassed or afraid to put that down on the page. And, it still won't be far enough because many of them are very timid. The exact opposite is true in your work. You push it so far that each movie is like a car accident where you want to look, but you're almost afraid to look because it's so painful and yet you need to because this is the human condition. When you're writing, are you drawn right into the heat? Do you struggle with it or do you know when you begin exactly where you need to go? Do you have advice on how to do it?

GA: I have two handicapped friends: one has polio and she uses braces and the other one has cerebral palsy. So, I am familiar with handicapped people and because of that I began working as a director on TV documentaries about handicapped people. I was considered the "fastest gun" in the business because people would ask me, "Man, are you busy tomorrow?" "No, why?" "Can you shoot a documentary?" I remember there was one about handicapped athletes and I went to go meet those guys without much of an idea of what was going on. There was a guy who had no arms and he was missing a leg. I saw him out of the water, but the moment he went inside the water, he became a dolphin. So, I said bring a submarine camera. They said they didn't have the money. And I said I would pay for it. I asked the camera operator to go as close to the part where the arm is missing. I don't want to be afraid of watching things. I'm not afraid of asking questions. I embarrass my family a lot because when I go to a dinner, I ask the most outrageous questions you can imagine. So, with my characters, it's nothing that I have planned, it's just the way I am. I think that we are too domesticated. We are too politically correct, especially in the middle and upper classes—and more in the first world like the United States—you cannot say anything because you might offend everyone. You are so careful in your conversations. You can even be sued. It's safe here in Mexico, no one's going to sue me. But, it's like "Man, you're going to get into deep trouble, if you continue doing that." But, I think there's no point in your being, as you say, shy. There's no point in constraining your characters. I hate the idea of likeable characters. Usually my characters are not likeable. In *Amores Perros*, we have a kid, Octavio [Gael García Bernal] who takes away the pregnant wife, Susana [Vanessa Bauche], of his brother.

NL: Right, but you do temper it with the fact that he's trying to protect her because of his brother's abuse. And, he's played by such a likeable actor.

GA: And, El Chivo [Emilio Echevarría] is a hitman. It's harmful. A man who kills for a living.

NL: But, he loves animals.

GA: Or, Charlize Theron [as Sylvia in *The Burning Plain*] who is a sex addict. Or, Benicio Del Toro [as Jack Jordan in *21 Grams*]. He's crazy, man.

NL: All true. I find that if characters are kind to children and to animals, even if they're horrible to each other, I'll find a soft spot for them. So, in *Amores Perros*, I had a soft spot for El Chivo and for each person. I thought you really found the humanity. In *Amores Perros*, it happens each time through an animal. The first of your movies that I saw was *Amores Perros*, and I never, ever, ever forgot the scene when El Chivo comes home and all of his dogs have been killed. And, it was an act of love from Octavio's rescued dog (Cofi), and El Chivo starts to cry. It's such a great moment. I'll never forget it. The idea that you can have love and loyalty and yet destroy at the same time. There's so many morally complex grey areas to that particular storyline. Now, you say that you don't start with anything, but you had the crash . . .

GA: I had my own dog. That story started from my own dog. That happened really. Where I grew up, there were dog fights. My dog was a horrible mutt. All of his brothers and sisters were Weimaraners, but he was black with long hair. There was a scene where he runs out of the house and someone goes to try to kill him, just for the sake of killing him. In real life, it was a German Shepherd against my dog who killed the Shepherd. I was eight years old when that happened. But, some people began taking my dog fighting without our permission. He began winning all these fights. When the economic situation of my parents changed, we moved from this middle class to a higher middle class neighborhood where my dog always escaped and he began killing pedigree dogs. So, we put him in an empty lot because he was a very strong dog and he had all the space he needed. But, once the wife of the President was living next to our house, and he bit one of the bodyguards who hit him in the head. So, we put him in the garage. The woman who was renting the second apartment loved animals. She thought that we weren't giving the right amount of attention to the dog without knowing what kind of dog it was. So, she stole it. The guy who was in charge of the three apartments said that the dog ran away and never returned, but years later, the nephew of this woman said, "You know, she stole your dog and took it to a dog refugee [place]." Without knowing who she was bringing in, and he killed all the dogs there.

NL: And, out of a sense of loyalty. So heartbreaking. There are always themes of faith being tested and always themes of forgiveness, redemption, and atonement that run through all of the work. Are you religious?

GA: I am an atheist. I have had no religious education at all. My father is an agnostic and my mother is a non-practicing Catholic. They made no effort to make me [either]. I have been an atheist since I was eight years old. Everything that I have written is an atheist movie.

NL: There's always the randomness of the universe and anything can happen. Most of the time there's no reason, no warning, and your whole life could change.

GA: I like people to first of all be challenged by circumstances. If they were going in one direction and the circumstances crush you, how strong are you to still go on in the same direction? For example, the character of Octavio in *Amores Perres*, he was in the direction of taking the girl away from his brother. Despite his crash and everything, he still goes, "Come with me" at the funeral. And, more than dealing with atonement and redemption, I want people to be able to endure. Like William Faulkner said, "The heavenly spirit will endure." How strong you are. How strong you are to get out of the depths. But, it has no religious component at all.

NL: Your movies are all about synchronicity. There are random events, but they bring people together. When I watch them, it doesn't feel like it's just random anarchy. It feels like there's some plan, and people are severely tested in their faith. When this happens, the only way out of it is through actions. And, most of the time, active protagonists need to take a risk or do the more difficult thing. Part of the vulnerability of your characters is that they're compelled to almost always make the more difficult choice. You don't let them off easy. When you construct a character, since you don't have a plan, do you just see where they take you or do you think what would be the most challenging thing that this character would have to face based on their limitations?

GA: I see two questions here. The first one is that being an atheist makes you humanistic. I have no sense of faith and no sense of God at all. Nothing religious in my life. I work at very atheistic schools. A non-believing family. It was like okay until the age of eight, you can believe in Santa Claus and God. After that, it's a fantasy. For these characters, it has to be inside them, something that can pull them out of the dark hole that they are in. Second, I remember I was forced to take a seminar with one of these writing gurus. Not the best one, it was a lesser one. And, this person said, "You must know everything about your character." And, I said, "What's the point? How then is your character going to surprise you?" So, I have no idea where the characters are heading. I have no plan for them. I'm even surprised how they come out. For example, when El Chivo puts the gun between the brothers, I said to myself, "How did I come up with this idea? Where did it come from?"

I don't like anything that constrains me to write a film. That's why I don't write an outline. Since I write about things that have happened to me, what's the point of doing research? It's not that I am against research. I know that someone like Peter Morgan who wrote *The Queen* needs to do research. But, I am not writing about the Queen. For the first time in my life, I am writing something that is not an original, but based on a journalistic piece about tigers in Siberia. I have never been to Russia. I have never been to Siberia and I have never hunted a tiger. But, I am a hunter. I understand wild animals. They are not cute kittens. I know animals enough to know how they are going to react. So, I have no need of research.

NL: Once you complete a first draft, do you then go back and unify all the themes and threads? Or, do the first drafts turn out pretty faithfully to what is shot?

GA: First of all, I consider screenplays to be literature because I was first a novelist. I consider it the obligation of a writer as having a rebirth—that means questioning all of his creative decisions. For example, the character of Benecio Del Toro in *21 Grams*, he was first a wealthy businessman. It's almost the same structure. I question, I question, and I question until I find the right character. I think that this is a business about seducing.

> *You have to seduce movie stars, producers, financiers, and VP's. And, the main way to seduce them is through the screenplay. To write a screenplay that is so powerful and intense with the construction of the language that they will be drawn into it.*

ASSIGNMENT

Review each "plot point" in your screenplay and/or outline, and identify your protagonist's emotional state in each scene. What are they doing in each scene and why? How does each action make them feel? What emotional response are you intending for the audience to feel? Determine the ultimate catharsis for each main character; some may undergo substantive transformation, some might barely change at all. But all must deal with the full spectrum of their emotions through acceptance or rebellion of What Is.

21

WHAT'S WRONG WITH THIS PICTURE?

~~Rewrites:~~ Revise and Refine Your Intention and Vision

After you've completed what will probably be your very rough, exploratory draft, you'll need to begin navigating the rewrite phase. Don't despair—every screenwriter in the world faces this always challenging and often exhilarating revision process. It's not a coincidence that the most successful screenwriters in the entertainment business also have the talent, vision, and stamina to continually refine and polish their work, draft after draft. Academy Award-winning screenwriter Michael Arndt purportedly wrote over one hundred drafts of *Little Miss Sunshine*. Writing is rewriting.

Given that this next phase could take many weeks, months, or even years, it's essential that you have a passionate investment in the project from the get-go. Why are you compelled to write this? Who is your intended audience and what would you (ideally) like them to come away with? What will compel them to care about your characters? These are the questions that will sustain your creative process and resilience as you renovate and refine your work-in-progress screenplay.

Strategies for the revision process.

Put your exploratory draft in a drawer for at least three days and do not allow yourself to look at it under any circumstances. This will facilitate your regaining some of your objectivity.

After 72 hours, go someplace quiet and give it a gentle read, dog-earing pages and making notes in the margins. These notes will become your roadmap toward your first revision in which your goal should be to smooth out the trouble spots, tighten the narrative, rake the dialogue, and shorten the page count to (ideally) less than 120 pages.

Get this new and (hopefully) improved draft to a few "trusted advisors" for their objective and constructive feedback. Finding an effective trusted advisor is critical to your career and you should be as willing to read their work, as they are yours. If seeking out untested, not-yet-trusted advisors, try to find movie lovers and/or other screenwriters you respect. Can you predict that their notes will be constructive versus destructive? Ask them specific questions before they read your screenplay: Does this basic premise appeal to you? Is this a genre you have ever enjoyed? Approximately how long will it take you to read it? Yes, propose a deadline so you're not sitting around, agonizing, waiting for the phone to ring.

Prioritize the big notes from the smaller concerns. Once you've implemented the larger script notes (known as the "heavy lifting"), many of the smaller notes will become irrelevant. Structural notes are always the most substantial and daunting to receive. If you're only getting very specific page notations—even if there are a lot of them—that's good news! To me, the more nitpicky the page notes, the better. It tells me the reader and note giver was really paying attention to detail. If I'm mainly getting an overall impression—which is more common because it's much less time consuming—then I'll need to find those extremely specific trouble spots by myself or from my detail man/woman (trusted advisor).

If you receive structural notes, you're going to need to re-outline your screenplay. Write each scene in your script on a separate index card and lay them all out on the floor or a big table or post them on a bulletin board (*see Chapter 8 on Structure*).

If the structure is deemed basically sound, no need to go back to the drawing board. Now your latest draft of the screenplay becomes your outline—so feel free to hand-scribble all over the pages (yes—I recommend that you do this part of the process on *hard copy* so you have a permanent record). Some pages you'll "X" out completely. Some pages you'll write a "Note to Self" about what needs fixing. Very often you will write "OVER" on the page and then write a list of objectives to accomplish in the rewrite of the next draft in your computer document. I often create a roadmap for myself on the pages with numbers, letters, arrows, and asterisks. It looks like a mess and nobody but me would ever be able to follow it. But when I go to type in all these changes, I can see if this new progression works, if there is indeed a method to my madness.

Filter through all the notes and decide which are useful and on-target for the genre, tone, and vision of your screenplay, and which ones are not. *You're looking for a consensus among your readers.* If one person bumps on something that no one else did, you might be able to disregard that particular concern. Weeding out the frivolously subjective notes is essential. You can't please everyone, and you don't want to end up with a revised script that pleases your critics at the expense of your original vision. On the flip side, some writers, known as "heel diggers," have the unfortunate trait of getting defensive and arguing the notes. It's such a waste of time for writers to push back against notes when someone is trying to help. At the end of the day, you want to be proud of your work and stand by its value, so do listen to all the constructive criticisms, but you are not obligated to implement all of the comments.

If you're being paid, you might have a fiduciary responsibility to your employer, but you should never implement a note that you absolutely hate because the studio executive, director, and/or producer will never remember (or disavow) the bad notes they gave you and they will blame you for whatever doesn't work. And, invariably, they'll take credit for the magic on the page that they may or may not have inspired. But, hey, if you're getting paid for being a screenwriter, that's usually the cost of doing business.

Keep your sense of humor and perspective. Always remember that you're rewriting a script, not finding a cure for cancer. It's great if you're invested in your screenplay to a high degree, but it's never worth having a nervous breakdown or ruining your life over it. Sometimes the best medicine is lightening up. There's a great quote that I'm told is attributed to Albert Einstein: "The highest level of creativity unfolds through play." So try to enjoy this part of the process. If you're having fun rewriting, editing, streamlining plot, and punching up dialogue, it's probably going to translate onto the page. If it's labored and arduous, it might read that way. Get through this crucial first revision and allow yourself the satisfaction of your labors. Super-successful screenwriter David Koepp believes that the biggest creative leap your script will make is from that nascent exploratory draft to your first revision—and he wrote *Spider-Man*.

Trust in the process and try to commit to a new direction for this next full rewrite. You can always do another rewrite after that . . . and another. But trust your Muse and have confidence in your talent so you can complete the full rewrite. You can get there from here.

Strategies for interpreting and implementing notes.

I frequently work as a professional "script doctor," which necessitates diagnosing script ailments and prescribing remedies. One of the biggest problems with professionally written screenplays is that snappy dialogue will usually camouflage larger story problems. It's such an entertaining read that it's a page-turner, but when I get to the end, I feel unsatisfied. I always try to read a script once all the way through without stopping before making specific page notes; I like to get the pace and overall feeling of the story first. My second read is when I start to seek out what's missing and where the dramatic tension drops out and/or where the plot goes slack.

When I'm given a script to rewrite, I'm usually told in advance what the producer, director, and/or studio executive believes the major problems to be. And what I usually discover is that they're always right. There *is* a problem with that part of the script, but what that usually translates to is *the note beneath the note*. That is, they've identified a perceived weakness in the screenplay, but not the actual cause. For example, a third act problem might actually be an issue that occurs in the backstory or in the first act. Or an unsympathetic character might actually be very sympathetic, but it's the supporting characters that are throwing him/her off kilter. For these reasons, I've structured the below primer on the rewrite process to address the perceived problem versus what may be the actual problem.

What they say versus what they mean: doctoring your own script.

"The protagonist is unlikeable." Translation: He/she is devoid of charisma and his/her goals are unsympathetic.
Rx: Give your protagonist a key vulnerability.

"The story is too superficial." Translation: Dig deeper.
Rx: The how and what are probably clear, but not the *why*. Clarify main characters' wants/needs, fears/yearnings.

"The beginning of the script was way too slow, and I almost put it down, but then it got better in the second half."
Rx: Start the story later; too much setup and heavy-handed exposition; cut to the chase.

"I got bored." Translation: Plot lacks dramatic conflict and urgency.
Rx: Make protagonist more desperate, the antagonist more formidable. Raise the stakes.

"Predictable ending." Translation: Unsatisfying or nonexistent central mystery.
Rx: You need to more effectively obscure a hidden truth.

"I just didn't find the character arcs compelling." Translation: The protagonist doesn't evolve enough from page 1 to The End.
Rx: Clarify and re-conceive setup; more effectively need to externalize an inner void in the protagonist's "ordinary world" that needs to be externally filled by the end of the movie; act three problems are almost always related to ill-conceived backstory.

"I got lost in the story." Translation: Confusing/illogical plot developments; plot is too complicated.
Rx: Simplify setup; streamline plot/possibly reduce number of characters; unify POV.

"I don't know what you're trying to say." Translation: The story is too intellectual and not emotionally engaging enough.

Rx: Dig deeper (per above); get them to think less and *feel* more. If they're laughing hysterically, crying, and/or at the edge of their seats, they're probably not going to over-analyze and note you to death. On the other hand, every studio development executive in Hollywood needs to justify their paychecks, so it's not an issue of *whether* you're going to get notes or not; it's an issue of how extensive the notes are going to be, and how they're disseminated to you. A good producer is golden in being a crucial buffer to receiving notes.

Getting notes and doing revisions is not for the weak of heart, but it is par for the screenwriter's course, so suck it up. The biggest irony in this profession is that writers are artists—which requires great sensitivity. And yet to sustain a screenwriting career, you'll need to have a thick skin (or pretend to have one and then go home to your loved ones—or to your therapist's office—and cry). Rejection and criticism can crush you or galvanize you. The choice is yours. Pardon the cliché, but for me, laughter is still the best medicine.

INTERVIEW: Screenwriter/Director Jeff Nathanson

Jeff Nathanson Filmography

Best known for:

Men in Black III (2012)
Tower Heist (2011)
Indiana Jones and the Kingdom of the Crystal Skull (story) (2008)
Rush Hour 3 (2007)
The Last Shot (also directed) (2004)
The Terminal (2004)
Catch Me If You Can (2002)
Rush Hour 2 (2001)
Speed 2: Cruise Control (1997)

NL: I wanted to start with the genesis of *Catch Me If You Can.* Do you outline? Do you have a set process or was it specific to that project because you were writing about a real person?

JN: That one was a little bit different because I had this audiotape of Frank Abagnale who used to go around the country giving a speech about his crazy youth. I didn't know much about it. I read a book which was written, I think, in the 70s. I went to Dreamworks and said, "Is this something you guys would be interested in doing?" I think that they were not so thrilled about it because it was very episodic. Certainly, it was interesting to imagine a guy, this kid, to pretend to be a pilot, a doctor, and a lawyer, but then what's the movie? I didn't have much to go on, so I went to the source, I went to Frank. I flew out to Dallas and sat with him for a couple days and just talked to him about his life. And, very early on, he started talking about his childhood in a way that was not in any of the audio recordings and not in the book. He started talking about his father, his brother, the dynamics of that family. I started to realize that there was a movie here about the relationship between this father and this kid going out in the world and trying to right the wrongs of his family. So, I spent a couple years writing that movie and yet it still wasn't a movie, it still wasn't quite enough. There was a small part in the book about this FBI agent who had been tracking him, and I realized that here was a whole second father that could become a central part of the story. So, I created [Carl Hanratty] this Tom Hanks character. And, once that happened, then that script really became a movie, and once it became a movie, everything happened very quickly.

NL: Was Carl Hanratty a composite or was he based on one person?

JN: There was an actual guy named Joe Shaye who was tracking him. But, Joe Shaye did not want to be interviewed, so I just created a character that I felt could be the audience. The main thing it did, because he became a second father, was it allowed me to have a clear thematic through line and allowed people to see it as a complete movie which a lot of people weren't able to do beforehand.

NL: Was the Christmas motif something he talked about in his real life or did you put that in? The idea how they would always communicate on Christmas Eve.

JN: It just happened. It was one of those things where I realized, "Oh, this is the second time they are talking around Christmas." And, then I thought, "Well, why not carry that through?" When I realized that it became about this kid searching for family, it seemed to fit in with this Christmas theme. The fact that the movie was released on Christmas Day, I think, was an accident.

NL: It was also interesting how you gave Carl Hanratty the backstory of also being estranged from his family. He had been through a divorce. He had separated from his wife and daughter. I guess they're in Chicago. There's that great scene where Hanks says, "Oh, I know why you're calling me, you don't have anyone else to talk to." But, it was the same for him.

JN: You could see that they really only had each other early on. You know, a lot of times screenwriting is luck. It's dumb luck, so I played it out.

Certainly, it took me well over two years to actually crack the screenplay. Had I thrown it in a drawer, gone on to do something else, or been more successful at that time where people wanted to hire me to do other things, I probably would have never figured it out. That movie would never have gotten made. I was just lucky that I was able to stick with it.

NL: It's a great insight for aspiring screenwriters to hear that. At UCLA, my students have ten weeks to write a screenplay. At USC, they have 14 weeks in the semester system. And, they're both frustrated if by week three, they haven't cracked it. And, I say, "It takes time. You have to find it."

JN: Some movies you do find earlier than that, but even those you find early are certainly not done. I'm sure other people have said this to you— screenplays are never done. They really are never done. You have to embrace the fluid life of a script.

NL: I think all scripts are creative experiments. You don't really know if they're going to pan out or work. There's a lot of faith involved. It seems to me with *Catch Me If You Can*, there could have been another version of that movie where it was just gags and episodic stuff. And, the reason I enjoy the movie so much is because of the emotional gravity that you created. The great scene toward the end, I think it's the climax, where he runs from the plane to go to his mother's home on Long Island, and he discovers she's remarried. He's on the outside looking in. You just see that all he wants is to be part of a family.

JN: I had written many endings that were closer to the truth of Frank's real life. And, I don't want to even talk about it, but there were things within his family that I actually wrote about that were very, very heavy. When I realized I could put this in the movie, I was so excited as a writer, thinking, "Oh my God, this really happened to this guy, and he discovered this about his family." I thought for sure that would be the end of the movie. To Steven Spielberg's credit, he understood that that would have been too much. That the film wasn't able to hold certain emotional truths. The story had to be what it was. You had to complete that story. So, I kept writing these endings, and he kept handing them back to me and saying, "No, no." We went back and forth so many times trying to figure out the actual end of the film. He really kept me true to what I started and I owe him a lot of credit for that.

NL: So, ending it with him going to work for the FBI—it's "the start of a beautiful friendship."

JN: Exactly. Basically, I think the realization that he was going to have this other family now and that Carl was going to be in his life was the right ending. It meant that he was going to be okay and he was going to stop running. Sometimes as a writer, you see things one way, and the director sees things another way. In this case, I'm glad that the director was Steven Spielberg who has done this before. I feel like he got it right.

NL: Now when you're writing an original, do you have a planning process? Do you outline? Do you use cards? What kind of architectural or planning structure do you use or do you just start writing?

JN: I'm not much of an outline guy. Even when I was in school writing screenplays, I just wasn't really an outline guy. And then, the first job I ever got, I had to write a lot of outlines—almost eight months of outlines. When I finished that, I vowed to never write an outline again. I just wasn't able to get excited when I sat down to write. I think in the last 20 years, I've maybe written one or two outlines on projects which were just so big or just so complicated, there was no choice. But, I find it to be limiting for me and boring if I have that much information. I really want to sit down fresh, completely unaware of how the movie's going to take hold. The danger there is you're going to go off on a lot of left turns and you're going to bump into a lot of blind alleys, but when you discover something during the day that pushes the script forward in a fresh, exciting way, that's what keeps me coming back the next day. It's kind of like in golf when you hit that one good shot—no matter how bad you are—if you have one good shot in a round, you'll want to play again. That's how screenwriting is for me—it's just finding those moments during the day that get you excited.

NL: Do you make notes about the characters? Do you start with a lot of notes? How do you know you're ready to sit down and start writing?

JN: I don't do any notes. I like to have one or two scenes in my head that I know are great scenes. A lot of times, that's just how I'll pick a project. If I have one or two scenes that I can envision completely that I know are going to be good, and it doesn't matter where they come in the script—if I have those scenes, I tend to be able to sit down and start, knowing that I'm heading toward something.

NL: Was one of the scenes in *Catch Me If You Can*, when his parents tell him he has to pick which parent he wants to live with? And then, he starts running.

JN: That was definitely one where there was something to write toward in the first act. I knew that was going to be the moment. *Catch Me* had a lot of those scenes, so it was easier than some scripts, there were three or four that I knew, "Oh, this is going to be fun to write." This kid getting on an airplane, and he's never been on a plane before, pretending to be a pilot. I knew that was going to be a fun sequence. So, there was stuff built into that one where I just was excited and able to be relaxed enough to start. But, I don't make cards, I don't make character notes, I don't put things on the wall. I don't do any of that stuff.

NL: From some of your other movies, do you have any examples of other scenes that became the spark for you to build the screenplay around? For instance, *Tower Heist* or *Men in Black* which I know David Koepp did also?

JN: In *Tower Heist*, I immediately imagined a moment when Eddie Murphy would look at all of these guys and tell them that they had to go to the mall and steal something. And, they each have to steal $50 worth of stuff in order to prove that they could actually be thieves. And so, I immediately imagined these guys who had never stolen anything in their lives having to go to a mall with Victoria's Secret and actually shoplift. Once that scene came to me, I felt that I understood a way to structure the whole thing because that was enough.

NL: It showed that they were novices who were then going to be entering a much bigger, challenging arena. Was Eddie Murphy already attached and some of the other actors, so that you were writing with them in mind?

JN: No, I think Ben Stiller was developing it at that time. It was in a meeting with him where he said, "What about Eddie?" So, from that point on, we didn't know if we could get him or not, but we certainly thought it was a great idea since no one had seen Eddie do this in a long time. I also wrote and directed a film called, *The Last Shot*, that had a scene where the FBI is giving notes to a screenwriter about his script from a movie he thinks he's making which is actually an FBI sting operation. When I heard that, and I had that scene, I knew that I could make that movie.

NL: I want to segue a little bit into revision. When you get a script for a rewrite assignment, you know that at least one other writer has been on it. Do you find that there are common weaknesses? When you read scripts that need work, are there things which kind of jump out at you?

JN: In terms of scripts I've read and in terms of my own scripts and in movies I go to, it's almost always the same, and really you don't have to be a screenwriter or a professional screenwriter, anybody can go to the movies on Saturday night and walk out into the parking lot and say, "It was good, but it was a little slow here or I really didn't understand why that guy did that." Or, "Really farfetched and that ending was terrible." I think we all have a built-in meter which runs when we watch a movie. I think I do look at it slightly differently in that my job is to fix it. But, my first instinct is just as an audience member. Looking at the movie and trying to see, "Do I like this? What's the problem?" Almost all the problems originate in the first act. If it's not set up properly, if the characters aren't set up, if the foundation isn't there, if the concept isn't clear—if any one of these is off in the first act, there's no way to complete a screenplay and have it work. And, you certainly couldn't get to a third act with that screenplay. Most of the time, they'll send me a script and say the problem is the ending. And, I'll call them back and say, "You're problem is on page 3." That happens a lot. Or, they'll say, "We have a second act that needs a lot of work." And, I'll say, "It's actually that the first act has absolutely nothing to do with the second act, so there's no way that the second act could ever work. So, we're going to have to build a first act that flows into act two." Generally speaking, it's the first act that's broken, and that's led to people writing a full screenplay that wants to work, that can work, but generally will not work.

NL: You talked about the thematic through line in *Catch Me If You Can.* How important is theme to you when you're starting either an original or a rewrite? Is it something you think about early in the process?

JN: Yeah, I think you have to. I think you can't allow it to direct the writing on a rewrite. I think if you're just talking a straight rewrite, they've already decided a lot of the times what that movie is. So, I can't say to them, "Hey, I'm changing the whole focus of your film, so now, it's going to be this, this, and this." Many times, you go back into the first act and you lay in things to make the theme of the film clear in the second act, and actually pay off in the third act and actually make sense. But, generally speaking a lot people will have one scene where they'll have a lot of people in one room, and they'll feel like that's the movie. Sometimes there's other ways of doing it. For myself, I feel like when I rewrite myself, I'm always very, very careful to make sure that the theme is there and present, but not hitting people over the head. The movies I write are not theme-heavy films. Sometimes they are, sometimes they're not.

NL: In terms of visual motifs that sometimes speak to theme, one that jumped out at me in *Catch Me If You Can* is how he peels the labels off of bottles—where you take something that is branded and you make it non-descript. You can strip away a label. Visual representations which can inform on character. Do you look for these kinds of things when you're writing or does that become more of a directorial discussion later?

JN: I feel that that's something that can be in screenplays, but of all the millions of things that you have to worry about in screenplays, I would put it at the bottom of the list of things to start to try to imagine because either the director is going to change it or replace it. Because immediately when you start putting things in that are visual, their Spidey sense goes up and they think, "Wait—is this guy trying to direct the film for me?" It really depends what your relationship is with the director. Certainly, if you're directing your own thing, that's one thing. For me, the writing process is not about trying to imagine where that camera's going to be. To try to imagine what they're going to be looking at. In *Catch Me,* that was Leonardo DiCaprio's idea to tear the bottles. He came to Steven at one point and said, "What if everywhere I go, I'm ripping [labels] off [of] bottles?" That's just an actor who's really in touch with the character and brings something to it that Steven and I did not see. And, it was a great thing to add into the script later on.

NL: It also helped because it created a little plot point later on when Hanratty shows up at the wedding, and he sees the champagne bottle with the label off, so he knows he's there. That kind of stuff, it's interesting when you track that through. When you're doing revision, probably, a relatively common thing is that it's anti-climactic or the climax doesn't have as much heat or power as it might. One of the things that I talk about with students is that one of the ways to think about climax is that the climax is the truth. That you're building to something that the audience doesn't know. Because as soon as they know everything, the movie's over. What audiences don't know is what generates a lot more suspense, because then you have anticipation. Do you agree with that? As a structural concept, and again, with new screenwriters, it can become very self-conscious, but it's something that I strive for, the idea that there's a central question or central mystery. Something that you're holding back, like a final trump card to play late in the movie. Do you think about that consciously when you're either writing an original or when you're doing a rewrite?

JN: Yes. I say I don't outline, but I certainly have a basic idea of what the ending should feel like. I don't need to know what it is, but I need to know how it's going to feel—the basic structure of it. And, always in my mind, there is room for an element of surprise. Not just for the audience, but for me as a writer. What am I going to get to which will surprise me as a writer and make it worth someone coming and driving and parking for? When I say that most films are broken in the first act, that's true, but most movies die because their endings don't work. And, something I've experienced at least a dozen times in my life is having a filmmaker say, "Come in, watch my film, and tell me how to fix my ending." I watch the movie and say, "Here's some ideas of how you can make this work." Sometimes it's a whole new ending, sometimes it's a new scene, sometimes it's a line, sometimes it's an edit. But, there's always something you can do. It's the single most important thing for a film. It's what the studio worries about the most. It's where they put all their money. It's the whole thing. I've seen a lot of bad movies that have a great ending. Where you walk out into that parking lot and you say, "You know that was pretty good." And, you don't even remember that the movie didn't work on any level because the ending was so good. So, it's a big deal and it's something that you have to be aware of in the screenwriting process, but you really have to be aware of it in the moviemaking process.

NL: In terms of movie marketing, because movies are made now to be global, you hear a lot about the four quadrants—that it needs to appeal to every age group. You also hear that the idea should be articulated in one sentence. Often with the word "but" in that sentence, so that it includes the conflict. When you're doing revision, do you think movies, especially now, need to be articulated pretty easily in order to be accessible?

JN: First of all, everything I do is about revision. My whole life is about revision. My writing from morning 'til night is revision. There's very little forward motion in my day. So, my day is always going backwards. Let's say I'm on page 35 of my screenplay, I'll start my day and maybe I'll read those

35 pages and edit them from the night before. I will then go back and rewrite those 35 and then get to 36 or 37, one scene. I'll print it out and then do the same thing again. So, it's literally maybe half a step forward and 40 steps backward at all times. I think if you're going to be afraid of rewriting and revisions in a screenplay, you're not going to be a screenwriter. You just have to be able to constantly go back and edit. And, if you can't do that, then you're looking forward. And, if you're looking forward, you're missing the mark. As I said, the whole structure and tightness of a screenplay will fall apart if that first act isn't working. If I have a 10-week job, I might spend seven weeks on the first act because it's that important. Those first 25 pages for people to read are so important because they could make or break whether someone wants to make the movie.

NL: Well, the first 25 are basically setting up what the movie's going to be about.

JN: I don't think you can look at it that way. I think you have to look at it as—that's all you're getting. That's it. You have to look at it this way: if you're handing people a 120-page script, they're only going to read 25 pages. And, that's true of me or a first-time screenwriter. So, literally, you're almost creating a mini-movie that is 30 pages long that's going to be unbelievable with great original characters and original scenes that grab people and completely change their perception of what they thought they were going to read. And, give them the desire to then go forward. If you haven't done that, they're not going to go forward. There's very little you can do about it. There's no saying, "Hey, if you just get to page 80, it gets good." It doesn't work that way, no one's getting to page 80, if they haven't gotten past page 30. The answer to your other question is I try to not think about the marketing of movies too much. It's a slippery slope. Obviously I work within the studio system. I'm aware that these people are hiring me to work on a film that's going to be on 3,000 screens, and they're going to want those people to go to those movies. So, I'm aware of it, but I try truthfully not to think about it too much.

NL: Do you ever get sent a script that needs revision, where you've finished reading it and you still don't know what the movie's about?

JN: All the time.

NL: Is it that it's about too many things and you have to pick one?

JN: All the time.

NL: Because that's a common issue, and what I try to do with my students is bring that question up early when I say, "I don't know what your film is about, and I don't think you know what it's about." Do you think you have to make those decisions pretty early on: this is what it's about, this is what it's not about? Am I staying on point, on story?

JN: Let's say it in the clearest way possible. There are good ideas and bad ideas for movies. Most people sit down and start writing a bad idea for a movie.

Nine out of ten people will sit down and spend two months of their lives that if they had just asked five people, "Is this a good idea for a movie?" they would have all said no. It's people, it's just our nature. It's what we do. I did it—anyone who's ever written a movie has done it. The reason is it's hard to come up with good ideas for a movie. People are impatient. They're excited or they're in a class at school or they're a bartender at night, and they're thinking, "I've got to get this done," so they start writing. They've shot themselves in the foot before they've even started.

> *The single most important thing someone can do is to be patient enough to come up with an idea for a movie that somebody else on earth says, "I think that's a good idea for a movie." If you're not going to be patient, you're always going to be fighting a tidal wave because there's nothing that can save you from that.*

Really, there's no escape. People send me scripts all the time, people send you scripts all the time, it is an epidemic in a lot of ways and I really just think it's the eagerness of a young writer. And, if you can have that patience, I think you'll find it pays off. Because when you finally sit down to write a script that is good enough for a movie, it's a lot easier.

NL: How important is it for you to find something personal to emotionally connect with in a script that doesn't originate as your own idea?

JN: There certainly was a time in my life when I didn't say "no" to anything. I was young and wanting to work. Now, I do say "no" to things that I just don't feel I know how to do. There has to be something about it that I know I'll be able to get up in the morning excited to do it. So, to answer the last question, I wait around until I hear a good idea or read a good idea or come up with a good idea. And, then it's worth doing. To be writing a bad idea, which plenty of those get made, I've done it and it's just not that much fun.

NL: Finally, I wanted to talk to you about writing dialogue. I think it's difficult to teach people how to do it. I think it's a natural gift. Do you have any pointers about how to write effective dialogue?

JN: No one can teach someone how to write dialogue. You can certainly tell people to listen more, and to go out in the world, stop talking, and pay attention. But, I feel the best way to teach someone to write good dialogue is that if they're having trouble writing dialogue, they're probably having trouble writing scenes. That their dialogue is not incorporated into an actual scene. A lot of times someone can write pretty decent dialogue, but because their scenes never have a beginning, middle, and end, or even a point to them—it doesn't matter. You start to dislike their dialogue and you get angry that these characters are still talking. They're not actually getting to the point. They're not actually moving the story forward. Or, they're just talking because someone has a good idea for a speech. So, a lot of times, it's not so much the dialogue that's the issue, it's the inability to understand what a screenplay scene should look and feel like. If you can understand the scene, you can probably craft dialogue to fit into the scene.

NL: I also think it's the difference between people who have never been produced versus someone who has been produced many times or has directed. Things you learn from page to screen, from page to prep, and even in rehearsals about what you thought you'd need and maybe don't really need on the page. Are there things you've noticed?

JN: There's a tremendous amount of learning. Look, you have to have a gut to be a screenwriter. You have to have an instinct for it. You're not going to be able to teach everyone to write a screenplay, you have to have a knack for it. But, I do think after doing it for 20 years that there's a lot you learn about how easy it is to edit and how vicious you have to be with yourself and your own material. You have to be willing to just go in and chop it up or start over. There's many days where I just print out the first 30 pages and half of those pages go in the trash can because they're bugging me—they don't work. I know they can be better or my favorite speech goes in the trash because it's just not really doing much for the story. So, you have to really have an eye as an editor and as an audience as you're going. You have to be able to separate yourself from the material and be the writer and then as a reader, be a completely secondary person who can look over your own stuff and tap yourself on the shoulder and say, "Hey, let's talk about this."

NL: Do you have trusted advisors? Any friends who read your drafts or do you just put it aside for at least a few days and then you're that person?

JN: I'm that person for most of the time. Some people like to give their scripts to 20 people and have readings. I've never been that person. I have basically two people in my life after all these years who are my go-to people. They get the scripts first before the studio. And, one of them is my wife and she's an excellent audience and can be truthful. The key is whoever you're handing that script to; you have to make sure that they're going to be honest. Find an honest person, two honest people on earth, who will actually tell you what they really think. That's all you need. You don't need ten people. You really need one.

ASSIGNMENT

Find a chunk of uninterrupted time—at least six hours—sit down, turn off the Internet and Facebook and Twitter and cell phone—and start your rewrite. There is an invaluable app called "Freedom" for Mac that disables all your social networking capabilities for a prescribed amount of time. If you can't avoid the temptation of distraction and e-commerce, this app's for you. Now get busy addressing the smart comments you agree with and consider the others that were in consensus. Sure, you can defend your script in its current condition to avoid the work, but in the time you spend equivocating, you could finish many new and probably much better versions of your screenplay. So, in the immortal words of Nike: *Just do it.*

ABOUT THE AUTHOR

Neil Landau is a professor in the MFA in Screenwriting Programs, both at UCLA School of Film, Television and Digital Media, and USC School of Cinematic Arts. His film and television credits include *Don't Tell Mom the Babysitter's Dead*, *Melrose Place*, *The Magnificent Seven*, *Doogie Howser, M.D.*, *The Secret World of Alex Mack*, *Twice in a Lifetime*, MTV's *Undressed*, and the 3D animated feature *Tad: The Lost Explorer*.

Also by the Author

101 Things I Learned in Film School with Matthew Frederick (Grand Central Publishing, 2010)

Anthologies

NowWrite! Screenwriting (Tarcher/Penguin, 2011)
Alchemy of the Word (CalArts Press, 2011)

INDEX